Envisioning Crimi

Michael D. Maltz · Stephen K. Rice
Editors

Envisioning Criminology

Researchers on Research as a Process of Discovery

Foreword by Alfred C. Blumstein

 Springer

Editors
Michael D. Maltz
University of Illinois at Chicago
Chicago, IL, USA

Ohio State University
Columbus, OH, USA

Stephen K. Rice
Department of Criminal Justice
Seattle University
Seattle, WA, USA

ISBN 978-3-319-37948-7   ISBN 978-3-319-15868-6   (eBook)
DOI 10.1007/978-3-319-15868-6

Springer Cham Heidelberg New York Dordrecht London

Springer International Publishing AG Switzerland is part of Springer Science+Business Media (www.springer.com)

Foreword

For the past 10 years, I have been teaching a course identified as "Ph.D. Seminar I." This course is required of all new Ph.D. students enrolled in the Carnegie Mellon University's Heinz College. We assume that all our entering students know how to get good grades, but not necessarily how to do research. Since a principal purpose of a Ph.D. program is the development of skills at carrying out research, the mission of that course is to develop in them the insights and skills needed to pursue a research career.

We start the course with a presentation by individual faculty members of one of their research papers, not as they would present the finished paper at a professional meeting, but taking them backstage to the shaping and development of the paper. The faculty members are asked to report on how they identified the problem, how they went about addressing it, what models and analytic methods they chose to use, what data they used and how they gained access, what results they found, and how they reached their conclusions. Finally, they are asked to identify the limitations of the paper, what further analyzes are needed, assumptions they made that may need further support, thereby indicating next steps in the research that are needed, and steps for which the author didn't have the data or the methodology to pursue. The students are encouraged to question the faculty members, asking them to explain the choices they made and challenging them to defend their choices against some reasonable alternatives.

After that diverse set of introductions to the research process, we require the students to prepare their own research proposals, critique each other, and then shape a second iteration of the proposal that is more targeted than the "moon shots" we too often see in their first proposals.

The chapters we see in this fascinating collection organized by Maltz and Rice would be a valuable addition to such a course. Each of the authors, in very different ways, has taken us behind the scenes, not so much to a particular paper, but rather to a particular facet of a research issue or a personal research career. Their stories confirm one of the themes of my seminar that "all research is research in progress." There is a striking continuity in the authors' individual stories as they moved from one completed paper to the next, even though it may appear that the next paper moves into a different area. Finding that different area could well have been provoked by issues raised in a previous paper, by methodologies introduced or developed in an earlier paper, or by needs to support a previous assumption. Of course, if the next steps were easy, the previous author would have taken them, but moving beyond provides an important challenge, either with new methodology or new data that were not available for the previous paper.

The original planned title for this volume was "Visualizing Criminology," reflecting a clear interest by Michael Maltz to highlight the value of graphical information, a habit he picked up in his undergraduate engineering education. And indeed his 3D graph depicting the frequency of homicide as a function of the ages of victim and offender is quite illuminating and providing useful insights that go beyond the expected offender-victim peak at age 19. It would have been interesting to have other authors pick up on such a visual theme, but the only other one who did so extensively was Jonathan Caulkins, also trained as an engineer. Indeed, I often find it helpful to provide a graphic display of my data and results, and that is probably also a product of my own engineering education. Stephen Rice brings visualization into another intriguing dimension, with his textual visualization of condemned inmates' final statements, an impressive methodology for capturing the keywords in a number of documents.

Policy research should be an important aspect of criminology, but it is particularly complicated by the high multidimensional nature of the criteria involved in policy choices. Obviously, crime reduction is one major choice, but there could well be trade-offs between directing effort at one kind of crime compared to another. Inevitably, there will be tension between efforts directed at crime reduction and the cost of those efforts, and the task is further complicated by the fact that any attempt to assign a dollar benefit to a particular crime reduction is fraught with difficulty in balancing personal cost against public cost. And the importance of justice embodied in at least five Constitutional Amendments often come in as further constraints.

Overlaying the analytic challenges is the ideology of the political actors who make the policy choices, whether those are legislators still afraid of being seen as "soft on crime" or executives who face a large array of policy choices to respond to immediate public concerns—and crime reduction is not a particularly salient demand in light of current low crime rates—and longer-term infrastructure development to respond to work slowly growing problem areas. Caulkins's paper on the development of his important contributions to drug policy provides a strong example of the process of bringing research to policy.

It was interesting to see the degree to which the various authors focused on their process of generating hypotheses rather than the more arduous and less exciting task of testing them. That testing is the work of science and what gets reported in detail in their published research papers, but in a macro volume like this one the exciting activity is finding interesting hypotheses to test, and especially to find data appropriate to that testing.

What is particularly striking about the collection here is its great diversity. Those who tell us about their intellectual development come from a wide variety of personal and academic backgrounds. Only a few started with a deep personal commitment to deal with crime or criminal justice. Most started with some more general education or disciplinary training, got fascinated by criminology and issues of criminal justice and ended up making some important contributions there.

It is also striking to see the diversity of methodological approaches and the questions being pursued, whether those be technical issues of the validity of surveys of defensive gun use highlighted by Cook and Ludwig or the richness of information Decker and Smith showed they can obtain by ethnographic inquiries. Larger structural issues are addressed by Sampson in shaping one of the largest social-science efforts in his Project on Human Development in Chicago Neighborhoods (PHDCN), an effort with an initial emphasis on an accelerated longitudinal cohort design that ended up with its major contribution in the relationship between neighborhood characteristics and crime. That project is quite different from the efforts by LaFree in trying to shape a research agenda on the broad issue of terrorism, starting with a broad base of rich but very diverse data. We get some diverse pictures of how impressive research careers develop by Land and by Piquero, and this is balanced by Moskos's story of how a researcher transitioned to a police officer. Skogan covers the diversity of approaches and issues in surveying police officers; in contrast, Turner covers many trials and approaches in the narrower and fundamental question of estimating risk. Weisburd takes us into the dynamics of how he came to focus on "hot spots," an important issue that has shaped police operations to a significant degree.

It was also interesting to see the reports of individuals who became immersed in a particularly rich data set, made major personal investments in organizing those data to serve their individual interests and needs, and then built careers with those particular data sets. This was the case with Lynn Addington's immersion in the NIBRS (National Incident-based Reporting System) augmentation of the FBI's Uniform Crime Reports and Janet Lauritsen's use of the NCVS (National Crime Victimization Survey). While they have occasionally ventured beyond those major data sets, they have become the world's experts in them. Those data sets are rich enough to provide for important contributions.

All of this and more fits under the rubric of criminology. In contrast to economics, for example, which has much more a sense of orthodoxy in the issues it pursues, the saliency of supply and demand and price, and how it pursues them, criminology is much more open to a wide variety of modes of inquiry. It tries to address quite a range of forms of crime, from the ordinary street crime that dominates the UCR to domestic disputes to white collar crime to official corruption to terrorism. It is also beset by an enormous array of causal factors that contribute to crime, including variations in personal characteristics like socioeconomic status, age, income, and gender, family structure, education, and environmental characteristics like lead, gangs, culture, formal social control instruments like laws, police, courts, and parole officers, and informal social control instruments like family, relatives, and neighbors. Many of these issues are addressed here, but bringing them all in would require an encyclopedia. Maybe that's the next step for Maltz and Rice.

Pittsburgh, PA, USA   Alfred C. Blumstein

Contents

Section 3   Mining Records

Section 4   Analyses of Existing Data

Section 5   Visual and Geographical Tools

Contributors

Lynn A. Addington American University, Washington, DC, USA

Alfred C. Blumstein Carnegie Mellon University, Pittsburgh, PA, USA

Jonathan P. Caulkins Heinz College, Carnegie Mellon University, Pittsburgh, PA, USA

Philip J. Cook Sanford School of Public Policy, Duke University, Durham, NC, USA

R. Brent Decker University of Illinois at Chicago, Chicago, IL, USA

Scott H. Decker, Ph.D. School of Criminology and Criminal Justice, Arizona State University, Phoenix, AZ, USA

Amy Farrell Northeastern University, Boston, MA, USA

Elizabeth R. Groff Temple University, Philadelphia, PA, USA

Matthew J. Hickman, Ph.D. Seattle University, Seattle, WA, USA

Valerie Jenness University of California, Irvine, Irvine, CA, USA

David Kennedy John Jay College of Criminal Justice, New York, NY, USA

Charis E. Kubrin University of California, Irvine, Irvine, CA, USA

Gary LaFree START Center, University of Maryland, College Park, MD, USA

Kenneth C. Land Duke University, Durham, NC, USA

Pamela K. Lattimore, Ph.D. RTI International, Research Triangle Park, NC, USA

Janet L. Lauritsen University of Missouri, St. Louis, MO, USA

Jens Ludwig University of Chicago, Chicago, IL, USA

Michael D. Maltz University of Illinois at Chicago, Chicago, IL, USA
Ohio State University, Columbus, OH, USA

Peter Moskos John Jay College of Criminal Justice, New York, NY, USA

Alex R. Piquero University of Texas at Dallas, Richardson, TX, USA

Nicole Rafter Northeastern University, Boston, MA, USA

Charles Ransford University of Illinois at Chicago, Chicago, IL, USA

Stephen K. Rice Department of Criminal Justice, Seattle University, Seattle, WA, USA

D. Kim Rossmo School of Criminal Justice, Texas State University, San Marcos, TX, USA

Randolph Roth Ohio State University, Columbus, OH, USA

Robert J. Sampson Harvard University, Cambridge, MA, USA

Wesley G. Skogan Northwestern University, Evanston, IL, USA

Gary Slutkin University of Illinois at Chicago, Chicago, IL, USA

Dietrich Lester Smith Chaminade College Preparatory School, St. Louis, MO, USA

Susan Turner University of California, Irvine, Irvine, CA, USA

Sudhir Venkatesh Columbia University, New York, NY, USA

David Weisburd The Hebrew University, Jerusalem, Israel
George Mason University, Fairfax, VA, USA

Cathy Spatz Widom John Jay College of Criminal Justice, New York, NY, USA

About the Editors

Michael D. Maltz is Professor Emeritus of Criminal Justice and of Information and Decision Sciences at the University of Illinois at Chicago. He is also Senior Research Scientist at the Ohio State University's Criminal Justice Research Center and Adjunct Professor of Sociology at OSU. He is the author of *Recidivism* (1984), which won awards in both criminology and operations research, and coauthor of *Mapping Crime in Its Community Setting* (1990) and was Editor of *the Journal of Quantitative Criminology* from 1996 to 2000. From 1995 to 2000 he was a Visiting Fellow at the Bureau of Justice Statistics (BJS), working on the development of graphical and geographical methods of analyzing data. For the past few years, he has focused his attention on two areas: assessing and improving the quality of crime data and improving the methods used to analyze criminal justice data. He is currently analyzing missing data in the FBI's Uniform Crime Reports and developing imputation methods to improve their accuracy. Maltz received his undergraduate degree from Rensselaer Polytechnic Institute and his Ph.D. from Stanford University, both in electrical engineering.

Stephen K. Rice is Associate Professor of Criminal Justice at Seattle University. He studies cooperation and defiance in individuals' interactions with the justice system (procedural justice, restorative justice; perceptions of racial profiling; police legitimacy; radicalization; final statements of the condemned); sentinel events; social media and criminal justice; data visualization; evidence-based law enforcement. He is co-editor of Race, Ethnicity and Policing (NYU Press, 2010) and Envisioning Criminology (Springer, 2015) and author of articles on topics to include guardian policing (Harvard Executive Session on Policing and Public Safety), radicalization, the variability of anger cross-culturally, and profiling of African Americans, Latinos, and Muslim Americans. His publications have appeared in outlets to include Criminology, Justice Quarterly, Deviant Behavior, and the Journal of Quantitative Criminology. He received his master's degree from Florida State University and his Ph.D. from the University of Florida.

About the Authors

Lynn A. Addington is an associate professor in the Department of Justice, Law and Criminology at American University in Washington, DC. She earned her Ph.D. in criminal justice from the University at Albany (SUNY) and her J.D. from the University of Pennsylvania Law School. Her research focuses on violent victimization with an emphasis on adolescents and school environments as well as the measurement of crime and utilization of national crime statistics. In addition to her faculty appointment at AU, she has served as a Visiting Fellow with the Bureau of Justice Statistics. In 2015, she will begin a 4-year term as editor of *Homicide Studies*. Her recent publications have appeared in a range of outlets including the *Journal of Quantitative Criminology*, *Justice Quarterly*, and *Trauma, Violence and Abuse*. She is the co-editor (with James P. Lynch) of a volume of original research entitled *Understanding Crime Statistics: Revisiting the Divergence of the NCVS and UCR* (2007, Cambridge University Press).

Alfred C. Blumstein is a University Professor and the J. Erik Jonsson Professor of Urban Systems and Operations Research and former Dean (from 1986 to 1993) at the H. John Heinz III College of Carnegie Mellon University. He has had extensive experience in both research and policy with the criminal justice system since serving the President's Commission on Law Enforcement and Administration of Justice in 1966–1967 as Director of its Task Force on Science and Technology. He has chaired NAS panels on Research on Deterrent and Incapacitative Effects, on Sentencing Research, and on Research on Criminal Careers. In 1998, he was elected to membership in the National Academy of Engineering. On the policy side, Dr. Blumstein served from 1979 to 1990 as Chairman of the Pennsylvania Commission on Crime and Delinquency, the state's criminal justice planning agency. He served on the Pennsylvania Commission on Sentencing from 1986 to 1996. He was the recipient of the 2007 Stockholm Prize in Criminology. Dr. Blumstein is a Fellow of the American Society of Criminology, was the 1987 recipient of the Society's Sutherland Award for "contributions to research," and was the president of the Society in 1991–1992. He recently chaired the Science Advisory Board for the Office of Justice Programs of the US Dept. of Justice. His education includes a degree of Bachelor of Engineering Physics and a Ph.D. in Operations Research, both from Cornell University. His research over the past 20 years has covered many aspects of criminal-justice phenomena and policy, including crime measurement, criminal careers, sentencing, deterrence and incapacitation, prison populations, demographic trends, juvenile violence, and drug-enforcement policy.

Jonathan P. Caulkins is H. Guyford Stever Professor of Operations Research and Public Policy at Carnegie Mellon University's Heinz College. He specializes in systems analysis of problems pertaining to drugs, crime, terror, violence, and prevention—work that won the David Kershaw Award from the Association of Public Policy Analysis and Management, a Robert Wood Johnson Health Investigator Award, and the INFORMS President's Award. Issues surrounding marijuana legalization have been a particular focus in recent years; other interests include optimal control, reputation and brand management, prevention, and black markets. He has taught his quantitative decision-making course on 4 continents to students from 50 countries at every level from undergraduate through Ph.D. and executive education. He has authored or co-authored over 125 refereed articles and 9 books including *Marijuana Legalization* (2012, OUP), *Drugs and Drug Policy* (2011, OUP), *Drug Policy and the Public Good* (2010, Oxford), and *Optimal Control of Nonlinear Processes: With Applications in Drugs, Corruption, and Terror* (2008, Springer). He is a past co-director of RAND's Drug Policy Research Center (1994–1996), founding Director of RAND's Pittsburgh office (1999–2001), and continues to work through RAND on a variety of government projects. Dr. Caulkins received a B.S. and an M.S. in Systems Science from Washington University, an S.M. in Electrical Engineering and Computer Science and Ph.D., in Operations Research both from M.I.T.

Philip J. Cook is ITT/Sanford Professor of Public Policy at Duke University. He received his Ph.D. in economics at the University of California, Berkeley in 1973. His substantive interests include topics in public health and social policy: alcohol and tobacco control, crime prevention, firearms regulation, state lotteries, structural influences on educational achievement, and sources of growing economic inequality. He has served as an advisor to the Criminal Division of the US Department of Justice, and to the Enforcement Division of the US Department of Treasury. He has also served on a number of expert panels of the National Academy of Sciences on violence- and crime-related topics, and in 2001 was elected to membership in the Institute of Medicine. He serves as co-organizer of the NBER Workshop on the Economics of Crime. He has authored or co-authored a number of books, including *Gun Violence: The Real Costs* (with Jens Ludwig, 2000) and *The Gun Debate: What Everyone Needs to Know* (with Kristin A. Goss, 2014).

R. Brent Decker has been with Cure Violence since March of 2003. He has worked with a wide range of United States and International partners to adapt, train, and provide ongoing technical assistance on the implementation of the Cure Violence model. Mr. Decker's focus has been on the development of systems to adapt, train, and implement the model to contexts outside of Chicago. The areas where Mr. Decker has worked with Cure Violence include Chicago, Baltimore, New York, New Orleans, Philadelphia, Kansas City, Honduras, Colombia, Iraq, Trinidad & Tobago, South Africa, Kenya, and

England. Decker holds a Masters of Public Health (MPH) in International public health and development and a Masters of Social Work (MSW) in clinical social work from Tulane University. Before joining Cure Violence, Mr. Decker worked on a number of public health and social justice projects throughout Central and South America.

Scott H. Decker graduated from DePauw University with a B.A. in Social Justice. He earned the Ph.D. in Criminology from Florida State University in 1976. He is Foundation Professor in the School of Criminology and Criminal Justice at Arizona State University. His main research interests are in the areas of gangs, violence, criminal justice policy, and the offender's perspective. He is a Fellow in the American Society of Criminology and the Academy of Criminal Justice Sciences.

Amy Farrell is Associate Professor of Criminology and Criminal Justice at Northeastern University. Her scholarship seeks to understand arrest, adjudication, and criminal case disposition practices. Professor Farrell also conducts research on police legitimacy and law enforcement responses to new crimes such as hate crime and human trafficking. Her recent research examines how changes in state human trafficking laws impact the identification and prosecution of human trafficking offenders. Professor Farrell has testified about police identification of human trafficking before the U.S. House of Representatives Judiciary Committee. Professor Farrell was a co-recipient of NIJ's W.E.B. DuBois Fellowship on crime justice and culture in 2006.

Elizabeth R. Groff (Ph.D. in geography, 2006, University of Maryland) is an associate professor in the Criminal Justice department at Temple University. Her research focuses on place-based criminology and policing which she investigates using geographic information systems, randomized controlled experiments, and agent-based simulation models.

Matthew J. Hickman is Associate Professor of Criminal Justice at Seattle University. He has been involved in applied police research for approximately 15 years, beginning as a doctoral student working on community policing and police integrity projects in the City of Philadelphia, and carrying into his first career as a government researcher with the Bureau of Justice Statistics. At BJS, he specialized in the development and analysis of national data collections relating to law enforcement operations as well as forensic issues in the United States. For the past 7 years, he has served on the criminal justice faculty and has an active research agenda focused primarily on issues in policing, quantitative research methodology, and the impact of forensic sciences on the administration of justice. His work has been published in numerous peer-reviewed journals and edited volumes. He is recent co-editor, with Kevin Strom, of Forensic Science and the Administration of Justice (Sage).

Valerie Jenness is a Professor in the Department of Criminology, Law and Society and in the Department of Sociology and she is Dean of the School of Social Ecology at the University of California, Irvine. Her research focuses on the links between deviance and social control; the politics of crime control;

social movements and social change; and corrections and public policy. She is the author of four books, including: *Appealing to Justice: Prisoner Grievances, Rights, and Carceral Logic* (with Kitty Calavita); *Making Hate a Crime: From Social Movement to Law Enforcement Practice* (with Ryken Grattet); *Hate Crimes: New Social Movements and the Politics of Violence* (with Kendal Broad); and *Making it Work: The Prostitutes' Rights Movement in Perspective.* She is the co-editor of *Routing the Opposition: Social Movements, Public Policy, and Democracy* (with David Meyer and Helen Ingram) and many articles published in sociology, law, and criminology journals. Her work has been honored with awards from the American Sociological Association, Society for the Study of Social Problems, the Pacific Sociological Association, the Law and Society Association, the Western Society of Criminology, University of California, and Gustavus Myers Center for the Study of Bigotry and Human Rights in North America. She has worked with corrections officials in the state of California, the Los Angeles Police Department, and Immigration and Customs Enforcement officials to develop innovative law enforcement policy and law enforcement training programs. She is the Past President of the Pacific Sociological Association and the Study of Social Problems.

David Kennedy is the director of the Center for Crime Prevention and Control at John Jay College of Criminal Justice in New York City. He directed the Boston Gun Project, whose "Operation Ceasefire" intervention was responsible for a more than 60% reduction in youth homicide victimization and won the Ford Foundation Innovations in Government award; the Herman Goldstein International Award for Problem Oriented Policing; and the International Association of Chiefs of Police Webber Seavey Award. He developed the "High Point" drug market elimination strategy, which also won an Innovations in Government Award. He helped design and field the Justice Department's Strategic Approaches to Community Safety Initiative, the Treasury Department's Youth Crime Gun Interdiction Initiative, and the Bureau of Justice Assistance's Drug Market Intervention Program. He is the co-chair of the National Network for Safe Communities, which includes more than 50 jurisdictions—among them Los Angeles, Chicago, Milwaukee, Cincinnati, Boston, Providence, High Point, North Carolina, Newark, and the states of California and North Carolina—that are dedicated to reducing crime, reducing incarceration, and addressing the racial conflict associated with traditional crime policy. He is the author of *Deterrence and Crime Prevention: Reconsidering the Prospect of Sanction*, coauthor of *Beyond 911: A New Era for Policing*, and a wide range of articles on gang violence, drug markets, domestic violence, firearms trafficking, deterrence theory, and other public safety issues. His latest book, *Don't Shoot*, will be released by Bloomsbury on September 27, 2011.

Charis E. Kubrin is Professor of Criminology, Law and Society and (by courtesy) Sociology at the University of California, Irvine. She has published widely on the intersection of music, culture, and social identity, particularly as it applies to hip hop and minority youth in disadvantaged communities. She has served as an expert witness and consultant in multiple criminal cases involving rap music as evidence of alleged underlying criminal activity. She recently gave a TEDx talk, Rap on Trial, on this issue (https://www.youtube.com/watch?v=cjTIhRtFJbU) and also co-authored an amicus brief about rap music for a rap lyrics case soon to be heard by the US Supreme Court. In 2005, she received the Ruth Shonle Cavan Young Scholar Award from the American Society of Criminology.

Gary LaFree is Director of the National Consortium for the Study of Terrorism and Responses to Terrorism (START) and a Distinguished Scholar Teacher in the Department of Criminology and Criminal Justice at the University of Maryland. He is a Fellow of the American Society of Criminology (ASC) and has served as President of the ASC. Much of Dr. LaFree's research is related to understanding criminal violence.

Kenneth C. Land is Research Professor in the Social Science Research Institute and the John Franklin Crowell Professor of Sociology and Demography Emeritus at Duke University. His research interests are in the development of mathematical and statistical models and methods for substantive applications in demography, criminology, economics, and social indicators/quality-of-life studies. Ken is the author or co-author of over 200 publications. He has been listed on the Institute for Scientific Information Highly Cited webpage as one of the 400 most highly cited social scientists in recent years. Ken is an elected fellow of five professional societies, including the American Statistical Association, the American Society for the Advancement of Science, the Sociological Research Association, the American Society of Criminology, and the International Society for Quality-of-Life Studies. He is well known in criminology for his research on structural covariates of crime rates across various levels of analysis, including neighborhoods, cities, metropolitan areas, and states/provinces, the effects of unemployment levels and fluctuations on crime rates, latent trajectory models of delinquent/criminal careers, and multilevel crime opportunity theory.

Pamela K. Lattimore is Director of RTI's Center for Justice, Safety, and Resilience, which focuses on improving understanding of crime and related problems, criminal justice systems, safety threats and responses, and prevention and intervention activities designed to ameliorate societal problems and increase community and individual resilience. Her research focuses on the evaluation of interventions; investigation into the causes and correlates of criminal behavior, including substance use and mental health; and development of approaches to improve criminal justice operations. Dr. Lattimore is an internationally recognized expert on prisoner reentry, having led the National Institute of Justice (NIJ)-funded multisite evaluation of the Serious and Violent Offender Reentry Initiative (SVORI), including a follow-on effort to examine desistance among SVORI evaluation participants, and currently is leading an NIJ-funded study of reentry programs supported by Second Chance Act (SCA). She is the principal investigator for the NIJ-funded evaluation of the Honest Opportunity Probation with Enforcement Demonstration Field Experiment and is also principal investigator for a Department of Defense multimodal study examining military workplace violence. She served as Chair of the Division on Corrections and Sentencing of the American Society of Criminology (2001–2003) and is a Fellow of the Academy of Experimental Criminology. Before joining RTI in 1998, Dr. Lattimore worked for 10 years at NIJ, most recently as director of the Criminal Justice and Criminal Behavior Division, Office of Research and Evaluation. Dr. Lattimore was also a professor in the Department of Criminology and Criminal Justice at the University of South Carolina (2003–2006).

Janet L. Lauritsen is Curators' Professor of Criminology and Criminal Justice at the University of Missouri—St. Louis. She received her Ph.D. in sociology from the University of Illinois in 1989. Her research is focused on the social distribution of victimization and its consequences, and the methods of measuring crime and victimization. She is a Fellow of the American Society of Criminology.

Jens Ludwig is the McCormick Foundation Professor of Social Service Administration, Law, and Public Policy at the University of Chicago, and Director of the University of Chicago Crime Lab. His work focuses on urban policy challenges related to crime, education, poverty, and housing. He has published in leading scientific journals across a range of disciplines including Science, New England Journal of Medicine, Journal of the American Medical Association, American Economic Review, Quarterly Journal of Economics, Criminology, American Journal of Sociology, and American Journal of Public Health. In 2012, he was elected to the Institute of Medicine of the National Academy of Sciences. In 2014, the Crime Lab was awarded a $1 million prize from the Macarthur Foundation for creativity and effectiveness, the organizational equivalent of the foundation's "genius prize" for individuals.

Peter Moskos is an associate professor at John Jay College of Criminal Justice in the Department of Law, Police Science, and Criminal Justice Administration. A former Baltimore City police officer and Harvard and Princeton trained sociologist, Moskos studies people the old-fashioned way: He talks to them. In addition to his primary duties at John Jay College, Moskos is a faculty member in CUNY's Doctoral Programs in Sociology and Criminal Justice, teaches introductory police classes at LaGuardia Community College in Queens, and is a Senior Fellow of the Yale Urban Ethnography Project. Moskos's three books—*Cop in the Hood*, In *Defense of Flogging*, and *Greek Americans*—have won high praise and earned him recognition as one of Atlantic Magazine's "Brave Thinkers" of 2011. He has also published in the Washington Post, Washington Monthly, the New York Times, Macleans, Pacific Standard, Slate, The Chronicle of Higher Education, and his blog, Copinthehood.com.

Alex R. Piquero is Ashbel Smith Professor of Criminology at the University of Texas at Dallas, Adjunct Professor Key Centre for Ethics, Law, Justice, and Governance, Griffith University Australia, and Faculty Affiliate, Center for Violence and Injury Prevention George Warren Brown School of Social Work Washington University in St. Louis. He has received several research, teaching, and mentoring awards and is Fellow of both the American Society of Criminology and the Academy of Criminal Justice Sciences. In 2014, he received the University of Texas System Board of Regents Outstanding Teaching Award.

Nicole Rafter a professor at Northeastern University since 1977 has authored five monographs; a sixth, *Toward a Criminology of Genocide*, will be published in 2015 by NYU Press. She has also translated (with Mary Gibson) the two major criminological works by Cesare Lombroso. She has won a number of awards, including the Sutherland Award of the American Society of Criminology and a Fulbright fellowship to Austria. One of the great pleasures of her academic life has been working in the same department as Amy Farrell, first as Amy's dissertation supervisor, more recently as a colleague and collaborator.

Charles Ransford is Director of Science and Policy of Cure Violence, a program of the School of Public Health of the University of Illinois at Chicago. He is responsible for advancing the theoretical basis for the Cure Violence Health Approach and building and leading a national effort to create a health sector framework around violence prevention. Over the years, he has been involved in many aspects of Cure Violence, including data and evaluation, strategic planning, communications, and dissemination of the model nationally and globally—and authored several papers on the Cure Violence health approach. He frequently presents Cure Violence policy initiatives, findings and results at national and international conferences and has authored several papers on a health approach to violence prevention. A graduate (MPP) of the Harris School for Public Policy at the University of Chicago, Charlie was named a McCormick Leadership Fellow and a Bowman Memorial Fellow.

D. Kim Rossmo is the University Endowed Chair in Criminology and the Director of the Center for Geospatial Intelligence and Investigation in the School of Criminal Justice at Texas State University. A former detective inspector with the Vancouver Police Department in Canada, he has researched and published in the areas of environmental criminology, the geography of crime, and criminal investigations. Dr. Rossmo is a member of the International Association of Chiefs of Police (ICAP) Advisory Committee for Police Investigative Operations and is the chair of the Austin Public Safety Commission. He has written books on geographic profiling and criminal investigative failures.

Randolph Roth is Professor of History and Sociology at Ohio State University and a fellow of the American Association for the Advancement of Science. He is the author of *American Homicide* (The Belknap Press of Harvard University Press, 2009), which received the Michael J. Hindelang Award of the American Society of Criminology and Allan Sharlin Memorial Award of the Social Science History Association. He is a member of the National Academy of Sciences Roundtable on Crime Trends. He is current working on a history of child murder in the United States from colonial times to the present.

Robert J. Sampson is Henry Ford II Professor of the Social Sciences at Harvard University and Director of the Boston Area Research Initiative.

A member of the National Academy of Sciences, American Academy of Arts and Sciences, and the American Philosophical Society, he served as President of the American Society of Criminology in 2012 and in June 2011 he and John Laub received the Stockholm Prize in Criminology. Sampson has published widely on crime, disorder, the life course, neighborhood effects, urban inequality, immigration, and the social structure of the city. His two books on life-course criminology were published with John Laub—*Crime in the Making: Pathways and Turning Points through Life* (Harvard, 1993) and *Shared Beginnings, Divergent Lives: Delinquent Boys to Age 70s* (Harvard, 2003). In 2012, the University of Chicago Press published *Great American City: Chicago and the Enduring Neighborhood Effect,* the culmination of over a decade of research based on the Project on Human Development in Chicago Neighborhoods, for which Sampson served as Scientific Director.

Wesley G. Skogan holds a joint appointment in Northwestern University's Institute for Policy Research and Department of Political Science. His most recent books on policing are*: Police and Community in Chicago*, and *Community Policing: Can It Work?* Prof. Skogan was co-editor of a policy-oriented report from the National Research Council, *Fairness and Effectiveness in Policing: The Evidence*, and he chaired the committee that produced it. From 1999 to 2004 he chaired the National Research Council's Committee on Research on Police Policies and Practices and was a member of NRC's Committee on Law and Justice. Another line of his research includes crime prevention; this led to his book *Coping with Crime*, and a number of articles on community responses to crime. Prof. Skogan has also been involved in research on criminal victimization and the evaluation of service programs for victims.

Gary Slutkin is a physician and epidemiologist at the University of Illinois at Chicago, and the Founder and Executive Director of Cure Violence, a scientifically proven health approach to violence reduction using behavior change and epidemic control methods. The Cure Violence approach has substantially reduced shootings and killings in areas where it is deployed. In 2013, Cure Violence was named one of the ten best nongovernmental organizations (NGOs) in the world by the Global Journal—and listed as the top NGO dedicated to reducing violence. His view of violence as contagious has been confirmed by the most recent Institute of Medicine Report, *The Contagion of Violence*. The Cure Violence method is working in over 60 communities in more than 25 cities in the United States and in 5 countries. Slutkin received his M.D. from the University of Chicago Pritzker School of Medicine, and completed his internship, residency, and infectious disease training at UCSF/San Francisco General Hospital. He ran the Tuberculosis (TB) Program for San Francisco (1981–1985), worked in Africa, and then joined the World Health Organization working in over 20 countries. Slutkin's work has been featured in The Interrupters, a documentary film about the work of Cure Violence and most recently in New York Times best-selling authors' Nicholas Kristof and Sheryl WuDunn's new book, *A Path Appears*.

He has received numerous national and international awards including the US Attorney General's Award for Outstanding Contributions to Community partnerships for Public Safety.

Dietrich Lester Smith has been the Director for Diversity at Chaminade College Preparatory School in St. Louis, Missouri, for the past 16 years. He has served as consultant to the US Department of Justice (NIJ), the US Department of Health and Human Services (ACF), and the US Department of Education (SE). In 1989, he joined the staff of the Criminal Justice Department of the University of Missouri-St. Louis, as a Field Research Analyst for three federally funded investigations. (Youth Gang, Burglary, and Armed Robbery studies). He served as consultant for the History Channel Gangland Series. Mr. Smith is coauthor of "A Woman's Place is in the Home: Females and Residential Burglary" and "A Snowball's Chance in Hell: Doing Fieldwork with Active Residential Burglars." He is a board member of Brothers Keepers SCI, a not-for-profit organization devoted to assisting spinal cord injury victims through violence and serves on the St. Louis County Commission on Disability.

Susan Turner is a Professor in the Department of Criminology, Law and Society at the University of California, Irvine. She also serves as Director of the Center for Evidence-Based Corrections and is an appointee of the President of the University of California to the California Rehabilitation Oversight Board (C-ROB). She received her M.A. and Ph.D. in Social Psychology from the University of North Carolina, Chapel Hill. She led a variety of research projects while she was a Senior Behavioral Scientist at RAND, including studies on racial disparity, field experiments of private sector alternatives for serious juvenile offenders, work release, day fines, and a 14-site evaluation of intensive supervision probation. Dr. Turner's areas of expertise include the design and implementation of randomized field experiments and research collaborations with state and local justice agencies. At UCI, she has assisted the California Department of Corrections and Rehabilitation in the development and validation of a risk assessment tool as well as an evaluation of a parole violation decision-making instrument designed to provide an orderly decision-making process for response to violations of parole. Most recently, she is involved in several evaluations of the impact of California's realignment on state and county justice systems. Dr. Turner is a member of the American Society of Criminology, the American Probation and Parole Association, a Fellow of the Academy of Experimental Criminology, and past Chair of the Division of Corrections and Sentencing, American Society of Criminology.

David Weisburd is Distinguished Professor of Criminology, Law and Society at George Mason University and Walter E. Meyer Professor of Law and Criminal Justice at the Hebrew University. He is author or editor of more than 20 books and 150 scientific articles that cover a wide range of criminal justice research topics, including crime at place, white collar crime, policing, illicit markets, terrorism, criminal justice statistics, and social deviance. Professor Weisburd is the recipient of the 2010 Stockholm Prize in Criminology and the

2014 Sutherland Award from the American Society of Criminology. He is also the founding editor of the *Journal of Experimental Criminology* and the editor of the *Journal of Quantitative Criminology*.

Cathy Spatz Widom, Ph.D. is a Distinguished Professor in the Psychology Department at John Jay College and a member of the Graduate Center faculty, City University of New York. A former faculty member at Harvard, Indiana, University at Albany (SUNY), and New Jersey Medical School, she has served on the editorial boards of psychology, criminology, and child maltreatment journals. She is an elected fellow of the American Psychological Association, American Psychopathological Association, and American Society of Criminology and has been invited to testify before congressional and state committees. Widom served on the Institute of Medicine Committee on Child Maltreatment Research, Policy, and Practice for the Next Decade and is a member of the Committee on Law and Justice at the Commission on Behavioral and Social Sciences at the National Research Council. She has received numerous awards for her research, including the 1989 American Association for the Advancement of Science Behavioral Science Research Prize for her paper on the "cycle of violence." In 2013, she was honored to receive the Edwin H. Sutherland Award from the American Society of Criminology. Widom and her colleagues have published over 130 papers and book chapters on the long-term consequences of childhood abuse (physical and sexual) and neglect, and she recently completed a major study on the intergenerational transmission of child abuse and neglect. Dr. Widom received her Ph.D. in psychology from Brandeis University.

Introduction

Michael D. Maltz and Stephen K. Rice

As Alfred Blumstein noted in the Foreword, we started out to edit a book describing the new visualization techniques that have recently been developed for research into crime and criminal justice. We felt that this was an important goal, since articles in social science and criminology journals usually present data analyses in tables, which can be mind-numbing, rather than in figures and charts. In contrast, most articles in hard science journals are usually filled with graphical representations of data rather than relying entirely on tables. Our feeling was that not enough attention has been paid to those techniques in the social sciences (Maltz, 1994). Specific to sociology, Healy and Moody (2014) argue that in its infancy sociology did, in fact, employ innovative visualizations, e.g., Du Bois's *The Philadelphia Negro*'s (1898/1967) choropleth maps, time series, and table-and-histogram combinations, but that in later years the employment of visualizations was hampered by thoughts that compared to causal-inferential modeling they were unduly descriptive, were thought to be unsophisticated, and tended to lag behind the computational abilities of the day (p. 107).

However, the deeper we got into our own exploration of these (and other) research methods, the more we realized that, in terms of new methods and approaches to help understand crime and criminal justice processes, visualization techniques were but a small part of the innovations that have been developed in the past few decades. True, they are an integral part of crime mapping, which has burgeoned since the early 1990s, both in terms of police use as a deployment tool and as a major component of the sociology of space and place, but other new methods have also contributed to our understanding of crime and criminal justice.

Better Understanding the "Meta-Research" of Crime and Criminal Justice

But there are limitations to our understanding of how these innovative ideas were developed. First, many journals have page limitations and often specify how the papers should be structured. This restriction prevents researchers from telling the full story, for example, of why they chose the topic or method they did.

Second, many studies cannot be easily separated from the personal and social context of the researcher, in terms of what the researcher chooses to study, how the study proceeds, and

M.D. Maltz (✉)
University of Illinois at Chicago, Chicago, IL, USA

Ohio State University, Columbus, OH, USA
e-mail: maltzmd@gmail.com

S.K. Rice
Department of Criminal Justice, Seattle University, Seattle, WA, USA

M.D. Maltz and S.K. Rice (eds.), *Envisioning Criminology: Researchers on Research as a Process of Discovery*, DOI 10.1007/978-3-319-15868-6_1, © Springer International Publishing Switzerland 2015

how it is received by the field. It also matters in a researcher's selection of a problem to study and in the researcher's decision as to how to approach the study of a problem. We feel that it is important to document this aspect of the research process, recognizing that researchers are not just "objective" measurement devices, and that their research is often shaped by turning points in their careers.

Before we turn to how these researchers describe their own personal journeys, we first look at what was, for a long time, the standard way of doing research and explaining findings. We then describe how this led to a standard way of presenting research in journals. The concept of "objectivity" in research is then discussed. The last section attempts to organize the disparate accounts of the contributors into a meaningful order.

Old Methods, New Methods

In the beginning was the random sample, accompanied by the test of significance. When Ronald Fisher wrote his classic book, *Statistical Methods for Research Workers*, almost a century ago, data were hard to come by. In some fields, it continues to be difficult to obtain large amounts of data, and some studies need be based on small samples and significance tests.

Moreover, the analytic techniques that were available to Fisher and his contemporaries were limited as well. Correlation, regression, analysis of variance: these were the primary statistical tools that were available, and significance tests were used to determine whether the relationships that the techniques discovered were more likely to be true, or just due to random variation.[1] And since tests of significance are used primarily to compare means, there is an implicit assumption that only the mean of a statistical distribution is important, and that the distribution is only important as a measure of variance around the mean.

At the time that these techniques were developed, and up into the 1960s, the "computer" was the desk calculator. It could just perform the basic arithmetic functions of addition, subtraction, multiplication, division, and finding the square root. This constituted the available technology when Sheldon and Eleanor Glueck (1950) conducted their studies of delinquency. The situation was noticeably better when Marvin Wolfgang, Robert Figlio, and Thorsten Sellin (WFS) published their landmark study, *Delinquency in a Birth Cohort* (1972). In both of these studies, a sample of juveniles was selected, and information about them, their families, and their infractions was collected.

The Gluecks' studies occurred prior to the use of computers in social science research, so their methods of analysis were restricted by what they could accomplish using calculators and card sorters. The WFS study, on the other hand, was able to use computerized methods, which had recently become available in the form of BMD, a biomedical software package. Although WFS had a digital computer available to them, it still required them to transcribe the data into computers; that is, individuals had to read the documents, code the data gleaned from the documents into numbers, transcribe the coded data onto punched cards, and then run the cards through the statistical package. Those of us who were doing computations during that era recall all too well the difficulty that a misspelling or an extra comma or omitted slash could bring about—especially when only the first error (of possibly many) was detected on each run, and the turnaround time for finding each error was 24 hours!

That was then, this is now: in many areas of research in criminology and criminal justice, we are blessed (or cursed) with a fire hose of data. Significance tests, when applied to large samples, are meaningless, since they often show that *all* results are significant. And this, in turn, has led to the development of many of the innovations we describe herein. For example, one can now easily parse data geographically, looking at differences among smaller and smaller units of analysis, thereby reducing the size of the groups being compared. Some researchers have taken advantage of

---

[1] Although statistical significance only has meaning in the case of random samples, it was (and still is) applied in all too many cases in which this and other assumptions (normality, independence of observations, homoscedasticity, etc.) are violated.

the computer's versatility and developed ways of visualizing and mapping data that tease out patterns heretofore undiscovered. Others have looked more closely at survey methods and found new ways of slicing and dicing data. Still others have looked through microscopes instead of telescopes, and found new ways of understanding previously untapped areas of study.

One of the goals of this volume is to display some of these methods that so far have not shown up in textbooks on research methods in criminology and criminal justice. We hope that it will serve as a one-stop shop for describing not the research innovations themselves, but how they came about, which we feel is important to document.

Publication Restrictions

While new methods have been developed and used, academic and professional journals have been less welcoming, not to publishing the *results* of these inquiries, but to publishing the ways that the new information has been obtained. That is, more and more journals (e.g., the *Journal of Quantitative Criminology* and *Journal of Experimental Criminology*) are specifying that papers be organized into specific sections: Objectives, Methods, Data, Results, Discussion, and Conclusions. As a result, we can expect that much of the spirit of discovery may be squeezed out of the articles published by these journals. This all but eliminates the excitement and fun (and travail) that constitute a major part of the discovery process. Another goal of this volume, therefore, is to have researchers describe some of the issues they contended with in their own research, along with the frustrations and blind alleys and insights that may be filtered out of the publication process. They include personal accounts by the researchers of the problem they were trying to solve, and how (and why) they developed their solutions. We hope that this gives readers some ideas as to how to think "outside the box" of the standard research paradigm.

The authors of these chapters all have different stories, depending on their own experiences,

what tickled their fancy, what problems they confronted, and how they approached the topics they studied. We want to give readers a feel for and appreciation of the different ways of "thinking like a researcher."

That is: when a research method is described, often omitted are the ancillary aspects. If we consider that there are three phases of research, the "pre-do," the "do," and the "post-do," what is published most often is the *doing*, and the results of that effort. Missing from most descriptions of research are what we feel are important pre-do and post-do contextual matters that, we believe, constitute much of the more interesting and enjoyable—and sometimes frustrating—aspects of doing research.

Pre-do: what made the researchers think of the topic, what problems did they see that they were trying to understand, how did they hit on this way of doing it? What difficulties did they encounter, were there false starts, did they have doubts (and how did they deal with them)? Quoting Isaac Asimov, Howard Wainer and Shaun Lysen (2009) noted that the most exciting phrase to hear in science is not "Eureka!" but "That's funny...." What were the researchers' "funny" moments?

Post-do: To throw in a cliché, Isaac Newton famously noted that he could see further because he was standing on the shoulders of giants. But even when he came back down to earth, he stepped on the toes of some of his rivals.[2] And in the policy-laden fields we inhabit, this is bound to happen to a much greater extent than in physics and mathematics. How have those authors for whom the shoe fits (pun intended) dealt with the pushback?

Obviously, not all of the authors deal with the same issues in their research, which is exactly the point of this book. Some developed more data-heavy methods, others focused on small-N situations, but all are looking to solve problems and extract information from their data sources (or to generate new data) that was not heretofore available.

---

[2] In fact, the battle between Newton and Gottfried Leibniz over who invented/discovered calculus got pretty bitter.

Objectivity

One of the points that these essays collectively make is the role of the researcher in conducting research. We all realize that, in social research, the measuring "instrument," the researcher, influences the "data." In particular, ethnographic studies, wherein the researcher embeds himself/herself into a neighborhood, situation, or network, are affected by the gender, ethnicity, attitude, age, etc. of the ethnographer. However, responses to a survey are similarly affected by the characteristics of the questioner—or by use of a computer or even by question order. But it is also true that the characteristics of those of us who do "hard" data analysis, unsullied (so to speak) by contact with the data providers, have influence on our analyses and our results. That is, none of us are truly objective in our search for knowledge. As Steve Heims (1980) notes:

> The ethos of science rests on two pillars, the politically useful myth of "value neutrality" and the article of faith most conducive to the growth of scientific bureaucracy, namely, that scientific innovations ("progress") and science-based technological innovations are a priori beneficial. While these two pillars clearly knock against each other, they continue to hold up the practice of science.[3]

---

[3] In a response to a review of his book, Heims (1982) wrote: "According to prevailing tradition the ideas in mathematics, physics, and philosophy are regarded as having no connection with the social circumstances or personal characteristics of their progenitors. Such a complete dichotomy between thoughts and the thinker, however tidy, seems to me artificial and naive. Indeed, one of my motives for writing the book was to address the paucity of literature exhibiting connections between a mathematician's or theoretical physicist's scientific style and social conditions, motivations, and personal themes."

In our field(s), this is especially true. First, most of us have been drawn into the study of crime and criminal justice, not just because they contain inherently interesting problems, but also because we can use our skills to understand, and therefore reduce, societal harms (clearly not an "objective" goal). That is not to say that we don't challenge ourselves (and each other) to test our propositions and findings to make sure that they are as accurate and useful as possible, even if they are not truly objective. But even this has its limits: the problems we study take place at a certain time and in a specific context, both of which are continually changing. This has the virtue of keeping us on our toes, as well as presenting us with new problems to study, new challenges to conquer.

Organization of the Book

This book is more like a collection of short stories than a novel that has a beginning, middle, and end. Each of the stories is different, as different as the authors and their backgrounds. A number of themes do come through in many of the contributions. For example, a number of the authors indicate, some explicitly, the value of tenure that permitted them to explore new or complicated issues that would not result in immediate results. Others describe the benefits of mentoring and of persistence and not being discouraged by initial failure. The specific methods used run the gamut from ethnographic ($N=1$) studies to research on big (or biggish) data.

Despite our reservations about creating pigeonholes for these chapters (so many of them fit into a number of categories!), we can consider five areas into which the chapters can be categorized: those that rely on information obtained from the street; those that generate new data; those that mine extant sources of data in new ways; those that describe analyses of existing data; and those that use visual and geographical tools. The following table sorts the chapters into these categories.

Voices from the street	Generating new data	Mining records	Analyses of existing data	Visual and geographic tools
Decker & Smith	Jenness	LaFree	Addington	Caulkins
Kennedy	Kubrin	Rafter & Farrell	Cook & Ludwig	Groff
Moskos	Rice	Roth	Land	Hickman
Slutkin with Ransford & Decker	Sampson	Widom	Lattimore	Maltz
Venkatesh	Skogan		Lauritsen	Rossmo
			Piquero	Weisburd
			Turner	

This selection of research (ad)ventures should give the reader an appreciation of the range and breadth of research in criminology and criminal justice, and of the differing viewpoints of the researchers themselves.

References

Du Bois, W. E. B. (1967). *The Philadelphia Negro.* New York, NY: Shocken Books. (Original work published 1898)

Glueck, S., & Glueck, E. (1950). *Unraveling juvenile delinquency.* Cambridge, MA: Harvard University Press.

Healy, K., & Moody, J. (2014). Data visualization in sociology. *Annual Review of Sociology, 40,* 105–128.

Heims, S. J. (1980). *John von Neumann and Norbert Wiener: From mathematics to the technologies of life and death.* Cambridge, MA: MIT Press.

Heims, S. J. (1982, May 13). "Scientists and Life," a reply to a review of Heims (1980). *The New York Review of Books.*

Maltz, M. D. (1994). Deviating from the mean: The declining significance of significance. *Journal of Research in Crime and Delinquency, 31*(4), 434–463.

Wainer, H., & Lysen, S. (2009). That's funny…. *American Scientist, 97*(4), 272.

Wolfgang, M. E., Figlio, R. M., & Sellin, T. (1972). *Delinquency in a birth cohort.* Chicago, IL: University of Chicago Press.

Although much of the data that criminologists and policy analysts deal with is in the form of official records (covered in another section), a great deal of it is based on what occurs on the "street," that is, in interactions between offenders and victims, and between citizens and the police. Getting an appreciation of these interactions is a major focus in the study of criminology and criminal justice. These chapters exemplify some of the issues involved in such studies. David Kennedy ("Warping Time and Space") notes the contradictions in police work: keeping the bad guys at bay while working with some of those same bad guys to keep them out of trouble. Kennedy also provides vivid examples of how "pulling levers"—imposing costs on offenders in their areas of vulnerability—can reduce chronic offending. Peter Moskos ("Observations on the Making of a Police Officer") details the tightrope he had to walk between town (in the form of becoming a police officer in Baltimore MD) and gown (in the form of his dissertation committee). Obtaining data from offenders themselves is another source of street data, as exemplified by the contributions of Scott Decker and Dietrich Smith ("A Conversation with Street Daddy") with active street offenders in St. Louis, and of Sudhir Venkatesh ("Why Criminals Tell Us the Truth") with "Michael" of Robert Taylor Homes, in Chicago. A different take on street interactions is provided by Gary Slutkin with Charles Ransford and R. Brent Decker ("Cure Violence—Treating Violence As a Contagious Disease"), who describe the similarity between the epidemiology of violence and the epidemiology of HIV/AIDS and other diseases, and show how this approach has been used to reduce its prevalence.

A Conversation with Street Daddy: Pulling Back the Curtain on 20 Years of Ethnography

Scott H. Decker and Dietrich Lester Smith

Introduction

From 1989 to 1995 my colleague Richard Wright and I studied hundreds and hundreds of active offenders. When I say "studied" I mean interviewed, followed, observed, created experimental conditions, re-interviewed, cross-validated results, obsessed about ethics, worried about their safety and ours, rode around with them in cars, read and reread transcribed interviews and most provocatively went on "walk-abouts" with them past the sites of their most recent crimes while they were "miked up."

We focused on three specific groups of active, serious street criminals: residential burglars, armed robbers, and street gang members. Officially, we interviewed 105 residential burglars, 99 gang members, and 89 armed robbers. More than half of these individuals were located and interviewed a second time. By the time these three projects were over—all funded with federal grants—we had talked with well over a thousand individuals who plied their trade as high level active offenders. It

S.H. Decker, Ph.D. (✉)
School of Criminology and Criminal Justice,
Arizona State University, Phoenix, AZ, USA
e-mail: Scott.Decker@asu.edu

D.L. Smith
Chaminade College Preparatory School,
St. Louis, MO, USA
e-mail: DSmith@chaminade-stl.com

almost didn't happen. Without the good fortune to be teaching at an urban public university where we each had "Street Daddy" as a student in class these studies may not have been completed.

In 1987, the National Institute of Justice issued a solicitation for proposals to fund research on residential burglary with active offenders. There had been a lot of research on burglars who had been caught and were interviewed in jail or prison, or "reformed" burglars who claimed to no longer be actively offending. Oftentimes, such individuals had been off the street for years, having time to forget some details and embellish others. NIJ was committed to funding research with currently active house burglars, and they deserve credit for taking the risks associated with such an endeavor. One of the proposals to NIJ offered to follow active offenders into houses and observe them as they disposed of their goods and used drugs. They were not funded.

My colleague Richard Wright had conducted field research on burglars with the noted English criminologist Trevor Bennett (Bennett & Wright, 1984). I had published on deterrence and was interested in offender decision making. It seemed a good fit. We responded to the NIJ Request for Proposals promising to interview 20 active residential burglars. The reviewers liked our proposal in every respect save one: no one believed we could find and convince 20 active residential burglars to participate in a research study. We connected with Street Daddy and found a dozen

M.D. Maltz and S.K. Rice (eds.), *Envisioning Criminology: Researchers on Research as a Process of Discovery*, DOI 10.1007/978-3-319-15868-6_2, © Springer International Publishing Switzerland 2015

active residential burglars who participated in a pre-test. We resubmitted our proposal and were funded in 1989. The rest is history. Sort of. History is recorded in a particular way, and there is a lot of "recorded" (i.e., published) history from the initial burglary project and the others that followed (Curry & Decker, 1997; Decker, 1995, 1996, 2000, 2001; Decker & Van Winkle, 1996; Decker, Wright, & Logie, 1993; Decker, Wright, Rooney, & Smith, 1993; Logie, Wright, & Decker, 1992; Wright & Decker, 1994, 1997a, 1997b; Wright, Logie, & Decker, 1995; Wright, Decker, Redfern, & Smith, 1992).

What hasn't been recorded in much detail is the process of finding and dealing with Street Daddy. Sandberg and Copes (2012) note that textbook depictions and accounts of ethnographic research are often very different from ethnography in practice. In this chapter, we attempt to identify the source of some of those differences. Throughout our own work we have tried to discuss, sometimes in excruciating detail, how and why we did what we did. We are not practitioners of "hanging out;" instead we carefully monitor our referral chains, their origins, density, saturation, and variation. Our samples were not haphazard and random; when we found promising nodes, we exploited them for the diversity of information and individuals that they provided. Some we abandoned quickly, others we plumbed for weeks and weeks. We also debriefed Street Daddy regularly, particularly early in the projects where we needed to be sure that our expectations for the kind of offenders we wanted to interview were clear to him, and to us.

Winnie Reed (now retired) was the project monitor and provided excellent guidance throughout the project and others that followed. We were fortunate to have Al Reiss and Carl Klockars assigned to us as outside research consultants who provided insight and suggestions throughout the project. Demonstrating the depth of his stature as an intellectual, Al also gave a guided tour of a Thomas Hart Benton exhibit at the St. Louis Art Museum during one site visit. He gave us a lesson in the history of the Regionalist art movement of which Benton was a major force. We were joined by a young Visiting Fellow at NIJ, Gil Kerlikowske, who went on to

be Chief of Police in Buffalo and Seattle and now serves as Director of the Office of National Drug Control Policy. As Richard often said, we had the Cadillac of projects.

The burglary project could never have achieved the success it did without Street Daddy. The project wouldn't have been funded and neither Richard nor I had the contacts to pull it off without him. Indeed, the relevance and importance of Street Daddy to the St. Louis street ethnography tradition can hardly be overstressed. Richard Wright, Scott Decker, Scott Jacques, Bruce Jacobs, Jody Miller, Chris Mullins, Volkan Topalli, and others benefited from the groundbreaking work that Street Daddy did in the early 1990s. The burglary project that promised 20 offenders produced in-depth interviews with 105, found 70 of the 105 and walked them past the three most recent residences they had burgled while wearing a microphone and recounting the details of the crime, and refound 48 of the original 105 for a series of experimental studies. It is clear that the early success in finding active offenders, convincing them to participate in a research study and providing good analysis laid the foundation for subsequent funding as well as sophisticated analyses of future offending behavior.

But it almost didn't happen.

Most books, articles, and final reports describe research in a seamless linear fashion. We contend that the reality is far different (Sandberg & Copes, 2012). Research designs are rarely implemented according to their blueprint, are fraught with unexpected challenges, and in the end may be useful road maps through uncharted territory. A lot of the uncharted territory has to do with relationships, whether with a street ambassador, with subjects or with both. We engaged in a particular style of fieldwork, one that depended on the credibility of our ambassador Street Daddy. Maintaining our relationship with him was even more critical than field relationships. While the use of such intermediaries solves a number of problems (access, prescreening, "posing" as an offender when one is not), it also has a number of challenges. We began each study (burglars, robbers, and gang members) with a clear set of criteria about who was eligible, how we would determine that and what we wanted to learn from them. Street Daddy did the initial eligibility screening on the street, did secondary screening in the car on the way to interviews, and debriefed offenders on the way back to their drop-off spot. As much as possible, but especially early in the projects, he debriefed with us about the offenders and what they told him. One dilemma that plagued us for the longest time in the burglary project illustrates an issue we struggled with for over a year; was this a study of burglars or burglary? If it was a study of burglars—individuals—then individual characteristics (motivation, emotions, risks, relationships with others) were of central importance. If it was a study of burglary—acts—then it was the steps taken that were critical and career concerns (initiation, progression, disengagement) were much less important. It doesn't sound profound now, but when we decided that ours was primarily a study of burglars who committed burglary (among other offenses) it was a real breakthrough moment. The credit for this breakthrough, as was the case with most of the enlightened moments in the study of residential burglars and armed robbers goes to Richard.

Ethnographic research involves the use of interviewing, observation and native terms, and concepts. True to that tradition, this chapter proceeds with an ethnography of the ethnographer. In this chapter, we address a number of issues: we review how we found Street Daddy and convinced him to participate in our study, his account of how he became involved in crime himself, his transition from street offender to shooting victim, to college student, to street ethnographer, to diversity counselor at one of the premier private Catholic high schools in the country. We conclude by discussing his life between two worlds, the world he grew up in as an offender and his life after that. With some narrative framing, the story is told from his perspective.[1] I conducted a series of interviews with Street Daddy and had them transcribed, as we had with the active offenders. Digital tape recorders are a great advance over the 30 min cassettes we used at the time.

---

[1] All quotes are reprinted verbatim, as was the convention Richard and I used in our work. Street Daddy's responses are in italics and the interviewer's questions are in bold.

Finding Street Daddy

The first step in working with Street Daddy was determining that he had the connections and the credibility to be our ambassador to the streets. We had to convince him, just as he later had to convince the offenders in our studies, that he had little to risk and something to gain by working with us. Just as they are on the street, issues of race, legitimacy, and trust played a role in building a relationship between the researchers and the street ethnographer. The role of race was particularly important across the three ethnographic projects in part because of the highly disparate representation of African-Americans in official crime statistics but also because St. Louis is a highly racially polarized city.

How did you get involved in these three projects? (The burglary, the robbery, the gang projects)

I was in class, in Richard's class. I think it was in delinquency or somethin'. And, he (Richard) was talkin' about how the streets were and so on and stuff. So, I didn't want to challenge Richard in class, like you know I'm, I'm the nigger—you know how some black students can be. "Nah, that ain't how it is." You know, wanna be that loud mouth and spokesperson for black life and white people don't know shit, okay? So, (laughter) I waited until after class, and I said, "Well, it's a little bit different than that." And then, I think he talked to you about, "I think we got the right guy for our project," and then I was introduced to you. But, I had had you in class before.

And, that's how we met. And then uh, Richard kind of proposed it to me and the next thing I know, I was talkin' to both of you guys. You got me.

So, what did you think when these two middle-class, white college professors asked if you would find offenders? I mean, were you skeptical? Did you think it was a scam?

Well, well, when you all kind of laid it out to me, you know, even when the first time we spoke; I felt it was okay 'cause you guys are my college professors. So, therefore, bein' a, a hustler,

I knew, first of all, you wasn't police, and I knew you guys were straight up professors. And, professors usually don't put everything on the damn line like, "I'm gonna have the police sting some criminals or somethin'." So, I knew right then and there by your status, and I had been in school for a while, with you guys.

So, I knew what you were doin' was on the legit side. So, I didn't have no fear in that.

Let's think about Richard and me in all this. Can white, middle class, college professors really understand the street? I mean, I think of you as our navigator, right? You kind of took us into a world we wanted to understand better. But, I mean, how much can we know what it's like to be a young black guy growin' up in a high crime neighborhood, doing crime?

Well, any time, now you got a good scout, and you guys got all your background to be able to you know, to structure it, and, and, and you go over to, investigate to where you talkin' with your scouts, and there was kind of like, if they got an honest scout, you guys can do it. I learned a lot from you by your strength in bein' a college professor. You were able to dig deep, deep down where I didn't have a damn clue. Having a navigator with my background will give you a direct line to various aspects of being black in a high crime neighborhood. My introduction of offenders to you and the research team will broaden your knowledge about high crime areas in St. Louis.

I mean, you're learning shit from each other in extractin' that data. You no longer that little cream puff just on the news, lookin' at the news and sayin', "Well, that's what the news people say." No, you guys are fact finders and uh, the way you strategizin', and to extract that thing, you, you know more than the most. So, yeah—a white guy can come and see it.

But, here's two white guys—why would you trust us?

Well, see, by then, let me tell you—there was a transformation when them bullets went in my ass. [Street Daddy was shot six times in the back; more on that later.] The first person came to my rescue was a white guy. He was, he was a nurse.

He came to my aid, and said, "Look, I'm gonna take care of you. Just be care—I think....let me do this, let me do that." And that transformation started, man. And then, I had white doctors fixin' me up. And then, I had white therapists. So, they gave me A-1 treatment down there. A-1 treatment, so, and like I say, the transformation started—here it is, at my weakest moment, look who came to pick me up.

Getting into Crime….and the Role of Race

As the quote above clearly identifies, St. Louis has a long history of racial struggles. While it did not experience the "race riots" which took place in other Midwest cities like Chicago and Detroit, African-Americans have been entrenched in the urban underclass and faced historic discrimination in schools, employment, and at the hands of the police for well over a century. Mistrust between black citizens and white authority has clearly been a core part of the city's history. Street Daddy experienced that discrimination firsthand when his family, upwardly mobile with middle class aspirations, moved to a better neighborhood (Walnut Park, a working class neighborhood on the north side of the city) when he was in high school. He attributes some of his involvement in crime, at least the early stages, to retaliating against the discrimination he faced from whites who didn't appreciate his presence in the neighborhood. Some of that attribution could be an attempt to legitimize his behavior some 30 years after the fact, but much of it does not seem misplaced.

Street Daddy saw two motivations for involvement in crime. One was in retaliation for the racial discrimination he faced; the other was that it was an easy way to get over. While he and his family faced mistreatment at the hands of his white neighbors, whites were just easier targets.

So, tell me, when did you first get involved in crime?

After I moved into the Walnut Park area my delinquency and the criminal behavior began.

I moved over there about my sophomore year [in high school], that's when you [black people] started gettin' the attention of [white] people; throwin' [things] at your house, trashin' your house, chasin' us, sayin' it was nigger day—you know, a bunch of white guys in cars hoppin' out with bats and chains sayin' it was nigger day. By junior year, I had got into the group of guys, me and my closest friends was doin' armed robberies.

....and then, I had friends who was lookin' to get even on these people on another tip. You know, let's steal from these people; it's an easy, you know, easy thing to do. And, that started me. Prior to that, I didn't have no hoodlum in me.

You have no what?

I had no hoodlum or thug in me. (laughter)

My junior year, a friend of mine introduced me to the car game. And then, after high school, I became like a full-time guy doin' it. And then, in between doin' that, around, leavin' high school, I started doin' the armed robberies.

And so, you graduated from high school in what year?

I was a seventy-five graduate, so my junior year was seventy-four.

Some of this was getting even for racial discrimination?

Yeah, it was gettin' even. We were not robbin' African Americans, Asian Americans, Hispanic Americans, only white Americans.

And, why was that?

It's because we had, we had came to this integrated neighborhood and was bein' treated badly by whites.

Gotcha.

And then, when, when white flight kind of kicked in, they became a much easier target. And, I don't mean that the composition of the population changed from like 80 percent white to 20. No, it, it changed maybe like to 75 [percent black], then we started gettin' busy.

So, what, why move it, so armed robbery was a way of gettin' even?

Uh, the car theft was too.

Because uh, my buddy had a philosophy that, that, that there was always somethin' wrong with black people's cars. So, he didn't want, you know, then that's a deduction on what you gonna get, because the people who buy it had to do some body shop work to repair that little dent or somethin'. I mean, a small dent would, would affect your money. But, my idea was uh, "Well, no— let's go out there and get them [white people's cars] 'cause we know there won't be no dents." My partner had one goal "steal quality cars [based on a stereotype that white people's cars were in better shape than black people's]. Guess who was buying our car parts? New car dealerships, body shops, and salvage yards. All own by white people.

Getting Shot

Being shot was a profound event in Street Daddy's life. He was shot by the brother of someone charged with first degree assault with a firearm. Street Daddy had testified against the shooter. The brother of the shooter threatened Street Daddy and told him if he testified he would be shot. Street Daddy was an old school offender, for whom the code of the street meant something. After his testimony, he was shot in the back and confined to a wheelchair. On many occasions, Street Daddy told me that being shot saved his life; that had he continued in "the game" he would have eventually put himself in harm's way and either killed someone or be killed himself. Being in a wheelchair posed all kinds of logistical problems for his mobility, but it was especially bad in the rain and cold. The sidewalks and alleys that were littered with broken glass posed additional hazards for the tires of his wheelchair. But being in a wheelchair provided an advantage for the kind of fieldwork we asked him to perform as it proved disarming for many of the offenders he approached, and as he pointed out, you were not nearly as threatening in a wheelchair at just under

4 ft as you were standing up at 6 ft. Street Daddy also had an interesting way of remembering the year he was shot as it coincided with the year of the assassination attempts on two world leaders.

So, what year did you get shot?

Oh....when was that? What year did the Pope get shot? Shit, I can't, I'm, I'm, (laughter) me, and the Pope, and Anwar Sadat got shot in the same year.

You and the Pope and who?

Anwar Sadat. I'm thinkin' eighty-one, Scott. But, they put me in good company. (laughter)

Tell me about getting shot. How did that come about?

A young guy next door to me (Elliott), who I liked came to help me take some groceries into the house. And then uh, uh, David "B" came across the street, and uh, still today, I can't remember what their altercation—they had some bad blood between them. So David pulls out a gun and shoots Elliott on the spot. Elliott was less than maybe six feet from me when he shot him, and uh, he hit him twice—on the leg and the side or somethin'. And, Elliott makes it, makes it to his house, which is next door to my next-door neighbors. David just walked back across the street like nothing happened. Uh, I went over and I knocked on the door for Elliott and asked him was he okay. He said he was hit, so I called the ambulance for him. Then, when the police came uh, I told 'em that little jerk David shot him because uh, you know, you didn't do that shit on my street. That's, that's just how I felt. You don't do that shit. But, this is a new thread of negroes comin' into the neighborhood and that was my biggest slip, not recognizin' how low class these little fuckers were, and how stupid they were. Uh, what applied in the old days was no longer applyin'—respect and shit. So, I, I testified against him.

The police came to the house and I told 'em, "The guy over there shot him,". So, when it came down to the juvenile hearin'. An altercation busted out right there with Terry "B" and Travis "B", picked up chairs, and I told 'em I'd whip both of their asses. So I went in the hearing and

he got adjudicated. He got maybe about, that I could say, less than 60 days of time. And then uh, Terry uh, took it upon hisself to get even with me, and uh, about a year later, within a year my house was broken into twice.

And uh, a good year later, they seen me comin' out the library on West Fourth, him and some more people. I didn't know that then, but I do remember that, that Ford Torino, chocolate, dark-medium brown with a chocolate uh, top on it, slowin' down in front of the West Florissant Library, and I'm lookin' but I can't pick them up. I got in my car. I pulled out and I went to my good friend's buddy's house and when I came out of his house, that Grand Tor, Torino was uh, comin' down the street. I said, "Damn, there that car again." So, when I left there, I went to my daughter's mother house. And, when I came out, I seen the car comin' down Lee Avenue near Newstead. I said, "Damn", and this time they lookin' up where I'm at, 'cause the house sits up on a hill like. "Like, like that's the same damn car." So, I, you know, they drove all down and I got back in the car and then I drove to the bank, and that's when uh, the lot was full, so I got on the external [drive through] lane, which I thought was the less full.

But, at Washington and uh, Jefferson, that's where I was at. So, he came, after they nodded their head, as if, "Yes, that's him." He popped his 9 mm and started shootin'.

And, this was Terry?

Yeah, that was Terry. So uh, he shot around about, mmm, they said about 17 casings down there. As Terry was shooting I begin to weave and bob. He hit me six times. Two of 'em was in my arm. It broke the right arm. It looked like a chicken bone. I couldn't even lift—it was in half. So, I couldn't even lift the right arm up. Uh, two of 'em went in my chest, one of 'em came out the middle of my chest where my St. Christopher medal hanged, and I mean, seriously Scott the bullet hole at the middle of my chest. Didn't touch the heart, didn't touch the spleen, didn't touch the liver, goin' in the lungs or nothin'. And then two of 'em went in my back. Uh, one is up high and that one just got near the spine, but the one is a T-11and that one severed the, the spinal cord.

And, that last time he shot is the one that para-lyzed. The last shot he shot.

I knew I was paralyzed cause the car took off and it run into a, actually, this African American grandmother like standing, you know, I pushed my foot, my right foot went on the accelerator. During the commotion, I put the car back in drive and, you know, when he was shootin' at the car, I started weavin' and bobbin', and then that last shot hit my spine and the foot dropped on the accelerator, and the car was in gear, so I'm pushin' cars out the way. I pushed two cars out the way, and now my car is headed straight across the street, and straight for this wall. And, I picked up my left hand—which I say my guardian angel picked it up—and I made a left turn to avoid runnin' into the wall and runnin' over that old lady.

I went to the hospital, then I went to rehab. I was in the hospital for maybe about 2 months. Then I went to rehab uh, for probably a month, and then they said I was a good patient, high, you know, low risk too, didn't bother the world that he could live like this. And then uh, came home, and then uh, I waited for about a good 2 years before I could get back into tryin' to do my edu-cation. First, I had to learn my body and stuff and how that shit works.

Right.

And, then I enrolled in UMSL [University of Missouri-St. Louis], and then, then voc rehab came in there.

Offending

Street Daddy succeeded in finding and convinc-ing offenders to participate in our study in large part owing to his own success as an offender and extensive contacts among offenders. His "old school" reputation as a stand-up offender who subscribed to the old code of the street was a major reason he was trusted on the street and able to engage high-level offenders. Even so, there were occasional struggles in convincing some offenders to participate and "lulls" in the process of finding and interviewing offenders. His past experience as an offender was a point of honor

for him in many ways, the facts that he was involved in higher level offending, never was arrested for a felony and was a "stand-up" guy.

And so, between the time you got out of high school in 1975 until 1981, you were mostly involved in armed robbery, auto theft?

Uh, armed robbery had stopped maybe within two years. Uh, that's a, you know, first of all that's a serious crime. And, we were very fortu-nate we never had to shoot nobody. But see, that's another thing, in those days, you could grab a victim with such physical force that let them know you knew business. And, that's where you go first, you first scarin' the shit out of 'em by grabbin' 'em the correct way. So, we did fair, we had weapons but we never had to use 'em.

How many armed robberies do you think you did?

Oh, a lot, Scott. Uh, Scott, we used to go on certain days and, and ride around and wait 'til white folks pulled into their driveway and clocked the time they got in and then go back. I'm gonna say, and I'm not gonna exaggerate, I would say more than 50.

And uh, what slowed us down, you remember this ol' cop, Lieutenant Brogan?

Yeah.

And uh, the thing about it is we had a philoso-phy too. You don't rob the bank—you rob the people comin' out of the bank.

When you went to a pharmacist, you robbed the people goin' into the pharmacist instead of comin' out of the pharmacy. 'Cause, they had money goin' in, and the pharmacist, they were, they were leavin' with less money when they came out.

Life Transitions for Street Daddy

To go from an active street hustler engaged in the most physical and emotionally demanding crime, armed robbery, to being paralyzed is an extreme transition. But as demanding as the physical transitions were in Street Daddy's life, the transitions in social class, education, and world view were perhaps more demanding. To go from a hustler's view of the world, getting over on the weak, exploiting situations ripe for the taking to working in a university with a college degree is quite the transition. Street Daddy often told us he "heard the street calling" even though he knew he could never go back. Dealing with the demands of the straight world could not have been easy, and we had occasional qualms about placing Street Daddy in harm's way, physically and emotionally.

Okay. So, let me ask you this question. Not every offender could make the transition. Not every guy who did armed robbery, or stole cars, or sold drugs, or whatever could move over and be part of a research project. What made you able to do that? What was it in your background?

But, then I knew, as a disabled guy, my criminal life was over. There's no respect for dudes in wheelchairs. You can hang if you want to and then try to be boys in the hood, but you gonna get fucked up again. When it's time to run, them, them motherfuckers gonna leave you. And, if I want to sell drugs, I'm an easy target to get knocked off. And, I'd heard stories where guys in wheelchairs had been found dead in they car. It was over. I had no choice. It was done. And, if you get caught, you're gonna do prison time in a wheelchair. So, the shit was over. I gotta go legit.

Working on the Project

Street Daddy had a variety of responsibilities. His primary tasks were to identify active offenders—individuals who had committed multiple crimes in the most recent months—and encourage them to participate in interviews. We actively encouraged him to move beyond networks of individuals he had offended with, knew or came from neighborhoods he lived or offended in. He was also tasked with contacting the research leaders (Richard and me) about upcoming interviews. Once he identified and screened appropriate individuals, he drove them to campus for interviews. Once the interviews

were over, he drove them back to the neighborhoods they lived in. Thus, the time in the car on the way to and from interviews was a critical preliminary and follow-up period in which Street Daddy could validate and probe for information. Perhaps most importantly, these conversations were a chance for Richard and me to cross-validate the results from interviews.

Conflict is a normal part of life. Certainly, there was conflict working on the three ethnography projects, and that included the faculty researchers, the street outreach worker, student assistants, and subjects. It would be easy to understand how the faculty researchers could decide that the street outreach worker had overstepped their bounds or for the street outreach worker to conclude that the faculty researchers really couldn't understand the street. The street outreach worker had to balance his street reputation and toughness with working in the sometimes-professional environment of a university. The balance between the two lives was sometimes difficult to maintain. This was particularly true when Street Daddy felt disrespected, as occurred during a time when another local university talked to him about a job.

So, tell me, lookin' back, were you treated fairly on the project? Were you an equal partner? Are there things that you didn't think were right that didn't get corrected?

I thought I got fair, very treated. I got uh, uh— I'm gonna be honest. When I got hired, I, I didn't know when Richard said, "You got academic status." [a university title] And, I was like, "Okay, what the fuck is that?" But you know, that was huge. I had a great salary and then when things got great, you guys fought, you actually fought for me, gave me a bad-ass raise. You gave me, you gave me a lot of respect—both of you did. And, and let me handle the street and the field relations. When it came to the instrument design, you let me input on that too. So, no—I got treated very fair.

But then…

When I got scolded, I was a little mad. I only got scolded like twice but I pouted about it. (laughter)

Yeah, I remember that, well, we all do. So, why -

Yeah, but I pouted about it, though. But, it, it wasn't enough for me to be uh, uh, say I'm gonna punk you out, you know. That professional maturity, you know, I hadn't had that growth in me yet.

You know, I had a Ph.D., I had a Ph.D. in the streets but I didn't have Ph.D. in the workforce.

Why do you think the offenders agreed to be interviewed? I mean, it's pretty risky to get in the car and come to the university.

Well, many of 'em knew me, and if they didn't know me, I knew people who knew those areas. And, those folks, when I talked to 'em that day, they, they hadn't exactly agreed. I said, "Well, you know such-n-such." Say if I'm at, say if I'm at Carr Square [housing project]. I said, "Well, you know, I know where all the bad motherfuckers hang out at. You go ask the motherfuckers who I am. They'll tell you who I am." Okay, say if I'm on the south side, motherfuckers know me over there. "Hey, you ask such-n-such over there. They'll tell you who I am." So, I knew everybody. If there was public housing, I knew. The only one I didn't know was Cabanne [housing project], and the only reason I know that motherfucker was 'cause in high school, we used to fight them son-of-a-bitches. (laughter)

So, what are the things you think that Richard and I did the best in the project? When you look back on what we did, what are the things—and I'm also gonna ask you what you thought we could have done better, we didn't do so well at? So, let's start with the good stuff.

I think the best thing that uh when we earned the trust, all the components for bein' trustworthy, and was on the same board as no tricks between nobody. I think that was the best thing you guys done. You allowed the relationship to grow and you didn't give me that feel that, "Okay, is he tryin' to bullshit us?" you know? Anything I done, you took from me and said, "It's real. It's legit." And, I made sure that it was. So, it was very solid. That was good. We bonded. You know, we fought afterwards about that armed robbery shit, but….the bottom line is we, we bonded with a trust level and that was a good thing. You let me do my job too.

Conflict is a normal and inevitable outcome of social interaction and our three projects were no different in this regard. The largest source of conflict occurred during the third and final of the projects, the robbery project. Street Daddy had been invited to talk to a group in Epidemiology at the medical school at Washington University during the spring of 1995. This was an extremely proud moment for him; Washington University has an elite medical school and it appeared clear that they were interested in employing him on several of their outreach projects. It was around this time that the pace of interviews slowed considerably to the point that the project could have been in jeopardy. We didn't see Street Daddy in the office as frequently, and contrary to our expectations, he didn't stay in touch very effectively. When Richard expressed his disappointment about these things, Street Daddy took it as a sign of disrespect, pouted, and continued to be diffident. Knowing that he took Richard's comments as an affront to his reputation and credibility, I tried to turn it to the advantage of the project. As Richard was preparing to spend much of the summer in England, I told Street Daddy that it was an opportunity for him to show Richard what he could do, and that by bringing in record numbers of subjects over the summer, he could reestablish himself as a premier street ethnographer. I also offered him something that he had wanted to do, but hadn't done fully up to this point, conduct interviews. Conducting interviews would, in Street Daddy's mind, certify him as a full member of the research team. He responded to the challenge, and we interviewed several dozen active armed robbers that summer.

Okay. So, what did we do that didn't go so well?

Mmm, mmm, let's see. I'll tell you this. Richard said something to me that I didn't like how he told me. And, I looked at that as if a white man had said, "I want to do some upward mobility," uh, it wouldn't be a problem. [This was in reference to Street Daddy considering the job at Washington University.] And, I was like, "I wasn't tryin' to pull a power play." I was really lookin' at Washington U. They were really courtin' me. I didn't want to say, "Damn. I'm gonna leave." But, what I did say was, "I'm gonna smoke his ass [generate a large sample] on that".

I remember that.

When he left [for the summer] and said, "Oh, it was kind of slow," well, it was right after that he kind of pissed me off. But the point was I was, I mad, during that time, I was makin' more promises to the guys.

So, tell me about a time in the project that you thought was dangerous. Were there any times when you thought, "Oh, shit. We're in trouble now."

Well, when we took xxxxx back to see the dope house that he burglarized, and they said, "Oh, there's Daddy-O in the car." And, I said, "Let's get the hell out of here."

Yeah.

And uh, actually one time when uh, that guy dead, the other guy's dead too. Uh, he wanted us to stop, we was on the Washington stroll, the Delmar stroll when he wanted to get out and whoop that guy's ass.

That was with Richard, right?

It was one [armed robber] wit' us. I, I don't, but he literally jumped from the other side of the car. Tell me, "Stop. Stop the car, man. Stop the car. I'm tryin', I'll get out." Ah, shit.

Uh, another time was in that Jennings spot uh, where I seen the shootin' from about maybe two block away, and I was goin' down there to get those guys. And, then the skinny guy who we did get [to interview], he had been shot in the spleen. He was a real skinny dark one, he said, "If I had been shot by somebody," a member of his kind of group or gang, "He would've finished me off." That was scary 'cause then the motherfucker, he was really down with the code. He didn't want to drink no coca cola 'cause it was a red can—remember that?

Oh, yeah. Oh, yeah.

Yeah, that little dangerous motherfucker, yeah. Uh, let's see what else. Me and Richard went to a burglary spot and they had the guns. And, the guy was uh, they did a burglary and they got some semi-automatic Uzi-like uh, weaponry—semi-automatic guns. And uh, they told us to come in the back door, me and Richard, 'cause they had fixing to make a transaction, and they started shootin'. Pop-pop-pop-pop-pop-pop.

Right.

I was like, "Damn." It was so bad they was shootin' up in the air, (laughter) 'cause I didn't know what the fuck that noise was. So, that was about....and maybe when my tire fell off the damn car on the highway. (laughter) Tie rod broke and uh, I remember Chase [a member of the burglary sample]said uh, "ah man, I was gonna have to sue ya." I'm like, "God Jesus".

Life Changes

Street Daddy has held a very responsible job as the diversity counselor at a highly respected private Catholic boys School in suburban St. Louis. He has been there more than 15 years and is a favorite with the boys, their families, and staff. He has a retirement account and legitimate respect, two commodities very different than his life on the street would have provided.

So, tell me a little bit about how your life changed, how your career evolved, workin' on this project.

Mmm. Let me tell ya one thing, it didn't bring up my past at all, because I didn't have any convictions which helped. Didn't people researchin', and researchin', and researchin', and say, "Oh, well he's a bad ass all the way." But, the non-conviction was able to keep me, not to be scrutinized as too fucked up. And then, Peter Hernon's article [a writer for the St. Louis Post-Dispatch who wrote a feature about Street Daddy], that was, that was huge. And then, all of a sudden, I started gettin' more publications like that, and then TV appearances and stuff, and that made things, you know, just pretty much grow and, and it just led me to other things like uh, many speak— that's how I got to Chaminade.

Tell me a little about, you know, I know you're a good Catholic boy and you ended up with the Catholics. But, you took kind of a different route than most folks do. How did the Chaminade thing come up?

It came up, the Coordinating' School District, they wanted uh, Chaminade wanted somebody for a character formation program.

(laughter) Okay.

(more laughter) And, by that time, I had done, ooh, mmm, you know, dozens and dozens and dozens of presentations, and uh, somehow uh, the coordinating' school district said, "Well, we think we have the guy for you," because they were tryin' to straighten out bad behavior of the boys. And uh, they took me on. And, I'll never forget that. That was a really good job.

Did you apply or did they come to you? How did you find out about it?

Well, the coordinating' school district had me in their, in their uh, file to do uh, speaking engagement. I did one or two for 'em and then they just kept me in the files, and they kept sendin' me, you know, speaking jobs. And then uh, the Chaminade came and said, "Well, we can send this guy".

Uh huh.

So actually a student had voted me as for middle school teacher of the year, but not bein' a member, I couldn't get it. So, they let me come to the graduation ceremony for the eighth grade, and they presented me with a, a, a nice plaque about it. And then uh, one of the board of trustees uh, and the principal did I want to take on this diversity job.

What year did you start then on the diversity job?

Uh, 1998.

So, you've been there 15 years.

Goin' on 16. So, that's another, I always did think take a look at, about my weak links.

So, then tell me a little bit about what offenders said in the car, after the interview was done. What did you talk about with 'em?

Oh, the first thing we talked about, you know, you say, "Well, how you feelin'?" "Oh, man. That was cool. That was a'ight, man." I say, "Believe me,"

"I told you it was like this they say man, I told you we wasn't gonna ask nothing. I told you we was gonna stay away from murders and all that shit that gets you in trouble. And, I told you we did it all on campus. And, if we do it on a college campus, ain't no way, and I'm gonna be honest, ain't

no way these white folk gonna let them do no experiment and try to sting nobody." And, we gettin' in the car and I say, "Look here, see we gone free, ain't no police on our ass or nothin'. I told you this was legit." And, not only that, you had just put a publication out about the burglaries study.

Right.

You had, in St. Louis Magazine. Well, Richard, I think you, I, I wasn't in the picture—just you two. And, and I took those books, [and showed them to the offenders] and I said, "Here, it's legit." So, that, that was the kind of conversation. And in the car, you'd say, look here you know, I'd tell 'em, I'd say, "Look here. You know how smooth and, you know, introduce me to some of your folks and I 'd say, you know, same deal— no, you know, no problems." Said, "A'ight, man. Cool." And that's how we did it.

Living Between Two Worlds

Elijah Anderson talks about "code switching" (1999), the existential duality of being of one world and living in another. Anderson discusses the concept in the context of young black men who live in the inner city with a separate set of normative beliefs and behaviors who must "switch" between the codes of the streets where they live and those of conventional society. In many ways, this is a dilemma that Street Daddy found himself in time and again. He had to be "street" enough to relate to offenders and convince them of his "chops" as a legitimate former offender, but also navigate the academic and agency world. The language, status, nature of relationships, and core values for each of these two worlds could not have been more different. But our experience in dealing with Street Daddy and his interactions in the two worlds he negotiated was that he didn't switch codes as much as he straddled them. After all, he was no longer an offender (or at least the offending he did do was sporadic and no longer his primary identity and source of income) and his future was not as a participant in crime (though perhaps it was as an ambassador to criminals). He felt the pushes and pulls of the two worlds in a number of circumstances.

I remember there were times when you said sometimes you felt like the street was still calling you, and you were kind of negotiating these two worlds. Now, you've got academic status, you're making an income, you got benefits, you got an office at the university, but you still got a foot back in the street. Do you remember talking about the street calling you?

Yeah, it's always callin' me, especially when uh, people are sayin', "Look here, Les. I got 25/30 pounds of weed, you can have 'em all up front." "Oh." "I got this guy who can get tech-nines [a semi-automatic handgun] and uh, he'll front 'em to you, you just make sure you get out." I remember I did indulge in that for a few minutes on the, on the gun tip. But that's the only thing I did illegal during the projects.

Uh huh.

And uh, there was a gun collector buyin' 'em. I didn't get caught up in it 'cause a friend of mines was a fireman, and he knew the guy. And uh, you know, and the fireman was my connection to him, so I start purchasin' 'em but I was sellin' 'em to legit people who I knew. Only for protection. To kill humans, none for deers. So uh, when one of the (Beys), told me that the Beys will buy as many as I can get. I said, "Oh, hell no." I ain't gonna get involved with these cutthroats. And, that was somethin' I made sure, that I didn't get involved with killers. Killers kill and I don't trust 'em, they steal life. I just don't trust 'em. The tech-nines were only costin' me $175 dollars, I'm unloadin' 'em at twenty-five-hundred. And that is the worst piece that anybody can buy. I call 'em Jam specials because they don't shoot the right ammunition, they jam up. That, that tech is crap. But, we were gettin' other things Taurus's, uh, Bulldog 45, gettin' in some Derringers uh, uh, you name.

So Street Daddy crossed the line several times back into crime, despite "going straight" and despite the fact that the time he would have done in prison would have been doubly hard because of his status in a wheelchair. He did draw the line when it came to selling to "cutthroats" rather than people who needed them for "protection." This moral

equivocation is not uncommon among offenders transitioning to higher levels of conformity.

Were there times that you felt that you had moved so far away from the street that you lost touch with what was goin' on?

It took me about 20 years to get back.

Uh huh.

"Cause, when I went back out on the streets for you, the south side changed, all them changed. Uh, I'm tellin' ya, Scott, I sat in my wheelchair on corners, many days, rollin' through streets, hopin' somebody would see me. Only ran across two of our burglars. I don't know where the hell they were at. But, the idea was that I didn't lose my contact. Right now, it's still kind of losin' a little bit, just a little bit 'cause, you know I'm not in the city every day.

So, let's, think a little bit about the trip we made to Washington to attend the first Administration of Children, Youth, and Families [Department of Health and Human Services] gang meetings.

Oh, it was huge. The point of uh, the work you're doin' is that now you're goin' up to D.C., up there where the people are funding you, and they want to hear what you're doin' and, obviously, they think what you're doin' is okay, and they want to bring all the people up here, in some cases, you know, to, to do what you're doin'. And then, they turn around and they say, "Well, we want you to review our stuff now".

Yeah, that was huge. You got to review grant proposals for Health and Human Services.

Department of Education I did too.

Okay.

Lisa Herman, she hooked me up with Paraquad, when I was at Paraquad [a St. Louis agency that works with individuals with disabilities particularly individuals in wheelchairs]. She liked the way I talked and then she said, "Well, come on and review for us." So, I reviewed for them, but FYSB [Family Youth Services Bureau] and Health and Human Services, a couple of them, and then NIJ had me do a few.

Okay. So, let, I want to talk about another part of the project. Had you been on an airplane before?

Uh, not, not paralyzed. (laughter). I rode on a plane only one time other than that. And, at that time the plane company was called Ozark.

Uh huh. What do you remember about flyin'?

Oh, well, I remember you tellin' me, you said, "You don't have to worry about the flyin' because the most dangerous part is takin' off and landin'." (laughter) And then, and then you told me, you said, "Well, I'll tell you what now, whatcha drinkin'?" I said, "What do you mean?" "Oh, we're first class, man." "Oh, damn." "Yeah, (just order what you want)." So, that's when I was doin', started drinkin' Bloody Mary's on the airplane.

Uh huh. (laughter) And so, do you remember when uh, Dick Gephardt and Joan Kelly Horn [two former members of the US House of Representatives from St. Louis] got on the plane with us?

Yeah. I do recall seein' them.

I think I remember this correctly, you turned, you had a big grin on your face and I said, "What the hell are you smilin' about?" And, you said, "All these people who get on the plane now, they just see a black guy in first class. Nobody says, 'Oh, look at the guy in the wheelchair.'" Do you remember that?

Yeah, I did. (laughter) Yeah. Well, they couldn't see that (the wheelchair) at that time.

Yeah. So, I understand, I remember somebody watched a couple movies they weren't supposed to watch and emptied out their mini bar.

Hey, hey, hey. That was by mistake.

Now, you got to remember I was new at this. I didn't know the mini bar, (laughter) and you had to pay for that. And, those, that, that few minutes watchin' the dirty channel, I didn't know you had to pay for that. (laughter)

Well, that's all water under the bridge for now.

How many of the folks, how many of 'em, after you dropped 'em off, do you think went to score dope?

I, I, remember the one with me and Richard? He told me, "Man, pull over just for a minute." I pulled up, you know, you know, sometimes I had to do, I didn't do dirty runs [taking them to the dope man] with them, where I knew what they were gonna do. He pulls in, and I drop him off and he say, "Well, just wait." Or, "I got to go in and get somethin'." He came back out with his heroin. And then he'd start fixin' it up as I'm drivin' down the street. So, for me to play my role as a cool guy ain't panicking, I said, "Man, hurry up with that shit, man." Hurry up. "You want some?" "No. I don't want none. Hurry up with that shit".

You know, you know, a lot of them want to keep that party goin', so and that's whether it was marijuana or heroin, so mmm, I would probably say the majority [bought drugs with the money we gave them for being interviewed].

Yeah. So....

So, they didn't go pay bills. I think, you know, they just went and got them some, maybe a good meal, and you know, things that party people do—get what they party with and, you know, get a good meal and then, you know, say, "I'm cool." Worry about tomorrow tomorrow.

But uh, I can't say exactly how many went to the drug dealer after me, but you know, I feel, I'm sure that out of the, the, the person who made the most money from us was probably the weed guy. You know, you know, a lot of their money, somebody probably bought a dime bag or some kind of way it's a little weed.

How'd you get the name Street Daddy?

Uh....actually, you want me to be truly honest?

Yeah.

My buddy, Al, I told him I was, I was, I was his, I was his street dad, and he told me he was world daddy, he was my world dad. So, then so -

So, Al told you that you were a street daddy?

No-no. I told Al that I was his street daddy. And, I told him, I said, "But, I'm your street daddy." And then he say, "Well, motherfucker, I'm your world daddy." 'Cause he said it like that, "I'm world daddy." So, that's how the name created. And then, when I entered the street, they said, "Well, what's your name?" I said, "My name Dietrich, just call me Street Daddy." So, it kind of, it kind of kicked out from my own self-promotion' it a little bit.

So, do people at Chaminade know much about your past?

Yeah, they, they uh, they know uh, quite a bit. They know quite a bit. Matter of fact, matter of fact, I did a, uh, a part about me uh, bein' a racist car thief. Bein' a racist car thief.

Tell me about that.

And, and it goes from me stealin' cars to me gettin' hurt, to where I say the good Lord say, "I got something I want you to do but you have to sit down." So, that's how it kind of ends. And then, I start the new life by sittin' down. My new mission. So, they got an inkling'.

Memories of the Projects

One theme of this chapter has been the duality between the street and research. That duality is reflected clearly in Street Daddy's participation as a member of the research team. Understanding the research process from his perspective is important, and we now turn to his reflections of the projects.

Pick one person from—one -one person from the burglary project, one person from the gang, one from the robbery that you'll always remember and why.

Okay. From the burglary, I'm gonna remember my, I can't think—the cable dude. It's like, do you remember the cable guy who brought in the kruggerands?

Yeah.

And, he said, "I brought 'em in just to let you know I'm legit. And, the reason I done it 'cause Dietrich know some guys I knew at the car game." He sticks out with me, tremendously. And, and another one was the young lady who was a stripper, who turned to a crack head that looked like

shit. And lived, and, and I never forget her house was so nasty, where I didn't even want my wheel-chair tires to touch it. But, before crack head, she was a fox.. Those two are the burglary I remember the most.

Yeah. How about the robbery project?

We uh, on, on the robbery, let's see. Mmm, mmm, let's see. I'm tryin' to think. Oh! When, when I got that dope addict involved, Mike. When I got his ass involved. And how uh, uh, I remember, he was a heroin addict, an active heroin addict in college. That fucked me up. I didn't think that was possible. I didn't think, I didn't think a heroin addict would sit his ass that long and, you know, and do that. That fucked me up.

How about of the gang project—who do you remember there?

Mmm. Let's see. Well, you know, the most thing that stick out with me is that I got a young man, cured and fixed with a broken foot, that the pins were pushin' out of him, tried to save his life from gangrene and blood clots and, and then he turns around and kills a girl and shoots a guy and gets life in prison. And, he broke his foot runnin' from the police.

What about the white guy from the east side?

Oh, that crazy motherfucker. Uh, well, let me go back to the burglary too, the two white guys. (laughter) 'Cause, we had a few of them in the burglary, Chris. The one that's got caught for burning KKK sign for the black folks' house.

Uh huh.

And, the day I took him out and brought him back, on the burglary study, we come down the highway and he, he yellin' at this Asian guy, every kind of frickin' name. But, in the gang project, it was a cool little white dude—I can't think of his name for shit now. I mean, he was one little wigger [a white guy who acts like a street-wise African-American]. You know, he was sayin', "They're my niggers, man." He dated black girls, you know? He said, "Man, fuck -," his parents had a nice, big ass, service station, and they had a huge confectionary, and he out there fuckin' around, and he got shot up after he done the interview with us. And, he got nipped a little bit in the chest, 'cause we do a second interview with him. And uh, he, he was a Disciple Gangster from the east side. The white guy.

Yeah. So -

Another thing was the gang project, when we were at a NIJ conference. You was on the panel, and the brothers and sisters, they tried to show you up about, "Well, what you mean there ain't no leadership structure? What do you blah-blah-blah?" And then, I got up and, and uh, what's the lady name? God! With the glasses?

Winnie Reed?

Yeah, Winnie. And uh, I stood up, I didn't stand up, but I said, "Well, it may be as sophisticated or may be intrinsic, we were not able to detect it. It could be like the mackerel in the sea. You know, we don't know which one triggered it which way to go." And then they, they mellowed out. But, they was tryin' to chew you up on the stand a little bit. I don't know if you remember that, but ask Winnie about the mackerel, 'cause she said, "I like that mackerel theory Dietrich."

Anything that you want to tell me about workin' on the projects? You know, you know from the questions that I've asked what I'm interested in. Anything I didn't ask that I should know about?

Mmm, I said one of the good things is that you guys did come out, I should say, you did come out to inspect the field. You come out the ivory tower, okay? Researchers are usually in the ivory tower the practitioners are using on the ground.

You guys came out enough into the field to get a feel, to know what you were lookin' at, and then talk with some of the guys. Y'all had a design in that instrument to uh, to do that. Y'all didn't just extract the information from me, y'all took rides with me, you all took rides with the sample too. So, that was real strong that connected to the whole deal, and then that's really, that's really strengthened the, the next projects that came behind, because these guys knew ya and seen ya, 'cause somewhere in uh, you know, 'cause your multiple criminal.

So, it was uh, uh, you know, that was cool. And, you all stressed that you didn't want to make it just a, a, negro thing.

You just didn't want to make it a black thug thing. And that's what I tell people about these, these Ph.D.s, I said, "They got a plan from A to Z. (laughter) Get that, but get that, get that, get that, and by the time the study is over, they got uh, say, 18 other alphabets—they pretty damn happy." (laughter) So, yeah, it's a lot of things, and not only that, givin' me the opportunity to get published and, you know, not just takin' me and usin' me, and sayin' okay, but actually gave me some fame behind it. I got a lot of fame behind it, and it's still, still out there.

So, speakin' of fame, if they were to make a movie about your life, who would they have to play you?

Oh, shit. Uh, I look like Bill Cosby but he too damn old to be me. (laughter) And, that guy, that guy playin' Ironsides right now, you know, he, he, you know, he ain't old, he can't do it either.

Conclusion

Are there other Street Daddy's out there? Certainly there are, though finding someone who was as uniquely qualified would be difficult. Indeed, it was serendipitous for Richard and I to each have him as a student in class. Street Daddy's qualifications stemmed from a variety of factors. First, he was actively involved in a variety of criminal offenses over an extensive period of time. The fact that he had committed armed robberies, auto thefts, and sold stolen property brought him into contact with a large number of other offenders in a variety of parts of the city. His involvement in crime over a period of several years (at least a decade) helped develop a network of offenders and a reputation that enabled him to successfully identify appropriate offenders and earn their trust. Second, being shot, ironically, only served to enhance his credibility on the street and render him less threatening. He also became somewhat of a novelty, rolling up and down the cracked and glass-strewn sidewalks of the city. Despite the lower profile, he was easily identifiable as "the guy in the wheel chair with the UMSL project." That identity was important to his ability to strike up conversations with people he didn't know and move across the different neighborhood-identified turfs of the city. Third, Street Daddy received a good deal of media attention. He was featured in the "Current" (the UMSL student paper), the St. Louis Post-Dispatch, the St. Louis American, and other media outlets. He was "Mr. February" in the calendar put out by the local dry cleaners in his neighborhood. All this publicity gave him a certain status as a "street celebrity," and he was not shy about showing the stories around to people on the street, especially when they enhanced his ability to make connections or secure an interview. While there was an element of serendipity in finding and working with Street Daddy, we each had the sense that many of our students had been involved in street life, or had friends or family members who had been. Being prepared to ask and follow up when these individuals presented themselves to us was an important part of the success of these projects.

We were less attuned to the extent to which he still was tied to the streets than perhaps we might have been. We learned after the studies were over about his involvement in gun sales while he had been working on the project. We did learn (and reported in *Burglars on the Job*) the fact that he had neither a driver's license nor car insurance. This information, though upon reflection not surprising, caused a lot of concern at the time, given the potential liability issues involved. I also secured his release from jail on a bench warrant for an incident involving him, his car, and the boyfriend of his ex-wife. To the best of our knowledge, Street Daddy didn't get involved in fencing any property, buying or selling drugs, or engaging in offenses with members of our samples whom he recruited.

A large part of the success of these projects rests with the nature of the relationship between Street Daddy, the researchers, and our research subjects. We showed respect toward the people we interviewed and tried to uphold a reputation for honesty. Our reputation on the street can best be measured through a number of the unobtrusive outcomes that we measured. We had always anticipated that the problem for us would be generating large enough samples and convincing people to participate in our interviews. About halfway through the burglary project, individuals began to show up in the Criminology department and tell the Administrative Assistant, "hello, I am a house burglar and I want to be interviewed." Little did we know that word on the street would spread and as the code of the street would lead you to expect, hustlers wanted to get in on the hustle (we paid participants $20). We huddled with Street Daddy and decided that we weren't going to take "walk-ins." During the robbery project, we received a call from the Office of Equal Opportunity. A young man was in the OEO office telling people he was an armed robber and wanted to be interviewed. We explained to him that we didn't take volunteers, and that study participants had to be recruited through channels. Street Daddy was never stopped with an offender in the car; the only time we were stopped was when I was in the car with him; apparently, a black guy and a white guy in the same car driving through an all black neighborhood attracts attention.

Can this kind of work be replicated without Street Daddy? Several practitioners of the UMSL fieldwork approach (using an "ambassador") have taken the strategy to new cities. I have found an outreach ambassador in Phoenix and worked with him to generate a sample of former and current gang members (e.g., Decker, Pyrooz, & Moule, 2013, 2014; Decker, Pyrooz, Sweeten, & Moule, 2014; Moule, Pyrooz, & Decker, 2013; Pyrooz, Decker, & Moule, 2014; Pyrooz, Moule, & Decker, 2013). Bruce Jacobs remains successful conducting active offender research in Dallas, and Volkan Topalli and Scott Jacques are finding success in Atlanta. And the inspiration for the entire project, Richard Wright has continued to interview active offenders in St. Louis working with another ambassador. When continuing in this line of work, there are several important directions to follow. We understand far too little about desistance from crime. There is not enough of a knowledge base to understand active car thieves and the illegal gun market. With few exceptions (most notably the really outstanding work by our colleague Jody Miller) very little is understood about the role of women on the street, especially their role independent of men.

Street Daddy has become Mr. Dietrich L. Smith, Diversity Director at Chaminade College Preparatory School. He serves as a High School Mentor and AYF Moderator. He is actively involved in raising his four grandsons. Sometimes, he still hears the street calling him.

References

Anderson, E. (1999). *Code of the street: Decency, violence and the code of the inner city.* New York, NY: W.W. Norton.

Bennett, T., & Wright, R. (1984). *Burglars on burglary: Prevention and the offender.* Aldershot, UK: Gower.

Curry, D., & Decker, S. H. (1997). What's in a name?: A gang by any other name isn't quite the same. *Valparaiso University Law Review, 31*(2), 501–514.

Decker, S. H. (1995). Slinging' dope: The role of gangs and gang members in drug sales. *Justice Quarterly, 11*(4), 1001–1022.

Decker, S. H. (1996). Collective and normative features of gang violence. *Justice Quarterly, 13*(2), 243–264.

Decker, S. H. (2000). Legitimating drug use: A note on the impact of gang membership and drug sales on the use of illicit drugs. *Justice Quarterly, 17*(2), 393–410.

Decker, S. H. (2001). Doing fieldwork with active gang members: Gettin' down on the set. *Focaal, 36*, 97–104.

Decker, S., Pyrooz, D. C., Sweeten, G., & Moule, R. C. (2014). Validating self-nomination in gang research: Assessing differences in gang embeddedness across non, current, and former gang members. *Journal of Quantitative Criminology, 30*(4), 577–598.

Decker, S. H., Pyrooz, D. C., & Moule, R., Jr. (2013). Disengagement from gangs as role transitions. *Journal of Research on Adolescence, 24*(2), 268–283.

Decker, S. H., Pyrooz, D. C., & Moule, R., Jr. (2014). Disengagement from gangs as role transitions. *Journal of Research on Adolescence, 24*(2), 268–283.

Decker, S. H., & Van Winkle, B. (1996). *Life in the gang: family, friends and violence.* New York: Cambridge University Press.

Decker, S. H. Wright, R., & Logie, R. (1993). Perceptual deterrence among active residential burglars: A reseach note. *Criminology, 31*(1), 135–147.

Decker, S. H., Wright, R., Redfern, A. K., & Smith, D. L. (1993). A woman's place is in the home: Females and residential burglary. *Justice Quarterly, 10*(1), 143–162.

Logie, R., Wright, R., & Decker, S. (1992). Recognition memory performance and residential burglary. *Applied Cognitive Psychology, 6*, 109–123.

Moule, R. K., Jr., Pyrooz, D. C., & Decker, S. H. (2013). From 'What the f#@% is a Facebook?' to 'Who doesn't use Facebook?': The role of criminal lifestyles in the adoption and use of the Internet. *Social Science Research, 42*, 1411–1421.

Pyrooz, D. C., Decker, S. H., & Moule, R. K., Jr. (2014). The contribution of gang membership to the victim-offender overlap. *Journal of Research in Crime and Delinquency, 51*(3), 315–348. doi:10.1177/0022427813516128.

Pyrooz, D. C., Moule, R., Jr., & Decker, S. H. (2013). Criminal and routine activities in online settings: Gangs, offenders, and the Internet. *Justice Quarterly.* doi:10.1080/07418825.2013.778326.

Sandberg, S., & Copes, H. (2012). Speaking with ethnographers: The challenges of research drug dealers and offenders. *Journal of Drug Issues, 20*, 1–22.

Wright, R., & Decker, S. (1994). *Burglars on the job: Streetlife and residential break-ins.* Boston, MA: Northeastern University Press.

Wright, R., & Decker, S. (1997a). *Armed robbers in action: Stickups and street culture.* Boston, MA: Northeastern University Press.

Wright, R., & Decker, S. (1997b). Creating the illusion of impending death: Armed robbers in action. *The Harry Frank Guggenheim Review, 2*(1), 10–18.

Wright, R., Decker, S. H., Redfern, A. K., & Smith, D. L. (1992). A snowball's chance in hell: Doing fieldwork with active residential burglars. *Journal of Research in Crime and Delinquency, 29*, 148–161.

Wright, R., Logie, R., & Decker, S. H. (1995). Criminal expertise and offender decision-making: An experimental study of the target selection process on residential burglary. *Journal of Research in Crime and Delinquency, 32*(1), 39–53.

Warping Time and Space: What It Really Takes to Do Action Research in Crime Control

David Kennedy

Time

Nearly 10 years ago, I moved to New York. At that time, I'd been studying policing for some 20 years and been actively and operationally engaged in actual crime control work—in action research—for a decade. My entry into that world had been heavily contingent and essentially backward: low-level field research for the high-level Harvard Executive Session on Policing[1] had gotten me into some of the worst areas of some of the most dangerous cities in the United States at the height of the crack epidemic. The violence, fear, and disorder I saw there had spurred an obsessive focus on the worst public safety issues in the country's most troubled neighborhoods: homicide, gangs, guns, drug markets, domestic violence, and the like. That, in turn, had led to a long focus on policing: what it was, how it worked, and especially how it didn't work and might be made to work better.

New York had played, perforce, a leading and constant role in my thinking and experience. I'd studied the Knapp Commission[2] and helped advise the Mollen Commission[3] on drug-market-related police corruption. I'd spent time with NYPD commissioners Patrick Murphy, Ben Ward, Lee Brown, Ray Kelly, and William Bratton; studied Ward's drug market disruption operation in Alphabet City; and read the evaluations of Brown's early community policing initiatives. I'd assessed CompStat, sitting in on the sessions and interviewing a range of department personnel about the changes it brought. I was close to George Kelling, who drove police strategy first in the subways through the transit police and then city-wide through NYPD, and talked with him endlessly about both. I'd been involved with both federal prosecutors and the department in conversations about implementing in New York the homicide strategy I'd helped develop. I watched as the New York crime decline began and continued, and followed and participated in the debates about what was going on. I was, by any reasonable standard, reasonably well informed about policing in New York City.

[1] http://www.nij.gov/topics/law-enforcement/administration/executive-sessions/Pages/past.aspx

D. Kennedy (✉)
John Jay College of Criminal Justice,
New York, NY, USA
e-mail: dakennedy@jjay.cuny.edu

[2] *The Knapp Commission Report on Police Corruption*, Knapp Commission, March 1973.

[3] *Commission Report*, Commission to Investigate Allegations of Police Corruption and the Anti-Corruption Procedures of the Police Department, City of New York, July 7, 1994.

M.D. Maltz and S.K. Rice (eds.), *Envisioning Criminology: Researchers on Research as a Process of Discovery*, DOI 10.1007/978-3-319-15868-6_3, © Springer International Publishing Switzerland 2015

I wasn't. It took living in New York to get it: and which point something I'd missed completely became unmistakable. Riding the subway in the city, one regularly gets off and finds a dozen police officers working the platform. Walking the streets, one sees motorcades of a dozen police cars streaming lights-and-siren across the city—post-9/11 antiterrorism drills. Going to work one morning, I walked into a brawl between two construction workers in my local subway station; returning that evening, there was a uniformed officer standing on the spot. Relatively ordinary incidents frequently bring responses from four, six, or more officers. All of these are features of what it means to have a very large number of police officers in a relatively confined geographic area: one can do things that are simply not possible in other settings, and that I have never seen anywhere else before or since. The longer one observes policing in New York, the more of this one sees, and the more unmissable it becomes. I had of course long known the size of the city and the size of the police force; I'd studied the research on the connection between officer/population ratios and crime rates; I knew the significant and standing differences between coverage in east coast and west coast cities; I'd done street work in both settings. None of it had conveyed a core, essential truth about the nature of policing in New York. And getting to that truth did not involve study, analysis, or special access, all of which I'd done or had already. It involved something both simple and precious: exposure. It took time on the ground.

This is in fact the nature of doing a certain kind of work in policing, and more broadly in crime prevention, or public safety, or criminal justice, or the equivalent frame for community research and work: there is no—literally, no—substitute for direct exposure. One cannot understand what is going on without it. No formal account, no empirical analysis, no qualitative study—nothing—can convey what is actually going on. That is neither to discount nor diminish other ways of understanding what is going on—we will turn to that next—nor is it to say that direct exposure is sufficient unto itself. But if one

needs to understand things in certain ways, one cannot do without it. One has to put one's time in.

When I was being initiated into the world of police research, I remember George Kelling talking about how police departments really worked. I'd read Egon Bittner, James Q. Wilson, Jerome Skolnick, David Bayley, Al Reiss, and many others. I had learned a tremendous amount. I was participating in intense discussions about the movement from the political model of policing to the reform model, about the shift of tactics from foot patrol to motorized rapid response, about what the shift to a focus on incidents and serious crime had meant with respect to order maintenance and community relations. And I remember sitting one day while George said, consider: when police are riding around in cars waiting for a radio call and not doing anything, they're considered "*in*" service," and when they've gotten a call and are actually doing something for a citizen, they're considered "*out* of service". It said more about how policing had gone astray than anything else I'd read or heard. And George hadn't gotten it by reading or studying or looking at deployment strategies: he'd gotten it by riding with cops and hanging around police stations. He'd been there until, in ordinary language, he "got it".

That is how it works. One cannot understand the "criminal justice system," or that it is in fact not a system—another one of George's early and most instructive insights—until one has seen the blind fury cops frequently direct at prosecutors (I've worked in two cities that I know of in which officers have drawn guns on assistant district attorneys), or a homicide detective refuse to even return the phone call of the gang officer who knows who did the killing he's investigating. One cannot understand what it means for an offender to go to court without sitting in that court while a defense attorney, a prosecutor, and the judge decide his future in shorthand language he cannot even understand while ignoring him utterly and his mother cries on the other side of the bar. One cannot understand stop and frisk without riding with drug cops in a hot neighborhood, seeing them stop every young black man they see, go through their pockets, and throw everything they find on the ground. One cannot understand police officers until one sees gang cops organize a grueling charity run to fund a summer job program, or the toughest tactical officer in a dangerous city talk endlessly about the new Israeli blood clotting powder he'd found, and how it had already helped his team save several shot street dealers. One cannot judge the "gangs are the family at-risk youth can't find at home" claptrap until one sees real gangs in action, for the chaotic, nihilistic, pointless enterprises they really are. One cannot understand police corruption until one sees the desperation good officers feel to get the job done, and the legal corners it drives them to cut, and the willing blindness their chain of command displays to what they know full well is going on. One cannot understand youth violence until a young man says straight out that he can't walk off his block without fear of being shot, and see the street shrines on that block that say his fear is real. One cannot understand police-community relations until one hears—over, and over, and over—that the police are working for the CIA to flood the neighborhood with crack.

All this takes time. That is really all that it takes. None of this, one finds, is hidden; if one goes to the streets and the stations and the neighborhoods, it's all there in plain sight. But it does take time, exposure, ride-along after ride-along, coffee after coffee, and conversation after conversation. And in my experience of doing this work, it then becomes nearly impossible to hang on to the mannered convictions of most criminal justice thinking. Most cops, one finds, are not in fact particularly tough. Most prosecutors don't go for the jugular. Most gang members love their mothers. Most gang members' mothers love their sons. Young gunslingers are neither remorseless "superpredators," (Bennett, DiIulio, & Waters, 1996) on the one hand, nor trapped in communities with no remaining status opportunities save violence, on the other. Police departments are ineffective in the main not because they don't have the laws, or the people, or the technology to do the work, but because their top management is utterly missing in action. Criminals aren't so much impulsive and irrational as they are confronting an official world that seems to them

utterly irrational and unpredictable. Violent communities aren't so much tolerant and complicit as they are profoundly alienated from the police and the outside. As I have written elsewhere, when I began working on youth violence in Boston, I found a remarkable coalition of police officers, prosecutors, community members, and others who had a very different, and it turned out extremely accurate, assessment of the problem. They knew it was a gang problem, and unlike everybody else thinking about gangs, they knew that gang members were neither hardened criminals using violence for economic ends nor underserved youth with no options or resources. They saw pretty ordinary kids trapped in deeply dangerous circumstances they couldn't handle, making rational but deeply destructive moves as a result, and thus needing both help and to be controlled. Their nuanced understanding, I soon came to see, was driven by what they in fact saw every day; the more mannered, broader convictions others held, and that dominated both the academic and the public conversations, simply couldn't survive that genuine ground truth.

So practitioners have that exposure, which comes with the territory for them and that the rest of us can to some extent get, with a bit of luck and the investment of time. What they do not have is space.

Space

My partners in Boston had extraordinary insight into the Boston street scene. But they had next to no running room: no capacity to step back, think, plan, strategize, conduct new inquiries, and experiment. Criminal justice and, more broadly, public safety work is usually carried out by agencies, both governmental and not, with overwhelming immediate demands. Police have calls to take and investigations to carry out, prosecutors have cases to process, probation officers have caseloads, social service agencies have programs to run and placements to make. Their leadership is almost completely taken up with running those organizations and securing funding. There is no capacity, no resources, no expectation, and frequently no reward for stopping and considering a problem—even a critically important one—anew. Such as does happen tends to be relatively cursory and superficial, a slight adjustment, a new initiative undertaken without overmuch thought, an application of an existing tactic in a somewhat different setting. Where it rises to the level of what police and police researchers might call "problem solving," it tends to be what Braga and Weisburd call "shallow" problem solving rather than a robust, open-ended, clean-sheet-of-paper exercise (Braga & Weisburd, 2006).

That kind of robust work, of course, is what researchers are supposed to be good at. We're accustomed to taking on inquiries that last a long time—years, sometimes. We're equipped with formal tools to make those inquiries: a range of research methods and statistical techniques. We have access to, and are supposed to be conversant in, data and information technologies. And we have, crucially, an enormous body of scholarship—theory, research, evaluation—on which to draw.

That scholarship is of enormous practical significance. If one is dealing with a gang member who speaks sorrowfully about violence when alone with one police officer—or one researcher—and then goes out and does drive-bys with this friends, understanding the very great deal that social psychologists have come to understand about pluralistic ignorance can make sense out of an otherwise nonsensical situation. If one is trying to understand communities that express bitter anger at police and seem inured to violence, then understanding the literature of legal cynicism will be very helpful. If one is working to build community capacity to prevent violence, then understanding the theory and research on informal social control and collective efficacy will be important. Very serious, very smart people working to a very high collective standard have spent generations building up these ideas and bodies of knowledge. They are an extraordinary resource.

So I certainly found it. It was the Boston cops who pointed me at gangs, and Boston gang members who immediately shattered any ideas about gang members I may have had, but it was David

Matza and *Delinquency and Drift*, with his idea that gang members fall largely thoughtlessly into readily understandable group dynamics that helped me understand what I was seeing (Matza, 1964). It was the cops who already knew that the dead and those who killed them had amazing criminal records, but the classical deterrence literature that offered the idea of "the experiential effect"—well documented in the research—that high-frequency criminality could actually teach offenders that they were likely to get away with it. It was our practitioner working group that was already convinced gang members had no idea of the legal risks they faced, but Zimring and Hawkins (1973) who contributed the classic insight that deterrence was a form of advertising, and that a penalty unknown was a penalty that could not deter—and fed the thought, crucial to the crafting of the actual intervention that communicating those risks directly to the gangs might matter. It was both the working group and the gang members—and our own subsequent research—that said that the violence was hardly ever about money and very often about respect, but Elijah Anderson and others who contributed the notion of the "code of the street" and how it governed young men who did not trust the police (Anderson, 1999).

And so on. We had the room to do what the cops, the probation officers, and the gang members could not: frame the problem, come at it from a variety of angles, ask questions, do formal research, let that suggest new angles, draw on a wide range of literatures, follow up on where they led. We could, in other words, do what researchers are supposed to do, more or less full time, and what practitioners have strictly limited time for: we could *think about it*.

Warping Time and Space

So. Outsiders—including researchers—do not usually know what frontline practitioners know. Frontline practitioners do not usually know what researchers know. Beyond that, neither group understands how potentially *practical* that combined knowledge is.

It is one thing, for example, to know that research shows conclusively that informal social control is on balance greatly more powerful than formal social control. It is another to know that the research on legal cynicism shows clearly that high-crime neighborhoods are not tolerant of violence, but rather mistrustful of police. It is still another to know that research shows that in the most troubled neighborhoods, low perceived police legitimacy is linked with higher violent crime rates. And it is still another to know that research on group dynamics shows that attention to the collectivity can have impact that attention to individuals cannot. All this has been understood for some time; it has not led to effective new crime interventions.

On the other hand, police and others close to the frontlines may know that many gang members' parents are trying desperately to get them to stop, but losing to peer pressure and street dynamics. They may know that people in the community believe that the police were allowing, even facilitating, the neighborhood drug trade in order to lock up their sons, and that view so angers the police that they have never stooped to responding to it. They may know what outsiders frequently do not, that the growing "stop snitching" culture is less about witness intimidation than a deep anger at, and a principled withdrawal from, the police. And they may know exactly what network of offenders is driving the violence. Many on the frontlines have in fact known all this for some time; it has not led to effective new crime interventions.

Take all of this in at once, however, with an eye to crafting an intervention, and something else emerges. Perhaps it would make sense to get together with those parents, address their conviction that the police are out to get their children, take concrete steps—such as offering services—to support them and their families, and on the basis of that new understanding and partnership arrange to have them directly communicate norms and expectations to the offending network their sons are part of. That is exactly the kind of process that led to the design of the Boston intervention, and many others like it.

This work has consistently revealed a very clear pattern. Street knowledge is essential to understanding what is going on, and researchers do not have it. Scholarly knowledge is also essential to knowing what is going on, and practitioners do not have it. Practitioners are relentlessly practical, but do not have the capacity to undertake ambitious problem-solving efforts. Researchers have that capacity, but do not have the background or the habits of mind to make what they know academically practical. When all of that is brought together—and it can be—quite remarkable things can happen.

In my own experience, the path has usually led from the street to the academy: it is what I have seen while in the field, and what my field guides have shown me, that has highlighted the areas that I have then been able to illuminate and unpack through existing scholarship and new research. I think it can work just as well the other way: those already steeped in the literatures will be equally provoked when exposed to the field. What is increasingly clear is that we need both sides.

References

Anderson, E. (1999). *Code of the street*. New York, NY: Norton.

Bennett, W., DiIulio, J., & Waters, J. P. (1996). *Body count: Moral poverty—And how to win America's war against crime and drugs*. New York, NY: Simon & Schuster.

Braga, A., & Weisburd, D. (2006). Problem-oriented policing: The disconnect between principles and practice. In D. Weisburd & A. Braga (Eds.), *Police innovation: Contrasting perspectives* (pp. 133–154). New York, NY: Cambridge University Press.

Matza, D. (1964). *Delinquency and drift*. New York, NY: Wiley.

Zimring, F. E., & Hawkins, G. J. (1973). *Deterrence: The legal threat in crime control*. Chicago, IL: University of Chicago Press.

Observations on the Making of a Police Officer

Peter Moskos

Like most graduate students, I entered the Ph.D. program pretty clueless. Because I love cities, I wanted to study something urban related. In sociology, that generally means race, education, or immigration. I'm not certain exactly when I started thinking about police as an academic field, but something odd was happening in 1995, my first year of sociology graduate school at Harvard. Crime was plummeting, and nobody knew why.

As an undergraduate, I learned the party line on crime. "Root causes" were to blame: poverty, racism, inequality, and deficiencies in education, housing, and health care; guns made the problem worse, and drug addicts needed to be "treated." Police, when they were mentioned at all, were at best only tangentially related to crime. At worst, police were a malign force of racial and class oppression. The job of police, then, was to arrest offenders and not be brutal or corrupt. Since the late 1960s, these attitudes were espoused by virtually the entire academic field.

In graduate school, I began reading scholars like Michael Tonry and Peter Manning, both of whom (just two among many, I should add) insisted that crime could not go down unless society addressed the root causes. While I was

reading their excellent works, the root causes were not improving. And yet crime *was* going down. Between 1990 and 1995, murders in New York City dropped 50% (in the rest of nation the drop was closer to 5%). Police were doing something in New York, and it seemed to be working. Criminology was in the midst of a Kuhnsian "scientific revolution." If all of academia was wrong about police and crime prevention, I figured this was a great field to get into!

Reading more of the literature, I discovered that noted police scholar John Van Maanen—who went through the Seattle police academy in the late 1960s as a participant observer—was just a few blocks away at MIT. George Kelling and David Kennedy were teaching a class at Harvard's Kennedy School. Police ethnographer Maurice Punch lived outside of Amsterdam, where I had lived tending bar at my brother's comedy theater after I graduated from college.

It was in Amsterdam, in 1998, that I started my police research because, unlike in the United States, police in most of the civilized world are generally open to academic researchers. Though little of published substance came from my extensive research in Amsterdam, I learned about policing in general and also the fun of participant-observation police research in particular. I saw a more European approach to police, crime, and drugs that shaped my worldview. Later, I like to think, this early research made me a better police officer.

P. Moskos (✉)
John Jay College of Criminal Justice,
New York, NY, USA
e-mail: mail@petermoskos.com

M.D. Maltz and S.K. Rice (eds.), *Envisioning Criminology: Researchers on Research as a Process of Discovery*, DOI 10.1007/978-3-319-15868-6_4, © Springer International Publishing Switzerland 2015

Initially, my Ph.D. dissertation plan was to copy John Van Maanen and write about the socialization of police. In discussions with him, we agreed that a replication/follow-up study was well overdue. Having gained access in Baltimore, I would follow a police academy class for 6 months in the police academy and then 6 months on the streets. I had little idea what I was getting into, much less what to expect or what I would find. Since I had conceived no formal hypothesis to prove or disprove, my committee and I agreed on a "grounded theory" approach, which, at least as I understood it, was a way to avoid pesky theory before starting my research. Though I didn't yet know it, what I was planning was an ethnography.

Jump to Baltimore, Wednesday, October 27, 1999, the first day of my fieldwork. I met with Major Kojack, the commanding officer of the Baltimore City Police Department's Education and Training Division, better known as the police academy (names that are not public record have been changed). The major was friendly to me, but pointed out that we probably wouldn't speak again because of "chain of command." There were four ranks between trainee and major. He joked that the only reason trainees usually entered his office was to be kicked out of the program.

I thanked him and proceeded to the quartermaster's office and picked up my trainee uniform and equipment, bundled unceremoniously in a black garbage bag. I wrote in my notes (emails and field notes have been slightly edited to correct grammar and typos):

> I get everything but the badge. I wish I were more into uniforms for their own sake, but the hat does look kind of snazzy. And the handcuffs, of course, have limitless potential. The academy starts Friday morning, at 7:39 a.m. No, not 7:40, but 7:39 a.m. Awfully early for a late sleeper like me.

Friday, 2 days later, I was in the academy wearing my police shirt and khakis, the seemingly universal uniform of police academies. When the class members were asked to stand up and say why they wanted to be police, it was with extreme nervousness when I admitted, as required by the IRB (the internal review board or human subjects committee), that I was a Harvard graduate student conducting research. But the sky didn't fall. A few moments later, the first class—a brief primer on the three elements of the criminal justice system (which was interesting to me because I had never taken an introductory criminal justice class)—began. Next, we ran to the gym to learn how to march in formation, which I found "very goofy, but kind of fun to learn how to stand at attention, left face, right face, about-face, parade rest, and salute. What it has to do with police work, I have no idea."

Then, with the command of "Trainee Moskos: front and center!" I was called out of formation and taken to Major Kojack's office. I figured this couldn't be good. It wasn't. The major told me he had orders from a Colonel Daniels to pull me from the program.

"Do you know why?" I asked.

"No," Kojack said. "Chain of command."

I had never heard of Colonel Daniels. I thought perhaps his first name was Colonel. He was, in fact, the acting police commissioner. Perhaps I should have known this, but I was new to the city, and this was a time of political and police transition in Baltimore. Also, newspapers were barely online and Wikipedia did not yet exist. I did know a new mayor was about to be elected and that Thomas Frazier, the police commissioner who had approved my research, had read the tea leaves and left Baltimore to take a job with the Clinton administration.

I asked to call Colonel Daniels from Major Kojack's office, which certainly wasn't respecting the chain of command. But then, best I could tell, I no longer had any place in that chain. Colonel Daniels was reached and sounded surprised to hear my voice. He agreed to meet. I suspect Daniels had no idea that I was even in Baltimore, much less was practicing my about-face in the police academy.

Being naive and not yet indoctrinated into the police world, it never occurred to me how unprecedented it was for a trainee to walk the few downtown blocks from the police academy gym to the office of the police commissioner. I was ushered in. Colonel Daniels now told me to my face that my research was over. All ties with the Baltimore Police Department were severed. My mouth was dry. My heart pounded. I pled for mercy.

I told the acting commissioner that I had come to Baltimore on good faith—my research had been approved—and to stop me now, to have to return to Harvard, would be an academic and life catastrophe. Colonel Daniels paged another high-ranking officer, Colonel Vrilakis, who called at once. Over the phone, best I could determine, Colonel Vrilakis pled my case. But Colonel Daniels remained unconvinced.

I had heard of Vrilakis, as he was probably my original "in." A Greek-American, Vrilakis was close to the previous commissioner, Frazier, and was known by a longtime Baltimore political operative, Peter Marudas. Marudas, another Greek-American, was a friend of my father, Charles Moskos. Because of this connection, Baltimore—unlike Boston, New York, and San Francisco—granted me access and permission to conduct my research. The only other city to approve my research, Knoxville, Tennessee, was where my uncle, Harry Moskos, just happened to have been the editor of the *News Sentinel* newspaper. I mention this not because the names are important, but to observe—eloquent as my letter of request may have been—that the only two American police departments that allowed me to do research as a participant observer were those in which I had some family, political, and/or Greek-American connections.

Back in the commissioner's office, Colonel Daniels explained to me in no uncertain terms that (1) "the people who approved my research had no idea what they were doing," (2) "the legal expert whose signature was on the letter no longer worked for the department," and (3) this expert was "incompetent." Daniels expressed shock that my research project was approved in the first place. All in all, his objections were presented in a mostly legal manner and though I was loath to admit it, they actually seemed like reasonable objections.

Daniels told me that a third colonel had been ordered by former commissioner Frazier to put me through the program (I learned there were nine colonels in total, who, pending Baltimore City Council approval of a new police commissioner, formed a sort of ecumenical council of whom Daniels was the first among equals). I can't be certain, but I suspect Colonel Daniels vetoed me simply because I had been approved by his much disliked former boss.

Since I couldn't see any room for negotiation, I just tried to keep the conversation going. At one point, Daniels asked me point blank, "Why don't you want to become a cop for real?"

"Who would hire me knowing that I only plan to remain a cop for a year, and that I'm doing it for research on my dissertation?"

After a very brief pause he said, "I would."

This was an opening I hadn't considered.

Daniels continued, "I would even waive the academy fee [$13,000 in 1999] we normally charge police officers if they quit the department before working for 2 years." Daniels also said that he could, without lowering the hiring standards, expedite the hiring process, which was well within his fiefdom as head of the Human Resources Bureau.

The meeting lasted 2 hours. I desperately needed water. I felt like a guillotine was hanging above my head. But in the end, Daniels said I could return to the academy on Monday, in plain clothes, and continue my research but *only if I could be hired as a police officer*. Since Daniels was the cause of my problems, I did not consider him to be an ally. But looking back, Colonel Daniels both showed mercy and remained true to his word.

When I returned home I wrote:

> This could be the end. Though if I were an optimist, I would see the silver lining. It's funny, because I did think that perhaps things were going too smoothly. I figured at some point there would have to be a little story about trouble with access. It seems only poetic. That is, of course, if it works out in the end.

I sent a brief email to my Harvard professors explaining my predicament and this unexpected turn of events. I opened up more to John Van Maanen, who was now also on my dissertation committee:

> If things don't work out, I'm screwed. It would be a catastrophe.... This is one of my nightmares coming true: the commissioner who approved my research is no longer the commissioner.... I don't know why this was not resolved months ago....
>
> He [Colonel Daniels] did seem to offer me the following: if I went through the normal channels to be hired, he would be willing to hire me as a cop, knowing full well that I would quit after one year. If that were to work, it would be great. I could stay in the same class, would be a full cop, their legal ass would be covered, and I would get paid for my

research. The other possibility, which I think is more likely, is that it all comes crashing down (they sure ain't getting their cuffs back, that's for sure!).

On Monday, after an uneventful weekend exploring Baltimore, my new home, I returned to the academy in jacket and tie (I had but two jackets, one of which came from a previous job waiting tables at Radius, an expensive Boston restaurant). I also began the hiring process by taking the civil service and psychological exams, both of which I apparently passed. Little did I realize that another scaffold was being erected for me on the sixth floor of William James Hall, Harvard University's Sociology Department.

The next day, Tuesday, November 2, I received an email from Harvard (which I did not manage to save) which told me that becoming a cop was not an option. I was to return to Harvard at once. But returning to Cambridge was problematic at many levels.

Police departments stress commitment to the job above all else, including family, friends, holidays, and even self. The police academy, at least from 7:39 a.m. to 4:12 p.m., is a paramilitary and total institution. You can't just take a personal day, no matter your educational pedigree. On weekdays, I couldn't even make a long phone call during the day. Cell phones were not yet common, and I didn't have one. There was a single pay phone in the windowless lunchroom, but the class—particularly the dozen women who were all single mothers—quickly queued up during break. It wasn't possible to hold any conversation that lasted more than a few minutes. My weekends were consumed with hassles and tests related to getting hired. I would later describe the academy as "more like the world's worst all-inclusive vacation than a finely tuned training machine.... The academy environment is less a learning process than a ritualized hazing to be endured."

From a research perspective, the difference between unpaid participant observer and paid active participant observer seemed relatively minor. And I had also made serious financial, emotional, and academic commitments in moving to Baltimore. I couldn't just split. I had rented and put down a deposit on an apartment. I had

sublet my Cambridge apartment for a year and didn't want to kick out my friend who was living there. I didn't own a car. Also, perhaps stubbornly, I didn't want to quit.

The next day, after work, I emailed a reply:

I was more than a little surprised by your reaction and intense urging to abort and return to Cambridge. In the frustration of the moment, I may have done a very poor job of communicating the goings-on around here. While I never expected my research to be easy, and things have certainly been frustrating beyond my wildest expectations, I do not yet see the situation as doomed. In fact, the potential for excellent research is greater than ever....

Let me now address the issue of me becoming a cop, as this may be the source of any misunderstanding between us....

While it was not my original intention, becoming a full-fledged police officer is an unprecedented opportunity for an academic researcher.... This whole plan may not work. The next few weeks will be difficult.... But I intend to push things to a conclusion in Baltimore before making that decision.

Second, I would like to emphasize that I do not intend to "go native" and forgo my academic career. I am much more committed to earning my Ph.D. than putting in 20 years as a cop. (Though if I did intend to remain a cop—which I don't—I would see nothing wrong with that choice.) I view becoming a police officer as an incredibly rich opportunity to break new ground with sociological research (and an interesting life-experience)....

The main reason why I did not more strongly pursue the option of becoming a cop for research purposes (though I did take the Massachusetts civil service examination) was one of honesty and ethics. It would be unethical for me to deceive a police department, knowing that my true goal is to write a doctoral dissertation, quitting my job after one year....

[I would not] be deceiving the other police academy trainees. They are fully aware of my research goals and my current status in limbo, auditing but out of uniform and no longer participating in the class (I might add that through the past few days they have been incredibly supportive of me and have helped raise my morale from its low point last Friday).

I find it impossible to believe that any effective research I may have conducted as an active participant observer would be tarnished, contaminated, or somehow less valid should I be able to continue as a full-fledged trainee.

Finally, I see no real point giving up and returning to Cambridge in defeat (don't get me wrong: I still may return to Cambridge in defeat yet!). I do not intend to give up the fight until I have no choice. Also, on a practical level (1) working out the obstacles I face here requires my continuous presence and does not allow me the luxury of even a few days off, and (2) I have made a large commitment to move to Baltimore and moving back is easier said than done....

In the meantime my research is continuing as scheduled despite the distractions....

I hope this clarifies my situation, and I eagerly await your response.

Almost 3 weeks passed. Though I found it odd and disconcerting that I hadn't received a reply, I didn't want to push the issue, so I continued my fieldwork. On November 22, a bit nervous, I wrote an email to my committee in which I updated them on my research and noted, "I have not heard from any of my Harvard advisers since my last letter. I can only hope that no news is good news." Around this time, I received a posted letter from the department chairperson. I found it strange to receive an actual letter, since even in 1999 there was email and telephone. It was as if correspondences from Harvard were being sent on a packet steamer.

The letter from the chairperson, whom I didn't know well, warned that I "will be asked to withdraw from the graduate program" by the end of that academic year for my failure to meet certain academic deadlines. The letter continued ominously:

Faculty members who have been working with you in the program indicated that you are currently away from Cambridge engaged in field research that you regard as preparatory to the development of a dissertation prospectus. They further related that there have been unanticipated changes in the arrangements for access to the prospective field sites, changes that seriously concern these faculty members. They explained that they had advised you to return to Cambridge to consult with them about the directions of the project in light of these changes, and that you have declined to follow their advice.

I replied via email stating that I fully intended to meet the department's deadlines and that my research had not fundamentally changed. I stressed that I was not *unwilling* to meet with my committee but temporarily *unable* to leave Baltimore "without completely abandoning my research." I asked "for the continued support and encouragement from the sociology department."

On November 29 I received a reply from my adviser:

No. It is not the case that "no news is good news." We are all very concerned about you and your work. I do not agree that you should remain in the police academy on the condition that you work as a policeman for a year afterwards. We are not in the business of training policemen here in the sociology department. I am also very concerned about not having received a statement indicating clearly where you are going with this project.... Had things gone smoothly, I would have been willing to continue supporting you, assuming that you sent me a statement of your research objectives. All this, however, has changed. COULD YOU KINDLY RETURN TO CAMBRIDGE IMMEDIATELY AND RESUME YOUR STUDIES TOWARD YOUR ORAL EXAM AND YOUR THESIS PROSPECTUS. I REGRET TO SAY THAT THIS IS NON-NEGOTIABLE. IF YOU DO NOT RETURN I WILL HAVE TO WITHDRAW FROM YOUR DISSERTATION COMMITTEE.

Clearly, as Bugs Bunny would say, what we had here was a failure to communicate. I replied the following day:

I am sorry to have alarmed you regarding my commitment to progress in the Sociology Department....

I would very much like to come back to Cambridge to meet with you and my committee. Up until now, however, for me to return to Cambridge would have been tantamount to abandoning my research. I doubt that you wish me to do that, especially after such a difficult effort to gain unprecedented access to a police department....

As for returning to Cambridge while I am at the police academy, my only free days are Saturdays and Sundays. I would, of course, be more than eager to come up on one of those days, if that were convenient for you. If you prefer, I would be able to return to Cambridge on a weekday, once police training is over....

To be sure, I will have a short commitment of approximately 6 months as a police officer after completing the academy. This will allow for far better in-depth observations of police activities and life. In no way does this development alter my academic career plans. Indeed, the potential for pathbreaking research is now greater than ever....

It should be noted that I have been in contact with the third member of the committee, Professor John Van Maanen. Having gone through the police academy process himself, he has been an enthusiastic supporter of my research endeavors.

In brief, I plead with you to empathize with my situation. The research methodology remains—despite the trials of the past month—as originally planned and extremely promising....

All in all, the time needed for completion of the projected research should be well within the bounds of doctoral dissertations. I stress this to alleviate any fears that I may have lost my calling as an academic in order to play cops and robbers.

Though the hiring process was proceeding in fits and starts, another deadline was approaching. I had to be hired before the first day of live shooting at the gun range. If not, I would be dropped to the next academy class. This would not have been the end of the world, but it was something I wanted to avoid, especially since any further change to my status in Baltimore would not go over well in Cambridge.

Four days later, another email arrived from my adviser:

> I am very relieved that you think it is now possible to come to Cambridge since your refusal or inability to do so would have had serious consequences for you here.... There are many other ethical concerns involved in your decision to do police work after graduating from the academy. I want to make it absolutely clear to you that the [human subjects committee] and the sociology members of your committee, myself included, are opposed to this decision on your part. If you are serious about continuing your studies with us you had better find a way to get out of whatever promises you made about working as a policeman....
>
> I am insisting on the following conditions:
>
> You will have to find some way of getting out of any agreement you made to work as a policeman after graduating. One possible way out for you might be a decision of the Human Subjects committee not to agree to this extension of your research. I do not know how this committee will react to the fact that you have changed your original plans to include police work, but I rather suspect that they will require you to get out of this agreement. In that case you can simply inform the commander down there that you have no choice but to back out of your agreement with him.
>
> If this is not possible, then you are out of luck and will have to change your research plans since THE DEPARTMENT IS ADAMANT THAT IT WILL NOT AGREE TO AN EXTENSION OF YOUR RESEARCH TO INCLUDE POLICE WORK AFTER GRADUATING FROM THE ACADEMY. I am writing this in big, bold letters so there can be no misreading of what I am saying. This e-mail will also be placed in your file.

Three days later, on December 6, 1999, I was hired.

There was much paperwork to fill out, retirement benefits explained, uniform measurements to be taken, and a very anticlimactic swearing-in ceremony. In the courthouse, I signed my name in a book and raised my right hand while a bored woman read a 15-second monotone oath. I couldn't follow everything she said, but upholding the Constitutions of Maryland and the United States were part of the bargain. At the end, I simply said, "Yes."

I was a sworn Baltimore City Police Officer in training.

I took a long, late lunch, got my police uniform back from the police officer who had secured it a month prior, and returned to the police academy at 15:30 hours (military time, of course), at the end of a lecture on search and seizure.

My academy class, the fifth class of 1999, or "99-5," was probably not the strongest group of police officers ever (after all, half the classes do have to be below average). But my classmates were very good to me. When I entered the room with my garbage bag of police belongings in hand, it was a clear sign I had been hired. The class broke out in applause. The instructor for that class, Agent Cassidy, beamed as he shook my hand. After class, my squad leader called me to the front of the room, congratulated me, and made me do a push-up for each class member present. Luckily, half the class was at the gun range.

I knew I was on the verge of a once-in-a-lifetime opportunity, but these few months were difficult for me. There was a certain irony to the whole situation. I thought of the cop-movie cliché in which a detective is ordered off the case, but throws his badge down and continues to work as a renegade. Here I was, in real life, working in the police department while being told I would have to give up my Harvard ID. In my notes I joked that I might have to go Times Square to buy an "Official University ID Card" to flash at people (very quickly) when my academic credentials were questioned.

My mother, ever supportive, pointed out that there were plenty of other graduate programs that might appreciate what I was doing. My father, a prominent sociologist himself, was equally supportive but more quick to point out that no respectable graduate program would accept another school's dropout. Oh well, were I kicked out of school, at least I had a job. I could always hit the streets as a true rogue sociologist.

It often surprises the liberal and well educated, but I received very little resentment about my Ivy League status from the conservative, no-college cops with whom I worked. Most police come from backgrounds without the resources to apply to or be accepted into college, much less an elite graduate school. For a large part of America, there is no "college track." And the Baltimore Police Department, like most police departments, requires no education beyond a high-school diploma or G.E.D. Harvard University is as foreign to most blue-collar workers as white, pickup-truck-driving, God-fearing, gun-loving Republicans were to me. And yet it was through these cops, some of whom are still my friends, that I began to appreciate the advantages I have, earned both through birth and hard work.

As to the Harvard world, there was one line I couldn't get out of my head: "We are not in the business of training policemen here in the sociology department." Well, I should hope not, but I didn't see why academics should look down on those who do. It wasn't as if, through my research, I would befriend criminals or learn how to engage in criminal enterprises, as others—such as Adler, Bourgois, Duck, Goffman, Jacobs, Mohamed and Fritsvold, and Venkatesh—have done with great and deserved acclaim. At some basic level, I was just taking a government job. A few in my academy class even admitted in private that they were becoming police officers not because of a lifelong desire but simply because "the post office wasn't hiring."

Eleven days after being hired, I was able to return to Harvard on a Friday and meet with my advisers. I had no idea what to expect. These meetings turned out to be cordial and blessedly anticlimactic. I was told that Harvard University was a "risk-averse place" and that the sociology department "has had enough." And yet the general tone was very supportive. My adviser implied, with no reference to the substance of the all-caps emails, that he was the last person on my side, in effect circling the wagons against other enemies in the department.

My other Harvard committee member was also supportive, which I found equally odd. "So just who is the 'they' that we keep referring to?" I asked him. He implied it was the human subjects committee and the department chair. During these meetings, I agreed to be "more sensitive and communicative and proactive about potential potholes." I would write a letter that stated my research goals (which would also help me complete my overdue prospectus), provide a timeline, and address potential legal and ethical issues.

I still don't understand why this needed be discussed in person, and not, say, with a 6 p.m. phone call. But supplication has its place, and ring kissing is certainly better than applying to new graduate school programs. I had another lease on life.

In the following months, to stay in good graces, I looked for any excuse to write my committee. I took extensive daily field notes, but most weeks I had nothing to report. Sometimes a job is just a job. In late March, right before the academy class's graduation, the newly elected mayor, Martin O'Malley, replaced Colonel Daniels (who had since become the commissioner) with Ed Norris (who would later do federal prison time). I wrote my adviser:

> Norris is a non-college-educated New York cop. He is known for his foul mouth and blunt talk. O'Malley and Norris are keen on Zero Tolerance and the New York style of policing. Daniels (never accused of being a "softy") was very concerned with Zero Tolerance vis-à-vis minority relations. Evidently, he also had reservations about not being in complete control and becoming a PR man for the Mayor's Police Department.
>
> Given the latest events, I'm wondering if perhaps I should focus specifically on racial perceptions and attitudes among the police going into a high-crime minority area?

I waited a few days, as was custom, and received an unexpectedly positive email from my adviser:

> This seems like one of those golden opportunities that sometimes fall in the lap of the lucky or blessed. I personally would not mind if you seized

the opportunity to explore what has become a major national problem re the police and minority communities. At the same time, you should be careful not to become too taken with the obvious topicality of the issue. You have to keep it sociological.

That I could do. The crisis was over. By comparison, my job and fieldwork were easy.

In my academic adviser's defense, he became my adviser at my urging and only shortly before I departed for Baltimore to begin my research. He took me on good faith and at my word as to my Baltimore research agenda. When things changed so quickly—when I was forced to be hired or go home—I knew my intentions were honest, but maybe he felt betrayed, as if I had pulled a quick one and was attempting a bait and switch.

I had switched advisers because I felt my previous adviser's quantitative bent wasn't a good match for my qualitative ambitions (though he graciously agreed to remain on my Ph.D. committee). Also, I wanted a fresh start after failing the sociology department's oral examination. I might be the only student ever to have failed this usually perfunctory departmental exam.

My final adviser also deserves credit for shaping my post-research writing. His hands-off style gave me the freedom to write in my own voice. He encouraged a dissertation that was readable, included no statistical regressions, and could be more easily adapted to book form.

I quit the Baltimore Police Department in 2001, moved to New York City in 2002, and completed my Ph.D. in 2004. Since then I have been teaching in John Jay College of Criminal Justice's Department of Law, Police Science, and Criminal Justice Administration. Based on my dissertation, both the University of Chicago Press and Princeton University Press were interested in publishing my book. I chose the latter and finished a book draft in 2007. It was completed and published the following year to some acclaim and sold surprisingly well.

I still don't entirely know what to make of these events. I never mentioned these research issues in my book, *Cop in the Hood*. They weren't relevant to the greater points about policing in the ghetto and the war on drugs. Plus I didn't want to sound petty or bitter. Until now I have purposely avoided even reviewing my notes relating to this incident. I saw no point in reliving the experience. I let bygones be bygones (or at least repressed a few emotions). Fifteen years later, I remain on good terms with my former advisers, who have all been very supportive of me and my career.

And yet maybe I was just lucky. Maybe I made bad choices and just happened to get by. Had I abandoned my research and returned to Harvard, I probably could have churned out some quantitative tome on police and crime without ever talking to a police officer or handling a criminal. But that's not what I wanted to do. I didn't want to write a dissertation without heart, one that nobody outside the ivory tower would read, much less understand. Returning to Harvard, as instructed, would have been a personal failure and an academic mistake. Both methodologically and socially, I felt like a black sheep in my graduate program. But then I doubt there is a graduate student anywhere in the world who feels emotionally supported and completely understood.

So after 6 months in the police academy and 14 months policing the streets of East Baltimore—20 months total in the field—I earned civil-service protection (which makes it very hard for police officers to be fired) and quit policing. Technically, I first took a year of unpaid leave, just in case things at Harvard didn't work out. On my way out of Baltimore, a friend and squadmate, one who had been a police officer longer than I had been alive, said in no uncertain terms: "When you leave, you better not come back here. I know that if you come back here, then you're a failure."

Had I been kicked out of Harvard and stayed in policing, I would now have 16 years on the job. I might be burnt out and counting the days till retirement. Or maybe I would have left Baltimore and moved to New York regardless. Perhaps I would have joined the NYPD. Or maybe I would be waiting tables and tending bar for a living. Would that be so bad?

Major Kojack and I talked a few more times after I was called to his office at the police academy. I never knew him well (the new commissioner replaced him before I was even out of the academy), but one thing he said stuck with me. At 7 a.m., he would often smoke a cigarette where I locked up my bike in the parking garage. I would jump to attention and salute, as required by chain of command. He would put me "at ease," and then we would chat a bit, more informally. Initially, we talked about the benefits and hazards of biking to work. But as a curious person anywhere might inquire about some foreign land, he would turn the conversation to Harvard University. One cold morning, he exhaled a cloud of tobacco smoke and declared: "You should really be proud of yourself that you got into that school."

These police officers were a lot more accepting of me, a Harvard-educated liberal, than most Ivy League students and faculty are of them. Being a Baltimore City Police Officer helped define me as a person and a scholar. So I needed to make good. Though I don't train police officers, I am in the business of educating them. Having actually walked the beat, however briefly, gives me a degree of "street cred" in the classroom. But on a more substantive level, I don't know how I could teach others about policing without the knowledge, understanding, and empathy I gained on the job.

Just a smattering of those I teach in the classroom are active police officers (and they tend to be excellent students). The vast majority of my students, at least at the undergraduate level, are immigrants or upwardly mobile children of immigrants who want to become police officers (New York City, unlike Baltimore, does have a college requirement). Through my research, writing, and teaching—especially at a public university—I actually do help people improve their lives.

When people ask me if I miss policing, I joke that being a professor is a much better job: the pay is about the same, but my hours are better, I get summers off, and nobody shoots at me. And maybe this is important to remember. Only some of us are lucky enough to get advanced degrees and conduct research for a living. Of course, we should all try

to discover new insights, do the right thing, and make the world a better place, but research, even in criminology, is rarely a matter of life or death. Meanwhile, we live the life that many other good and smart and hardworking people—perhaps the same people we study—can only dream of.

References

Adler, P. A. (1993). *Wheeling and dealing: An ethnography of an upper-level drug dealing and smuggling community.* New York, NY: University of Columbia Press.

Bourgois, P. (1995). *In search of respect: Selling crack in El Barrio.* Cambridge, England: Cambridge University Press.

Duck, W. (2015). *No way out: Precarious living in the shadow of poverty and drug dealing.* Chicago, IL: University of Chicago Press.

Glaser, B. G., & Strauss, A. L. (1967). *The discovery of grounded theory: Strategies for qualitative research.* Chicago, IL: Aldine Publishing.

Goffman, A. (2014). *On the run: Fugitive life in an American city.* Chicago, IL: University of Chicago Press.

Jacobs, B. (1999). *Dealing crack: The social world of streetcorner selling.* Boston, MA: Northeastern University Press.

Kuhn, T. S. (1962). *The structure of scientific revolutions.* Chicago, IL: University of Chicago Press.

Manning, P. K. (1997). *Police work: The social organization of policing* (2nd ed.). Prospect Heights, IL: Waveland Press.

Mohamed, A. R., & Fritsvold, E. D. (2010). *Dorm room dealers: Drugs and the privileges of race and class.* Boulder, CO: Lynne Rienner.

Moskos, P. (2008). *Cop in the hood: My year policing Baltimore's Eastern District.* Princeton, NJ: Princeton University Press.

Punch, M. (1979). *Policing the inner city: A study of Amsterdam's Warmoesstraat.* London, England: Macmillan.

Tonry, M. (1995). *Malign neglect.* New York, NY: Oxford University Press.

Van Maanen, J. (1972). *Pledging the police: A study of selected aspects of recruit socialization in a large, urban police department* (Ph.D. dissertation). University of California, Irvine, CA.

Van Maanen, J. (1973). Observations on the making of policemen. *Human Organization, 32*(4), 407–418.

Venkatesh, S. (2008). *Gang leader for a day: A rogue sociologist takes to the streets.* New York, NY: Penguin.

Wilson, J. Q., & Kelling, G. L. (1982, March). Broken windows: The police and neighborhood safety. *Atlantic Monthly*, pp. 29–38.

Cure Violence: Treating Violence As a Contagious Disease

Gary Slutkin with Charles Ransford and
R. Brent Decker

The Cure Violence Health Model is a health approach for reducing violence. This model is based on established methods that have been shown to control other epidemic diseases. It is derived from a synthesis of the fields of epidemiology, infectious diseases, behavioral science, social psychology, and neuroscience.

The methods used in the Cure Violence Health Model came out of my prior experiences in health and epidemic control with tuberculosis, cholera, and HIV/AIDS (Slutkin et al., 2006), mostly, but not exclusively, in developing countries—in concert with conversations and discussions with researchers and practitioners in violence prevention the United States—and in particular those persons most intimately involved and affected from the community and the street. Persons most affected from the community and the street became the core of the intervention, as is usual in health and disease control efforts.

Cure Violence is therefore a merging of several scientific disciplines and the street. It was not initially planned that way. Initially, strategy was designed in the usual way the World Health Organization (WHO) devises strategies for many infectious and noninfectious problems, but with time it became clear that violence has an intrinsic contagious nature, and as a result a new theory emerged—that of seeing and treating violence as a contagious process. It also became clear that difficulties emerging from other approaches may have been a result of following old theories, for example with an emphasis on moralism. Likewise, prior successes may have been from knowingly or unknowingly using contagion control methods, or in some cases just from the natural history of epidemic processes—i.e., that epidemics do reduce or die out on their own under certain, sometimes predictable, conditions.

I am a physician trained in infectious diseases. I spent 15 years working on preventing epidemic diseases, mostly in Africa, and did not intend to work on preventing violence. What I expected was to continue working on preventing the spread of more "usual" infectious epidemics. When attempting to take a break, my career diverged when I came to see that violent behavior was also an epidemic process and then with others gradually tried out new methods based on epidemic control. I have learned along with many others in cities across the United States and in other countries that this new approach can be effectively adapted if principles and practices are followed as for other similar diseases, and that the theory of violence as a contagious disease is becoming even more validated by the practice itself and the results of independent evaluations.

G. Slutkin (✉) • C. Ransford • R.B. Decker
University of Illinois at Chicago, Chicago, IL, USA
e-mail: gslutkin@uic.edu

M.D. Maltz and S.K. Rice (eds.), *Envisioning Criminology: Researchers on Research as a Process of Discovery*, DOI 10.1007/978-3-319-15868-6_5, © Springer International Publishing Switzerland 2015

Working with Epidemic Diseases

During my training in infectious diseases at San Francisco General Hospital (SFGH), I was asked to run the tuberculosis control program for San Francisco. This was my first real experience in epidemic control and this is where I first learned the methods of controlling things that *spread*, which is largely done by identifying the most infectious persons and putting them on therapy as well as identifying and treating contacts. We used outreach workers with trust from the same communities to accomplish this. After my training, I signed on to work in Somalia. When I told my mentor at SFGH that I was making this move, he told me that it was the biggest mistake I'd ever make. I landed in the middle of a dire refugee situation: a million refugees in 40 camps, where infectious diseases were common and I was one of only six doctors. I was brought on to work on preventing the spread of tuberculosis, but when the epidemic of cholera struck my responsibilities immediately expanded to helping inhibit the spread of cholera as well.

Because of our limited resources, we recruited and trained refugees to become specialized health workers. This was the same method we used in San Francisco for tuberculosis control and offered the best method for gaining access and trust with the local population. This was a new category of worker—an indigenous worker that was trained at the location of the outbreak to help doctors stop the spread of disease. We relied on these indigenous workers because we had no other options, but we also saw how the trust and credibility they had with a fearful refugee population made them extraordinarily effective at changing behaviors and norms to prevent the spread of the diseases beyond what any other workers had been.

Following 3 years of work in Somalia, I began working for the WHO on the newly exploding pandemic of HIV in Africa—my assignment being the epicenter of central and east Africa— Uganda, as well as Rwanda, Burundi, Zaire (now Democratic Republic of the Congo),

Tanzania, Malawi, and several other countries. To rapidly combat the spread of HIV, we used many of the same methods the Somali team and I had previously employed in Somalia—most notably carefully selecting and training indigenous workers to change behaviors and norms, in this case on sexual behavior. After several years, and a relatively successful program of behavior change in Uganda, I was called on by WHO to use what we had learned in the field to run a unit at WHO where we were responsible for designing interventions to guide countries to prevent the spread of disease. In this capacity, the Intervention Unit of WHO formalized the methods of changing behaviors and norms using indigenous workers, methods that are used today in many countries.

After 10 years overseas, I was feeling physically exhausted, chronically jet lagged, and emotionally isolated and wanted to come home. I had seen a lot of death, and in particular epidemic death. Epidemic death has a different feel to it— it is full of not only fear, but panic. I had repeatedly heard hundreds and thousands of women wailing and crying in the desert. In the face of so much death, for my own health and well-being, I felt the need to come home and take a break and maybe start over.

Coming back to the United States, I was not aware of any epidemic problems that I could be involved in addressing. In fact, I was not aware of very many problems at all by comparison—there is running water in every home and many other luxuries are commonplace. After all my experiences, I really didn't know at all what I would do next.

My Introduction to Violence and the Responses to Violence

I returned to my hometown of Chicago, where my parents lived, and it was not long before friends began to tell me about how children were shooting other children. I asked my friends what was being done about this, and what I heard boiled down to essentially two approaches.

The first approach involved different kinds of punishment—what generally falls into the field of suppression. In the health field, which in many ways is based on the understanding of behavior and behavior change, punishment is not considered as a tool, and we find it to be highly overrated in the public mind.

Additionally, the punishment approach reminded me of what happened in historic epidemics when people did not have a scientific understanding of the causes of diseases. Epidemics such as plague, typhus, leprosy, and smallpox in past centuries were thought to be caused by bad people, "bad humors," or bad air. In some instances, this misunderstanding of the causes led to blaming, exclusion, or punishment of victims. These responses not only caused additional pain and suffering, they caused more spread when persons affected or carriers do not seek care, or go into hiding.

The other prevailing approach to the problem of violence that I heard came out of what I call the "everything" solution. This approach calls for us to fix schools, families, poverty, racism, drugs, and everything else that is wrong in chronically violent communities. There is no question that all of these factors can and do exist in the context of community violence, but in our work in disease control we found that sometimes you don't need to wait for the solution to everything in order to stop the spread of diseases. In Somalia, we had no ability to solve the refugee crisis with only six doctors, but we found a way to stop the diseases.

Regardless of my experience with these types of approaches, it was clear to me that the field of violence reduction was stuck. This has happened with many problems in our society. For example, this was true with diarrhea and malaria for decades until the strategies for these were rethought.

I did not know what had to be done with violence, but it did appear that the perspective on the problem as a health problem, and an understanding that violence as a type of behavior could lead to a new approach, or at least fill a gap. We thought there was a likely possibility that the methods of behavior change and norm change that we had used for epidemic diseases might be productive in addressing violence as well.

Violence as a Disease

When we first started exploring this issue, as for many others, we looked at the data. What we saw in the maps of violence in most US cities showed characteristic clustering—just like the maps that I had seen in other epidemics such as cholera (see Fig. 1). The graphs also showed that violence rose and fell in wave upon wave configurations. In my work with epidemics, I was used to seeing exactly these types of graphs as well—because all larger epidemics are combinations in time and space of many small epidemics, rising and falling as the disease transmits and spreads (see Figs. 2 and 3), leading to new foci or epicenters.

As we were beginning to make these connections, I began to look into what really predicted a case of violence. I found that the greatest predictor of violence is a preceding case of violence. This characteristic of violence reflects other epidemics as well. If someone has a case of flu or upper respiratory infection (URI), it is known to have been preceded by another case of flu or URI. I was beginning to see that violence was behaving like an epidemic disease.

In a way, we all are intuitively aware of this connection from reports that discuss the "spread of violence" in fights, gang wars, civil wars, riots, as well as for genocides. With gang wars, one shooting often causes one or many retaliations, with each retaliation in turn causing many more, and so on—so that over time a single shooting could lead to a great number of deaths.

Similar Characteristics, Similar Approach

Counterintuitively, the finding that violence behaves like an epidemic disease was very good news to me and our team—because there is a way to reverse epidemics. My colleagues at WHO and

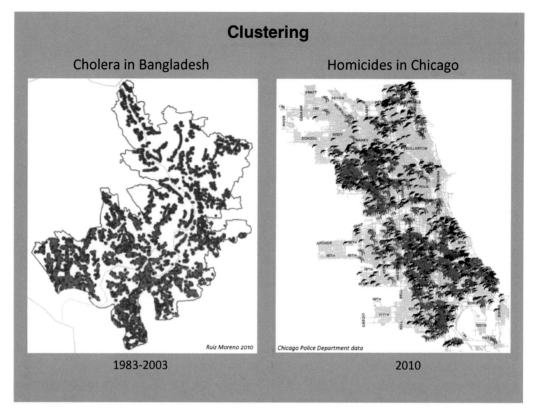

Clustering

Cholera in Bangladesh   Homicides in Chicago

Ruiz Moreno 2010   *Chicago Police Department data*

1983-2003   2010

Fig. 1 Maps showing similarities in clustering between infectious diseases and violence: The timeframe for these two events are vastly different, with the cholera cases taking place over 20 years and the homicide cases over a single year. The speed of the clustering is not relevant here. Contagious processes have differing incubation and latency periods and take place in places with different population characteristics that affect the rate at which they cluster. These charts are intended to demonstrate the similarity in clustering patterns typical of contagious processes

I had used this method many times in many countries. The method for reversing epidemics has essentially three main elements:[1]

1. Interrupt transmission
2. Prevent future spread
3. Change group norms

To interrupt transmission, you need to detect "first," or active cases and stop the transmission to others. With tuberculosis, for example, you find those persons that have active or currently infectious tuberculosis; and then you prevent them from spreading the disease to other people. [For violence, a "first" or active case can be someone who is very angry because he feels he has been disrespected or someone who is angry about an unpaid debt, and who is contemplating violence. In these cases, if you can neutralize the tensions that lead to violence or change the thinking such that violence will not be used, transmission is interrupted.]

To prevent future spread, you need to find those who have already been exposed to the disease and treat them before they can spread the disease further. With AIDS work, it could be sex workers or clients who already may have HIV/AIDS or are at least at high risk who need to be reached (Slutkin et al., 2006). Once you find people who are able to reach and have the trust of these high-risk people, you need to help them change their behaviors so that persons are less likely to contract the disease—e.g., by using condoms or by reducing the number of sexual

---

[1] Other elements are also important including environmental control.

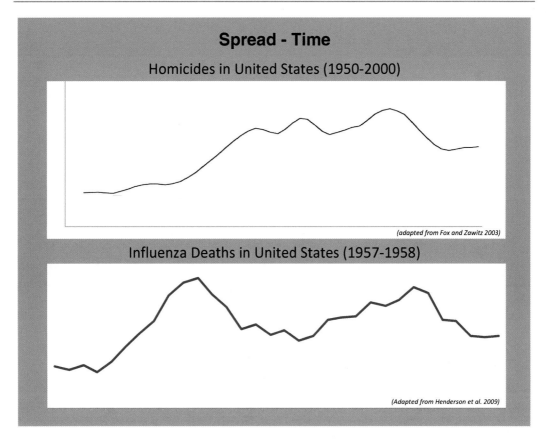

Fig. 2 Sample epidemic curves of violence and infectious disease

partners. For violence, we find those persons that are most exposed to violence, who are involved or "hanging out" in networks with other violent people, and we work intensively with them—again using the most credible and trusted but trained workers to change their behavior to become less violent.

Finally, to change norms we need to challenge unhealthy or harmful norms and replace them with positive and healthy norms. With epidemics we do this by spreading information through public education, specific events, and other activities. The spread of information and skills makes possible group immunity, where a population becomes resistant to a disease because its (new) norms support behaviors that protect them from infection. We thought a very similar approach could be used to treat violence.

Beginning with a small staff, we spent the next 5 years working on how to adapt this epidemic control strategy to the epidemic of violence. This process involved simultaneously talking to people in the community about what was thought feasible, looking at the scientific literature in violence prevention and related behavioral fields, and actively working with a mixed technical and community steering committee to prioritize interventions using the methods we had learned and helped to develop at WHO. Our goal was primarily about developing a clear objective to focus the research and planning. In this case, it was about ensuring that the focus would remain strictly on addressing violence in the form of shootings and killings, rather than becoming distracted by or specifically concerned with gangs, drugs, or poverty—although these other issues also have the potential to be affected by an intervention for reducing shootings and killings.

With this focus in mind, we developed a logic model and a specific plan. Our first plan was a

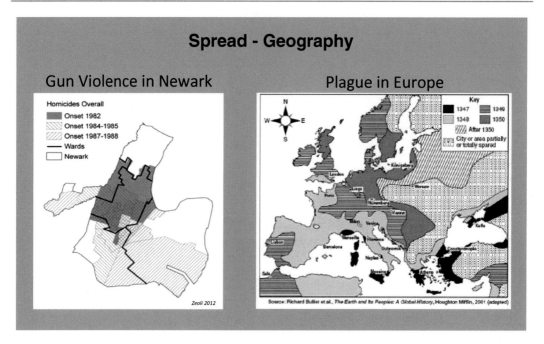

Fig. 3 Epidemic spread of gun violence and infectious disease: Onset is defined in the study as the years in which clusters emerged in the pattern of homicides, as determined using mapping software

collective effort that involved the community, law enforcement, and researchers. The Office of Juvenile Justice and Delinquency Prevention and the Centers for Disease Control and Prevention supported this strategy development work from 1995 to 1999, as well as for years later.

Starting to Treat Violence as a Disease

In 2000, we began to operationalize this plan to address violence in the Chicago neighborhood of West Garfield Park, which at the time was the most violent community in the United States. The initial pilot was made possible largely by the support of the Robert Wood Johnson Foundation, the Chicago Community Trust, the MacArthur Foundation, and an Illinois State Senator named Lisa Madigan, who now serves as the Attorney General for Illinois. West Garfield Park was specifically chosen because of its high level of violence as well as the presence of a good community partner organization, Bethel New Life, who was already operating in the neighborhood.

For the pilot program, we hired a new category of worker: people who were from the community and who then became trained in the methods of disease control. While other programs had employed outreach workers for decades to address gangs, drugs, and crime, they had never before been trained in epidemic control or operated as community health workers. In addition, their focus was sharply defined as stopping shootings and killings. These outreach workers were specifically hired for their access and credibility among the highest risk population—coming out of the same community and with real experience in the same gangs. These indigenous workers were just like the workers we had used in Somalia and Uganda, but their training was designed for a different type of problem.

Through these new workers, our staff put in place an outreach system that worked to change behaviors and stop conflicts among those at highest risk for violence. This evolved into a system which also included a street-level public education component using yard signs, leaflets, and photocopied fliers—the same tactics we had employed in many developing countries. Workers made a point of encouraging multiple messengers from the community to convey messages that were designed to change norms around the use of violence. To push this norm change, whenever a shooting occurred we organized shooting responses, where clergy and residents gathered to speak against the violence in a very public way. Responding to each and every shooting was a new idea and many people initially objected to it. For many in the community and the general public, the death of a gang member was not a tragedy—the attitude was essentially, "he asked for it" or "let them kill each other"—not realizing or prioritizing the effect on the community overall or not fully appreciating how there are carriers, and how this group is affecting the norm. Previous to this being part of the system to change norms, outpourings, demonstrations, and rallies from the community—in Chicago as well as most other cities—were usually limited to when there was considered to be a young child or others considered an "innocent victim." We came in with responses to all shootings to firmly establish the idea that every death and shooting is awful and against the newly proscribed norm, and began to spread this idea among the peer group as well as the community itself.

As the work began, my colleagues and I were surprised by a couple of developments. First, we had intended the shooting responses to create a role for the community to become active in establishing new norms, but we found that individuals at high risk for violent behavior would often come out for the responses as well. This allowed our outreach workers and the community members a chance to interact with them and talk to them about the violence in the community. Essentially, the norm change had opportunities to happen on the spot. Second, the outreach workers became quite popular in the community. People looked up to them. This gave our workers even more ability to influence and change the behavior of those at high risk for violent behavior to persuade them against using violence as well as the credibility to mobilize the rest of the community.

The first year of implementation resulted in a 67% drop in shootings in the West Garfield neighborhood, while comparison areas saw a much lower reduction of 20% (Ransford et al. 2010). That year included long periods without shootings, up to 90 days at a time—previously unheard of in that community as we were told by community residents. The community also started to look different. For the first time in as long as they could remember, families began coming out onto their front lawns and sidewalks in the afternoons and evenings. People were now enjoying parks that had gone unused for years.

The funders then asked us to "do it again"—in other words, repeat the result. With the help of Senator Dick Durbin from Illinois, we obtained funds from the United States Department of Justice to expand this pilot to four more communities over the next three years. Collectively these communities showed a 42% drop in shootings in their first years of implementation, while comparison areas had a 15% reduction, neighboring areas had a 14% reduction, and the city of Chicago had a 12% reduction (Ransford et al. 2010).

Developing a Model

At this early point, the model was focused on changing individual behavior and community level norms. To accomplish these goals, outreach workers were called on to perform two functions with their high-risk clients: (1) focus on the problem of violence by working to change violent behaviors and stop violent events, and (2) help their clients with any other problems in their lives.

This multi-pronged approach was common in my experience with epidemic diseases. While specialized health workers focus on the problem of greatest concern (in this case, stopping and reducing shootings), during interactions with clients workers are often called on to help with a variety of other daily and life issues and crises. With tuberculosis, outreach workers helped to make sure clients took their medicine but also addressed problems clients were having with alcohol or finding work or homes. With HIV, outreach workers helped teach people how to use condoms, but also assisted with daycare and financial needs. With violence, our outreach workers were helping to change the behavior of those at highest risk for violent behavior, but also assisting with multiple other areas of their clients' lives. One of the things that they often helped with was mediating conflicts to prevent them from escalating into shootings. This mediation and behavior change was part of the outreach workers' role, but a tension soon developed between these and with other client needs. This was brought to our attention by two of our first outreach workers named Evans "Chip" Robinson and Antonio "Lil Tony" Pickett (referred to as Batman and Robin in the community).

The tension occurred because outreach workers were being called on to do much more expansive and time-consuming behavior change, largely daytime and continuous interactive work, as well as life-saving conflict mediation, which is mostly nighttime and frequently urgent work. Because the workers could not always work at night or were busy with other client activities, some conflicts did not get mediated, which resulted in shootings. It became clear that a new specialized worker was needed to focus on interrupting conflict. In 2004, we separated out these job descriptions and developed a new type of worker called "violence interrupter" to focus like a laser on detecting and interrupting potentially lethal events that were simmering in the community.

In 2004, because of the statistical results in the first five communities, the state of Illinois funded a tripling of the whole program in Chicago—from 5 to 15 communities and from 20 to 80 workers, with a large concentration in the West Garfield area and in Logan Square, and started a particularly strong program in Maywood, a heavily affected nearby suburb to Chicago that had 22 killings in the previous year. That year, there was an immediate 47% drop killings in Cure Violence Chicago sites, with the city as a whole experiencing an unprecedented 25% reduction in killings. West Garfield and Logan Square had particularly large drops, which suggested a possible dose-dependent relationship. Maywood, Illinois also had a 50% drop in killings (Ransford, Kane, & Slutkin, 2013).

Scientific Validation and Growing the Movement

The impressive results caught the attention of the National Institute of Justice, which funded a multi-year, multi-method, external evaluation of the Chicago program led by Northwestern University. This evaluation showed that shootings dropped by 41–73% overall in program communities with 100% reductions in retaliation homicides in five of eight communities.[2]

These were compelling results that the lead evaluator, Wesley Skogan, called "as strong as you could hope for." The findings led to a cover story in *The New York Times Sunday Magazine* focusing on the new theory and the results, *The Economist* (World in 2009) referring to this work as the "approach that will come to prominence," a subsequent official endorsement by the U.S. Conference of Mayors, and years later to the approach being featured in an award-winning documentary called *The Interrupters*.

This positive evaluation also increased interest among other cities with chronic violence problems in replicating the Cure Violence approach. The first replication of this approach, outside of Illinois where there was already widespread replication, began in Baltimore in 2007. A subsequent evaluation of the Baltimore replication funded by the Centers for Disease Control and performed by the Johns Hopkins University School of Public Health reported that homicides were reduced by up to 56% and shootings by up to 44% (Webster, Whitehill, Vernick, & Parker, 2012). A replication in New York City which began in

---

[2] Overall reductions in shootings in the seven program sites were between 41 and 73%. When comparing to control communities to control for other factors such as law enforcement, statistically significant reductions that were specifically *attributable to the CeaseFire program* were found to be between 16 and 28% in four communities by time series analysis. Hot spot analysis found reductions of shooting density between 15 and 40% in four partially overlapping communities. Six of the seven communities examined had reductions due to the program as determined by either time series analysis or hot spot analysis. The seventh community had 100% drop in retaliation homicides and large reductions in shootings, but the neighboring comparison community had similar reductions.

2009 was evaluated by the Center for Court Innovation and found to have resulted in a rate of gun violence that was 20% lower than comparison neighborhoods after implementation of the program (Picard-Fritsche & Cernaglia 2012). Today, the Cure Violence program has more than 50 sites in more than 25 cities in the United States as well as programs in 8 countries outside the United States. Several additional evaluations are currently being completed, including evaluations of Cure Violence replications and adaptations in Cape Town, South Africa; Loiza, Puerto Rico; and a program adapted to a youth prison in England. The Chicago program has also had an additional independent evaluation showing statistically significant reductions that showed a 38% greater decrease in homicides, 1% greater decrease in total violent crimes, and a 15% greater decrease in shootings (Henry, Knoblauch, & Sigurvinsdottir, 2014).

More About Understanding the Health Approach

It's still new for many people to see violence as a health problem. Some are not yet aware of the science of violence as contagious, or understandably feel most comfortable with the view of people as "bad" as a dominant lens. Our theoretical framework still requires accountability for violent behaviors, but attempts to approach the problem from what is known about behavior from brain and social science.

Also, many people are not yet aware of the theoretical and practical experience of public health in hiring persons from similar backgrounds as a proven and necessary health and public health technology and resist the hiring of people who have formerly been involved in violent activity. Relapses of personnel occur as they do for all diseases and the press or others can amplify these effects. However, relapses in other fields that use peer-based workers have also occurred—with one study showing a 48% relapse rate for drug counselors with previous drug issues (Rhodes et al. 1974) and another study showing a 37.5% relapse rate for alcohol counselors with previous alcohol issues (Kinney 1983). Even law enforcement agencies experience occasional criminal activity by their staff.

By comparison, the Cure Violence workers relapse rate is incredibly small—estimated to be approximately 1.5% of workers. This low rate is likely a result of the sophisticated relapse prevention system put in place in Cure Violence sites. This system includes the use of hiring panels to screen applicants, community checks on applicants and staff, periodic drug and alcohol screening, and weekly discussions and support of relapse prevention with workers. Cure Violence is also developing increasingly sophisticated counseling and self-care training for staff to offer additional resources to prevent relapse.

We realize that it takes time for new policies or practices to take hold; however, the practice of viewing and treating violence as a health problem is growing. Not only is the Cure Violence approach spreading in the United States and around the world, but many other programs that take a health approach to violence are also arising. Health Departments are now getting much more involved in running programs to address violence—with health departments in Baltimore, Kansas City, and New York City leading the way. Law enforcement agencies in many areas are also embracing this approach—either by working with health departments or other departments using health approaches such as youth agencies, or in some cases by adopting health approaches in their own work. Trauma centers and hospitals, an innovation added to the Cure Violence Health Model in the last 10 years, are getting involved by implementing programs to address the effects of exposure to violence and for preventing retaliations. And there has been a very fast acceptance of the approach in the international community, where health is increasingly seen as a logical and effective approach in a more complete strategy to effectively reduce violence in communities.

Continued Learning, Continued Development

At Cure Violence, we work with others to actively research and learn how to make the model and the full health approach more effective. To this end, we have a process of continual development, redesign, and feedback. We started our work by strategizing, then implemented something, learned some lessons, made some changes, learned more, and so on. We continue to learn—from the workers on the street, from the literature on the science of behavior, as well as from other health approaches. Then, we combine the knowledge gained from the street with the science to make adjustments to the model to make it more effective. The first major change was the addition of the violence interrupter position in 2004, but many other changes have followed, including the hospital component, and substantial revisions to the training, and data usage.

The independent evaluators, who spent years studying the implementation of the program to figure out what made the model work, accelerated this learning process greatly for us and for everyone. Skogan's team's evaluation confirmed the effectiveness of both the outreach workers and interrupters and helped us to crystallize this aspect of the model. He found that the outreach workers were acting as role models to their clients and providing significant assistance in connecting the clients with the social services that they needed. The clients reported that the outreach workers were the most important people in their lives aside from their parents. His team found that the interrupters were surprisingly effective in preventing retaliation—actually eliminating retaliation homicides in five of eight communities. Skogan called the innovation of violence interrupters "an original and important development in the violence prevention arena." We learned a lot of unexpected and very useful findings about the approach from this evaluation.

Daniel Webster, the lead evaluator for the Baltimore study, concluded that the work of interrupting conflicts seemed to be very important to achieving results. Looking at four communities, he found that differing results correlated with differing numbers of mediations—communities with three times the number of mediations per month had much stronger results.

Webster's team also found that there was evidence of norm change in persons who were not associated with the program. A survey of young adult males in one program community and two control communities found that after program implementation youth in the program site were much less likely to approve of the use of a gun to settle disputes and four times more likely to support little or no use of violence than their cohorts from the control communities. Because the survey measured attitudes towards use of violence in individuals not directly involved in the program, his findings suggest that the norm change work of the program was spreading beyond the program participants, as it is intended to do.

We are also examining data on our own to make improvements, such as determining the optimum number of workers and types of workers for different communities. The original 67% drop shootings in the first program site was accomplished with 8–10 workers per community site. The subsequent smaller reductions were accomplished with 4–5 workers.

Finally, the rapid expansion into other countries has resulted in much additional experience in both adapting the model and helping us to understand even more about what makes the model work in different circumstances. While political context, culture, and levels of violence may differ in many of the areas we work, it goes back to the same practice we used years ago in Somalia, Uganda, and so many other places: employing highly trusted indigenous workers with the right training and support to change behaviors.

The first country where the model was adapted internationally was Iraq, in 2008. On the surface, the context of southern Iraq could not have been more different from the west side of Chicago, east side of Baltimore, or central New Orleans. However, as we started working with a local Iraqi organization to adapt and implement the model it became apparent that many of the conflicts leading to violence, which may have been labeled as "sectarian" or "tribal," actually began as small interpersonal disputes. As in Chicago, Baltimore, or New York when workers who belonged to the same (in this case) religious and tribal groups focused on preventing the spread of violence among their own peers, the model was able to mediate hundreds of conflicts that otherwise would have led to more deaths.

Since the work in southern Iraq, the Cure Violence Health Model has been successfully implemented in a range of contexts around the globe, including Puerto Rico, Honduras, South Africa, and England. The use of epidemic control methods to (1) map out likely causes of violence, (2) recruit and train indigenous workers with access and credibility with those likely to be involved in violence, and (3) develop behavior and community norm change messages has been universal in application—even if the end result looks widely different on the ground. In each context where our community and implementing partners work, most people are relieved to move beyond the old view of punishing "bad people" and instead to work towards interrupting conflicts, and changing behaviors and norms.

Disease: More Than a Metaphor— Epidemiology and Neuroscience

Years ago, it became clear to me that violence behaves like a contagious disease in virtually all of its critical characteristics, as a result of multiple lines of research from the health, epidemiologic and other disciplines mentioned above, and now summarized in a report from the Institute of Medicine (IOM, 2013; Slutkin, 2013). What has become additionally clear from applications described here and elsewhere, is that violence can be successfully treated like an epidemic disease as well. In other words, the theory is being validated by the treatment. Further, as scientists learn more about how behaviors are formed, we have found that violence has all of the specific population and individual characteristics, meets the specific criteria of a contagious and epidemic disease, and meets the dictionary definitions of both contagious and disease (Slutkin, 2013).

Further, we have learned a great deal from recent studies on the mechanisms of behavioral acquisition, maintenance, and change from recent developments in neuroscience and behavioral science, many of which are highlighted in the IOM report as well. And we can now make a more cohesive picture of how this fits together including at other levels of analysis. Of greatest

relevance perhaps is research over the past 20 years that has repeatedly demonstrated in greater detail that exposure to violence—not just as a victim, but also as an observer—makes people more likely to commit violence. And that this effect happens across violence types.

The synthesis of these studies from different fields, and the expanded understanding that they offered, had a tremendous effect on our thinking. For example, a recent longitudinal study of youth in a public housing project in Mobile, Alabama, found that those chronically exposed to violence were 30 times more likely to engage in violence (Spano, Rivera, & Bolland, 2010). Another longitudinal study of youth in Chicago showed that exposure to violence approximately doubles the probability that the subject will perpetrate serious violence (Bingenheimer, Brennan, & Earls, 2005). These and other studies demonstrate that there is dose dependency between exposure and likelihood of expression of violence—a critical characteristic of infectious processes. This type of dose–response relationship has also been demonstrated in other types of violence, including for child abuse (Ball, 2009; Egeland, 1993, Ertem, Levanthal, & Dobbs, 2000; Widom, 1989), war violence (Archer and Gartner, 1976; MacManus et al., 2013), intimate partner violence (Baldry, 2003; Black, Sussman, & Unger, 2010; Duman & Margolin, 2007; Ehrensaft et al., 2003), elder abuse (Yan & Tang, 2003), and suicide (Gould, Greenberg, Velting, & Shaffer, 2010). What defines infectious disease epidemiology and separates it from other epidemiology is when the outcome variable is a risk factor for itself (Giesecke, 1994).

We are also beginning to learn about *how* this exposure to violence plays out in the brain and how the brain picks up behaviors. For example, we knew that people tend to pick up behaviors from people they are around; now, we have learned that the brain unconsciously learns through observation (Bandura, 1977), possibly using mirror neurons or similar circuits—even when the observer does not "intend" to pick up behaviors as far as can be determined (Iacoboni et al., 2005). We knew that people are compelled to perform certain actions in response to social influence or pressure (Gilovich, Keltner, & Nisbett, 2011); now, we can turn to findings that show that human beings experience social rejection in neurologically similar fashion to physical pain (Eisenberger, 2012; Eisenberger and Lieberman, 2005). Finally, we now know that repeated exposure has been shown to hardwire dissociative and hyperarousal responses to violence into the brain (Perry, 2001).

Understanding this is good news to practitioners and policy makers from all fields—because we can now understand violence scientifically rather than relying on moralistic judgments to guide both policy and practice including intervention design. Moralistic approaches and emotions have a very poor record historically in solving major problems. The scientific approach moves us away from using emotions as the tool box of problem solving; instead, we can apply what we now know—which *is* more than we did before—from the sciences of behavior, epidemiology, infectious diseases, and neuroscience. This can not only ground us in a new theory of violence as a contagious process and epidemic disease, but also in the solutions that follow. This lens and approach has the advantage of understanding behavioral acquisition in a contagious framework and in understanding behavioral and normative change at individual, group, and community levels.

Next Steps

The theory of violence as an epidemic and contagious brain process was not something that we intentionally sought. The original Cure Violence team and I viewed this as a problem of science and of behavior that called for behavior change approaches—relevant, essential, but incomplete. Through research and practice it does now appear that violence behaves like a contagious disease: it operates like a disease in how it spreads and transmits and it lends itself to health-based epidemic control solutions. It is now even more relevant and very feasible to consider violence a health problem—in other words brain based, brain acquired, trauma facilitated, and contagious. The people who are both engaged in it and affected by it have a health issue.

At Cure Violence, we are not arguing that the health approach is the only and entire solution to violence—just that the health sector can make a much more significant contribution to the solution—and that this sector is currently being underutilized. Successful societal efforts require more than one angle or approach. For HIV prevention, we utilize behavior change, norm change, as well as antiviral treatment. With diarrheal disease control, we use water and sanitation improvements, as well as oral rehydration. To reduce motor vehicle fatalities, we use enforced speed limits, as well as innovations such as changing behaviors around seat belt usage and reducing drunk driving, designing divided highways, and better designed cars.

For reducing violence, the role of law enforcement is already fully accepted. But the effort to address violence must be about more than enforcing laws. We can now take into account a lot of new science that provides not only a new theoretical framework based on a new understanding, but can help us to create new methods of prevention and epidemic control. The health system is very experienced at changing behaviors—consider exercise behavior, eating behavior, smoking behavior, and sexual behavior. Violence is simply another behavior that the health sector can be more actively involved in helping to change.

We *all* need safer, more livable, and healthier neighborhoods and cities. Nothing is more essential to all of us. We all see an enormous problem in violence—but this problem is not insurmountable. We can challenge ourselves to understand violence more clearly, utilizing science, health, and epidemiology as well as all the usual fields of research already established. We must keep an open mind about what we have learned scientifically about how the brain works and what this brain research says that gives us new understandings to stop violence in new ways. Just as the discovery of microorganisms by Anton van Leeuwenhoek in the late seventeenth century opened the door to unlocking the causes of epidemic disease—and effective ways to prevent them—the new science of how behaviors are formed and the view of violence as an epidemic disease process are revealing a new path and set of possibilities for all of us—and for new hope for our future and for generations to come for the possibility of life without violence.

References

Archer, D., & Gartner, R. (1976). Violent acts and violent times: A comparative approach to postwar homicide rates. *American Sociological Review, 41*, 937–963.

Baldry, A. C. (2003). Animal abuse and exposure to interparental violence in Italian youth. *Journal of Interpersonal Violence, 18*, 258–281.

Ball, J. D. (2009). Intergenerational transmission of abuse of incarcerated fathers: A study of measurement of abuse. *Journal of Family Issues, 30*, 371–390.

Bandura, A. (1977). *Social learning theory*. Englewood Cliffs, NJ: Prentice-Hall.

Bingenheimer, J., Brennan, R., & Earls, F. (2005). Firearm violence exposure and serious violent behavior. *Science, 308*, 1323–1326.

Black, D. S., Sussman, S., & Unger, J. B. (2010). A further look at the intergenerational transmission of violence: Witnessing interparental violence in emerging adulthood. *Journal of Interpersonal Violence, 25*, 1022–1042.

Bulliet, R., Kyle Crossley, P., Headrick, D. R., Hirsch, S. W., Johnson, L. L., & Northrup, D. (2001). *The earth and its peoples*. New York, NY: Houghton Mifflin Company.

Chicago Police Department's CLEAR (Citizen Law Enforcement Analysis and Reporting) System. (2010). Retrieved from https://data.cityofchicago.org/Public-Safety/Crimes-2001-to-present/ijzp-q8t2

Duman, S., & Margolin, G. (2007). Parents' aggressive influences and children's aggressive problem solutions with peers. *Journal of Clinical Child and Adolescent Psychology, 36*(1), 42–55.

Egeland, B. (1993). A history of abuse is a major risk factor for abusing the next generation. In R. J. Gelles & D. R. Loseke (Eds.), *Current controversies on family violence* (pp. 197–208). Newbury Park, CA: Sage.

Ehrensaft, M. K., Cohen, P., Brown, J., Smailes, E., Chen, H., & Johnson, J. G. (2003). Intergenerational transmission of partner violence: A 20-year prospective study. *Journal of Consulting and Clinical Psychology, 71*, 741–753.

Eisenberger, N. I. (2012). The neural bases of social pain: Evidence for shared representations with physical pain. *Psychosomatic Medicine, 74*, 126–135.

Eisenberger, N. I., & Lieberman, M. D. (2005). Broken hearts and broken bones: the neurocognitive overlap between social pain and physical pain. In K. D. Williams, J. P. Forgas, & W. von Hippel (Eds.), *The social outcast: Ostracism, social exclusion, rejection, and bullying* (pp. 109–127). New York, NY: Cambridge University Press.

Ertem, I. O., Levanthal, J., & Dobbs, S. (2000). Intergenerational continuity of child physical abuse: How good is the evidence? *The Lancet, 356*, 814–819.

Fox, J. A., & Zawitz, M. W. (2003). *Homicide trends in the United States: 2000 update*. Bureau of Justice Assistance. Retrieved from http://www.bjs.gov/index.cfm?ty=pbdetail&iid=968

Giesecke, J. (1994). *Modern infectious disease epidemiology*. Boca Raton, FL: CRC Press.

Gilovich, T., Keltner, D., & Nisbett, R. E. (2011). *Social psychology* (2nd ed.). New York, NY: W.W. Norton.

Gould, M. S., Greenberg, T., Velting, D. M., & Shaffer, D. (2010). Youth suicide risk and preventive interventions: A review of the past 10 years. *Journal of the American Academy of Child and Adolescent Psychiatry, 42*, 386–405.

Henderson, D. A., Courtney, B., Inglesby, T. V., Toner, E., & Nuzzo, J. B. (2009). Public health and medical responses to the 1957–58 influenze pandemic. *Biosecurity and Bioterrorism: Biodefense Strategy, Practice, and Science, 7*(3), 265–273.

Henry, D. B., Knoblauch, S., & Sigurvinsdottir, R. (2014). *The effect of intensive ceasefire intervention on crime in four Chicago police beats: Quantitative assessment*. Chicago, IL: Robert R. McCormick Foundation.

Iacoboni, M., Molnar-Szakacs, I., Gallese, V., Buccino, G., Mazziotta, J. C., & Rizzolatti, G. (2005). Grasping the intentions of others with one's own mirror neuron system. *PLoS Biology, 3*(3), e79.

Institute of Medicine. (2013). *Contagion of violence*. Forum on Global Violence Prevention. IOM and National Research Council of the National Academies.

Kinney, J. (1983). Relapse among alcoholics who are alcoholism counselors. *Journal of Studies on Alcohol, 44*(4), 744–748.

MacManus, D., Dean, K., Jones, M., Rona, R., Greenburg, N., Hull, L., …, Nicola, F. (2013). Violent offending by UK military personnel deployed to Iraq and Afghanistan: a data linkage cohort study. *The Lancet, 381*, 907–917.

Perry, B. D. (2001). The neurodevelopmental impact of violence in childhood. In D. Schetky & E. P. Benedek (Eds.), *Textbook of child and adolescent forensic psychiatry* (pp. 221–238). Washington, DC: American Psychiatric Press.

Picard-Fritsche, S., & Cerniglia, L. (2012). *Testing a public health approach to gun violence*. New York, NY: Center for Court Innovation.

Ransford, C. L., Kane, C., Metzger, T., Quintana, E., & Slutkin, G. (2010). An Examination of the Role of CeaseFire, the Chicago Police, Project Safe Neighborhoods, and Displacement in the Reduction in Homicide in Chicago in 2004. In Youth Gangs and Community Intervention. Ed. Chaskin, R. J. Columbia University Press: New York.

Ransford, C. L., Kane, C. M., & Slutkin, G. (2013). Cure violence: A disease control approach to reduce violence and change behavior. In E. Waltermaurer & T. Akers (Eds.), *Epidemiological criminology*. London, UK: Routledge.

Rhodes, C. & White, C., & Kohler, M. F. (1974). The role of the so-called paraprofessional in the six years of IDAP. In E. Senay, V. Shorty, & H. Alksne (Eds.). *Developments in the field of drug abuse* (pp. 1051–1066). Cambridge, MA: Schenkman.

Ruiz-Moreno, D., Pascual, M., Emch, M., & Yunus, M. (2010). Spatial clustering in the spatio-temporal dynamics of endemic cholera. *BMC Infectious Diseases, 10*(51), 10–51.

Skogan, W., Harnett, S. M., Bump, N., & DuBois, J. (2009). *Evaluation of ceasefire-Chicago*. Chicago, IL: Northwestern University Institute for Policy Research.

Slutkin, G. (2013). *Violence is a contagious disease*. The Contagion of Violence. Institute of Medicine. Retrieved from www.cureviolence.org/wp-content/uploads/2014/01/iom.pdf

Slutkin, G., Okware, S., Naamara, W., Sutherland, D., Flanagan, D., Carael, M., …, Tarantola, D. (2006). How Uganda reversed its HIV epidemic'. *AIDS and Behavior, 10*, 351–360.

Spano, R., Rivera, C., & Bolland, J. (2010). Are chronic exposure to violence and chronic violent behavior closely related developmental processes during adolescence? *Criminal Justice and Behavior, 37*, 1160–1179.

Webster, D. W., Whitehill, J. M., Vernick, J. S., & Parker, E. M. (2012). *Evaluation of Baltimore's safe streets program: Effects on attitudes, participants' experiences, and gun violence*. Baltimore, MD: Johns Hopkins Center for the Prevention of Youth Violence.

Widom, C. S. (1989). Does violence beget violence? A critical examination of the literature. *Psychological Bulletin, 106*(1), 3–28.

Yan, E., & Tang, C. S. (2003). Proclivity to elder abuse: A community study on Hong Kong Chinese. *Journal of Interpersonal Violence, 18*, 999–1017.

Zeoli, A. M., Pizarro, J. M., Grady, S. C., & Melde, C. (2012). Homicide as infectious disease: Using public health methods to investigate the diffusion of homicide. *Justice Quarterly, 31*(3), 609–632.

Why Criminals Tell Us the Truth

Sudhir Venkatesh

I have been conducting ethnographic research on crime for two decades. My fieldwork is most often situated in urban neighborhoods—disproportionately among the poor, but occasionally with the middle and upper classes. As an ethnographer, I need individuals to trust me enough to provide truthful information over an extended period of time. My observation will last at least 2 years, so I'm depending on a high level of commitment from my research subjects.

I anticipate that individuals will be hesitant to disclose their criminal behavior. I also expect them to have many reasons to forgo participation entirely. Perhaps I'm stating the obvious here, but most perpetrators of crime do not wish to be caught. So, they have little reason to trust the promises I or any other researcher make about confidentiality of data. Social science researchers have no privilege that mirrors the assurances that physicians, therapists, and members of the religious clergy can provide those with whom they work. And, of course, simply because they participate, I have no guarantees that they will be truthful. Given that they are committing illegal acts, inaccurate or impartial disclosure is inevitable.

A researcher can certainly make promises to their subjects that all data will be kept confidential. She may rely on her past record of achievement or she may buttress her promises with impressive documentation, like the Certificate of Confidentiality offered by Health and Human Services. But all of this means relatively little if the courts wish to obtain the researcher's data. Either she turns over the data to law enforcement or she will face some form of punishment.[1]

Unable to give my respondents complete assurances of confidentiality, I am never surprised when potential research subjects say they are uninterested in my study. The rational course of action is not to be involved.

And, yet, immediate declination is quite rare. More often than not, those whom I study are cooperative and forthcoming. In fact, there is no shortage of persons who agree to allow me to document their illegalities.

Why?

One reason could be that that crime has altered their capacity for astute judgment. But, if they have the gumption and wherewithal to carry out criminal actions—some of which entail a fairly high degree of complexity, it is probably safe to assume that they have the capacity for critical thought. But, participating in *crime* and participating in a *study about crime* are two different things. The first yields all sorts of potential benefits—symbolic and

---

[1] For an interesting discussion of human subjects protection in the Internet age, see Bassett, E. H., & O'Riordan, K. (2002). Ethics of Internet research: Contesting the human subjects research model. *Ethics and Information Technology, 4*(3), 233–247.

S. Venkatesh (✉)
Columbia University, New York, NY, USA
e-mail: sv185@columbia.edu

M.D. Maltz and S.K. Rice (eds.), *Envisioning Criminology: Researchers on Research as a Process of Discovery*, DOI 10.1007/978-3-319-15868-6_6, © Springer International Publishing Switzerland 2015

material, while the latter would seem to only increase risk and vulnerability.

For this reason, I do not think we can take for granted the willingness of persons to participate in research. In my case, I do not feel that my experience differs from the majority of my colleagues. Most of the ethnographers I know who study crime experience low rates of attrition, and they report receiving candid and truthful information. To be sure, I have encountered my fair share of errors of omission, partial renditions, and hemming and hawing. But I have experienced very few instances of outright lies or refusal to participate in my academic game—and this holds across demographic categories of criminals, whether rich or poor, native, or immigrant, old or young, male or female.[2]

The challenges of obtaining truthful data are a topic of great concern among social scientists. I have seen very few explanations for why criminally minded individuals seem desirous of being research subjects. For much of my tenure as a fieldworker, I have not responded well to the question, "Why do your research subjects participate in your studies?" I find it difficult to come up with a very good answer.

I have certainly asked the subjects themselves—before, during, and after the study is completed. Most shrug and answer, "You said it was important, so I'm helping you." I could ask them for additional information, but it is not a conversational topic that I am anxious to visit over and over. As long as they don't complain, I'm okay not exploring all their inner drives and motivations.

Then, a few years ago, I met a young man named Michael. Michael was turning 25, but he was already a seasoned gang leader in Chicago. Michael was someone with influence in his neighborhood. He not only dictated the behavior

of the several dozen people in his gang, but he had deep relationships in the community. He gave money away to homeless people to buy their allegiance, he ran a protection racket for local stores, and he distributed money to poor individuals in exchange for storing cash and guns in their homes. His social ties reached much further than the young members in his gang organization.

I use the term "broker" to refer to people like Michael who hold sway as a result of their criminal success. A broker could be a gang leader, a pimp or madam, or the director of a trafficking network. I call them "brokers" because of their capacity to make connections and facilitate the exchange of resources across multiple social worlds. They fill "structural holes," the sociologist Ron Burt would say.[3]

I depend on brokers for *continued* access to others in their world.[4] This is so because, in ethnographic work, involvement can never be presumed. Participant-observation is premised on the capacity to have sustained contact with a person of interest—as opposed to a one-time interview or survey that might bring researcher and subject together for a few hours at most. By contrast, ethnographers must return to their field site and their subjects must return to them. Since I am returning to my field site for many years, a simple introduction is never sufficient. I need people who can help me maintain relationships over time. Michael is one of the brokers in his neighborhood who helps others gain confidence in my research—enough so that they also will continue to participate. Michael liked to remind me of this basic fact.

Michael worked in several of Chicago's low-income neighborhoods. I had spent a year observing his gang, when, suddenly, he began sharing his feelings about life as a father. He spoke to me about his worries about dying, and he started telling me about his fears of ending up in prison, unable to be a role model for his children. As he

[2] A number of ethnographers have examined the relationship to the criminal in great detail. See Bourgois, P. (2003). *In search of respect: Selling crack in El Barrio* (Vol. 10). New York, NY: Cambridge University Press; Goffman, A. (2009). On the run: Wanted men in a Philadelphia ghetto. *American Sociological Review, 74*(3), 339–357. See also Venkatesh, S. (2013). Underground markets as fields in transition: Sex work in New York City. *Sociological Forum, 28*(4), 682–699.

[3] Burt, R. S. (2009). *Structural holes: The social structure of competition.* Cambridge, MA: Harvard University Press; Burt, R. S. (2001). Structural holes versus network closure as social capital. In *Social capital: Theory and research* (pp. 31–56).

[4] For another discussion of brokerage, see Pattillo, M. (2008). *Black on the block: The politics of race and class in the city.* Chicago, IL: University of Chicago Press.

spoke, sometimes on the verge of tears, I felt I had crossed an important barrier in our relationship. I have always found it easier to solicit information about criminal activity from criminals. The harder task is getting them to open up about the mundane parts of their lives—coping with school, applying for jobs, keeping up friendships. The more difficult bridge to cross is emotional.

Michael also felt as though he was crossing a threshold. However, whereas I felt relief and excitement at his disclosures, he was feeling nervous and vulnerable. I knew intimate details about his life, many of which he had not told to friends or even the members of his own gang.

One afternoon, we were in his car trying to stay warm in the unforgiving November chill that Chicago brings. We were waiting for the rest of his gang to show up. Michael didn't like to turn on the car heater because it was "a waste of gas." He attributed his success as an underworld business figure to such thrift. Michael had called for a meeting in a neighborhood park.

"You know I could kill you right now and nobody would notice," he said, sipping on his cup of coffee.

"Someone would hopefully hear us!" I laughed, nearly spilling my own coffee.

There was silence. I couldn't tell whether he was joking with me.

"No, they wouldn't," Michael said matter-of-factly. "My uncle showed me a lot of ways to kill someone without any noise. No blood either—and no prints."

"Are we having a serious conversation," I said. "Really. I want to know." At this point, Michael exchanged his coffee for some beer in his backpack. One after another, the beer slid down his throat.

"It's hard, I know," Michael said, wincing at the carbonation stuck in his chest. "*You* just don't know if I'm going to act crazy. Even *I* don't know if, all of a sudden, I might just pop one off the side of your head. It's kind of—like a mystery movie!"

He had his finger pointed at my head to mimic a gun. A sinister smile swept across his face.

"Why haven't you done it already?" I said incredulously—although the thought of him shooting me was starting to appear more real as a result of this conversation. "You could have killed

me a while back. So, I don't think you really would do it."

Michael turned to me and said, "You're probably right. But you never can be sure, can you? Isn't that what makes it interesting?"

Michael was turned on by the fact that he could control the quality and duration of our relationship. He enjoyed making me uncomfortable and unable to predict his behavior. He would tell me that he was more "complicated" than any of my sociological theories. At times, I wondered whether the ability to tease in this fashion was the primary attraction of my research.

Michael could threaten me, but up to a point. Michael couldn't force me to continue my fieldwork—I could leave at any point. And, if he withdrew from my study, it wouldn't be a final blow to my research—I would be disappointed, but I wouldn't beg him to stay on. He couldn't dictate what I write about, nor did he have any editorial control over my choice of publication. And it is worth noting that in any altercation, the police would undoubtedly take my side. And, yet, his threats to inflict physical harm felt very real at times and I wasn't about to test his resolve.

We began to have these conversations on a regular basis. Every few weeks, Michael would feel it was necessary to threaten me. I didn't think much of it until I took notice of its regularity. There was a ritualistic aspect to his sudden outbursts. Sometimes they would occur in public—he might take out a gun and ask if I'd like to play Russian Roulette. At other times, he might interrupt a private conversation by asking if I had prepared a will for my family.

It started to become clear that, in our asymmetrical relationship, the capacity to interject dark humor gave Michael the feeling of self-efficacy. When he exposed my vulnerability, I was sure to react. If he saw that I stood in fear of a physical attack, he could infer that I would be hesitant to leave him any time soon. Like any abusive partner, it was conceivable that Michael felt that his behavior was the real basis for our bond.

But, I believe another dynamic was actually unfolding. To see this, I borrow a concept from sociologist Jack Katz. Michael enjoyed being mean because he was a street *badass*. And, I was his muse.

The *badass* is a notorious urban legend. It comes to us in full force in the 1960s as black Americans sought to take control over their ghetto streets. The badass liked to roam the neighborhood looking for ways to inculcate fear in others as a means of demonstrating his own stature and authority. As Jack Katz elegantly reminds us, for the *badass*, crime is a seduction and daily interaction is motivated by thrill seeking.

> Being mean produces its awful air by intimating that where the self is coming from is a place that represents chaos to outsiders and threatens constantly to rush destructively to the center of their world. The ultimate source of the seductive fascination with being a badass is that of *transcending rationality*.[5]

Katz's observation can be exported into the area of research. As I have noted, the rational response of a criminal to any research inquiry should be to forgo participation altogether. In practice, however, many of them accept the proposition to be placed under an academic microscope. We cannot presume that their motivations are those of the researcher. That is, throughout my studies of crime, I have given prospective participants sound reasons to enroll in my study: *I'm trying to advance science, I hope to use your answers to produce more effective social policy*, etc. For the most part, these invitations ring hollow. The criminal typically cares little about such highfalutin motives.

In my work, most perpetrators of crime bypass these justifications and immediately pose the question, "I still don't understand why I should work with you. Can you give me a reason?" As I search frantically for other reasons, I usually begin with a series of disclaimers, e.g., involvement will never financially rewarding, their name cannot appear in my publications; there is little benefit that will accrue either immediately or in the long term.

It is at this point that people like Michael quickly seize upon another motivation to join my study. Participation could be a great deal of fun

because it enables them to assume the role of social threat. The criminal knows that saying "yes" to a researcher's invitation offers them a chance to be intimidating. It is their way of "rushing into the center of the [researcher's] world," Katz might say, and showing off.

My invitation to participate in a research study becomes Michael's opportunity for thrill seeking. Although the rational response would be to walk away—to better protect his criminal ventures, his emotional needs push him into my research. Like so many criminals, Michael is not simply in need of telling his story—such motivations exist for many people whether they are involved in criminality or not. Michael's role as a criminal *cum* badass requires that he seek every opportunity to *upend traditional moral boundaries*. What better way than to pretend to be the compliant research subject! After I grow comfortable in his presence, he can have some fun at my expense. Michael is correct in thinking that I "can never be sure" about his behavior. Involvement could be precarious and my fear of his erraticism sustains his hold.

Too often, ethnographers who study crime write about access to their subjects as a one-time affair. But it would be incorrect to think about access as a single point-in-time phenomenon. I needed to affirm my partnership with Michael throughout my research. I could not rely on a formal contract that specified the terms of exchange. Our obligations toward one another were held in abeyance each time we met. They had to be affirmed during the course of the interaction. And by being mean or off-putting on occasion, Michael was reminding me that his participation required such continuous negotiation. I had no claims on his allegiance or loyalty over the course of my study.

At the same time, there is a *crying wolf* constraint to the work of the *badass*. At some point, a threat must be followed up with action if it is to have an effect. If Michael threatens physical harm, but never actually assaults me, then I will not fear him. If he raises the prospect of withdrawal from my study, but never quits, then I know that he is simply looking for attention. Michael could not assume a threatening position each time we were

---

[5] Katz, J. (2008). *Seductions of crime: Moral and sensual attractions in doing evil* (p. 112*)*. New York, NY: Basic Books.

together. He was important for my research, but not expendable. He knew there were other gang members whom I could befriend—others who could slowly help me to feel comfortable in the neighborhoods I traveled. So, he would evoke a cooperative air at times.[6] He willingly nurtured my research by helping me gather data. He introduced me to other gang members or other criminal figures in the underworld. He also took an interest in my interview protocols: he helped me pilot questionnaires and adjust question wording. And he listened quietly as I described a research problem in sociology.

And, then, a few weeks later, he would remind me that he liked to be in control. Typically, this reminder took on a sinister form.

Threat is also a key feature in the broker's gestalt. The broker connects people in different worlds together, but as important, she can *sever* those connections. Michael could both put me in touch with others in his neighborhood whom I wanted to interview, but he could also persuade people to withdraw from my study. And, on many occasions, there were criminals who said they were going to participate in my work because Michael had promised them I was someone to be trusted.

Once Michael agrees to participate in my study, our interests become aligned. If he chooses the research game as a means by which to gain emotional satisfaction, power, and stature, he is invested in playing by the rules of that game. Perhaps the most important rule in this game is simply that *Michael must provide me honest and useful information*. His capacity to play the *badass* role depends upon it.

In the researcher-informant couplet, then, Michael and I shared a common constraint: neither of us could continue working together if the information he presented me was not an accurate depiction of his world. If I learn that he is lying about his gang's monthly revenue or other details about their illicit affairs, it will put our partnership at risk. If I find that his aim is to jeopardize my research, he quickly became useless as a research subject. He must work as hard as me to ensure the success of the research project. Only then are the foundations in place for him to threaten me and pursue his thrill seeking.

In my experience, this is one important reason why brokers in the criminal world give ethnographic researchers accurate information. Truthful data becomes a social contract that permits the relationship to continue. Not every criminal I meet will draw upon our relationship to voice threats and insults, but they all arrive with a complex set of emotional needs. Michael required affirmation that he was a *badass*. But other underworld figures want me to listen to their life story or help them solve problems in their criminal organization. And nearly all of them desire the validation that accompanies observation. Faced with a society that sees them as marginal, thuggish, an object of fear, etc. Michael and others enjoy a researcher's judgment-free observation. But, whatever their needs, they quickly discover that we are partners only to the degree that the capacity to collect truthful data is upheld.

So, we come upon the curious fact that, in the context of the research game, the criminal becomes an obedient figure. She must adhere to the rules that I set in place at the outset of my work. And, in my experience, most serious criminals take pride in ensuring that the data has great value. They go out of their way to protect the social contract that is in place. Otherwise, their fun might end.

---

[6]As I begin to learn more about his world, I threaten Michael's capacity to bridge the structural hole. For a broader discussion, see Moody, J., & White, D. R. (2003). Structural cohesion and embeddedness: A hierarchical concept of social groups. *American Sociological Review 68*, 103–127.

Section 2

Generating New Data

Although much research is done using data collected by criminal justice agencies and other sources, there are many cases where such data do not suffice and original data collection is required. This is the case when obtaining data of a personal nature from untapped populations, such as Valerie Jenness' study ("Gender & Sexuality as Methodological Confounds in the Study of Transgender Prisoners") of transgender prisoners. Charis Kubrin pulls her data from the lyrics of rap music, which in many cases have been used in court cases ("Come Along and Ride on a Fantastic Voyage"). Stephen Rice's chapter ("Getting Emotional") explores the statements of offenders about to be executed and shows how they can be assessed for feelings of not only defiance, but also for desires for forgiveness. Robert Sampson ("The Making of the Chicago Project") details the trials and tribulations of mounting a community-based data collection effort, one that has produced varied new concepts in the social sciences (e.g., collective efficacy, ecometrics) and a major body of research. And Wesley Skogan ("Surveying Police Officers") deals with the ins and outs of obtaining information from police officers on sensitive issues such as police culture and procedural (in)justice.

Gender and Sexuality as Methodological Confounds in the Study of Transgender Prisoners

Valerie Jenness

In the summer of 2007, Alexis Giraldo, a transgender parolee who served over 2 years in California prisons, sued the California Department of Corrections and Rehabilitation (CDCR) and individual prison staff members who allegedly allowed her to be serially raped by her male cellmates while in Folsom State Prison.[1] After successfully navigating a complex and exhausting extralegal and legal complaint process, Giraldo, a young Puerto Rican transgender woman—a biological male who identifies and presents as female—had her day in court. During the 2-week trial in San Francisco Superior Court, the plaintiff and her attorney communicated to the jury, the witnesses in the courtroom, and the press how she was placed in a men's prison without regard for the obvious risk of sexual assault from the male prisoners she was housed with, endured daily beatings and brutal sexual assaults by her cellmate, begged for help from prison staff and was told to "be tough and strong," reported the injuries to doctors and therapists, and officially documented her situation and experiences.

In turn, the state's attorneys representing the CDCR contested these claims. They argued that Giraldo's allegations were unsubstantiated and discredited him as a disgruntled parolee with a history of manipulative and deceitful behavior. They explained that inmates with male genitalia are, of course, housed in men's prisons, and they emphasized the plaintiff's request to be placed in the housing assignment where the alleged sexual assaults occurred and subsequent refusal to transfer to alternative housing when given multiple opportunities to do so. They pointed to the consensual nature of his sexual liaisons with other inmates, including the alleged rapist, and to his failure to clearly and unequivocally inform CDCR staff of sexual assaults at the time they occurred. They claimed he had financial motivations for filing suit. They argued that he is a convicted felon who, by virtue of his previous convictions, has demonstrated he is capable of—and well rehearsed at—engaging in fraudulent endeavors in the obvious pursuit of self-interest.

Both sides in this high-profile legal dispute emphasized that the plaintiff is a gendered subject, but they differed—in fact, they were

This is an edited version of "From Policy to Prisoners to People: A 'Soft-Mixed Methods' Approach to Studying Transgender Prisoners," originally published in the *Journal of Contemporary Ethnography*. 2010, 39(5):517–553. Reprinted with permission of Sage Publications. All rights reserved. Reader should consult the original publication for the original acknowledgments as well as the full text, footnotes, and references. Direct all correspondence to Valerie Jenness, Department of Criminology, Law and Society, University of California, Irvine, 92697-7080. E-mail: jenness@uci.edu

[1] *Giraldo v. The California Department of Corrections and Rehabilitation*. Case No. CGC-07-461473, Superior Court of California, City and County of San Francisco.

V. Jenness (✉)
University of California, Irvine, Irvine, CA, USA
e-mail: jenness@uci.edu

M.D. Maltz and S.K. Rice (eds.), *Envisioning Criminology: Researchers on Research as a Process of Discovery*, DOI 10.1007/978-3-319-15868-6_7, © Springer International Publishing Switzerland 2015

diametrically opposed—in their assessment of the plaintiff's gender and attendant standing as a legal subject: the plaintiff's attorney maintained that Giraldo is, for all intents and purposes, a female and should be understood as such, while the state's attorney maintained that Giraldo is, for all intents and purposes, a male and should be understood as such. The jury charged with wading through these claims and counterclaims considered the evidence, including a report on which I was the lead author (Jenness, Maxson, Matsuda, & Sumner, 2007; see also, 2014). They assessed the credibility of the parties participating in the trial and rendered a verdict. Without explicitly taking sides in the gender dispute that characterized this case, the jury found in favor of the CDCR on the alleged civil charges. To quote one legal observer, the CDCR "dodged a bullet."

Shortly after this high-profile trial, I was commissioned by CDCR to conduct a study of transgender inmates in CDCR institutions. Described in detail elsewhere (Jenness, 2014; Jenness, Sexton, & Sumner, 2010), this study relied primarily on structured interviews with transgender prisoners, and it necessarily included an ethnographic component as a result of being *in* many prisons, *among* many prisoners, and *engaged* with many CDCR personnel. The main goal, at least originally, was to provide insight into the basic policy question—where best to house transgender inmates if keeping them safe is the primary goal. Herein I focus on how experts, CDCR officials, researchers (including the author of this article!), and transgender prisoners who participated in my study constructed gender and sexuality as applied to transgender inmates. I faced no small task: searching for an unknown number of needles in lots of haystacks. That is, I was looking for an unknown number of transgender inmates within hundreds of housing units in 33 prisons spread across the largest state in the USA (for a detailed review of the larger study, see Jenness et al., 2010).

Defining the Population

Determining who is and is not transgender and, related, how transgender is understood in the context of prison life is tricky business. In large part, this is because gender and sexuality are replete with ambiguities and contradictions—the very things that can derail a research project anchored in categorical understandings of the social world built around the establishment and reification of social boundaries that define categories of people. For example, a consultant I hired because of her background in the social sciences and because I thought she is transgender (she was born physically recognizable as a male and underwent surgery as an adult to become physically recognizable as a female) suggested that the research team use language like "others like you," "women like you," or "those presenting as female" when addressing the target population. She encouraged me to avoid using the term "transgender" with transgender inmates. Odd, I thought. Later, I discovered she offered this advice at least in part because she does not identify as transgender; despite the fact that I hired her precisely because I assumed she is transgender only to find out she identifies, simply, as "a woman" (who underwent "anatomical corrections" to reflect that identity).

In contrast, other experts encouraged me to use the term transgender because it is, they argued, well equipped to capture a range of identities. As one well-known transgender activist in the Bay Area who has considerable experience working with transgender prisoners said to me: "Just use transgender, they'll get it." When I explained that I wanted to be sensitive about language and labels and questioned the degree to which the "target population" would feel comfortable with the term transgender above and beyond just getting it, he said:

> Val, the cutting edge term is gender variant, but I wouldn't use this term. It's too academic. These folks in prison do not have the room, space and luxury to think about distinctions between those who wish to be seen as transgender, those who wish to be seen as women, and those who just wish to be seen. They don't care about identity politics like you think.

He went further to admonish me for wasting valuable research time trying to parse all this out and said something mildly snide about "us more educated folks" who sit around and make sense of it all while often forgetting "their" realities.

As I would learn, "their realities" include securing the standing of "girl" in an alpha male environment (Jenness, 2010; Jenness & Fenstermaker, 2014). From his point of view, my concern with getting language "right" was misguided—what he called "a waste of time and energy"—and in some ways beside the point for a group of people who want to be seen and heard but others often ignore. As I later learned, he was right. The girls in men's prisons would be happy to talk with me and other interviewers on the research team under conditions of confidentiality. Indeed, 95% of the transgender inmates with whom we made contact consented to be interviewed and completed a usable interview (Jenness et al., 2010).

Given that there is very little consensus on how best to define the term transgender and that "transgender" is often used as an umbrella term for a plethora of identities, I decided to focus data collection on those inmates who (1) self-identify as transgender (or something analogous); (2) present as female, transgender, or feminine in prison or outside of prison; (3) have received any kind of medical treatment (physical or mental) for something related to how they present themselves or think about themselves in terms of gender, including taking hormones to initiate and sustain the development of secondary sex characteristics to enhance femininity; or (4) participate in groups for transgender inmates. Meeting any one of these criteria would qualify an inmate for inclusion in this study. By deploying these criteria, I hoped to bypass larger debates about who is and is not transgender and, instead, rely on a comprehensive understanding that would maximize inclusion without diluting the target population beyond recognition. In short, my intention was to move from questions of policy to comprehension of prisoners.

Working with CDCR Administrators to Identify Transgender Inmates in CDCR Prisons

For CDCR personnel, evaluating various definitions and attendant understandings of "transgender" was decidedly unproblematic. Before data collection commenced, I presented an overview of the research plans to wardens and other CDCR officials in attendance at a wardens' meeting in Santa Barbara, California, on February 5, 2008. During and after this presentation, I solicited the assistance of the wardens to identify all transgender inmates in their respective facilities. After delineating the four-pronged criteria by which I hoped to identify transgender inmates in California prisons, as described previously, the first warden to ask a question said: "So you want our homosexuals?" Sincerely delivered, this question came off as reasonable and attentive as he was genuinely trying to ensure he understood who should and should not be on the list produced at his prison. At this moment, it became clear to me that, for this group of professionals, who have considerably more experience with the target population than I or anyone on my research team, "transgender" and "homosexual" are conflated social types in a perceptual scheme that sees very little distinction between the two. Recognizing this "misunderstanding," I politely responded: "Well, some transgender inmates might be homosexual, but some might not; and, in any event, we want to select transgender inmates, not homosexual inmates." I then went over the four-pronged criteria again, emphasizing that we are selecting transgender inmates quite apart from whether they are homosexual. My review of the criteria for including study participants, in turn, evoked a few blank stares and an ensuing discussion about the difference. It was a discussion that, I am convinced, did not lead to much shared understanding despite our—theirs and my—best efforts.

Throughout this project, CDCR officials routinely indicated that transgender prisoners in men's prison are, in the first and last instance, male homosexuals. Thus, they effectively conflate gender, homosexuality, and transgender. The substantive variation was in how much I responded to the conflation at various moments in the field. In other moments, I simply did not respond to indications of this conflation. For example, on the heels of the wardens' meeting at which the project was introduced and described by me and the point person in the CDCR, a high ranking CDCR administrator sent a letter to the wardens to formalize the request for assistance and to remind them of the four-pronged criteria by which transgender inmates were to be identified for participation in the study. Presented below, some of the text of her letter rightly directed the wardens to err toward overinclusiveness when producing rosters, knowing that we could eliminate inmates from participation in the study once an interviewer asked them a few eligibility-related questions when face-to-face in a confidential setting at the prison:

> To ensure the research team has the most current data and because there is no system-wide code that identifies inmates as transgender, please provide a list of all transgender inmates (name, CDCR#, and housing location in facility as of that date) in your institution. To ensure consistency across all prisons and to ensure that no inmate who might qualify as transgender is excluded, please include all inmates that fit any of the following criteria:
>
> • Male inmates who present themselves as female, transgender, or feminine while in prison.
> • Who participate in any transgender related groups in your facility.
> • Who receive any kind of medical treatment (physical or mental) for something related to how they present themselves or think about themselves in terms of gender.
> • Who self-identify as transgender (Official letter sent to CDCR wardens, dated March 11, 2008).

I drafted the letter containing this text and, in the main, the director used my text verbatim. However, before sending the letter to the wardens on official CDCR letterhead, the director made a key revision. Namely, she inserted the word "Male" in the first bullet point, effectively ensuring the gender categorization is unambiguous from an institutional point of view.

Unlike my carefully delivered rejoinder in the discussion of the distinction between transgender and homosexual in the wardens' meeting described previously, this time I simply noted the difference (to myself and my research team) and thanked the director for her assistance. I did not contest the director's revisions to the letter for a host of reasons, including estimating that another discussion about why inserting "male" might be problematic and simply desiring to get on with the next phase of the research. I did so because

I wanted to advance the project rather than waiting for pristine conditions to enact well-considered research protocols. I have long since accepted that pristine field conditions rarely exist, and they never exist in prisons. By casting a wide net, however, we found that many inmates on the list provided by the prison officials did not qualify for our study because, as they would tell us once face-to-face in an interview room, "I'm just gay," "I'm not a girl," and "You're barking up the wrong tree here."

This kind of misidentification often created an awkward moment as the interviewer had to explain there was, no doubt, a clerical error, apologize for making an inappropriate assumption, and assure the person that, of course, no one thinks of him as anything other than what he is. In some cases, this was no big deal and in other cases, interviewers had to do more interactional work to respond to the awkward moment and engage in interactional repair work. In one instance, for example, I wrote the following in my field notes about a "non-interview":

> I sat down to interview an inmate, a large, African-American, bald, muscular man who kept calling me "Miss Val." He explained to me that he was not gay, that he is "100% real man. The real deal." He also said he is a 49 year old drug dealer from [another state] and was happy to talk with me, but "You shouldn't do it here. People see people coming in here and they are going to wonder what is going on and think I'm telling on people." He suggested that we do interviews in another building—a building where inmates can't see who is going to meet with us. I asked him if he wanted to leave and he said, "No, I'm here now." Because I had to wait for [another interviewer] to finish an interview anyway, I asked "Bruce" how things were going and he went on and on about prison politics as "so much about race. It isn't like this in [his home state]. I was down 10 years in [his home state] and I never saw anything like this—blacks don't talk to whites, whites don't talk to blacks, it's crazy shit. That's the problem in California—this race shit. It really is unbelievable. Race. Gangs.

Shit, it's all a mess. It isn't like that in [home state]. In [home state] you can associate with anyone you want, I mean, as long as they aren't a sex offender or something. Someone needs to study this race thing. I've never seen anything like it!" I asked him about the transgender inmates. He said: "They are what they are. Some of them are taboo. You don't mess with them. Some of them are okay."

Val: "Who is taboo?"
Bruce[2]:   "The ones with AIDS. The ones who sleep around and spread diseases. Those are the ones you need to stay away from. They are dirty."

I then asked him how [transgender inmates] were thought of by other inmates and he said: "Some guys are weak. They can't hold their own in here. There's no women and it gets old using your hand to get off. Oh, I'm sorry; sorry about my language."

Val: "No, please, explain it to me in whatever language makes sense to you and will help me understand."

Bruce: "Ok, you're locked up, you have no women, you get tired of using your hand, so you dump in them. They are like a dumping ground. You just dump your load in them. But, we know they are men. You have to act like they are women, but we know they are men. C'mon, man, they have what men have. Still, you can dump your stuff in her."

Val: "Why would she let you do that?"

Bruce: "Hey, I didn't say I do it! I'm not weak. But they want what women want: security, protection, comfort, companionship, someone to be nice to them, and take care of them. But, also, some just want the sex. Some really like it. Others just do it to get what women want. They are not all the same. Ask them why they do it."

Val: "Are they good for anything other than sex?"

Bruce: "Yeah, some guys like to talk with them and use them to, you know, keep the cell clean, wash their clothes, iron, sew, cook, you know, all the shit women do. I've done that, too. I mean, I don't want to do that shit. And, like I said, some of them do it because they like it—it makes them feel like women. But, others do it just to get what women want: men, protection, comfort, companionship, someone to talk to, you know. I guess, really, it's like on the outside. But, like I said, we know they are men. We don't get fooled in that way. But, we've got to talk to her like a woman because that's what she wants."

He then went on to explain he has a wife and kids at home and that he's always provided for them (via selling drugs), "just like men are supposed to do." Throughout our conversation, he routinely apologized for his language and indicated that he did not mean to be disrespectful. At the end, as I was escorting him out of the office and down the hall, he said "Miss Val, don't think I'm not a gentleman. I treat women well. I know women like you don't get treated the way these girls in here get treated. I bet you get treated real nice. I know the difference. My momma raised me to respect women and I do. I hope I didn't show you any disrespect, did I?" I said "No, not at all. I'm glad you helped me understand how things work in here, that's why I'm here. You've been very helpful."

This impromptu commentary says a lot about the nexus between prison life and the structure of gender and sexuality in men's prisons. As I reported in another publication, this was upsetting to me on multiple levels (Jenness, 2010); however, because this "non-case" was effectively providing substantive data related to key concerns related to the larger project, I remained in research mode. I simply listened and nodded as he spoke, periodically signaling him to continue rather than thank him for his time and move to the next potential interviewee.

---

[2] "Bruce" is a pseudonym.

Working with CDCR Personnel in the Field

The director's decision to insert the word "male" into previously gender-neutral text anticipated what I observed again and again in the field while working in prisons. As the research team traveled to 28 prisons to interview over 300 transgender inmates, I spent hundreds of hours with prison officials in prisons. This included countless hours meeting with wardens and their administrative delegates "on-site," being escorted in and out of prisons and housing units within prisons by staff, and simply "hanging out" with officers and inmates alike as I waited for interviewees to be escorted to confidential interview rooms. Countless serendipitous ethnographic observations gathered during this "non-interview" time associated with the research revealed that CDCR staff routinely referred to transgender inmates in men's prisons by using masculine generic pronouns and/or by using their male names rather than adhering to transgender inmates' preference to be referred to with feminine generic pronouns and/or by using their female names.

The practice of ordaining transgender inmates in prisons for men as men was particularly vivid when I was walking across a prison yard with two other interviewers and the lieutenant with whom we had been working for days. A Cuban transgender inmate described by an officer on-site as "very flamboyant" was sauntering across the yard with her CDCR-issued blue shirt tied at the waist such that it appeared like a female blouse, rubbing her butt, and announcing to anyone within earshot that she had just had a hormone shot. She made it clear the shot was both painful and welcome. As other inmates made note of her visibility on the yard and directed her way what could be perceived as playful or rude comments—for example, "Hey, aren't you looking fine, I'd like a piece of that ..."— the lieutenant amicably and matter-of-factly told the transgender inmate to stop drawing attention to herself. He said: "Okay, Mr. Hernandez, that's enough." She smiled and quickly retorted: "That's Ms. Hernandez." The officer called her Mr. again and she corrected him

again. This exchange happened three times, with Ms. Hernandez and the lieutenant finally just walking off in different directions—her toward the center of the yard and us inside a programming building. Once inside, I respectfully asked the lieutenant if that kind of exchange is typical and he said "Yes, but we try to keep it to a minimum." I then asked: "Why not just call her Ms. Hernandez? What does it cost you?" He respectfully explained that Mr. Hernandez is in a male prison, he's a male, and policy requires forgoing the use of aliases. He went on to explain that the use of aliases constitutes a threat to security. What made this particularly telling to me was that this lieutenant proved to be one of my favorite officers to work with in the field because he helped us get our work done in an efficient and effective manner and because, in the process, he struck me as a CDCR official who genuinely respects the transgender inmates and truly cares about their welfare. In my field notes, I wrote "helpful and nice guy."

In another memorable moment, I was in the administrative segregation unit in what is considered to be an old, violence-prone prison, waiting for officers to bring a potential study participant to be interviewed, when an officer with whom I was chatting made a distinction between a "real one" and "not one" as he brought inmates to us. At one point, he went further and made a reference to "a real winner" and "a real one." I asked the officer closely stationed by a bulletin board with photo identification of all inmates in the unit posted how he knew which inmates were transgender. At first, he seemed hesitant to tell me, but then he said with confidence: "It's obvious, just look at them." I proceeded to look at the many photographs on the board, one by one, and in a focused and sustained way. I shook my head in a negative direction as I moved from photo to photo and declared "I can't tell who's who." When I asked him to help me figure it out, he gleefully did so by pointing to specific cards and calling out the ID numbers. He treated this identification exercise as unproblematic until he came across a particular inmate photo. He pointed to it, paused, and said "Now, that one, who knows ... I'm not sure. Can you tell?" My response—"I can't"—was greeted with an awkward silence; thereafter, we went through the cards one by one, and he began to indicate less confidence in his assessment abilities, saying "sometimes it's hard to tell" and "sometimes we're off." He seemed embarrassed to confess to this confusion, concluding with "but they all know who they are." I didn't know what to make of this, but I was thinking "if only it were that easy." In another memorable exchange in the field, a lieutenant made of point of distinguishing between homosexual inmates and transgender inmates. After completing interviews at the prison at which he works, I secured approval from the warden to take a few pictures of transgender prisoners who consented to having their pictures taken. When I went back to the prison to take pictures of transgender inmates, this lieutenant—with whom I had been working a few weeks earlier when my team was there doing interviews—enthusiastically showed up with his own camera to assist me with our mission to secure photographs. As we were walking through the administration building and toward the yard, each of us with camera in hand, the following dialogue unfolded:

Lieutenant: How will we know who to take pictures of? Do you think you can tell?

Val: Yes, let's just look for the female-looking inmates.

Lieutenant: But what if they are just gay?

Val: Let's just look for [plucked] eyebrows and makeup.

Lieutenant: But that might just be the gay ones.

Val: Okay, let's look for breasts.

Lieutenant: Really, are you serious?

Val: Yeah, I think that's our best bet.

Lieutenant: I think you're right. Let's go to the yard first.

The value of reporting this exchange lies in its exceptional status. It is, quite simply, the only time—after hundreds of hours in the field with officers and administrators—a CDCR official explicitly expressed a distinction between homosexual and transgender inmates. In every other instance in which the two descriptors were used by CDCR officials, conflation between the social types was assumed. When I asked the lieutenant

how he arrived at this nuanced understanding, he looked quizzical and then went on to inform me that he was a single dad for many years during which time his daughters taught him quite a bit about gender and how it is different than sexuality. He went further to ask: "It's complicated, but distinct, right?" He was sincerely looking to me—the professor and the lead researcher in the exchange—for an answer and I gave him one: "Yeah, it's complicated." I would like to say I was purposely being vague, if not evasive, in choosing this response. Alas, the truth is, I said all I could think of that best reflected my understanding at the time. It was what undergraduate students tell me is a "duh" response, and I suspect that is exactly how he heard it.

Debriefing with Fellow Researchers

Almost without fail, interviewers followed each day of data collection with some "debriefing," usually in the car on the way home or back to the hotel. Predictably, this debriefing was sometimes humorous and sometimes shocking. For example, I had to laugh when an interviewer reported that a transgender inmate mistook her for being pregnant. When the interviewer informed the inmate that she was not pregnant, the inmate apologized for her rudeness by saying, "Oh, I'm such a cunt!" What a thing for a transgender inmate in a men's prison to say about herself. I found myself thinking: "Well, that's an awful thing to call yourself." But, I also thought: "What does calling yourself a cunt mean in a context in which having female body parts, especially breasts and vaginas, is desperately desired and creatively pursued as a necessity for the Self (with a capital S)?" It occurred to me that maybe a transgender inmate calling herself a cunt has meaning I do not understand, and, in any event, I now like to think of it as a playful, positive, multifaceted comment—a comment defined more by context than cliché.

Debriefing was predictably disturbing as interviewers shared reported incidents of sexual assault in prison, difficult lives outside of prison, and the complicated nature of the relationship between gender identity, sexual orientation, and self-presentation. Doing so amplified all of our exposure to the highlights of others' interviews and hopefully prompted insight that otherwise would not have occurred. At the same time, sometimes the debriefing took the form of "Yeah, well, I did an interview with someone who …" as the comparisons became the basis for what occasionally struck me as a subtle form of friendly competition over who did the most interesting, illuminating, and atypical interview as well as a venue for much-needed catharsis at the end of long and often emotionally taxing days. One day, the interviewer who interviewed the "lesbian transgender couple" trumped. Another day, the interviewer who interviewed the transgender inmate who used to work in porn movies trumped. Another day, the person who interviewed an extremely mentally ill transgender inmate trumped. Another day, the two interviewers who interviewed a transgender couple who were making plans to parole and move in with a lesbian couple in another state and set up a middle-class household trumped. The examples are endless, but the point remains: there was seldom a day of interviewing that did not generate a "case" to add to the pool of cases discussed in our debriefing sessions that effectively diversified the population and forced us to think in more complicated terms about transgender inmates. Reality continually defied stereotype.

As data collection unfolded, I could not predict what the new case would be, but debriefing always generated a provocative case to be shared and a venue for challenging our individual and collective views of the transgender population. Although I occasionally cringed when I sensed the debriefing session could be read as "gossipy" or we could (wrongly, I think) be accused of treating the transgender inmates like a "zoo exhibit" more than an oral "case study comparison" (to use the official words of social science), I looked forward to debriefing at the end of a long day of interviewing. During debriefing sessions, I occasionally thought that someone should study us, with an eye toward trying to make sense of how we do gender, make attributions related to our human subjects, and otherwise reveal the social fabric in which we were—and are—inevitably and inextricably entangled.

Most notably for my purposes here, what was not predictable to me was when we, members of the interview team, "slipped" and, in the process of debriefing among ourselves, referenced a transgender inmate in our study by using a masculine generic pronoun. We all did it more than once. The "slip" usually took the form of saying something like, "Well, he said …," "His situation included …," "The guy I interviewed …," "I told him …," and so on. These slips occurred despite our commitment to enact the interview training that dictated referring to the transgender inmates as they would like to be referred to (i.e., as transgender or female) and despite a genuine desire to be respectful of their self-designations and gendered identities. Sometimes these slips were followed by immediate self-correction, such as "uh, I mean her …" or "I mean she …," but sometimes they went unmarked. An e-mail exchange with a graduate student who worked on the project, including interviewing many transgender inmates, is informative along these lines. After the graduate student referred to a transgender inmate as "his," I pointed out the slippage when I wrote: "'his'—you little assimilationist, you." The graduate student wrote back:

> Ugh—I know. Sometimes I cringe at myself these days when I can tell I'm just doing what's needed to get it done and do it quickly—and what results is slippage. In these cases via e-mail regarding the lists [of potential subjects for the study] I've actually somehow convinced myself it's not awful because technically we don't know if "he" is transgender.

I responded: "Oh, that makes two of us. I cringe daily … the worst is when I slip in an interview after the person has told me how much 'he' is a girl. CRINGE." I report this exchange because it reveals what I experienced throughout this project. Namely, we very much wanted to get it "right" from a research point of view, from a humanist point of view, and from a political point of view. Without malice, and despite our best efforts, however, we too sometimes reinscribed a seemingly intractable gender order on "the girls." We did so even as we (sometimes self-righteously) adopted a critical stance toward CDCR officials for doing the same. Related, toward the end of data collection, my neighbor said in passing: "You still studying the guys in the big house?" I righteously corrected him: "The ladies in the men's prison." He responded "Yeah, right, whatever." And I said: "The 'whatever' matters."

Engaging with the Transgender Prisoners

Finally, engagement with transgender prisoners in the field serves as a catalyst for revealing both hegemonic assumptions about gender and the decentering of gender and sexuality. Consider, for example, three particularly memorable exchanges in the field: one that created a moment in which I was orienting to the interviewee as a male, one that created a moment in which I was orienting to the interviewee as a female, and one that created a moment in which I was being tutored into a prison-specific gender and sexuality order.

The first example came in the middle of an easygoing interview with a tall, slender, African-American transgender inmate with a gentle demeanor and inviting smile. The transgender inmate surprised me by asking, seemingly out of the blue, "Do you like animals?" Caught off guard, I said "sure" and then I immediately went back to my line of scheduled questioning. With what I perceived to be a coy smile, she then said: "Do you want to see my snake?" I thought "snake" was a reference to a part of the male anatomy and immediately thereafter thought, "Okay, here we go." I said "No, that's okay" and she responded with "But I really want to show it to you" as she proceeded to pull out of her shirt pocket a snake—an elongated reptile of the suborder Serpentes. I laughed, and she asked, "What's so funny?" I said, "Nothing" and then proceeded to admire what appeared to be a small garden snake. As I was petting the snake, she explained that she found the snake on the yard, has been taking care of it in her cell, and now feels very responsible for the snake. I suggested

that the snake might be happier back out in the yard and perhaps in the fields beyond the walls. She said she had never thought about that, but that now the snake might not survive on its own because it has gotten accustomed to being taken care of. She seemed chagrined when she said: "I can't set her free now, she won't survive." I didn't know if this was a reference to just the snake or to herself as well, but I regretted pointing out that she imprisoned the snake just as others imprisoned her. Even more, I regretted that my response to her original question—"do you like snakes"— was heard through the lens of orienting to her as, in the first instance, a him and thinking the reference to his snake was a reference to his penis.

In sharp contrast, in another exchange, I was struck by how, in the first instance, I found myself "naturally" orienting to an interviewee as female. On the way out of the interview room, a very warm and talkative Latina transgender inmate and I walked through a day room that had a television on with Hillary Clinton giving a stump speech during her run for president. Noticing this, the transgender inmate turned to me, asked me about the presidential race, and made a point of telling me "we girls want Hillary." She explained that they—the transgender inmates in this prison—want "the girl" to be president because (a) it was about time a girl was president and (b) Hillary is "tough and smart and can handle herself." She clearly related to Hillary's campaign as, to quote her, "the chance for the first woman president." For her, this campaign signaled that tough and smart women who can handle themselves can go far (now). When I revealed that I too was a Hillary supporter she seemed pleased and asked: "Are you a real girl?" When I said "yes," she spontaneously gently touched my forearm—something inmates are never supposed to do (i.e., touch a visitor) but is a routine feature of many interactions outside of prison—smiled, and said, "Oh, that must be nice." She went on to emphasize that the "other girls" are all for Hillary, too, and asked me if I thought Hillary would win in a world that, according to her, "is not easy on girls of any type." Despite her making a distinction between "real girls" and herself, I oriented to her in this interaction as "another girl."

The final example occurred outside the parameters of an interview and involved a moment of engagement with an inmate who does not self-identify as transgender but was nonetheless happy to explain "prison types" to me while we were both waiting in a hallway. While I was standing in a hallway waiting for officers to escort another inmate to the building in which I was conducting interviews, a Latino inmate who appeared to be in his mid-20s was sitting on a bench waiting to be escorted back to his housing unit when he initiated a discussion. He began by revealing to me that he knew why I was waiting in the hallway, indicating that I was "the professor in charge of the research by the university" as opposed to one of the other interviewers. Because he had been escorted to an interview room but was not interviewed, he rightly surmised that we were there to interview some inmates and not others. He volunteered to me that he is not transgender and is not on hormones, but that he is a "gay boy from [name of his home town]." I seized the moment to ask him the difference between being a gay boy and being transgender, and he gladly described the difference between three (easily confused) types of inmates:

> Gay boys are men who have feminine characteristics. They don't want to be girls. They are more like pretty boys, but they are boys. Transgenders want to be the girls. They want hormones, they want boobs to look like girls. They tend to think they were born to be girls and they are always bottoms. I don't want boobs, no way; and, I'm not always a bottom, but I like that. Homosexual men are just masculine men—they don't want and they don't have feminine characteristics. They are men men—like the Village People, you know that group?

I answered "yes" and asked "what about sexually?" He replied: "You wouldn't know they were homosexual, they are almost always tops, but you'll find about 25% go both ways. Have you heard about gunslingers?" I said: "I've heard of them." Thereafter he explained: "The gay boys and the tgs are all in one group, we get along, we're like community. We have to stick together in here." According to him, getting along was made easier insofar as the CDCR personnel can't tell them apart. When I commented that his eyebrows were shaped in the same way many transgender inmates do their eyebrows, he gleefully replied: "Oh, thank you, I try to keep them looking good." Throughout this study, I came to learn that carefully plucked eyebrows designed to reveal high—some would say exaggerated—arches is a key signifier of something important related to gender presentation, gender identity, sexual orientation, and sexual attraction—a recognizable marker of femininity. Their own sense of self along these lines complicates any picture of transgender prisoners as a homogeneous group.

Discussion

The research described in this chapter turned out to be the opposite of what Cullen (2010) calls "antiseptic criminology." While antiseptic criminology removes people from the real world, the research protocol for this work entailed going into the world of the target population and spending hundreds of hours in that world—their world. By going into prisons to collect original data from transgender inmates, I benefitted immensely from multiple points of view related to transgender prisoners—who they are, how they present and behave outside the confines of a formal interview, and how they are seen by the people who surround them and contribute to their environment and fate.

I was able to gain an invaluable ethnographic sense of the context in which transgender prisoners live and to which they respond. This type of engagement in the field routinely served to complicate the questions asked, the empirical portrayal of transgender inmates, and the sociological sensemaking surrounding both the policy and basic concerns that undergird this work. Indeed, it is difficult for me to make sense of this diverse population without the ethnographic engagement that, at times, only punctuated the work. Fortunately, this punctuation served to make the project messy by revealing the uncontested gender order that underpins prison life as well as the lived experience of gender and sexuality that contextualizes and thus permeates the lives of transgender inmates in prisons for men.

References

Cullen, F. (2010). Elliott Currie: In tribute to a life devoted to confronting crime. *Criminology & Public Policy, 9*(1), 19–27.

Jenness, V. (2010). From policy to prisoners to people: A 'soft-mixed methods' approach to studying transgender prisoners. *Journal of Contemporary Ethnography, 39*(5), 517–553.

Jenness, V. (2014). Pesticides, prisoners, and policy: Complexity and praxis in research on transgender prisoners and beyond. *Sociological Perspectives, 57*(1), 6–26.

Jenness, V., & Fenstermaker, S. (2014). Agnes goes to prison: Gender authenticity, transgender inmates in prisons for men, and the pursuit of 'the real deal'. *Gender & Society, 28*(1), 5–31.

Jenness, V., Maxson, C. L., Matsuda, K. N., & Sumner, J. M. (2007). *Violence in California correctional facilities: An empirical examination of sexual assault* (Report to the California Department of Corrections and Rehabilitation). Irvine, CA: University of California, Irvine.

Jenness, V., Sexton, L., & Sumner, J. M. (2010). *Transgender inmates in California's prisons: An empirical study of a vulnerable population* (Report to be submitted to the California Department of Corrections and Rehabilitation). Irvine, CA: University of California, Irvine.

"Come Along and Ride on a Fantastic Voyage"[1]: My Journey Through Rap Music Lyrics

Charis E. Kubrin

In 1982, when I was 12 years old, I cashed out my piggy bank and made my first big purchase on my own: a cassette tape by rap group Grandmaster Flash and the Furious Five. I bought the tape for one simple reason—it contained a song that I had heard on the radio, a song I could not get out of my mind called The Message. One of the earliest rap songs to offer social commentary, The Message exposes the conditions faced by America's urban poor, chronicling the daily obstacles they must overcome to survive. From the song's first few lines, a sense of entrapment looms large:

[Intro]

"It's like a jungle sometimes

It makes me wonder how I keep from goin' under"

[Verse 1]

"Broken glass everywhere

People pissin' on the stairs, you know they just don't care

I can't take the smell, can't take the noise

Got no money to move out, I guess I got no choice

Rats in the front room, roaches in the back

Junkies in the alley with a baseball bat

I tried to get away but I couldn't get far

Cause a man with a tow truck repossessed my car"

I was too young to understand this at the time, but now I know the song's power and resonance come not only from its candid depiction of inner-city life but also from its ability to capture the physical and emotional suffering wrought by American inequality. As a 12-year old, I was simply enamored with the song's amazing beat, stories about the challenges of life in the projects—a world so far away from my own—and one of the most captivating refrains of all time:

"Don't push me cause I'm close to the edge

I'm trying not to lose my head

It's like a jungle sometimes

It makes me wonder how I keep from going under"

Little did I know this purchase would set me down a path that would change my life forever and bring me right to where I am today—writing an essay about my research on rap music, which I have conducted over the last decade, and perhaps more importantly, discussing the implications of this research. In the pages that remain, I'll take you on my journey, describing how my love of rap music transformed into a research agenda that involved analyzing rap lyrics as a means to examine the intersection of music, culture, and social identity, particularly as it applies to rap and minority youth in disadvantaged communities.

---

[1]This is a line from Coolio's song, Fantastic Voyage, from his 1994 album, *It Takes a Thief*.

C.E. Kubrin (✉)

University of California, Irvine, Irvine, CA, USA

e-mail: ckubrin@uci.edu

M.D. Maltz and S.K. Rice (eds.), *Envisioning Criminology: Researchers on Research as a Process of Discovery*, DOI 10.1007/978-3-319-15868-6_8, © Springer International Publishing Switzerland 2015

"I Got a Story to Tell"[2]: Rappers' Lyrics as Data

Once I bought The Message, I became committed to learning the lyrics of this nearly 8 minute song by heart, down to the very last line. I set to work with my parents' tape recorder and my Apple IIE computer. The plan was to type out the lyrics line by line (remember, this was back in the day before the internet and websites like lyrics.com existed). It was a painstaking process that took weeks to complete. I would listen to a line of lyrics, type them out, rewind the tape, and do it all over again—hundreds of times. After finishing, I challenged myself to memorize the lyrics perfectly, which I did. My love of rap music took root right then and there.

I ardently listened to rap all throughout high school, college, and graduate school. My parents, who are not fans (and that's putting it mildly!), were dismayed my love of rap was not a passing phase. And very few of my friends matched my enthusiasm for this music genre. As I got older and more reflective, especially in college, I questioned my own reasons for embracing rap, especially gangsta rap, the most controversial subgenre of rap music known for its sexist and misogynistic lyrics, as well as its violent depiction of urban ghetto life in America. Each time I purchased a CD by Dr. Dre, Snoop Dogg, or Too Short, something felt "not quite right," clashing with all that I had been learning at the small liberal arts women's college I attended. Yet I couldn't forgo rap music, no matter how violent the lyrics or offensive the language. Instead, following each purchase, I would rush back to my dorm room, shut the door, and listen to my new CD with headphones on so others wouldn't be offended.

In graduate school, I briefly considered studying rap music but quickly abandoned that idea the moment I looked around and saw what my peers and professors were researching. Rightly or wrongly, I perceived the study of rap music to be "fringy" and "not sufficiently serious." And I certainly didn't want to jeopardize my chances at landing a tenure track position later on. I kept my love of rap music mostly to myself.

When I received my Ph.D. and started my job as an assistant professor, my research interests and love of rap music finally intersected. You know the saying "Your teaching should inform your research and your research should inform your teaching"? That expression meant little to me until one fall afternoon in 2002, when I was teaching a Race, Ethnicity, and Crime graduate seminar. The topic for the week was Understanding the Race–Crime Relationship: New Subcultural Explanations, and we were discussing Elijah Anderson's (1999) book, *Code of the Street: Decency, Violence, and the Moral Life of the Inner City*. Anderson's basic argument is that in impoverished, disadvantaged communities, there develops a street code that encourages the use of violence to gain respect and as a way to resolve disputes. During our discussion, a student pointed out an important omission in Anderson's work, asking: What about rap music? If Anderson is interested in inner-city youth culture and violence, why is rap music not a part of his explanation? My first thought was—great questions! My second thought was, hey, why didn't I think of that?

The student was right. In fact, Anderson's work said next to nothing about rap music and its relevance in the lives of the young boys he observed and interviewed in his ethnography of inner-city Philadelphia. One explanation is that rap music simply wasn't relevant in this context, but I seriously doubted this was the case. I wondered whether this important omission was unique to Anderson's work or was a common feature in the urban ethnography literature. I began reading other urban ethnographies that examined youth culture and violence and found that none explicitly considered rap music. Upon reflection, I realized this was likely a structural issue, reflecting the larger organization of academia. How many academic sociologists and criminologists listened to rap music, let alone gangsta rap? I knew exactly none (which is, by the way, one reason I kept my love of rap music to myself at the time).

---

[2] This is a song from Notorious B.I.G.'s 1997 album, *Life after Death*.

I then decided to read what academics who were writing about rap music had to say on this issue. Perhaps this group of scholars, nearly all outside of criminology and sociology, was exploring rap music, youth culture, and violence in the inner city in their work. While I was able to find much more "action" on this topic outside of my field, on the whole, I was not particularly impressed with this body of work. My main criticism was the lack of empiricism in much of the literature. Most of the work at this time was ideological, with scholars making grandiose claims—rap music is filled with misogyny; rap music causes violence—and supporting their arguments by relying on anecdotal evidence and the selective use of lyrics from songs. I wondered: where is the systematic empirical evidence to back up these claims?

I decided I wanted to contribute. In my own study, I would build on the urban ethnography literature by incorporating rap music into discussions of inner-city youth culture and violence. And I would develop the literature on rap music by conducting a large-scale empirical study that addresses some of the most fundamental claims being made about rap music. Using Anderson's (1999) work as a frame, my goal was to explore how the street code is present not only in "the street" but also in rap music and to more broadly consider the complex, reflexive relationship between the street code, rap music, and social identity. To that end, I created a list of questions I wanted to address: To what extent does rap music contain elements of the street code identified by Anderson (1999)? How is the street code manifested in the lyrics? How do rappers' lyrics actively construct violent identities for themselves and for others? How is violence accounted for and justified in the lyrics in terms that resonate with the code of the street? Exactly how prevalent are misogynistic themes in this music, and what specific messages are conveyed to the listeners? How do rappers, many of whom come from inner-city neighborhoods, experience and interpret their lives, and how do they respond to conditions in their communities?

Devising an actual study to answer these questions proved much more difficult than I had anticipated. For starters, I had never worked with music lyrics as data; in fact, I had only ever analyzed crime data in my research. And I had no training in content analysis, the methodological approach I'd be using to analyze the lyrics. Then there was the concern of my ability to be objective. In previous research, I had never been "so close" to my data. Would my love of rap music interfere with—taint even—my efforts at conducting the objective study I was so committed to pursuing?

And there were dozens of questions about how I would actually collect the data and conduct the study itself. In the beginning, my approach was largely deductive. I used Anderson's street code thesis as a framework, helping to guide my efforts about what to "look for" in the lyrics and providing a context within which to analyze the data. A priori I developed a list of themes (and related subthemes) central to Anderson's thesis: (1) respect, (2) willingness to fight or use violence, (3) material wealth, (4) violent retaliation, (5) objectification of women, and (6) problematic policing. These themes encompassed the major points raised in Anderson's discussion of the street code. But more challenging methodological questions remained—questions about sampling, measurement, and the analytical approach I would take.

As I pondered answers to these questions, I set out to secure funding to support my research. Whatever methodological decisions I would make along the way, I knew this project would be extremely time intensive and require lots of resources that I didn't have. In fact, for these reasons as well as others, many of my colleagues discouraged me from conducting this research. Amid frequent jokes such as "I really don't think listening to rap music all day constitutes 'research'" were more serious warnings about whether it was wise to pursue this project with the tenure clock ticking away. Pushing aside their concerns, I spent months writing grant proposals, applying to federal agencies and private foundations alike. While I waited for the responses, I set to work finalizing my methodology.

I read as much of the literature on rap music as I could. Then I started making decisions.

I decided to focus on the time period, 1992–2000, in order to capture the height of gangsta rap. According to the literature, gangsta rap emerged in the late 1980s and early 1990s (thus, my start date of 1992, when gangsta rap was beginning to hit its stride), and while still popular today, in the late 1990s, it became highly commercialized. Therefore, the year 2000, my end date, represents a turning point in the rap music industry whereby production values more clearly addressed commercial competition, pushing cultural production aside.

In an ideal world, I would have obtained a list of every single rap song produced during this time period to reflect the universe of music. Of course this was impossible to do as no such list exists and much rap music is produced and distributed underground, absent ties to a record label. I had to instead turn to the Record Industry Association of American (RIAA), which catalogs and produces all kinds of music lists over time, as a source from which to create my sample. From their website, I identified rap albums that went platinum (1,000,000+ copies sold) from 1992 to 2000. I included rap albums generally, rather than only gangsta rap albums, because rap albums typically mix subgenres and many songs with street code elements would have been excluded from the analysis if only gangsta rap albums had been included. During this time period, there were 130 rap albums that went platinum. Those 130 albums contained 1,922 songs. For purposes of generalizability, I randomly selected one-third of these songs for my sample, creating a final sample of 632 songs to analyze.

My next big challenge was locating this music. Where would I find all of these songs and their lyrics for analysis? Fortunately as a fan, I already owned a lot of this music. Also lucky for me, these were the days when Napster and other music-focused online services provided free peer-to-peer sharing. So for weeks on end, I used Napster to find all remaining songs in my sample and started downloading them, one by one, onto my computer. I next went on a mission to secure the lyrics for each of the 632 songs, most of which I was able to find on the website, The Original Hip-Hop Lyrics Archive

(http://www.ohhla.com/all.html). It was time consuming and exhausting but I managed to find the lyrics for all the songs in my sample. Several weeks and five printer cartridges later, I had all the lyrics printed out and neatly organized in enormous three-ring binders. I was officially ready to start analyzing the data. Instead of jumping right in, I froze in anticipation of what awaited me. How, exactly, would I go about doing this?

It was right around this time that I started hearing back on the grant proposals I had submitted. The news was dismal, one rejection after another. The pinnacle of disappointment came when I got a phone call from a program officer at one of the foundations I had applied to for funding. I answered my phone and the program officer said she was calling to discuss my grant proposal; I brimmed with excitement—finally, some good news! Wrong. She was calling to tell me that not only did my project "not get selected for funding," but that she thought the project itself was "doomed to fail" and that I should, essentially, abandon it (she gave me some reasons why but in my stunned state I didn't actually hear them). After she was done speaking, I politely thanked her and hung up the phone, more despondent than ever.

This phone call and my growing collection of rejections, not to mention the lack of enthusiasm about this project from my colleagues, did more than just knock the wind out of my sails. It led me to question whether what I thought was a good idea was, in fact, a good idea. I started questioning the very essence of this project. I was fortunate to have a good friend and mentor in the department, Ronald Weitzer, someone I respected and with whom I had published previously. I remember going out for coffee with him one afternoon, telling him about my project and listing the various setbacks I had recently faced. I decided to ask him point-blank: Is this project a waste of time? Do I think I have a good idea when really I don't? I pleaded with Ron to be absolutely up front with me and tell me if he thought the project was a waste of time. Ron's response was short but encouraging. He told me he thought I was "on to something" and should follow my research instincts despite all of the setbacks and negative feedback I had been receiving. I took his advice and plunged forward with my analysis of the lyrics, funding and naysayers be damned.

Of course before I could analyze the lyrics, I had to code them. But with no experience, I wasn't sure how to go about doing this. I read as much as I could but most helpful was talking with colleagues who had done content analysis before. After much consultation, I decided to code each song in two stages. First, I listened to a song in its entirety while reading the printed lyrics in order to get a feel for the song, understand what it's about, and so on. Second, I listened to the song again, this time coding each line of lyrics to determine whether the street code themes identified earlier were present in the song. I coded whether each theme was present or not present in the lyrics, choosing to create overlapping rather than mutually exclusive categories. As such, one line of lyrics could potentially contain references to all six themes. I coded the data conservatively, identifying themes only where it was clear that the lyrics reflected the street code. I also used all manner of Post-it notes to mark lyrical passages that were illustrative of each theme, that reflected a subtheme within one of the larger themes, or that mentioned something I had not previously considered but thought was noteworthy and significant.

Regarding this latter category, almost from the start of coding, I noticed I was routinely marking lyrical passages that reflected a sense of nihilism among rappers, no doubt an outgrowth of living in an environment filled with violence and limited opportunities. In their songs, rappers described their bleak surroundings in great detail and recounted the inescapable violence they encountered daily. The lyrics also frequently revealed rappers' preoccupation with death and dying. Nihilism was not one of the original themes I was coding, in part because it was not a central feature of the street code as discussed by Anderson. Yet after recognizing that a sizable number of the songs in my sample referenced some aspect of nihilism, I decided to include this theme along with the others. This decision was a costly one, since it meant I had to go back to the first song in my sample and recode all of the lyrics from the beginning. Yet, the result is that my

study was not just deductive but also inductive since nihilism was not theorized a priori, rather it bubbled up from the data.

Something that surprised me during data analysis was how often I would come upon words or expressions in the lyrics that I did not know or recognize (I thought I had most of the lingo down but apparently my perception was incorrect!). When I didn't know what a lyrical passage meant, I consulted The Rap Dictionary (http://www.rapdict.org/Main_Page), an online dictionary of rap and hip-hop terms. This was helpful but did not eliminate the challenges associated with coding. There were other situations that stumped me. For example, the words "bitch" and "ho" were ubiquitous in the lyrics, even in songs which otherwise had no references to the objectification of women or the street code more generally. At first I was tempted to code each reference to "bitch" and "ho" as reflective of misogyny. But after reading the literature more carefully and reflecting on this some, I realized that in rap culture, these terms are not necessarily intended to be derogatory; rather, it depends largely on the lyrical context. Ice Cube, for example, raps about a "wholesome ho" and Too Short refers to his "finest bitches" and a "topnotch bitch." Although recognizing that some listeners consider such terms offensive in all usage, I coded conservatively by including only lyrics that were unambiguously derogatory. During the coding, I thus paid careful attention to the context in which the lyrics were stated. This was necessary given that rap is rooted in the Black oral tradition of signifying and other communicative practices. Signifying is a way of speaking that involves ritual insult (often referred to as "playing the dozens") and double entendre. With signifying, words have alternate meanings beyond their conventional usages and should not necessarily be taken literally.

It took me over a year but I finished coding a final sample of 403 songs (64% of the total sample). During the course of coding, after about song 350, I no longer encountered lyrics that described new aspects of the street code themes. I coded another 53 songs to ensure that I had reached saturation and then stopped. Altogether, 1,588 minutes of music were coded for the analyses.

Exhausted but content, a new concern swept over me. How can I be sure my analysis or interpretation of the lyrics is correct? Might I have misinterpreted lyrics? Would critics or reviewers claim my interpretation is but one interpretation? I realized I needed to consider the issue of intercoder reliability or the extent to which two or more independent coders agree on the coding of the content of interest with an application of the same coding scheme. To do this, an independent researcher (read: a graduate student who I paid using my own money—recall my failed attempts at securing funding for this project!) identified a random subset of the sample ($n = 64$, 16% of the final sample) and listened to the songs, read the lyrics, and coded the cases. I then calculated agreement percentages, which reflected how often the researcher and I agreed that the street code was present (or absent) in the lyrics. Although the percentages vary slightly by theme, I was relieved to find that all were over 70%, suggesting the results are reliable.

For the next several years, I was busy writing papers using these data. The first, "Gangstas, Thugs, and Hustlas: Identity and the Code of the Street in Rap Music" (Kubrin, 2005a) considers how structural conditions in inner-city communities have given rise to cultural adaptations, embodied in a street code, that constitute an interpretive environment where violence is accountable, if not normative. In this paper I theorized the complex and reflexive relationship between the street code, rap music, and social identity. In the analysis, I explored the ways in which rappers justify and account for violence in terms that clearly resonate with the code of the street. My findings reveal that portrayals of violence serve many functions including establishing social identity and reputation and exerting social control.

In a second paper, "I See Death around the Corner: Nihilism in Rap Music" (Kubrin, 2005b), I investigated other aspects of the street code and, in particular, nihilism, which as I mentioned earlier represents a neglected area of study. In this paper I was particularly interested in how rappers experience and interpret their lives and how they respond to the harsh

conditions in their communities. The content analysis of lyrics identified several subthemes that I explored in depth including bleak surroundings with little hope, pervasive violence in the ghetto, and a preoccupation with death and dying.

In "Misogyny in Rap Music: A Content Analysis of Prevalence and Meanings" (Weitzer & Kubrin, 2009), Ron Weitzer and I focused on misogyny and the objectification of women in rap lyrics. Although misogynistic messages appear less frequently in rap than is commonly assumed (misogyny was present in only 22% of the sample, a figure much lower than the other themes, including nihilism), we identified five gender-related themes in the sample, themes that contain messages regarding "essential" male and female characteristics and that espouse a set of conduct norms for men and women. These include: (1) derogatory naming and shaming of women, (2) sexual objectification of women, (3) distrust of women, (4) legitimation of violence against women, and (5) celebration of prostitution and pimping. In the paper Ron and I also theorized the social sources of these themes, situating rap music within both the context of larger cultural and music industry norms and the local, neighborhood conditions that inspired the music in the first place.

Following this piece, Ron Weitzer and I coauthored a book chapter, "Rap Music's Violent and Misogynistic Effects: Fact or Fiction?" in Deflem's (2010) edited volume, *Popular Culture, Crime, and Social Control*. In this chapter we identified critical weaknesses in the literature that limit researchers' ability to draw firm conclusions about rap music's effects. These weaknesses included the nonempirical nature of most writings on rap; vagueness regarding the precise relationship between rap music and attitudes and behavior, and the associated lack of theoretical perspectives in the rap literature; the exclusion of the perspectives of rap music listeners in most studies; and drawbacks of both experimental research and existing ethnographic studies in this line of research. This essay brought me full circle (in that I returned to the original reasons that motivated my doing this work in the first place) but also helped to create a research agenda that I enthusiastically planned to tackle in the near future. While I was pleased with the contributions I had made thus far, I was eager to dive into "phase 2" of my research agenda studying rap music. Well, phase 2 never happened. Instead, a phone call that I received in March of 2011 changed my research agenda (and life!) in ways I could never have anticipated.

"You Can't Judge a Book by the Grain of Its Cover or the Name or the Color"[3]: Some Implications

Before I describe this major turn of events, I will mention a few of the smaller (but no less interesting!) implications of my work in this area. One of the most intriguing is best reflected in personal correspondence I received. In December of 2005, just a few months after my first paper *Gangstas, Thugs, and Hustlas* was published, I received an e-mail from someone whose name I did not recognize. I almost deleted the e-mail, thinking it was spam, especially given what was written in the subject line: "Why did you choose to focus on these things?" But I opened and read the e-mail, and am glad that I did. It read:

> Hello, my name is G_____ and I am a Black single mother in Los Angeles, California. I am currently at the end of a sociology research methods class and I'm doing a paper analyzing the methods used in your article [*Gangstas, Thugs, and Hustlas*]. It caught my attention because I am the single mother of two boys, aged 13 and 16. I have worked very hard to help my sons develop a different mentality than the one your paper speaks of (with success), and I thought your paper would make for good conversation between my sons and me. I assumed, for some reason, that you were a Black male, so when I looked you up on the Internet and saw your picture I was very surprised. When I saw the list of papers you've written and classes you teach, I became intrigued. Personally, the things I am most interested in are things that have affected me personally. I want to be a college counselor because my counselors have had a great influence on me. I care about special education because my son is a special education student. I am interested in mental illness because it runs in my family, etc. From what does your interest stem?

_____
[3] This is a line from Ransom's 2012 song, Pray for Me.

The e-mail did not end there. G_____ went on to describe how, to her good fortune, her sons have "successfully avoided the code of the streets" and that both are on the "road to success." But even as I read through to the end of the e-mail, I kept returning to her comment, "I assumed for some reason that you were a Black male" and her question, "From what does your interest stem?" This statement and question crystallized a number of experiences and feelings I had been having (and would continue to have) since publishing and speaking about my research on rap music. Nearly every talk I had given on my work in this area was, to some degree, "uncomfortable." At professional conferences, I could see the confused (disappointed?) expressions on audience members' faces when my name was called, and I stepped up to the podium to speak. I don't know who they were expecting to see (perhaps a "black male" in the words of G_____?) but apparently it wasn't me—a short, middle-aged, white woman (these reactions, by the way, were particularly noticeable when I was presenting while hugely pregnant with my son). These expressions, I suspect, were linked with doubts about my credibility, authenticity, and legitimacy as a scholar in this area. I have given hundreds of professional talks and presentations on my research, and none have evoked such fundamentally challenging questions as the ones where I present on rap music. In these presentations, I've noticed, audience members are, quite literally, quizzing me on my basic knowledge and history of rap and hip-hop to determine if I am "legitimate" and thus worthy of their attention. While this sort of thing happens much less today, it was routine 10–15 years ago.

Reinforcing these experiences and G_____'s assumption was the fact that, over the years, when others wrote about my rap research or cited my work in this area, they frequently referred to me as "he" (as in, for example, "It was interesting that the author mentioned on page 372 that the rap lyrics suggest one learns the value of having a reputation for being tough in order to survive. *He* suggests that violent imagery in rap lyrics serve two purposes..."). They still do. While my first name, Charis, does have some gender ambiguity, I have not experienced this with any of my publications in other areas. This gender assumption seems to be unique to my research on rap music.

Also unique to my research in this area is other people's curiosity, bewilderment, and even shock that I conduct research on rap music, a response I believe that is once again linked to my race/ethnicity, gender, age, and other personal characteristics. If I had a dollar for every time I've been asked, "What made you interested in studying rap music?" I'd be rich! Mirroring G____, others seem particularly interested in finding out what has led me down this research path, or as the subject line of her e-mail reads, "Why did you choose to focus on these things?" Once again, this is something I have not experienced with my research in other areas and on different (but no less interesting) topics.

There are, of course, other implications I could discuss, but the one of perhaps greatest significance is what I'd like to spend the remainder of time discussing. So, now, back to the phone call that changed my life and drastically altered the direction my research would take me.

"Murder Was the Case that They Gave Me..."[4]: Rap Lyrics Stand Trial[5]

In March of 2011, I was contacted by a lawyer who had come across my paper "Gangstas, Thugs, and Hustlas: Identity and the Code of the Street in Rap Music." He was interested in knowing if I'd be willing to serve as an expert witness in a case involving his client, Olutosin Oduwole, an aspiring rapper (stage name Tosin) charged with making a terrorist threat. In July of 2007, Oduwole's car ran out of gas, forcing him to abandon it on the Edwardsville campus of Southern Illinois University, where he was a student. When school authorities found his car,

among the many items they retrieved was a discarded piece of paper lodged between the seats. On one side of the paper were scribbled rap lyrics, written in verse, with lines such as "follow that thang to da ground when she drop it; pop it mami, pop it." The other side of the paper also had rap lyrics jotted down ("I Lead she a follower, / I'm single and I'm not wit her, but she / gott a throat deeper than a Sword / Swallower..."). These lyrics were followed by six unrhymed lines of text at the bottom of the paper—upon which the entire case rested. The six lines read:

glock to the head of
SEND $2 to … paypal account
if this account doesn't reach $50,000 in the next
7 days then a murderous rampage similar to the
VT shooting will occur at another prestigious
highly populated university. THIS IS NOT A JOKE!

Upon discovering this piece of paper, the police searched Oduwole's apartment, where they found a handgun, which was legally acquired but forbidden in a campus dorm. The police also discovered spiral-bound notebooks filled with, among other things, Tosin's violent and misogynistic rap lyrics. All of this, in combination with the officers' learning that Oduwole had been trying to purchase additional guns, led the police to charge him with attempting to communicate a terrorist threat. Tosin admitted to the gun possession charges but adamantly denied he was a terrorist planning to carry out acts of violence. He claimed the six lines of text were simply notes for a new rap song, reflecting early stages of the lyrical process.

Four years later and despite repeated attempts by the defense to have the case dismissed, in October of 2011, Oduwole went to trial in Madison County, Illinois. Around that time is when I was contacted about serving as an expert witness on the case. The attorney asked if I would review the notebooks with rap lyrics and provide my opinion regarding the six lines of text in question. After reviewing 146 pages of Tosin's rap lyrics, I testified in front of a jury, describing first what rap music is and, in particular, defining and discussing the subgenre of gangsta rap. I provided evidence that Tosin was indeed an aspiring gangsta rapper, as reflected in his desire to market

---

[4] This is a line from Snoop Dogg's song, Murder was the Case, from his 1993 album, *Doggystyle*.

[5] This section draws largely from my paper, "Rap on Trial," published in *Race and Justice*.

himself as "a hood symbol" and "G"; his frequent references to lyrics written by well-known artists such as Tupac, Lil Wayne, Young Jeezy, Rick Ross, Three 6 Mafia, Trick Daddy, 50 Cent, and Bounty Killa; and most importantly, the lyrical content of his raps. From my content analysis of Oduwole's lyrics and in comparison to my own research, I explained that the themes found in Tosin's lyrics were consistent with those found in gangsta rap more generally, namely, establishing credibility as a skilled rapper, money and material wealth, misogyny and the objectification of women, and most prominently, violence.

I then explained to jurors why violence and the threat of violence are commonplace in gangsta rap, citing, among other reasons, the need for aspiring artists to create a persona worthy of respect in the rap community and record industry conditions that often push would-be artists toward violent themes. Given these points, I argued it was predictable that Tosin's lyrics would be extremely violent and that the themes of violence portrayed in his raps would be consistent with those found in popular gangsta rap songs: portraying a violent persona, being prepared to use violence if necessary, violent retaliation, and the glorification of guns and other weapons. Finally, I testified on the process involved in creating rap music, noting that lyrics can reflect different stages of creative development (thus, they may be incomplete or reflect only rough ideas and not all lyrics rhyme or flow), that lyrics are often written on random pieces of paper or whatever may be available at the time an idea strikes, and that rappers often include unrhymed intros and outros in their lyrics, which can serve the critical function of introducing or concluding a song by emphasizing an important message. In making each point, I offered examples from Tosin's notebooks. At the end, I rendered my opinion—that the six lines in question represent initial ideas or concepts for a song or may constitute the intro or outro to a song.

The jury wasn't convinced. After deliberating less than 3 hours, they declared Oduwole guilty, and he was sentenced to 5 years in prison. The verdict drew widespread scrutiny from journalists and academics alike. I started seeing op-eds featuring the case, many of which were written by Erik

Nielson, an assistant professor at the University of Richmond who researches rap, hip-hop culture, and African American literature. Erik and I were eventually put into contact with one another by Oduwole's attorney. After talking and agreeing these developments were concerning, we decided to begin working together to draw attention to the Oduwole case and the issues it raises.

Little did Erik and I know that once we started investigating things more closely, we would discover that the Oduwole case, it turns out, is far from unique; rap lyrics are increasingly turning up as evidence in courtrooms across the country. We quickly got to work documenting recent cases in which rap music has been used as evidence in criminal trials as well as discussing the implications of this practice. We publicized all of this in op-eds, media interviews, and most recently in our paper, "Rap on Trial," published in *Race and Justice*. In each of these venues, we argue that rather than treat rap music as an art form whose primary purpose is to entertain, prosecutors have become skilled at convincing judges and juries that the lyrics are either autobiographical confessions of illegal behavior (what we call the "lyrics as confessional" argument) or evidence of a defendant's knowledge, motive, or identity with respect to the alleged crime (what we call the "circumstantial evidence" argument). Our research, as well as our experience as expert witnesses in such trials, suggests that rap lyrics are of questionable evidentiary value and that their use in court can result in unfair prejudice—a point I'll return to in just a minute.

While the scope of the practice is not entirely clear, our early research suggests that rap lyrics have been used against defendants in hundreds of cases across the country. And keep in mind that the cases we have been able to identify reflect only cases that have received media attention. In fact, both Erik and I are currently testifying in new cases involving the use of rap lyrics, neither of which has reached the national media. My point is that this is not an isolated practice.

Perhaps more troubling, though, is that all indicators suggest this practice is on the rise: from the increasing number of cases reported in the media, to the growing number of commentaries by academics, to the recognition among prosecutors that the practice is effective—so effective, in fact, they have begun promoting it. A training manual produced by the National District Attorneys Association, for example, advises prosecutors to use music lyrics so that they can, in the words of former Los Angeles Deputy District Attorney Alan Jackson, "invade and exploit the defendant's true personality." No other form of fictional expression is treated this way in the courts.

While the exact number of criminal cases that involve rap lyrics as evidence may be up for debate, what is less debatable, we argue, is the harmful impact this practice may have. The movement to criminalize rap lyrics reflects a broader effort to redefine the meaning of rap music—from art or entertainment to autobiographical confessions that provide clear insight into a defendant's thoughts or actions. The problem from our standpoint, as scholars who study rap music, is that the fictional characters portrayed in rap songs are often a far cry from the true personality of the artists behind them (Google "rapper Rick Ross" and "Smoking Gun" for a case in point). The near-universal use of stage names in rap is the clearest signal that rappers are fashioning a character, yet the first-person narrative form and artists' assertions that they are "keepin' it real" (providing authentic accounts of themselves and "the 'hood'") lend themselves to easy misreading by those unfamiliar with rappers' complex and creative manipulation of identity. This is particularly problematic with gangsta rap, where artists adopt larger-than-life criminal personas and weave embellished, graphic accounts of violence. If audiences don't appreciate that these are genre conventions, they can easily conflate artist with character and fiction with fact. In effect, they end up putting rap on trial.

But they are indeed genre conventions. Metaphor and hyperbole are among the many common poetic devices used by rappers, something I witnessed over and over in my content analysis of rap lyrics. And while one can find isolated examples of rappers with real-life connections to crime (name one art form where you can't!), as we argue, it would be a mistake to extend this characterization to rappers generally. If rappers were guilty of even the tiniest fraction

of violence they project in their music, we'd all be in big trouble, a point Erik and I have repeatedly emphasized while testifying. Unfortunately, judges and juries do not always understand this—an ignorance prosecutors either share or exploit. In case after case, the results have been devastating for the accused. Social science research helps explain why.

In one study psychologist Stuart Fischoff conducted an experiment to determine the impact gangsta rap lyrics might have on potential jurors. His test subjects were presented with basic biographical information about a hypothetical 18-year old African American man, but only some were shown a set of violent, sexually explicit rap lyrics that he had written (the lyrics had been used as evidence in a 1995 murder trial). The subjects were then asked about their perceptions regarding the young man's personality (e.g., caring–uncaring; selfish–unselfish; likeable–unlikeable; capable of murder–not capable of murder). Fischoff found the lyrics exerted a significant prejudicial impact on his subjects, generating more negative evaluations on all dimensions. Most relevant, perhaps, was his finding that the subjects who read the lyrics were significantly more likely to think the man was capable of committing murder.

In another experimental study, social psychologist Carrie Fried presented two groups of subjects with an identical set of violent lyrics (the opening stanza of the song Bad Man's Blunder by Kingston Trio) but removed any information that could identify the true source of the lyrics. One group was told the lyrics came from a country song, while the other was told they came from a rap song. As Fried hypothesized, respondents found the lyrics more threatening and dangerous when they were represented as rap compared to country. The racial dimensions are pretty obvious here; whereas country music is traditionally associated with white performers, rap primes negative culturally held stereotypes of urban blacks.

Here is where another critical implication of putting rap on trial begins to surface. In these trials, authorities are often prosecuting a young man of color, someone who already looms as a threatening stereotype in the minds of society. In nearly every case we've encountered, the individual being accused and tried is a young African American or Latino male. Using rap lyrics as evidence, then, is not just a matter of art being sacrificed for the sake of an easy conviction. Rather, the practice also constitutes a pernicious tactic that plays upon and perpetuates enduring stereotypes about the inherent criminality of young men of color. The lyrics must be true because what is written "fits" with what we "know" about criminals—where they come from, what they look like, and so on.

Finally, we argue putting rap on trial raises serious questions about the equal application of First Amendment protections and the right of all Americans to receive a fair trial. Will there be a chilling effect as more and more aspiring rappers find themselves locked up for their lyrics? In such a climate, we are left with a freedom of speech that comes with caveats, or as Rapper Ice-T ironically put it, "Freedom of Speech…Just Watch What You Say!"

"The Struggle Continues"[6]: Rap's Uncertain Future

I opened the last section of this essay with an illustrative case and I'd like to conclude the essay with another. As I write this, a man by the name of Vonte Skinner sits in a jail cell waiting to learn his fate. He's been waiting for 6 years. In 2008, Mr. Skinner, a New Jersey drug dealer and aspiring rapper, was tried in the attempted murder of Lamont Peterson, a fellow drug dealer. When Mr. Skinner was arrested, police found pages of his violent rap lyrics in the backseat of his girlfriend's car. With lines like "In the hood, I am a threat / It's written on my arm and signed in blood on my Tech [Tec-9 handgun] / I'm in love with you, death," prosecutors jumped at the chance to introduce the lyrics at trial to establish Mr. Skinner's "violent state of mind." During the trial and over repeated objections from the defense, the prosecutor read the jury 13 pages of Mr. Skinner's violent lyrics, even though all were composed before the shooting—in many cases

3–4 years before—and none of them mentioned Peterson or details about the crime. The only other evidence against Mr. Skinner was testimony from witnesses who changed their stories repeatedly. And yet the jury found him guilty of attempted murder, and he was later sentenced to 30 years in prison.

But in 2012, Mr. Skinner's conviction was overturned by an appellate court which ruled that the lyrics should never have been admitted as evidence in the first place. The majority wrote, "we have a significant doubt about whether the jurors would have found defendant guilty if they had not been required to listen to the extended reading of these disturbing and highly prejudicial lyrics." The state appealed this ruling to the New Jersey Supreme Court, which recently heard arguments in the case, and this brings us to where we are today, waiting to learn the court's decision. Although appellate courts in Massachusetts and Maryland recently reversed convictions after citing prosecutors for their improper use of rap lyrics or videos as evidence, most similar appeals, we have discovered, are unsuccessful. Recently, the Supreme Court of Nevada upheld the admissibility of rap lyrics as evidence in a first-degree murder case. A definitive ruling by the Supreme Court of New Jersey rejecting this use of rap music could help turn the tide. Regardless of what decision is ultimately handed down, there is clearly much more work to be done.

---

[6]This is a song from KRS-ONE's 2002 album, *Spiritual Minded*.

References

Anderson, E. (1999). *Code of the street*. New York, NY: W.W. Norton.

Kubrin, C. E. (2005a). Gangstas, Thugs, and Hustlas: Identity and the code of the street in rap music. *Social Problems, 52*, 360–378.

Kubrin, C. E. (2005b). 'I see death around the corner': Nihilism in rap music. *Sociological Perspectives, 48*, 433–459.

Kubrin, C. E., & Nielson, E. (2014). Rap on trial. *Race and Justice, 4*, 185–211. doi:10.1177/2153368714525411.

Kubrin, C. E., & Weitzer, R. (2010). Rap music's violent and misogynistic effects: Fact or fiction? In M. Deflem (Ed.), *Popular culture, crime, and social control* (Sociology of crime, law, and deviance, Vol. 14, pp. 121–144). Bingley, England: Emerald.

Weitzer, R., & Kubrin, C. E. (2009). Misogyny in rap music: A content analysis of prevalence and meanings. *Men and Masculinities, 12*, 3–29.

Getting Emotional

Stephen K. Rice

> Everyone has an anthropology. There is no not having one. If a man says he does not, all he is saying is that his anthropology is implicit, a set of assumptions which he has not thought to call into question. (Walker Percy, p. 228)

Elevator Speeches

Around the time Ross Perot ran for president (c. 1992), attention was given to how he made a fortune at IBM through his ability to articulate a value proposition—the benefit of a product or service, relative to the competition, that can be articulated within a brief "elevator speech."

Each year in my department's undergrad capstone course and grad student orientation, I encourage the outgoing and incoming students to consider their own elevator speeches within criminology and criminal justice—an incredibly rich discipline (or disciplines, depending on where one falls) that Todd Clear rightly depicts as multidisciplinary always and interdisciplinary at its best.

By engaging in this conversation, students also channel Ed Koch, the mayor of New York, who had a habit of approaching residents on the street with the simple question "How am I doing?" probing for ad hoc, street-side assessments of his

S.K. Rice (✉)
Department of Criminal Justice, Seattle University, Seattle, WA, USA
e-mail: ricest@seattleu.edu

performance at City Hall. It's no small endeavor to tackle questions like "How am I doing?" (or here, "how are *we* doing?") in a criminology and criminal justice which spans administration of justice, criminological theory, criminal justice theory, forensic science, environmental criminology, investigative criminology, research and evaluation, crime analysis, and so forth.

Amid these learning moments, it's not only Seattle University students who engage in questions about what works or what matters. So too does their professor, regularly and existentially. As university faculty, we're provided with the gift of a profession which affords latitude in how we make meaningful contributions, insomuch as the contributions fill a gap and do so rigorously.

Within the contours of my own grad school experience, I remember the (too few) moments when published work transcended expectation: Braithwaite, tapping the seemingly impenetrable processes of restoration, reconciliation, and reintegration; Weisburd, demonstrating how experiments and micro places serve as crime prevention applications; Maltz, making the case for visualization and the declining significance of significance (Mike, there's a better way than 20% explained variance and cross-sectional treatises on longitudinal phenomena?); Fagan, actually pulling off the intersection of criminology and law; Sampson and colleagues, tackling collective efficacy block by block, neighborhood by neighborhood; plus Sherman, demonstrating not only the power of professional networks (*how* exactly does one get PDs to open themselves up to such risk?) but also the power of the personal anecdote—that of a young man (Sherman's son), a movie theater, and sanction effects (defiance, deterrence, irrelevance).

The "Hot" and the "Wet"

Research "sticks" to some scholars in personal ways—in ways that suggest that even if the scholars were not incented for doing so, they would still figure out a way to contribute to law enforcement in the backstage, popular culture and the code of the street, stylized scripts and stop and frisk, violence interruption, or pulling levers. In my case, it's fair to say that my anthropology has been shaped by biographical influences: an NYPD patrolman father, half his career spent in Harlem in the 1960s, and his young son asking for blow-by-blows at end-of-shift (could this tie years later to my scholarship on racial and ethnic profiling, profiling of Muslim Americans, procedural (in) justice?)[1] or a lived life spanning working-class Queens to the Upper West Side, NYC or Seattle metro (interest in community-level processes, gentrification and disorder, theory testing (strain, self-control, shaming), racial threat?).

Put simply, my biographic situates itself contrary to the self-interested, coldly rational actor responding to calculations of risk and reward; instead, my efforts coalesce around the "hot" and the "wet" (my term, imperfect but useful), or how matters such as humiliation, shame, and rage condition defiance and criminal behavior, and how, conversely, desires for reconciliation and repentance afford softer avenues of understanding. These insights come from the interactional level of explanation—intimate, visceral, microsocial dynamics where negative affect takes shape. While there's little doubt that additive models of rational choice and deterrence hold influence, can we honestly say that the moral philosophies of

Beccaria or Bentham provide adequate guidance for the 2 a.m. traffic stop gone south—a microsocial environment impacted by far more than the usual host of internal and external controls (e.g., officer demeanor, driver demeanor, interactive effects both ways, driver assessments of law enforcement legitimacy, perceived procedural and distributive injustice, substance use, other legal-realistic inputs related to emotionality)?

Certainty and severity, meet the hot and wet.[2]

My "pre-do's" and "do's" have also been impacted by public scholarship which receives scant attention for its ability to shape the criminological imagination: outlets such as *The New Yorker* and the *The Atlantic,* op-eds like David Brooks' "Social Science Palooza," long form articles such as Elliott's "Invisible Child" about NYC's 22,000 homeless children, and Boston Globe reporters on the Boston Marathon bombing in "The Fall of the House of Tsarnaev."[3]

---

[1] It's wonderful to reflect on Owen Rice's time patrolling Harlem, a decade with no discharges of firearm and 2 babies delivered by my late father, each baby now roughly 45. One of these babies was named after my father but given the name Otis, a by-product of his mother's unfamiliarity with the Irish name Owen. Otis, here's to soft policing.

[2] When my wife and I lived in NYC, one night we went to Agave, our favorite Mexican restaurant. While in transit from the subway station to the said restaurant, a gentleman approached and inquired about our willingness to contribute. Being experienced New Yorkers, this was no big deal—panhandling is a reality. But then within seconds, the gentleman *touched* me: first on the shoulder, and then more obliquely. My wife, being more in touch on such matters, extricated us from the situation with a strong tug and an NYC "places to be" comportment.

I ask you, criminologists, where are the theoretical insights in this vignette? What if I'd met my wife at the restaurant instead, sans the benefit of her extrication? What if it were 12 a.m. instead of 7 p.m., incorporating the <interaction term> of Agave margarita(s), altering the microsocial environment? Do routine activities keep up with this moment-by-moment panorama?

[3] In "Social Science Palooza IV" (7/2014), Brooks demonstrates an appreciation for social science but also remarks that "Most social science confirms the blindingly obvious." While an exploration of Brooks' comment is best suited for another day, I'll draw attention to the fact that at the time of this writing (July, 2014), the American Society of Criminology fails to include a Division of Public Criminology (or some division with that explicit mandate). Further, at the time of this writing, the editorial board of ASC's most "applied" journal, *Criminology & Public Policy,* features editors and an editorial board drawn almost without exception from the ranks of academia. While better understanding scholars' "pre-do's," "do's," and "post-do's" is important, so too are considerations of selection effects—of conversations which are so constricted by organizational/disciplinary norms so as to render the conversation club-like.

Student readers: I'd recommend you have a conversation with your profs about their requirement that no public outlets (e.g., newspapers) be included in term papers. In your one hand, hold the readership (click) totals for Alice Goffman's *On the Run* on vice.com. In your other hand, hold the citation counts for your profs' published scholarship. Professor Goffman may well win that battle. As a backup, bring along the real-world (legal, correctional) references made to David Grann's article "Trial by Fire" in *The New Yorker* about the 2004 execution of Cameron Todd Willingham. Have the journal articles assigned in your corrections, law and social control, criminal law, or forensic science courses displayed this degree of *texture?*

Over the years, I've also paid close attention to *AP* reporter Mike Graczyk's work outlining hundreds of Texas inmates' experiences prior to, and during, their executions (overview provided by Dave Alsup). While it's fair to say that Mr. Graczyk is understated about the implications of his reporting, where else within criminology can one find data which tap into not only the expanse of inmate defiance but also desires for forgiveness and repentance?

Drawing on this intersection of criminality and affect, not to mention how emotions are rooted within the criminal justice system itself, consider Oklahoma's failed execution of Clayton Lockett in 2014.

The Body in Pain, Embedded in Defiant Presentation

As opposed to the years preceding *Furman* when executions could be conducted in relative obscurity, transparency in death penalty administration threatens to expose injustices that damage the moral order that penology and capital jurisprudence rely on. The finer points of Mr. Lockett's failed execution ("writhing," "gasping," "calling out") illustrate that failures in procedure tie to a coalescence of pity and terror, a mix that reduces the condemned to tragic in the public's mind rather than recipient of right and just punishment.

As Garland argues, punishment is a form of *communication*, and the prominence afforded

Mr. Lockett casts a bright light on not only unregulated compounding pharmacies, being tasered in the hours preceding the planned execution, and the possibility of a collapsed femoral vein (explored via groin catheter, a medically challenging procedure), but also assertions of racial bias in death penalty sentences and of the recent study estimating that 4% of all death row inmates are innocent (Gross et al.).

If one were to frame the execution as degradation ceremony, Mr. Lockett's was a high-stakes game: despite wardens' hopes for routinized procedures afforded by correctional officer and medical personnel training and straightforward drug "cocktails," Lockett's writhing and apparent calling out of "oh man…" *appropriated the moment* in that his narrative emphasized coercion and pain as violating justice.

Further, Lockett joins others who have experienced errors in the administration of gas, current, and lethal injection. As outlined by Radelet and Bedau, the more visceral include Jimmy Lee Gray's asphyxiation in Mississippi, tied to an executioner under the influence, marked by the expulsion of witnesses from the chamber as Gray struggled to breathe while banging his head against a steel pole in the gas chamber. Due to faulty hardware, Pedro Medina's electrocution in Florida featured flames shooting from his headpiece, while the placement of Allen Lee Davis' mouthpiece prior to electrocution in Florida was thought to have caused partial asphyxiation; legal filings post-execution described it as: "After Davis' airflow had been blocked by the mouth strap, the face mask, and his own blood, Davis made several sounds under the face mask which were described variously as muffled screams, moans, or yells." Lethal injections have been marked by malfunctioning syringes and tubing, allergic reactions, or technicians unable to find a suitable vein. And then there are the concerns for semiconscious suffering in Mr. Lockett's case.

Touching on work by Anthony Giddens, these procedural errors speak to a threat on the state's ability to assert its monopoly over penal "meaning" and the state's ability to eliminate unwanted noise in the symbolic system (and the symbols are many: the gurney, the chair, the gallows, supermax). Within the present context, the state's desire to open its walls has had the unintended effect of bringing injustice to light, evoking performances which question the morality of the state and damage the viability of such punishment.

More Explicit Renderings: Assessing Death Chamber Final Statements

It's a good day to die. I walked in here like a man and I am leaving here like a man. I had a good life. I have known the love of a good woman, my wife. I have a good family. My grandmother is the pillar of the community. I love and cherish my friends and family. Thank you for your love. To the Hancock family, I am sorry for the pain I caused you. If my death gives you any peace, so be it. I want my friends to know it is not the way to die, but I belong to Jesus Christ. I confess my sins. (Earl Behringer's final statement, 1997)

Well, first of all I'd like to address the MacPhail family. I'd like to let you all know that despite the situation—I know all of you still are convinced that I'm the person that killed your father, your son and your brother, but I am innocent. The incidents that happened that night was not my fault. I did not have a gun that night. I did not shoot your family member. But I am so sorry for your loss. I really am—sincerely. All that I can ask is that each of you look deeper into this case, so that you really will finally see the truth. I ask to my family and friends that you all continue to pray, that you all continue to forgive. Continue to fight this fight. For those about to take my life, may God have mercy on all of your souls. God bless you all. (Troy Anthony Davis' final statement, 2011)

Inspired by failed executions, data provided by the Texas Department of Criminal Justice (http://www.tdcj.state.tx.us/death_row/index.html), insights by scholars such as David Dow and Samuel Gross, and Graczyk's work documenting inmates' moment-by-moment experiences facing death in Huntsville, TX, several years ago my graduate student colleague Danielle Dirks (now an assistant professor at Occidental College) and I began digging into the emotional makeup of condemned inmates' final statements.

As far as Danielle and I could tell, despite the critically important issue of inmate final statements (see Sherman on emotionally intelligent justice; Sarat on the technologies for taking life),

circa 2006 there had not yet been a systematic assessment of final statements. This, despite sending criminals to penitent-iaries. Researchers dabbled here and there but nothing systematic. How this came to be still perplexes me, but then again there are many scholarship analogies to the centuries humankind went without post-it notes.

As a result of this realization, Danielle and I embarked on an effort to make sense of the public final statement transcripts. Because of the gap in the literature, for the research design we decided that a descriptive component and an analytical component would be appropriate. First, descriptively, how many and what types of emotions are articulated by inmates in the moments prior to death? Second, for the analytical piece, we considered a number of possibilities such as offender demographics, criminal background, offense types, administrative changes in the TDCJ, and legal aspects.

After considerable discussion plus a review of Marquart and colleagues' *The Rope, the Chair, and the Needle: Capital Punishment in Texas, 1923–1990*, we came to realize that a type of natural experiment was available to us: effective January 1996—several years post-*Gregg* (and therefore years past a number of executions in Texas)—the TDCJ adopted a rule permitting "homicide survivors" to attend executions (homicide survivors meaning family and friends of the deceased). Prior to that date, only relatives or friends of the condemned inmate, members of the media, spiritual counsel, and criminal justice officials were permitted to attend.

Given thoughts of the execution as theater (Garland), wouldn't it be fair to assume that the emotional makeup of final statements might be altered by the inclusion of these parties? Was there a "victims' rights effect," if you will?

Texas was chosen because at the time of manuscript preparation, Texas was where more than a third of executions in the United States had occurred since 1976, plus the state was at the forefront in permitting homicide survivors to attend executions. Further, and of relevance to an effort which wished to gauge the range of emotions as offenders contemplated their deaths,

Fig. 1 Texas execution chamber

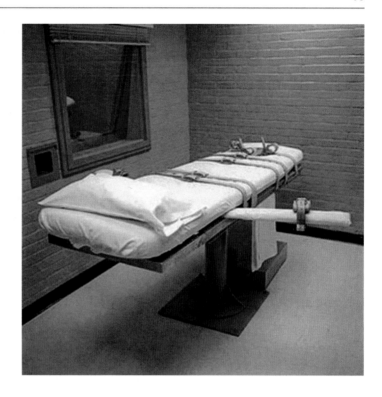

approximately half of all capital cases in Texas had been overturned on appeal, a number of innocent inmates had been exonerated, and a number of the condemned had been represented by attorneys disciplined for misconduct (Berlow).

For the research design, we chose a mixed method design informed by content analysis. Thematic codes were created to capture constructs linked to emotions, crime, and the law: namely, expressions of guilt, desires for forgiveness, repentance, expressions of innocence, expressions regarding the unjust nature of capital punishment, expressions regarding a lack of procedural fairness in the inmate's legal proceedings, and statements of religiosity. In addition to the thematic codes, a number of inmate demographic and legal characteristics were collected.

Once thematic codes were defined, the codes were applied to the textual accounts of final statements for a 23-year period beginning December 1982, an interval whose start date marked the advent of lethal injection in Texas. We applied the thematic codes to the set of final statement narratives independently, and our interrater reliability was good.

First, descriptives were compiled to provide the reader with a sense of what the emotional makeup of the final statements looked like—statements which are uttered in very close quarters (Fig. 1).

Narratives were then analyzed with regard to the date at which homicide survivors were provided with the opportunity to attend executions (1/96), and statistical effects were estimated by whether an emotional element manifested before or after that date. Baseline comparisons were obtained through descriptives and measures of association, and logit techniques regressed restorative emotions (i.e., expressions of guilt, desires for forgiveness, repentance, expressions of religiosity) on the pre/post-survivor attendance date (1/12/96) amid sociolegal controls. Conversely, logit techniques were also utilized to regress defiant emotions (i.e., expressions of innocence, expressions of the unjust nature of capital punishment, expressions of the unjust nature of the inmate's legal proceeding(s)) on the survivor attendance date amid the same controls.[4]

With regard to data collection, 345 executions took place during the 23-year period. The control variables included legal and demographic information such as inmate age (at time of offense, at received, at execution), education, race/ethnicity, sex, the inmate's county of conviction, whether the inmate had a prior Texas prison record, the race/ethnicity of victim(s), whether inmate had a codefendant(s), whether the inmate dropped the appeal, whether the inmate had evidence of mental retardation, and years on death row. Of the 345 executions, 269 inmates chose to make final statements when provided the opportunity to do so (approximately 80%). For detailed information, I'll leave it to interested parties to read the article; also, note that some analyses outlined here (e.g., re: inmate repentance) have been updated/made more recent in the years since the *Justice Quarterly* publication.

The trends: inmates roughly 50% white/50% nonwhite. Overwhelmingly male (only two females in our population: one, Karla Faye Tucker, chose to make a final statement[5]). Age received: late 20s. Age executed: late 30s. Low degree of education. Recidivists. Large number had codefendants (several of whom copped pleas). Relatively few dropped appeals (referred to as "volunteers" in prison nomenclature). Publicly available, documented evidence of mental illness rare (repeat: *publicly available, documented evidence* of mental illness). Victims predominantly white (see victim race hypothesis?). Info not collected, but true: overwhelmingly poor.

Interestingly, based on major demographic and case characteristics, we did not find statistically significant differences between those who chose to and chose not to make final statements when provided the opportunity to do so. In the full manuscript, we reminded readers that in light of our lack of information about each inmate in the weeks and months prior to execution with regard to mental health or the manner in which the inmate contemplated the impending execution and his or her culpability, innocence, etc., it was difficult to interpret statements versus no statements.[6]

Emotions were coded with somewhat of a blunt knife: dichotomously (0/1), with "1" indicating the presence of the expression within a statement. However, with regard to repentance—a variable which led Danielle and I to collaborate with psychologist Julie Exline to better understand the construct—it's important to note that it was coded as a combinatorial variable. That is, in order to remain consistent with scholarship which describes repentance as including elements such as confession, desire for forgiveness, and spirituality, the repentance variable required that an inmate have scored affirmatively (1) on guilt, the expression of sorrow toward/desire for forgiveness from the homicide survivor(s), and an element of religiosity (e.g., God's forgiveness).[7]

The study hypothesized that the inclusion of homicide survivors at executions would be associated with expressions of guilt and repentance in inmates' final statements, while the inclusion of homicide survivors would not be associated with emotions that are generally thought to be unrelated to the inmate ↔ homicide survivor dyad (defiance, broadly: expressions of innocence, statements of the unjust nature of the inmate's legal proceeding, statements of the unjust nature of capital punishment as a punishment), and then

---

[4] The homicide survivor attendance measure was treated as a proxy because we lacked execution-by-execution measures of when victim witnesses were in attendance post-1/96. In the aggregate, however, homicide survivors attended approximately 80% of executions in Texas after 1/96, to include a high of 91% in 2004.

[5] "Yes sir, I would like to say to all of you—the Thornton family and Jerry Dean's family that I am so sorry. I hope God will give you peace with this. Baby, I love you. Ron, give Peggy a hug for me. Everybody has been so good to me. I love all of you very much. I am going to be face-to-face with Jesus now. Warden Baggett, thank all of you so much. You have been so good to me. I love all of you very much. I will see you all when you get there. I will wait for you."

[6] Social psychology suggests that avoidance may represent a transgression-relevant response (angry individuals may avoid contact and withdraw). However, for this research question, one should probably use care in tying social psychology to stony silence. In its own way, silence may be a form of non-articulated defiance; that is, the inmate chooses not to validate the ceremony.

[7] We employed a conservative standard. If we were unable to definitively link a statement of sorrow/desire for forgiveness with a homicide survivor (e.g., as opposed to generalized society), we referred to AP or UPI news wires to compare the homicide survivor names to the content of the narrative. If a clear link between inmate and survivor could not be made, a statement was coded 0.

HOMICIDE SURVIVOR ATTENDANCE X
ADMISSION OF GUILT, REPENTANCE

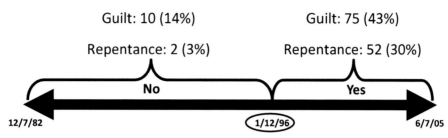

Guilt: 10 (14%)   Guilt: 75 (43%)

Repentance: 2 (3%)   Repentance: 52 (30%)

No   Yes

12/7/82   1/12/96   6/7/05

Homicide survivor attendance x Guilt (χ^2 = 18.7; p < .005; phi = .28)

Homicide survivor attendance x Repentance (χ^2 = 21.5; p < .005; phi = .30)

For clarification: during the period in which homicide survivors were not permitted to attend executions (pre- 1/12/96), 10 final statements included expressions of guilt (representing 14% of the final statements during that period). During the period in which homicide survivors were permitted to attend executions (post- 1/12/96), 75 final statements included expressions of guilt (representing 43% of the final statements during that period).

The trend is even more striking for repentance: whereas only 3% of final statements expressed pre-1/12/96 were repentant in nature, 30% of the final statements expressed post- 1/12/96 were.

N = 269 total final statements.

Fig. 2 Homicide survivor attendance × admission of guilt, repentance

finally, as in any such analysis, that any effect of the inclusion of homicide survivors at executions would not be found to be statistically insignificant upon the introduction of controls.

We found that as a group, the Texas final statements were more likely to contain statements of guilt (35%), desires for forgiveness (30%), and repentance (22%) than expressions of innocence (20%), expressions of capital punishment as unjust (11%), or expressions of unfair legal proceedings (10%).[8] While I can't speak for Danielle, I was surprised by this finding given threads within the psychology of offending and psychology of punishment literatures which say that serious offenders develop barriers against feeling of responsibility for their actions. Techniques of neutralization, if you will. Plus of course there's

the adage "there are no guilty men on death row"—an assertion typically articulated by death penalty supporters who say that under no circumstances will the condemned (or the merely incarcerated, for that matter) admit guilt. This study demonstrated this not to be true.

Looking at the question of homicide survivor attendance (pre-/post-1/96), analyses indicated a moderately strong relationship between survivor attendance and admission of guilt, a strong relationship between attendance and desire for forgiveness, and a strong relationship between attendance and repentance. The contrast was particularly striking for repentance: for the period in Texas when homicide survivors were not eligible to attend executions, only two inmates' final statements met the standard for repentance (guilt, desire for forgiveness, religiosity), representing less than 3% of the final statements during the period. Once homicide survivors began attending, 52 final statements were repentant in nature, representing 30% of the final statements during the period (see Fig. 2).

[8] Detailed statistics can be found in the article. Some statements included more than one emotive within themselves (e.g., capital punishment illegitimate + legal proceeding unfair).

Consistent with the study's second major hypothesis, the inclusion of homicide survivors at executions was not associated with defiant emotions which are not thought to be related to the inmate ↔ homicide survivor interchange.

Based on these findings, it appears that the two subsets of emotions (repentant, defiant) present themselves quite differently in this correctional context. Further, the incorporation of the sociolegal control variables did not wash away the major findings.

By referencing odds ratios, inmates were *24 times* more likely to repent after homicide survivors were in attendance.

Taken as a whole, there is something emotionally palpable under way when witness lists are made up of not only media representatives, criminal justice officials, and inmate witnesses but also loved ones of the deceased. When one includes emotions tied to defiance, the findings stand in contrast with those who suggest that inmates go to their deaths in quiet, resigned states.

Closing

For a project conceived of at Starbucks, understanding the implications of techniques I'd learned in class struck me like a lightning bolt. Just as there's a lexicon available to explain *mens rea* such as intention, knowledge, recklessness, and negligence (Katz), might too be emotions that manifest as inmates contemplate their deaths? Could Danielle and I have been contributing in some small way to Sampson's call for "dynamic contextualism" by joining event structures, qualitative narratives, and causal explanation? Overall, can forgiveness play a much more central role in criminal justice (Tullis)?

As far as "post-do's" go: as has plagued corrections research (Cislo/Trestman), reaching out to TDCJ Executive Services and TDCJ Victim Services has been unproductive. Exactly why

I'm not sure, given the Texas Crime Victim Clearinghouse's (TxCVC) effort to manage matters related to Texas victims, plus the trove of execution data TDCJ makes available at their website (515 executions as of this month, July 2014).

One obvious million dollar question is how variation in the emotional makeup of inmates' final statements relates to homicide survivor "closure," or the end of (or at least reduction of) pain associated with a loved one's murder. For her dissertation at the University of Texas-Austin, Danielle utilized discursive textual analysis to assess aspects and goals of closure in the popular press, legislative hearings, case law, and scholarship—one element being the instrumental use of the concept for justifying the continued use of capital punishment. The question of closure would of course require TDCJ's cooperation in identifying homicide survivors' contact information for ethnographic exploration.

Straightforward post-do elaborations are many. For example, finer cuts by way of inmate race, victim race, and the relationship between the two; the impact of spiritual counsel; the impact of breakdowns in routine procedures; the additive effects of psychosocial health and social and human capital; plus how, in the spirit of the Capital Jury Project, capital jurors and capital jurists feel about the emotional makeup of executions they were a part of (esp. jurists, as learning moments). Plus there's textual visualization of the most common words in final statements of inmates with particular personal or case characteristics (see Fig. 3).

At the end of the day, we may find that we're ill prepared to find "meaning" in final statements—that the penal system's desire for minimization of physical pain has led to a theatrical representation of pain: punishment which plumbs the depths of the offender's heart. Drawing on the range of scholarship about the intersection of emotions and crime is one good place to start.

Fig. 3 Text visualization—most common words in Texas final statements ("last words"). Size of words illustrates frequency of occurrence

Bibliography

Alsup, D. (2009). Texas reporter's seen unrivaled number of U.S. executions. *CNN*.

Bedau, H. A., & Radelet, M. L. (1987). Miscarriages of justice in potentially capital cases. *Stanford Law Review, 40*(1), 161–170.

Berlow, A. (2003). The Texas clemency memos. *Atlantic Monthly, 292*(1), 91–97.

Braithwaite, J. (1999). Restorative justice: Assessing optimistic and pessimistic accounts. In M. Tonry (Ed.), *Crime and justice: A review of research* (Vol. 25, pp. 1–127). Chicago, IL: University of Chicago Press.

Brooks, D. (2014). Social science palooza IV. *New York Times*.

Cislo, A. M., & Trestman, R. (2013). Challenges and solutions for conducting research in correctional settings: The US experience. *International Journal of Law and Psychiatry, 36*(3), 304–310.

Clear, T. R. (2001). Has academic criminal justice come of age? ACJS Presidential Address Washington, DC, April 2001. *Justice Quarterly, 18*(4), 709–726.

Dirks, D. (2011). *American capital punishment and the promise of "closure"* (Doctoral dissertation).

Dow, D. R. (2008). Last execution: Rethinking the fundamentals of death penalty law. *The Houston Law Review, 45*, 963.

Elliott, A. (2013). Invisible child: Girl in the shadows: Dasani's homeless life. *New York Times*.

Exline, J. J., & Baumeister, R. F. (2000). Expressing forgiveness and repentance. In M. McCullough, K. I. Parament, & C. Thoresen (Eds.), *Forgiveness: Theory, research, and practice* (pp. 133–155). New York, NY: Guilford.

Garland, D. (2010). *Peculiar institution: America's death penalty in an age of abolition*. Cambridge, MA: Harvard University Press.

Garland, D. (2012). *Punishment and modern society: A study in social theory*. Chicago, IL: University of Chicago Press.

Giddens, A. (1985). *A contemporary critique of historical materialism: The nation-state and violence* (2). Berkeley, CA: University of California Press.

Goffman, A. (2014). *On the run: Fugitive life in an American city*. Chicago, IL: University of Chicago Press.

Grann, D. (2009). Trial by fire: Did Texas execute an innocent man? *The New Yorker*.

Gross, S. R., O'Brien, B., Hu, C., & Kennedy, E. H. (2014). Rate of false conviction of criminal defendants who are sentenced to death. *Proceedings of the National Academy of Sciences, 111*(20), 7230–7235.

Jacobs, S., Filipov, D., & Wen, P. (2013). The fall of the house of Tsarnaev. *The Boston Globe*.

Katz, L. (2012). *Bad acts and guilty minds: Conundrums of the criminal law*. Chicago, IL: University of Chicago Press.

Maltz, M. D. (1994). Deviating from the mean: The declining significance of significance. *Journal of Research in Crime and Delinquency, 31*(4), 434–463.

Marquart, J. W., Ekland-Olson, S., & Sorensen, J. R. (1998). *The rope, the chair, and the needle: Capital punishment in Texas, 1923-1990.* Austin, TX: University of Texas Press.

Percy, W. (2000). *Signposts in a strange land: Essays.* New York, NY: Macmillan.

Radelet, M. L., & Bedau, H. A. (1998). The execution of the innocent. *Law and Contemporary Problems, 61,* 105–124.

Rice, S. K., Dirks, D., & Exline, J. J. (2009). Of guilt, defiance, and repentance: Evidence from the Texas death chamber. *Justice Quarterly, 26*(2), 295–326.

Sampson, R. J. (1993). Linking time and place: Dynamic contextualism and the future of criminological inquiry. *Journal of Research in Crime and Delinquency, 30*(4), 426–444.

Sampson, R. J., Raudenbush, S. W., & Earls, F. (1997). Neighborhoods and violent crime: A multilevel study of collective efficacy. *Science, 277*(5328), 918–924.

Sarat, A. (2001). Killing me softly: Capital punishment and the technologies for taking life. In A. Sarat (Ed.), *Pain, death, and the law* (pp. 43–70). Ann Arbor, MI: University of Michigan Press.

Sherman, L. W. (1993). Defiance, deterrence, and irrelevance: A theory of the criminal sanction. *Journal of Research in Crime and Delinquency, 30*(4), 445–473.

Sherman, L. W. (2003). Reason for emotion: Reinventing justice with theories, innovations, and research—The American Society of Criminology 2002 Presidential Address. *Criminology, 41*(1), 1–38.

Tullis, P. (2013). Can forgiveness play a role in criminal justice. *The New York Times.*

Weisburd, D., & McEwen, T. (Eds.). (1998). *Crime mapping and crime prevention (No. 8).* New York, NY: Criminal Justice Press.

The Making of the Chicago Project

Robert J. Sampson

Many social science studies appear rather anti-septic in their description, as if data cleanly appeared on the analyst's computer screen without any blood, sweat, or tears. The Project on Human Development in Chicago Neighborhoods (PHDCN) generated lots of the latter, and I believe that the story of its making is relevant to an understanding of how social science works, how cities work, and the interplay between them in producing a human outcome. The role of scientific investigators in such endeavors is usually overlooked, as is the process by which ideas generate the construction of data. Paraphrasing Goethe, one might say that "data are theory." Also underappreciated are the twists, turns, and compromises that researchers encounter once the research design texts are closed and data collection commences. I thus make an effort to breathe life into those key moments in the project. I begin with the intellectual backdrop to PHDCN, which might be subtitled: "What happens when social science gets into bed with big science?"

Intellectual History

The story begins in 1982, when a study group funded by the John D. and Catherine T. MacArthur Foundation was appointed to make recommendations for a major new study, a kind of "Framingham" for criminology. The two key players in this early group turned out to be James Q. Wilson, a leading political scientist who at the time was writing *Crime and Human Nature* with the psychologist Richard Herrnstein at Harvard, and Lloyd Ohlin, a sociologist best known for his classic book with Richard Cloward, *Delinquency and Opportunity*. The tensions, not surprisingly, revolved around a vision of crime as an individual trait, perhaps biologically rooted, as suggested by Wilson and Herrnstein, versus crime as a social and thus contextual phenomenon, favored by Ohlin.

Another relevant backdrop was the appointment of a National Academy of Sciences (NAS) panel, *Research on Criminal Careers*, chaired by Alfred Blumstein, an operations researcher at Carnegie Mellon University. The NAS issued a

This is an edited version of Chap. 4 in *Great American City: Chicago and the Enduring Neighborhood Effect*. Reprinted with permission: © 2012 by The University of Chicago. All rights reserved. Readers should consult the original chapter for the full text, footnotes, and references.

In their introduction, the editors note that terms like "collective efficacy" and "ecometrics" have made their way into textbooks, but there is little indication of how they came to be, and how difficult it was to mount the project that generated these and other concepts that are now in the mainstream of sociological and criminological thought. The full story (see Chap. 4 in *Great American City: Chicago and the Enduring Neighborhood Effect*) is considerably richer and more descriptive of the personalities, challenges, and opportunities of the project.

R.J. Sampson (✉)
Harvard University, Cambridge, MA, USA
e-mail: rsampson@wjh.harvard.edu

M.D. Maltz and S.K. Rice (eds.), *Envisioning Criminology: Researchers on Research as a Process of Discovery*, DOI 10.1007/978-3-319-15868-6_10, © Springer International Publishing Switzerland 2015

highly visible report in 1986, shortly after the publication of *Crime and Human Nature* in 1985. Together, these works set forth the notion of the "career criminal," foreshadowed by the work of Marvin Wolfgang. In *Delinquency in a Birth Cohort*, Wolfgang and colleagues reported that 6% of the members of a Philadelphia birth cohort had committed about two thirds of the offenses of the entire cohort. Crime was produced, it appeared, by relatively few individuals. Wolfgang had identified the "career criminals" retrospectively, and a consensus emerged that the field needed to design a major new prospective study of criminal careers. The provocative arguments put forth by Wilson, Wolfgang, Blumstein, and others set in motion a research agenda on "career criminals" (later "super-predators") and in particular a widespread return to what had been an early focus in criminology—prediction.

At that time, American cities were said to be dying, under siege by record levels of violence, disrepair, and outmigration. Violence in urban areas skyrocketed in the late 1980s and early 1990s, and the tenor of the times was one of despair. There was a public outcry for solutions to the violence problem in cities, and the PHDCN was conceived as a scientific effort to provide empirical evidence in support of urban crime policies.

With support from the MacArthur Foundation and later the National Institute of Justice, the initial investment of the study group led to a 1986 book by David Farrington, Lloyd Ohlin, and James Q. Wilson titled, appropriately, *Understanding and Controlling Crime: Toward a New Research Strategy*. Subsequently, the MacArthur Foundation was convinced to host a large working conference in Dallas in February of 1988 to hash out the details of an actual design. Instead of generating a research agenda, it produced nothing that MacArthur was able to use. After another try, with support from both MacArthur and the National Institute of Justice, a project was initiated.

Phase I of the project was born in 1988, with working groups chaired by Lloyd Ohlin, David Farrington (psychology, Cambridge), and Felton Earls (child psychiatry, Harvard), and the overall effort directed by Michael Tonry (law, University of Minnesota). The original title deliberately laid emphasis on crime and individual development: Project on Human Development and Criminal Behavior. The emphasis on crime reflected the widespread challenge that cities were facing, and the individual developmental focus reflected the increasing influence of what would later become known as the decade of the brain—a medical model conception of human behavior. These twin foci foreshadowed intellectual battles to come. The planning effort envisioned a prospective study of thousands of youth in multiple cities, aged 0–25, in a cohort-sequential longitudinal design and hopefully an experimental component. The measurement plans were heavily tilted to individual difference constructs, psychiatric diagnostic criteria, and family processes. Sociological factors and community were nodded to, but the latter in particular appeared perfunctory and in service of providing just another variable to add to the prediction of individual differences.

A key turning point for my personal situation came with the appointment of Albert J. Reiss Jr. to the steering committee later that year. Steeped in Chicago sociology, Reiss urged the inclusion of contextual and sociological features in the study. It helped that he had recently edited *Communities and Crime* for the University of Chicago Press and (for me) that I had written a commissioned article in the volume. Reiss enlisted my help, and in late 1988 I began serving on a planning committee.

That's when my hair began to turn gray, as I learned that interdisciplinary "big science" was as painful as it was exhilarating. I had to listen to neurobiologists and read behavioral genetics while interacting with leading scholars. Arguing over beers with a behavioral geneticist can also be a great deal of fun. There were many battles, but the main flare-ups centered on the proper role of individual and contextual factors in the etiology of crime. James Q. Wilson and a diverse group of criminologists and developmentalists favored a design that would include biological factors, while Lloyd Ohlin and other sociologists championed a focus on contextual factors. Al Reiss and I argued for community-level factors, and, in the end, we prevailed in at least getting the issue a place at the table. This was no small feat, considering the diversity of the committees, funding sources, and intellectual backdrop. Many more details could be elaborated, but it is sufficient to say that after much haggling and input from dozens of scholars, a design finally emerged. It was to be an "accelerated longitudinal" or cohort-sequential design, from ages 0 to 18, each followed for up to 8 years. In other words, the idea was to follow multiple cohorts of different ages over the same historical time. In turn, the cohort study was to be embedded in a community design, with independent data collection on the social organization of communities. The victory, from my view, was a commitment to the study of contextual variations as an important endeavor in itself, prior to and independent of the study of individual pathways to crime. Equally important, the study shifted from a focus on crime to a more general and interdisciplinary investigation of human development across the life course.

The original plan was to carry out the study in several US cities, but budgetary and pragmatic concerns quickly intervened. Only one city could realistically be studied intensively, so we searched for the ideal fit. Data were collected on numerous aspects of candidate cities, including LA, Chicago, Baltimore, NYC, and New Orleans. These included primarily census data, health records, and crime records. After site visits to each city that included meetings with local officials, Chicago was officially selected, and the collaboratively constructed research design was finalized.

Why Chicago?

I am an American, Chicago born—Chicago, that somber city—and go at things as I have taught myself, free style, and will make the record in my own way: first to knock, first admitted; sometimes an innocent knock, sometimes a not so innocent.

Opening proclamation in Saul Bellow's *The Adventures of Augie March*

A major goal from the outset was to obtain sufficient representation of the three largest race/ ethnic groups in American society—blacks, Latinos, and whites—combined with variation in socioeconomic status (SES). That eliminated most cities, and the remaining ones were ranked according to intellectual resources, cooperation from a variety of local officials, available archival data, estimated costs, and an established record of prior study that could be used as a comparative frame for understanding contemporary city life. Chicago emerged as the obvious choice, with its unparalleled history of community research being the icing on the cake.

There is another, less tangible factor, and that is simply the notion that Chicago is arguably the quintessential American city. As Saul Bellow, Nelson Algren, Norman Mailer, and a long line of literary, political, cultural, and criminal characters attest, Chicago captures the full range and intensity of American passions.

To be great is hardly to be flawless, of course. Quite to the contrary and to the dismay of would-be boosters, some of the worst excesses of American life, such as inequality, violence, racial segregation, and corruption, are on major exhibit in Chicago. Disasters are a regular part of the landscape as well, including deadly heat waves, crippling snowstorms, and the infamous Great Fire. Perhaps for these reasons, Chicago has motivated deep social scientific study as well as literary, intellectual, architectural, and political passions and has emerged on the international stage as the place that introduced Barack Obama to politics and produced his world views. Chicago is not absolutely average, to be sure, but Chicago has faced the dynamics that have confronted all the major cities in the country—growth, decline, riots, crime, and boom times. In this sense, Chicago is both unique and broadly representative, grounded in a thoroughly documented history and context that helps us understand key patterns. While attuned to observations and keeping closely grounded to contextual nuances, my goal is thus to identify what is typical rather than merely unique—to study regularities and structural patterns, in other words, with comparison to other cities wherever possible. This balancing between abstract principles and concrete instantiations is the most compelling intellectual route to take, I believe. It is not the pure lab model of scientists, where reality is kept at bay, or the type of field ethnography that focuses on particularistic knowledge only. Warts and all, Chicago is my exemplar of "truth spot" to work out empirical processes and theoretical ideas. Certainly, the place is an interesting one that, like Bellow's Augie March, is knocking its way headlong into the twenty-first century.

The Data

Data collection turned out to be a massive undertaking, described in detail in the book. Following several more years of fundraising, protocol development, pretesting, and open bidding for pieces of the large-scale data collection, a research shop was eventually set up in 1994, under the title PHDCN. The name was changed to reflect the integration of the two major themes of the study: development and context. There was also a concern that the original focus on crime was too narrow. Phase II of the project got started, and the really hard work began.

We carved up the city into 343 neighborhood clusters (NCs)—groups of 2–3 census tracts that contain approximately 8,000 people. Major geographic boundaries (e.g., railroad tracks, parks, freeways), knowledge of Chicago's local neighborhoods, and cluster analyses of census data guided the construction of NCs so that they were relatively homogeneous with respect to racial/ethnic mix, SES, housing density, and family structure. A total of 80 sampled NCs were then randomly selected for intensive study after stratifying across 21 cells defined by the cross-classification of SES and race/ethnicity. Census data were used to define the two stratification variables: racial/ethnic mix (three homogeneous strata and four heterogeneous strata) and a SES scale divided into equal thirds. Reflecting the pattern of segregation that is predominant in American society, the number of NCs falling into the 21 strata created by the cross-classification of racial/ethnic mix and SES was uneven. Although the aim of the PHDCN was to obtain nearly equal numbers of NCs from each of the strata, three of the 21 strata came up empty, and an additional

three cells had fewer than five NCs. Thus, in these three cells, all NCs were selected (the population). In other strata, NCs were selected systematically after sorting by SES and housing density. The resulting probability sample of 80 NCs capitalized on, to the extent possible, the range of race/ethnic diversity and SES stratification in the city of Chicago.

Extensive in-home interviews and assessments were conducted with the sampled children and their primary caregivers. Rather than farm out the data collection for the cohort study, the decision was made to create a research and administrative staff dedicated to the study over a number of years. At one point, some 200 people were employed with a base in rented office space in the West Loop area of downtown Chicago. Data collection took place over about 8 years on a rolling basis at 3 points in time, at roughly 2½-year intervals (wave 1 in 1994–1997, wave 2 in 1997–1999, and wave 3 in 2000–2002). The subject and parental assessments were intensive and in most cases conducted separately by two interviewers depending on age. Types of information gathered include health, temperament, personality, cognitive functioning, ethnic identity, moral development, social competence, exposure to violence, substance abuse, delinquency, family structure and process, and peers. In the infant cohort, some 500 babies were randomly selected for participation in a repeated observational study in which children and parents were videotaped and observed as a means to capture aspects of temperament and personality.

Owing largely to the dedication and hard work of the local staff, participation rates and retention were excellent for an urban sample in this time era. The PHDCN managed to enroll over 70% of the hardest-to-reach 18-year-olds and over 76% of the birth cohort; the overall participation rate was 75% of the intended target at wave 1. Many of the children and families moved frequently after the first visit, both within and outside Chicago. In fact, over 40% of PHDCN members moved, covering virtually all of Chicago and extending throughout the metropolitan region. Each move was geocoded to an address, and I exploit these residential mobility flows in the book's analyses.

PHDCN families were followed wherever they moved in the USA and beyond, such as Mexico. PHDCN staff spent a considerable effort tracking people down despite the widespread movement and managed to achieve a follow-up retention of 87% at wave 2 and 76% at wave 3. In the contemporary era of urban data collection, this retention rate is rather remarkable.

Community Survey

We executed three independent community studies apart from the families studied in the seven age cohorts. The largest leg of the community design was a survey in which the goal was to use residents as informants about their neighborhood using a "clustered" or multistage sampling approach. Since there had been a lot of work in community psychology and urban sociology relevant to our goals, we convened a workshop in Chicago in the fall of 1990 to gather advice on how to go about asking questions. Major scholars offered generous advice that continues to guide the study. A key outcome of the meeting was ratification of the idea to treat neighborhoods as independent sampling units and not simply an appendage of the cohort members. A number of core concepts were proposed, such as social control and disorder, and leading scholars presented their experiences in how best to measure them across neighborhoods.

Following this meeting, it was left to Al Reiss and me to construct the community survey and design the specifics of the sampling plan. This charge sounds deadly dull, but in fact, the process turned out to be an intellectual treat that reached its apex in a marathon session at the Yale Club in NYC. My memory of this event is especially vivid. Reiss and I worked almost nonstop until we hashed out a blueprint. Questions were written by day over a large wooden table in a windowless library study, and progress evaluated over dinner and single-malt scotch late into the night. At marathon's end, we produced a draft survey protocol and sampling plan to measure a number of concepts such as social cohesion, informal social control, friend/kinship ties, moral cynicism, organizational participation, and still others to be described later.

The community survey (CS) was a multidimensional assessment by residents of the structural and cultural organization of their neighborhoods. Our objective was to assess all Chicago neighborhoods, whether the individuals in our core sample resided in them or not. This was partly motivated by the expectation that many subjects would move within Chicago and that we would want to be able to characterize the receiving neighborhoods. But it was also done because of our affirmative focus on processes of neighborhood change and spatial mechanisms involving neighborhoods that adjoined the neighborhoods where LCS subjects resided. Thus, the community survey used the same NC sampling frame as the LCS, but independent data were collected on all 343 Chicago NCs. In total, 8,782 individuals 18 years of age or older were interviewed in their homes in 1995, with an average of 25 individuals per NC (average of 50 interviews conducted in 80 target NCs and average of 20 interviews in nontarget NCs).

We also conducted two other studies within the sample of 80 focal NCs linked to the LCS. The biggest non-survey component of the community design was the systematic social observation (SSO) of all the street segments within the 80 NCs. A third and somewhat separate component was the key informant study, composed of interviews with approximately 2,800 community leaders representing the institutional domains of business, law enforcement, community organizations, education, political, and religion. I describe each of these components below. But before I do, it is important to sketch out some of the challenges we faced in carrying out the community survey and initial enrollment of the PHDCN cohort members. They are tied in interesting ways to the characteristics of the neighborhoods and the city we set out to study.

Challenges and Solutions, Chicago Style

The naked truth of the origins of the PHDCN is that it was on the brink of failure at the starting gate. Not only did the project risk failure, but each of the major investigators fell into despair in the early stages, certain that the project was about to come crashing down.

Things started in earnest when a national survey firm won a national bid to carry out the household listing, screening, identification of eligible participants for the cohort study, and the community survey. These tasks entailed a massive undertaking with a budget in the millions. Yet neither the contractor nor PHDCN senior investigators fully comprehended how difficult a challenge awaited as data collection "ramped up" and attempted to hit stride in 1995. Readers from Chicago may remember 1995, for it spawned the most intense heat wave in the city's history. It was miserable much of the summer, with temperatures reaching 100° on a number of consecutive days. Some 700 people died. The contractor hired to do the screening for cohort participants, and the community survey stumbled badly, and in addition, it turned out later that they had underbid the project. Things simply broke down. The survey firm ran out of money with only about 10,000 households screened and the community survey incomplete.

This turn of events led to one of the more unpleasant and bizarre experiences of my academic career. Lawsuits and lawyers entered the picture; at one point, we found ourselves in a room arguing details of research design before attorneys and corporate administrators. A painful settlement was eventually reached—the survey firm would finish the community survey at an apparent financial loss (future grants were at stake), and we would have to pick up the pieces and do the screening and listing for the cohort study ourselves. Things looked disastrous as PHDCN lost about a year's time and costs spiraled.

Even when data collection was back on track, it ran into the realities of both old and new Chicago. Interviewers not only (literally) collapsed in the heat, some were robbed at gunpoint, others sexually harassed. Two research assistants on the way to a cohort interview came across a drive-by shooting and witnessed a dead body on the sidewalk. This was Chicago in the mid-1990s. Yet contrary to what many would expect, response rates were high in the "inner city." What nearly broke the back of the project was the North

Side lakefront. Residents of the new Chicago in lakefront high-rises—typically white, affluent, childless, professional, busy, and assertive—had effectively sealed themselves off from the neighborhoods west of them. As network theorists might have predicted, the lives of many of these people were extralocal in nature. Yet, paradoxically, local space was crucial, and it manifested itself in doormen to block outside entrance, elaborate security devices and gates, and powerful condo or homeowner associations vigilantly guarding property values and local conditions. It was not that the local neighborhood was unimportant—how could it be with seven-digit real estate values and development galore? Rather, it was that these neighborhoods were tightly defended, more by hired security guards than by residents. In screening households and interviewing for the CS, the project was thus at one point "locked out."

In response to the obstacles posed by residents' reclusiveness and the building security, the survey firm resorted to another Chicago tradition—they bribed or flattered the doormen to let them into the building. The clincher was an outside team known as "The Travelers," two women, one from New England and the other from the South. According to field notes from one of our interviewers and compiled by the site director, these women were in their 40s, petite, charming, dressed in the latest fashions, and "utterly elegant—adorned with jewelry, diamond earrings, and pearl necklaces." They were high-energy, fast-thinking, and able to cross race and class boundaries with savoir-faire. Working as a team, they cracked the North Side.

Data collection was also virtually halted in one Southwest Side community. Residents there refused to answer the door, much less the questions. Instead, they directed us to the local alderman, again in good Chicago form. After repeated attempts at contact, the alderman informed us that he had to first read the interview to see what information was being collected before he would put out the word that we were to be trusted. If this is not a measure of power and social organization, I don't know what is. He also offered to "consult" with us on adding questions of interest to his constituents. This situation required lots of ego massaging, negotiation, and some quid pro quo to get back on track. Even so, our participation rate in that NC was only 65%. To play good politics, we had to brief the mayor's office, police department, and on down the line before going into any neighborhood.

There was more. One morning we woke up to an ominous headline in the Chicago Tribune to the effect that a massive federal initiative on crime had targeted Chicago. An activist from Washington was quoted as linking us—inaccurately and without any evidence—to the so-called Violence Initiative, an ill-fated attempt by Fred Goodwin, who was head of the National Institute of Mental Health (NIMH), to coordinate research activity on crime and focus on biological determinants. We were charged with seeking to draw blood from participants to identify biological markers so that we could eventually identify and incapacitate criminals from the inner city. Another story charged that our goal was to sterilize black women. A group of local activists called the Chicago Coalition against the Violence Initiative soon joined the fray and called for the study to shut down operation and for residents to refuse participation.

Fortunately, we were blessed with strong leadership and had recruited a committed, ethnically representative, and streetwise local staff. Our site director, an African American, was appalled at the scurrilous charges and led a counterattack that took enormous social organizational effort. He and other project staff gave presentations and seminars throughout the city and met with community organizations over the course of many months. Aldermen were also brought in on the plans, along with key church leaders in the lower-income communities. The principal investigator, Tony Earls, spent countless hours articulating the scientific goals of the project and navigating a thicket of challenges both political and administrative.

In the end, we received the strongest support from the citizens in the very neighborhoods that many activists sought to represent. We even received an endorsement from the *Defender*, Chicago's oldest and biggest black newspaper, along with the left-leaning *In These Times*. I should note too that our design, with equal measure of black, white, and Latino areas and low and upper SES, belied the charges of limiting the study to the inner city or "ghetto"—in fact, the design might be read as an implicit criticism of the underclass "poverty paradigm" in urban sociology. It is also ironic that attempts to shut us down were followed by support from community activists. At one point, I was approached by a campaign manager for someone running for mayor against Richard Daley. As an aspiring politician, he had warmed to the idea of appropriating the concept of "collective efficacy" for his campaign. I declined to get involved in politics, but having seen the project be criticized by both the left and the right, I came to the conclusion that we must be doing something right.

There was one major substantive casualty to the design. For a variety of reasons, biological measures were considered but dropped from the final data collection plans. James Q. Wilson left the project soon thereafter, I suspect partly because of this turn of events. Some have claimed the study is flawed for not being on top of recent advances in biology. Although at the time I felt that sociology had in a sense won a battle, I no longer feel that way and have come to the broader conclusion that sociology's typical position on biology risks its credibility in the interdisciplinary world that characterizes recent trends in science. Disciplinary barriers are breaking down fast, and in 10 years, the way we currently cut up the academic landscape may have little relevance for understanding human behavior. Moreover, because context is necessary for the expression of genetic variation, sociology should be an intellectual player in the explanation of gene-environment interactions. That said, the PHDCN could not be everything.

These are just a few examples of the challenges of large-scale social science research in the modern city. A confluence of factors—race/ethnic segregation, suspicion of different paradigms, high-rise towers, fears of eugenics and biological determinism, gated communities, anonymity, and old-fashioned politics—conspired to make household interviewing and comprehensive assessments of individual development a difficult art. Yet the project overcame these challenges, hit its groove, and ended up pulling off both the community survey and longitudinal cohort studies with a better-than-anticipated cooperation rate.

Systematic Social Observations

A major linchpin of the community design rested on observation rather than on what people say. In the spirit of the early Chicago School of urban sociology, the project directors believed that direct observation was fundamental to the advancement of knowledge. As Andrew Abbott has emphasized, one of the hallmarks of the Chicago School was its concern for observing public places—not just abstract variables, but the sights, sounds, and feel of the streets. More than 25 years ago, Albert J. Reiss Jr. advocated systematic social observation as a key measurement strategy for natural social phenomena. By "systematic," he meant that observation and recording should be done according to explicit rules that permit replication. He also argued that the means of observation, whether a person or technology, must be independent of what is observed. By "natural social phenomena," Reiss meant that "events and their consequences, including properties of organization, can be observed more or less as they occur." Although he studied police-citizen encounters in his own research, Reiss noted the general import of the SSO method for assessing the physical conditions and social interactions within neighborhood settings that survey respondents may be incapable of describing.

One of the primary obstacles to our bringing independent and systematic social observation to bear on this conundrum is methodological uncertainty. This uncertainty includes not just how to properly conduct such observations but also how to properly assess their measurability at the neighborhood level. Another concern is cost, although direct observations are potentially less expensive than household surveys, since listing, screening, broken appointments, and response rates are eliminated. To address these issues, we developed systematic procedures for collecting observational assessments of public space.

Between June and October 1995, observers trained by NORC at the University of Chicago drove a sport utility vehicle (SUV) at a rate of 3–5 miles per hour down every street within the stratified probability sample of 80 NCs. The geographic unit of recorded observation was the "face block": the block segment on one side of a street. For example, the buildings across the street from one another on any city block comprised two separate units of observation. At each intersection, a unique geographic identification code was assigned so that adjacent face blocks could be pieced together to form higher levels of aggregation. To observe each face block, our team fielded a driver, a videographer, and two observers. As the SUV was driven down the street, a pair of video recorders, one located on each side of the SUV, captured social activities and physical features of both face blocks simultaneously. At the same time, two trained observers, one on each side of the SUV, recorded their observations onto an observer log for each block face. The observers added verbal commentary when relevant (e.g., about accidents or a drug bust), and that was captured by an audio recorder. One may wonder how we managed to do all this without suspicion. The answer is twofold: the windows were tinted, and even by 1995, SUVs had become commonplace. Despite our fears, no one seemed to notice. This became apparent upon viewing video extracts.

Observing and videotaping face blocks took place between the hours of 7 a.m. and 7 p.m. The SSO team produced videotapes, observer logs, and audiotapes for every face block in each of the 80 sampled NCs. In all, 23,816 face blocks were observed and video recorded for an average of 298 per NC and 120 per tract. The data collected from the 23,816 observer logs focus mainly on land use, traffic, the physical condition of buildings, and evidence of physical disorder. Unlike the observer logs, which could be directly entered into machine-readable data files, the videotapes required the expensive and time-consuming task of first viewing and then coding. We selected a random subsample of all face blocks for coding. A total of 15,141 face blocks were sampled for videotape coding, an average of 189 per NC and 77 per tract. From the videotapes, 126 variables were coded, including detailed information on physical conditions, housing characteristics, businesses, and social interactions occurring on each face block.

Much like the original Chicago School of urban sociology, SSO takes researchers to the streets and provides the sights, sounds, and feel of everyday life. As James F. Short Jr. has argued, summoning the legacy of Park and Burgess, the essential spirit of the Chicago School was to "observe and record social life in every conceivable setting and to generalize its forms and processes." Through new technologies and methodological strategies, coupled with a theoretical lens that recognizes the changing nature of the city, PHDCN tried to keep this spirit alive and well in community research.

Conclusion

The result of over a decade's worth of data collection, the Chicago Project resembles a web of data deliberately spun from theoretical ideas about community-level processes and contextual effects on individuals in the modern city. *Great American City* integrates and exploits this complex web of data in service of a theoretically guided assessment of how cities, neighborhoods, and individuals interact. But the contextual, intellectual, and historical backdrop of the data collection is itself an important part of the story, prompting me to present in this chapter an overview of the project's social origins and evolution. In fundamental respects, data are theoretical—they only take on meaning within a conceptual framework and guiding question. In my opinion, research design is thus theoretical and takes precedence over statistical analysis. PHDCN and the emergent Chicago Project reflect an empirical embodiment of this core idea.

Finally, I should disclose that I spent 18 years living in Illinois and consumed with all things Chicago. For 12 of those years, I taught at the University of Chicago and observed the city's neighborhoods (especially from downtown and the Near North Side to the Far South Side and reaching into the southern suburbs) on a daily basis as part of my normal rounds. Obviously, this is not ethnography, but I was immersed, and local knowledge of place helps to make sense of the larger picture. I also personally led focus groups, carried out selected interviews with community leaders, and took field notes and pictures of city streets on numerous occasions over the years. The bulk of the data are nonetheless more quantitative and systematic in nature, and I "detached" myself as a regular from Chicago (both the university and the city) in 2002, perhaps to better appreciate it from a distance and reflect on personal biases. Like Howard Becker, however, ultimately I believe that the canonical distinctions made between qualitative and quantitative research are not sustainable. I would further argue that key principles and impulses that motivate ethnography can guide quantitative work. What counts is the quality of empirical information and the veracity of inferences and claims drawn from it.

Surveying Police Officers

Wesley G. Skogan

In 2012, the Chicago Police Department (CPD) decided that it had to be nicer to people. A new Chief of Police had arrived on the scene from out of town and, after about a year of looking around, settled on that as one of his key problems. The problem was both external and internal. Externally, he could see that the relationship between the police department and many poor and minority communities was broken. Contention between them threatened to undermine the very legitimacy of the police—and perhaps the rest of government. Internally, he sensed a parallel collapse of authority. The leaders he found in place upon arrival were unimpressive. Plum job assignments and promotions were distributed in response to politics, cronyism, and nepotism and not in recognition of hard and effective work. The procedures in place to monitor and discipline officers, especially for serious misconduct, were in shambles.

So, he set out to fix these problems. While he made important moves on the community front, he sensed that he had to address the department's internal problems first. The organization needed modern leadership and management; a personnel system that identified, nurtured, and promoted qualified people; and a functioning disciplinary process. Only when they got their own house in

W.G. Skogan (✉)
Northwestern University, Evanston, IL, USA
e-mail: Skogan@Northwestern.edu

order could the CPD hope to develop a sustainably better relationship with the community. As one senior manager put it to me, describing motivating change among his employees, "We can't kick their asses until they are nice to people."

As one small contribution to understanding the success or failure of this effort (and perhaps encouraging its success), I conducted a survey of Chicago police officers. The project was paid for by a local foundation, and the field work was carried out by a professional, university-based survey research organization. As a descriptive tool, the survey was designed to help quantify the real depth and breadth of some of the concerns that the new chief sensed among his troops in the field. The CPD is a huge organization. In a world awash with rumor and blogging, dogged by leaks to reporters from jealous insiders, and operating in a political environment of legendary dysfunctionality, it would be hard for anyone to gauge the morale of more than 12,000 employees just by walking around. As a research tool, the survey was designed to test a theory of organizational effectiveness called "procedural justice." In a nutshell, procedural justice theory identifies key aspects of authority relations—be it between police officers and their bosses or between officers and the public. The theory promised to be useful for understanding the department's internal and external problems. In addition, the Chief bought into the theory, and he started talking about it during public and private appearances

M.D. Maltz and S.K. Rice (eds.), *Envisioning Criminology: Researchers on Research as a Process of Discovery*, DOI 10.1007/978-3-319-15868-6_11, © Springer International Publishing Switzerland 2015

around town. This is the first time I have worked with a police chief who had a theory!

Developing the Survey

When it came to leadership and supervision within the department—internal procedural justice—I began on solid ground. There is a very large literature on procedural justice in the workplace, including a number of solid studies of police officers and members of related occupations, such as FBI agents and army officers. This work is quite well known, and modern managers (still only a subset in these occupations, unfortunately) are well versed in the lessons of procedural justice research. As a result, I could stand on the shoulders of the research giants and reuse their survey questions. I started with a list of procedural justice concepts—for example, "voice," or giving officers an opportunity to describe their situation and express their opinions about a problem when their supervisors are deciding on a course of action. There were about a dozen of these categories, but my list was quickly filled in with the four or so questions that I wanted to measure. I was on my own when it came to asking about specific local initiatives, such as gauging support for the new Chief's hard-nosed "CompStat" management style. I also had to develop questions testing support for the city's homegrown community policing program and for discerning what officers think about their union (answer: it's complicated).

By contrast, external procedural justice, measured by officers' views of how they should be treating members of the public, was unexplored territory. Many surveys of police include questions about the community. On repeated occasions I have asked Chicago officers if they think the public likes and supports them or fears and hates them. But there have been precious few studies that have used the elaborate conceptual framework provided by procedural justice theory to frame a survey asking officers about their relations with the *public*, rather than their own bosses. The opposite, surveys of the public asking how they are being treated by the *police*, are common

beyond belief, but there have been few studies of the view of encounters from the police side.

So, I proceeded carefully. When possible I phrased these questions so they paralleled the officers-and-their-supervisors questions, for there could be some analytic elegance in comparing the two. A big problem is that the questions had to be pointed; they could not be sappy. Few officers are going to reply in a survey that they should be disrespectful and shout obscenities at the citizenry. And, actually, few of them believe that. Instead, the questions had to expose edges that would free officers (or some officers) to allow that life on the street can be complicated. Here are some examples; all of them were asked in a "strongly agree" to "strongly disagree" format and gave the officers six response categories. The various modifiers in the questions were inserted to increase diversity in the answers.

People should be treated with respect regardless of their respect for the police.

It is necessary to give everyone a good reason why they are being stopped, even if it is not required.

People who break the law do not deserve to be treated with respect.

There is little sense in officers trying to be impartial, because that is impossible in this job.

Because this segment of the survey was unknown territory, I also tried to include *more* questions about each key component of procedural justice. The analysis stage of a survey study starts by developing scales, or index numbers, that combine responses to multiple questions about "the same thing" into one summary number. For example, I wanted scales reflecting the extent to which officers support offering "voice," "neutrality," "respect," and "trust" to the public, including in those edgy situations. The criterion that responses to questions being considered for a scale are measuring the same underlying procedural justice dimension is met by combining questions with highly intercorrelated responses. This criterion was easy to meet when it came to internal procedural justice, for officers have well-developed ideas about their bosses, and some bosses are bad. The external questions were somewhat more hypothetical and a proper response would actually be situationally dependent, so I knew that I was probably going to have to drop some because they just did not fit with others that were supposed to measure "the same thing." My hope was to identify a minimum of three strong questions (one drawing numerous agreements and disagreements) for each procedural justice concept.

Other parts of the questionnaire presented "political correctness" issues. A key concept in police research is police culture, so I wanted to have multiple measures of its various elements. Some widely recognized elements of police culture lent themselves well to my Chicago study. "Isolation from the community" is one example, and officers split 50–50 in response to the question "How would you rate the relationship between the police and the people of Chicago?" I was also good with the solidarity commonly displayed by officers. Chicago is a high-solidarity place, and 75% of the officers agreed that "Officers need to stick together because we can't count on anyone else to protect us if we get in trouble." Cynicism was also in fashion. Ninety percent agreed that "Many arrests go nowhere because prosecutors and judges aren't serious about punishing criminals," and three-quarters stuck with "Most top managers know that rules must be broken or bent to get the job done, but won't admit it." They were split in terms of what the police culture literature calls "glorification of crime fighting." Just under 60% agreed that "the main focus of the police should be reducing violent crime and not addressing lesser matters."

But I would not touch other topics. Reputedly, one key element of police culture is racism. Others, the literature says, include homophobia, sexism, and political conservatism. Elsewhere I might have asked officers if they were Republicans, but this is Chicago, where none have been sighted for decades. I was not going near any other topic on this list. I am not alone. One feature of research on police culture is that it is almost completely ethnographic. The ideas I described above emerged from hanging out with police and participating in what the British call "canteen culture." It would be tricky, to say the least, to devise a short set of questions validly assessing the racism of a public employee or the extent of their presumed homophobia. The pointed questions this would require would have rocked the station houses, and my name would have been in the newspapers, for sure.

The first pages of the survey had to cover some basic, federally required issues. Academic research is conducted under the watchful eye of human subjects review committees, which is found wherever federal funding for research is found—which is everywhere. They are concerned about risks to study participants. In this case, the principal risk would be the disclosure of individuals' responses to the survey questions. Our respondents were all adult, sworn police officers, so they were not an "at risk" population that might be upset when confronted with questions about crime (I've had that issue raised in other studies). Some surveys involve deception, as when subsets of respondents are told different sets of "facts" or offered different "quotes" from supposedly the same source, but that was also not the case here. My study had no difficulty being approved by my local committee.

To meet federal requirements, the questionnaire opened with a brief description of the purpose of the study (always claim "we want to hear from officers like you"). Respondents were warned that they would receive no compensation for participating and that it was likely there would be no direct benefits to them for agreeing to be involved. We noted that a cost to them was that we would take about 20 min of their time. To be upbeat, we observed that "The results of this study may bring about improvements in the policies and procedures of the CPD." They were assured that their participation was voluntary, they could skip any questions they desired, and they could stop any time they wanted to. They were given my name and telephone number, in case they wanted to contact me for more information (no one called). The officers had to check off that they had read and understood all of this, before they could continue on to the actual questions. No one got this far and checked "no."

Mode of Interview

A key feature of the study was that it was going to be a lengthy, sit-down interview. I needed to gather a lot of information, because the survey was essentially covering two different (if related) topics: internal and external procedural justice. Police officers are accustomed to being offered surveys and in recent years have gotten choosey about which they will participate in. If we handed them a familiar but fat-enough paper-and-pencil survey, they might not get through it. One option for making this a serious and engaging survey was to conduct it as a personal interview. Trained interviewers could read questions to the officers and record their replies. Professional sample surveys have been conducted in this fashion for more than 80 years, but there were problems in this context. The respondents would not be anonymous to the interviewers, and—police being a suspicious bunch—some were certain to fear that "calls" would be made to discuss their answers with "higher-ups." We also would have to isolate each lengthy interview in a separate, private, and quiet space, and that is in short supply in most police stations. It would also be very expensive, because our interviewers were well paid (commensurately so, for their training and experience), and the survey would have taken more than an hour to complete. To handle this study, we would have to station a squad of interviewers in every police station house, around the clock.

Rather, we chose to go for CASI, or Computer-Assisted Self-Interviewing. Instead of a team of interviewers, one survey representative could handle the job. Officers could read the questions on a laptop screen and click on their response. Our representatives came to their stations at scheduled times, set up laptops around tables in the roll call room or community room where the study was being housed, broke open donut boxes, and opened the door. Police officers are quite computer savvy; they use them every day in their work and carry a portable data terminal in their car, so that would not be a problem. This survey project was different enough in its use of CASI that they found it, perhaps only at first, a bit inter-

esting. They picked their own machine, and the laptops' internet connections were turned off, lending a further air of anonymity to the task.

At our end, CASI meant that we did not have to enter any data; the survey software stored it for future retrieval. The laptops would have been a bit expensive, but fortunately our survey contractor had just completed a large public health CASI study and their earlier client had paid for the equipment. The laptops did raise logistical and security concerns. Different representatives were shuttling in and out of multiple stations at different hours of the day and night, so carrying them around in car trunks and passing between representatives would have been a nightmare. Instead, we bought the biggest plastic tubs that Rubbermaid© makes and stored laptops in the stations while we were active there. During my initial visit to each station, I walked around with the commander to identify a suitable survey room, and we also had to find a secure place to keep the laptop tub. It had to be a place where someone would always have a key, even at 5 a.m., yet from which the laptops would not "walk." Literally hundreds of employees flow through the back-office spaces of district stations every day, and this was a real risk. In one older station, the district commander volunteered the floor of his office, about the only private place there.

Logistics and Sampling

I wanted to interview a representative sample of officers. This would necessarily include officers serving on all watches, not just those conveniently (for me) working the day shift. Once selected, actually having a representative group complete their questionnaires also involved accommodating officers' days off, court appearances, and other circumstances that keep them away from their station. Our initial goal (which had to be revised in practice) was to complete 50 interviews in each of the 22 police districts, 40 with police officers (the bottom rank in the organization) and 10 with sergeants. Because there were only 16 or 17 sergeants in total serving in all but the largest districts, we did not sample them.

Instead they were all invited to participate. When it came to POs, we accommodated differences in the size of the districts by drawing somewhat larger samples in the largest districts and smaller ones in the smallest districts. Everywhere we selected officers proportionally to the number who worked on each duty shift, to ensure that people who worked midnights and those who came in during the day were accurately represented. Finally, once the data were collected, we used sample weights (see below) to put everyone into their correct proportions before analyzing the data.

To make this work, I need to "sell" participation, at several levels. First I had to secure the support of each district commander. It helped that when I first contacted them by email, I also attached a letter from their boss, the Chief of Police, endorsing the project and encouraging them to get involved. Given this support they would never say "no" to my survey, but I needed the active cooperation of their staff as well as easy access to their facility if I was going to get the project off the ground. To meet with each of the 22 district commanders and "seal the deal," I put 500 miles on my car—the project was a reminder of how physically big Chicago is.

One of my requests during our meetings was that the commander identify a district contact that I could rely on for information and assistance and whom (I assured the busy commanders) I would bother with my follow-up requests. The commanders were generally well informed and helpful, but the contacts they steered to me were more of a mixed bag. Some were interested; many were not. Many had the technical skills the job needed (see below), but some did not.

During my initial visits, I also dealt with another key issue at each station: where to park. At midnight, in the dark, I wanted my representatives to be safe, so at every station I arranged that our people could park in the staff lot.

The technical and logistical problem I faced was sampling officers from the active duty roster in ways that would protect the anonymity of respondents. Outsiders like me would never be allowed to lay hands on (actually, stroke the keys of) the department's personnel management software,

and I had to select respondents without knowing who they were. After talking about the task for more than an hour with a helpful sergeant in our test district, here is what we came up with. Each contact person was to generate an Excel spreadsheet listing every district police officer and sergeant, after sorting them by their watch number (into day, evening, and overnight shifts). Then they were to number the names on the list from top to bottom, beginning with "1." They would save this spreadsheet, make a copy of it, and then delete the officers' names from the copy. The copy was e-mailed to me, and at my end we randomly sampled an appropriate number of officers from each shift and mark those who were to be in the sample. On receiving this, our local contact was to match it to the original list that included officers' names, thus identifying (to them) those falling in the sample. The final step was to notify each sampled officer of their opportunity to participate. In some stations our contact could put a postcard-sized announcement in their mail slot. It listed the days and times that our representatives would be at the station and encouraged them to participate. But many stations do not have mail-slot facilities, so there our contact had to figure out how to get invitations passed on to individual officers as they came and went from roll calls.

One downside to this procedure was that our contacts knew who was in the sample. But since *someone* had to know in order to contact prospective respondents, it seemed best that this knowledge stayed in-house. Another plus was that, because the sample was selected locally by a station-house regular, we were able to forestall suspicion that somehow "downtown" had selected their favorite officers or that officers were being individually spied upon. A final subject protection was that our contact person by and large had no way of knowing which of the invited officers chose to actually show up and complete the survey. This was taking place across multiple days and shifts and generally out of view.

Encouraging sampled officers to turn out was our second "sell job." They could not be required to participate; this is a human subject's ethical no–no. We began the promotional campaign by having survey "sales representatives" appear at roll calls to describe the upcoming survey and answer officer's questions about it. Like the survey itself, we had to do this across shifts and days of the week in order to reach our target population. As we approached each district's start date, we hung large and colorful promotional posters in the lunch room and other back-office locations. The poster is reproduced here; smaller versions were also passed around as flyers.

Once the survey began, our representatives appeared multiple times on several different days of the week, on each shift. The officers who fol-

lowed the schedule on their invitation card and appeared were ushered into the survey room where they could select a laptop to work on. As our promotional poster promised, coffee and donuts were on hand for all respondents. The introductory screen on their laptop offered respondents a brief primer on how to go through the pages, enter their answers, skip questions they did not want to answer, and change mistakes. The practice question was "Do you have a dog?" The representatives continue to revisit a station until we completed interviews with a pre-established number of respondents there.

The Results

How did the survey actually go? It was mixed. We first conducted a pilot of the entire operation in one police district. Based on that, we lowered our expectations. We had hoped that 50% of invited officers would choose to be surveyed, but the pilot figure was 40%, and a few districts later, we revised it downward again, to 30%. This meant that we were drawing larger and larger samples from the duty roster, to try to hit our interviewing goal.

But the sampling did not run smoothly, either. Some of our district liaisons bought into the study and worked hard on our behalf, but others could care less. In addition, not all of them were computer savvy enough to follow our detailed, step-by-step description of how to draw the lists we needed to sample from, nor were they engaged enough to take a look at the samples we provided them. Our liaisons sometimes appeared with a tub of computers only to find that no invitation postcards had been distributed and that our contact person was off for several days. In a few districts we had to just announce over the PA that we were there and invite officers to come in for an interview. We had to abandon some interviewing visits entirely because the watch commanders told us their "troops" were too busy due to a local spike in 911 calls.

In the end we completed interviews with 621 police officers (not the 880 we had hoped for) and 95 sergeants, not 220. The final response rate was about 25%, but in several shaky districts, we could not calculate a firm number because our local contact had bungled the sampling. But respondents came in good numbers from each district, and based on their personnel counts, I calculated adjustment weights for each PO and sergeant. Using them, when I run the data, the respondents are distributed across rank and district in the right proportions.

When I met with the station commanders, I promised them that I would get back with some relevant findings. I suspect they were skeptical. Academics are usually not good at doing this and find it more congenial to get to work on the scholarly article. Once I had the data straight, my first task had been to get back to the Chief of Police who had authorized it. I produced an 8-page overview of the findings, one that included a number of graphical summaries of the data and a bullet-point summary of the summary on the first page. Then I met with him and a few of his confidants to discuss their implications. The officers were particularly unhappy about the department's internal processes. Few (10%, which is few) thought that they could get promoted by working hard, for example. He was depressed, seeing the glass at best a quarter full. I was more upbeat—he was new in town, while I had seen worse in the past. At the conclusion of our meeting, he asked me to make a presentation to the 125 "exempt staff" members who run the department. I gave them a 20-min talk with lots of illustrative slides. My commanders were in the room, so I gave them a shout-out for being supportive and reminded them that this was my promised feedback. The crowd had some good questions, and the effort seemed worthwhile. Then I got to work on the scholarly article.

Data sources are found not only in current agency records but also in other places. Historians pore through documents finding relationships that make us rethink core concepts, as shown in the chapters by Nicole Rafter and Amy Farrell (by way of their expansive methodological autobiography, "Playing in the Sandbox") and by Randolph Roth (on homicide, "Getting Things Wrong Really Does Help, as Long as You Keep Trying to Get Things Right"). Gary LaFree ("Criminology, Terrorism, and Serendipity") created a new terrorism data set by combining and checking the quality of other information on the topic. And Cathy Spatz Widom ("Twists, Turns, and Tears on the Path to the Cycle of Violence") describes her efforts in putting together records and interviews that informed her research on the cycle of violence.

Criminology, Terrorism, and Serendipity

Gary LaFree

I was attending a relatively uneventful Department of Homeland Security meeting several years ago, and the keynote speakers' topic was success. I can no longer remember the speaker's name, but I do recall that the gist of his message was that three things were essential for success: (1) get good at something, (2) be smart enough to respond when something you are good at comes along, and (3) hope for good luck. I pursued a Ph.D. with the aspiration of learning how to become a respectable social scientist. I have tried to remain open to new theories, methods, and opportunities throughout my career. And of course I have always hoped for good luck.

The Origins of the Global Terrorism Database and START

I studied for my Ph.D. in the Sociology Department at Indiana University in the 1970s, a period that was the high watermark for labeling critiques of mainstream criminology, including the idea that deviance is not a quality of the acts individuals commit, but rather a consequence of the application by others of rules and sanctions to suspected "offenders." Among other things, this

G. LaFree (✉)
START Center, University of Maryland, 8400 Baltimore Avenue, Suite 250, College Park, MD 20740, USA

labeling view suggested that social surveys—a major source of data in the social sciences—might simply be repeating widespread biases and stereotypes rather than capturing important aspects of social reality. Although the IU program required all students to complete an MA based on a statistical analysis of social surveys, I found the labeling critique of survey data compelling. Responses to surveys seemed so ephemeral, depending on the characteristics of the interviewer, the social connection between the interviewer and the interviewed, the time of day, the time of year, the order of the questions, and the interviewee's presentation of self. Accordingly, I started believing that the most defensible route for criminology was for researchers to become what could be called social "archaeologists"—that is, to look for archival data left behind by others that might shed light on key questions about deviance and crime. As in archaeology, we would approach these data realizing that they are incomplete but expecting that based on interpreting the bits and pieces of this admittedly imperfect data, we could arrive at an assessment of the underlying reality. This way of thinking probably came naturally for me because my undergraduate major in history had already encouraged me to favor archival data over other sources. For the past three decades, this approach has led me to spend most of my academic career looking for, digitizing, and analyzing archival data sets on crime and violence. The discovery of one such database was a major factor

M.D. Maltz and S.K. Rice (eds.), *Envisioning Criminology: Researchers on Research as a Process of Discovery*, DOI 10.1007/978-3-319-15868-6_12, © Springer International Publishing Switzerland 2015

in the creation of the National Consortium for the Study of Terrorism and Responses to Terrorism—the START Center—which I helped create and have directed for the past 10 years.

On a cloudy afternoon in late November 2001—just 2 months after the 9/11 attacks—I rode the Washington, D.C., area metro from suburban Maryland to the offices of the Pinkerton Global Intelligence Service (PGIS), located in a modern office complex in Northern Virginia. A graduate student at the University of Maryland who had served in the military told me that PGIS had been collecting data on terrorist attacks around the world for nearly three decades in order to provide risk assessments for their corporate clients and that they might be willing to share this information with a university researcher. The PGIS data appealed to me because it was a large archive on terrorist attacks and I had spent much of my time examining databases that contained information on violent deeds: homicides, robberies, and rapes. I explained to administrators at PGIS that I was a university professor and that I thought many in the research community would be interested in the data on terrorism that had been collected by PGIS. Apparently I was convincing because the administrators agreed to let me transport the original PGIS data—over 50 storage boxes of event records handwritten or typed on 5×7 index cards—to the University of Maryland for analysis.

I quickly learned that starting in the late 1960s, a small cottage industry had sprung up comprised of individuals and companies in several countries (especially the United States and the United Kingdom) collecting data on terrorist attacks from unclassified media sources. Many of those collecting data on terrorism in the early days of event databases had armed forces backgrounds, and many had worked for military intelligence before starting new careers as terrorism data collectors in the private sector. What was especially unique about the PGIS effort was that they collected information not only on international terrorism—which was also being done by a half dozen other companies—but also on domestic attacks. This turned out to be critical because we

later learned that domestic attacks outnumber international attacks by as much as 10 to 1.

So, barely 2 months after 9/11, I found myself in possession of what appeared to be the most comprehensive, unclassified database on terrorist attacks in the world. At this point I figured that if I can't get funding to code and analyze an extensive set of terrorism data shortly after 9/11, I had better retire early! But in fact finding funds to do the study turned out to be challenging. The Department of Homeland Security did not open its doors until March 1, 2003, and even after it was open for business, social science research was not at the top of its agenda. At the time, the National Institute of Justice (NIJ), a major source of funding support for me in the past, had sponsored very little research on terrorism. So, I enlisted the help of my colleague Laura Dugan, also at the University of Maryland, and together we received a small but strategic grant from the National Consortium for Violence Research (being led by Al Blumstein and Rick Rosenfeld) to explore innovative methods for the collection and analysis of terrorism data. And shortly after, Laura and I were successful in obtaining a grant from NIJ to digitize and begin to analyze the PGIS data.

My analysis plan at this stage was quite simple. I had been working for several years on compiling data on international homicide based on UN World Health Organization data which included homicides in its very long catalog of causes of death. I thought that I could use the same methods to examine cross-national data on terrorist attacks that I had been using to study cross-national data on homicides. This of course turned out to be a wildly optimistic assumption!

While large by NIJ standards, the grant Laura and I received was not nearly large enough to allow us to record and fully investigate the approximately 60,000 records that PGIS had collected between 1970 and 1997—let alone gather additional data. But a significant new opportunity surfaced in early 2004 when the US Department of Homeland Security announced a major national competition for a "Center of Excellence" that would be focused on the human causes and consequences of terrorism. In truth, at this point I was primarily interested in finding a few hundred thousand dollars to continue my own project with Laura rather than $12 million dollars to set up a major new social science research center. The proposal group that I led eventually included some 30 universities from around the United States and several other countries. After prevailing over a field of other university teams, including a demanding 2-day site visit, the START Center was born on January 1, 2005.

To announce the award, the Department of Homeland Security Secretary Tom Ridge brought an entourage to the University of Maryland to introduce this new center that would focus on social and behavioral science research on terrorism. After listening to the speeches and escorting the guests back to their cars, I remember returning to my office in the Criminology Department to find 40 or 50 messages from the media asking questions about my plans for the new center. My email traffic also skyrocketed. I began to realize that these developments were going to have a major impact on my life. A few months later, Mel Bernstein, the first Director of the Office of University Programs at DHS, summed it up nicely when he told me and the other three professors who were running the first of these centers at the time to "watch out what you wish for."

The Role of Criminology at START

The team that I assembled for the proposal that became the START Center was highly interdisciplinary, including not only criminologists, but anthropologists, computer scientists, engineers, geographers, political scientists, psychologists, sociologists, and others. In fact, one of the hallmarks of our team's grant submission was the idea that research on terrorism could progress most rapidly by taking advantage of theories and methods from other disciplines with obvious relevance for understanding terrorism. Thus, we assumed that knowing something about organized crime and gangs might tell us something about terrorism; that difficulties first responders face in reacting to major weather events might help us understand their problems in responding to major terrorist attacks.

To me the idea that explaining terrorism and the legal processing of terrorism should be a part of criminology was obvious. Edwin Sutherland's classic definition of criminology as the study of "…the breaking of laws and reactions to the breaking of laws" unambiguously encompasses terrorist attacks (Sutherland & Cressey, 1978: 3). Indeed, Clarke and Newman (2006: vii) have stated directly that "terrorism is a form of crime in all essential respects" and predict that terrorist attacks will cluster in time and space in the same way as more ordinary crimes. Rosenfeld (2004) argued that criminology theories are highly relevant to terrorism, and in recent years a growing number of researchers have begun to apply criminological theories to the understanding of terrorism. Criminal events share many characteristics with terrorist events. Both can be counted, both exhibit nonrandom temporal and spatial patterns, and I strongly assumed that both were likely to be associated with characteristics of offenders, targets, and situations. I figured that because much criminological research emphasizes the understanding of crime patterns across spatial and temporal dimensions, research methods commonly used in criminology should be highly relevant in the study of terrorism. There are also obvious forensic similarities: the same methods used for crime scene investigation are likely to be useful for investigating terrorist attacks.

However, I quickly learned that not all criminologists agreed with this assessment. Indeed, I remember presenting a paper on terrorism research in the early 2000s at a workshop that mostly included established criminologists and found that only about half of those in the room during my presentation raised their hands when I asked them whether they thought terrorism should be included as a standard topic in criminological research. It is true that there are clear differences between terrorism and more common types of crime. Terrorist attacks often constitute multiple crimes (e.g., murder, kidnapping, extortion); compared to common crimes, responses to terrorism are less likely to be local; and most terrorists, unlike most common criminals, view themselves as altruists. But on the other hand, both are disproportionately committed by young men, both exhibit major differences between how laws governing the illegal behavior are written and applied, and both can undermine social legitimacy of communities and institutions.

The Problem of Data in the Study of Terrorism

With some notable exceptions before 2001, there were few criminologists studying terrorism. In their encyclopedic review of terrorism, historians Schmid and Jongman (1988: 177) identified more than 6,000 published works but pointed out that much of the research is "impressionistic, superficial (and offers) … far-reaching generalizations on the basis of episodal evidence." More recently, psychologist Andrew Silke (2003) concluded that only 3% of articles in terrorism journals used statistical analysis compared to 86% in forensic psychology and 60% in criminology. Similarly, criminologists Lum, Kennedy, and Sherley (2006) reviewed over 14,000 terrorism articles published between 1971 and 2003 and found that only 3% were based on quantitative analysis.

One of the major challenges facing those interested in studying terrorism was the difficulty of collecting valid data. Data on illegal violence in criminology has come traditionally from three sources, corresponding to the major social roles connected to criminal events: "official" data collected by legal agents, especially the police, "victimization" data collected from the general population of victims and non-victims, and "self-report" data collected from offenders. Victimization surveys have been of little use in the study of terrorism. Despite the attention it gets in the global media, terrorism is much rarer than more ordinary types of violent crime. This means that even with extremely large sample sizes, few individuals in most countries will have been victimized by terrorists. Moreover, because victims of terrorism are often chosen at random, they are unlikely to know the perpetrators, making it impossible to produce details about offenders. And finally, in many cases, victims of terrorism are killed by their attackers, making it impossible for them to share their experiences. For all these reasons, terrorism data that relies on the reports of victims is likely to be of limited use.

Self-reported data, where researchers collect information about terrorist acts told by those who committed those acts, have been more fruitful than victimization data, but they also face serious limitations. Most active terrorists are obviously unwilling to participate in interviews. And even if willing to participate, getting access to known terrorists for research purposes raises evident logistical challenges. As terrorism researcher Ariel Merari (1991: 88) explains it, "The clandestine nature of terrorist organizations and the ways and means by which intelligence can be obtained will rarely enable data collection which meets commonly accepted academic standards." And again, data that rely exclusively on the accounts of perpetrators, even when available, are likely to be biased and incomplete.

Although governments in some countries do collect official data on terrorism (e.g., the US State Department, the Israeli Security Agency), data collected by governments are regarded with suspicion by many, either because they are influenced by political considerations or because of the fear that they might be so influenced. Moreover, while vast amounts of detailed official data on common crimes are routinely produced in most countries by the various components of the criminal justice system, this is rarely the case for terrorism. For example, the majority of offenders suspected of terrorism aimed at US citizens are not legally processed for terrorism-specific charges, but rather for other related offenses, such as weapon violations and money laundering (Smith, Damphousse, Jackson, & Sellers, 2002). Thus, Dzhokhar Tsarnaev, the surviving bomber in the 2013 Boston Marathon bombing case, has been charged not with terrorism but with one count of using and conspiring to use an improvised explosive device and one count of malicious destruction of property by means of an explosive device resulting in death. Finally, much primary data collected by officials working for intelligence agencies are simply not available to researchers working in an unclassified environment.

In response to the limitations of victimization, self-report, and official data on terrorism, for nearly half a century, researchers have relied on open-source unclassified terrorist event data. Terrorism event databases generally use news reports from electronic and print media to collect detailed information on the characteristics of attacks. These are then assembled into files that can be analyzed. From a research standpoint, the four most important event databases to the present have been the International Terrorism: Attributes of Terrorist Events (ITERATE) database, which began coverage in 1968 and has been periodically updated through 2009 (Mickolus, Sandler, Murdock, & Flemming, 2010), various data collection efforts by the RAND Corporation also going back to 1968 (Hoffman & Hoffman, 1995), the Worldwide Incidents Tracking System (WITS) data collected by the National Counterterrorism Center (Wigle, 2010: 5), and our Global Terrorism Database, which began with an updated version of the PGIS data from 1970 to 1997 and is now collected by a team at the START Center. While ITERATE and the RAND data have been very influential, ITERATE has never collected data on domestic terrorism cases and RAND only began doing so in 1998. WITS was a very comprehensive effort, but it only lasted from 2004 to 2011. This leaves the GTD as the longest running, most comprehensive of the existing event databases, including more than 120,000 cases from 1970 to 2013 when this chapter was being prepared. In the next section I consider some of the major strengths and weaknesses of the GTD and other event databases.

Strengths and Weaknesses of Terrorism Event Databases

Not surprisingly, terrorism event databases have serious limitations. The media may report inaccuracies and lies; there may be conflicting information or false, multiple, or no claims of responsibility for attacks. Because they rely on news sources, it is generally impossible to know the extent to which reported events reflect real outcomes or the freedom of the press in a particular country or region. Government censorship and disinformation may also affect results. When closed societies like North Korea, Sudan, or Myanmar report extremely low terrorism rates, we cannot say for sure whether it is because of an actual low incidence of attacks or the ability of these societies to minimize coverage by the print or electronic media. It seems incontrovertible that news sources will be more likely to report more serious than less serious attacks. The extent to which countries are covered by the international press also varies by region and over time. Data collection efforts have no doubt been biased toward coverage of English language sources. And to the extent that newspaper and electronic media are not archived, availability of original sources may erode over time, causing underreporting or missing data. This is likely to be especially problematic for small, regional, and local newspapers.

But despite these considerable limitations, compared to more traditional data options or even compared to crime data in general, event databases have important advantages. In particular, there is good reason to believe that the compelling interest that terrorist groups have in media attention makes open-source information uniquely useful in the study of terrorism. Unlike virtually all common criminals, terrorists actively seek media attention. Emphasizing this characteristic of terrorism, Brian Jenkins (1975) famously declared that "terrorism is theatre" and explained how "terrorist attacks are often carefully choreographed to attract the attention of the electronic media and the international press." The media are so central to contemporary terrorist groups that some researchers and policy makers have argued that the birth of modern terrorism is directly linked to the launch by the United States of the first television satellite in 1968. The fact that many terrorists are specifically seeking to attract attention through the media means that compared to media coverage of more common crimes, coverage of terrorism can tell us far more. Thus, while no responsible researcher would seriously suggest tracking burglary or fraud rates by studying electronic and print media, it is much more defensible to track terrorist attacks in this way. It seems a safe supposition to assume that in the massively interconnected world in which we live, it is becoming increasingly difficult for an aerial hijacking or a politically motivated assassination—even in remote parts of the world—to elude entirely the watchful eye of the global media.

And because of the importance of publicity to terrorists, event databases on terrorism also have another important advantage: one of the most serious limitations of cross-national crime research is that it has been focused overwhelmingly on a small number of highly industrialized Western-style democracies. For example, reviews of cross-national research on homicide show that most prior research has been based on fewer than 40 of the world's countries. And of course these countries are not a random sample of the nations of the world but rather strongly overrepresent Europe and North America while almost entirely excluding countries of Africa, the Middle East, and Asia. By contrast, open-source terrorism databases offer at least some coverage for all countries. While it is the case that traditional media underreport news stemming from developing countries or in highly autocratic states, the salience of terrorism as a phenomenon today makes it more likely than ever that media will report such incidents as information becomes available.

In sum, open-source event databases have important limitations. But to be clear, so do all crime databases. For example, official data sources like the Uniform Crime Reports have long been criticized for many of the same issues as those outlined above for event databases (e.g., O'Brien, 1985). Victimization surveys and self-report interviews with current or former terrorists also face major limitations as a source for estimating total rates. The bottom line is that despite their drawbacks, there is no obvious alternative to event databases for those interested in tracking terrorism.

Then and Now

To collect the original data from 1970 to 1997, PGIS trained researchers to identify and record terrorism incidents from wire services (especially Reuters and the Foreign Broadcast Information Service [FBIS]), US State Department reports, other US and foreign government reports, and US and foreign newspapers (e.g., the *New York Times*, the *British Financial Times*). The current collection of the GTD relies entirely on unclassified sources, primarily electronic media articles, to identify terrorist attacks and systematically record details of the attacks (Miller, 2013). At present, this process begins with a universe of over one million articles published daily worldwide, in order to identify the relatively small subset of articles that describe terrorist attacks. We accomplish this using customized search strings to isolate an initial pool of potentially relevant articles, followed by more sophisticated techniques to further refine the search results. By using sources that translate stories into English, we now cover news stories in 80 different languages. In order to maximize the efficiency of the data collection process, we use natural language processing techniques to identify and remove duplicate source articles by measuring similarities between pairs of documents. In addition, we have developed a machine-learning model using feedback from trained GTD coders that classifies the remaining documents in terms of how likely they are to be relevant to terrorism. This model is continuously refined using input from the research team regarding the accuracy of the classification results. To facilitate this iterative process, we have developed a web-based interface that our research team uses to provide feedback to the system through their review of the source documents and identification of false positives (media sources that appear to be about terrorist attacks but are not) and false negatives (media sources that appear not to be terrorist attacks but are).

Our workflow for identifying and coding unique terrorism events leverages the same interface. The GTD team reviews all the sources that have been classified as relevant by the machine-learning model and generates database entries for individual attacks that satisfy the GTD inclusion criteria. We facilitate this process by clustering similar documents together based on key identifying features of the text. In addition, as the set of identified incidents expands, we use this information to supply coders with details of already created events or related sources that are potential matches for a given attack under review. At present, 10,000–15,000 articles are manually reviewed, and 900–1,200 attacks are identified and coded for each month of data collection. Once the attacks have been identified, domain-specific coding teams record data on over 120 variables pertaining to the location, perpetrators, targets, weapons, tactics, casualties, and consequences of each attack, according to the specifications of the GTD Codebook.

We welcome you to take a look at the data yourself by going to our website: www.start. umd.edu/gtd. You can search the database for specific terms or browse the data by date, region, country, perpetrator, or weapon, target, or tactic type. You can also click on the GTD Data Visualization program to see how terrorist attacks (at least, the ones we are aware of) are distributed around the world or in specific countries or regions. On the top of the page, you can find more information about the GTD, how to use the database, and some commonly asked questions about the data. There is also a link to the START home page that includes a wealth of related information.

The Importance of Good Luck

In the 10 years since the START Center opened its doors, we have generated more than $60 million in research funding. We have developed a consortium that includes dozens of faculty and hundreds of students. The Global Terrorism Database is now used by the US State Department as its unclassified source of data on terrorism (START Center, 2013). There were nearly 1.2 million web visits to the GTD in 2013. In the same year the complete database was downloaded more than 3,800 times in 49 US states and more than 100 countries. Also in 2013, the START website received over 27.2 million page views with users from nearly every country in the world. In the same year START's website was visited by over 1,700 educational institutions and 880 government agencies.

In describing the origins of the START Center, I am reminded of the well-known proverb that begins "for want of a nail the shoe was lost" and after a long series of if-then statements concludes with "for want of a battle the kingdom was lost." If I had not accidentally run into a graduate student who had contacts at PGIS, I would never have known about their database; if they had not accidentally been in the process of shedding this part of their work product, they would never have allowed me to have the data; if I had not been looking for a way to code and analyze the GTD, I would never have sought research funding for the START Center; and without the START Center, the GTD project as well as 70 or 80 other research projects would either have been quite different or would never have happened at all. As the unidentified keynote speaker from DHS pointed out in the speech I mentioned in opening, there is no substitute for good luck.

References

Clarke, R. V., & Newman, G. R. (2006). *Outsmarting the terrorists*. Westport, CT: Greenwood.

Hoffman, B., & Hoffman, D. K. (1995). The RAND-St. Andrews Chronology of international terrorism incidents. *Terrorism and Political Violence, 7*, 78–229.

Jenkins, B. M. (1975). International terrorism: A new model of conflict. In D. Carlton & C. Schaerf (Eds.), *International terrorism and world security*. London, UK: Croom Helm.

Lum, C., Kennedy, L., & Sherley, A. (2006). Are counter-terrorism strategies effective? The results of the Campbell systematic review on counter-terrorism evaluation research. *Journal of Experimental Criminology, 2*, 489–516.

Merari, A. (1991). Academic research and government policy on terrorism. *Terrorism and Political Violence, 3*, 88–102.

Mickolus, E. F., Sandler, T., Murdock, J. M., & Flemming, P. (2010). *International terrorism: Attributes of terrorist events (ITERATE)*. Dunn Loring, VA: Vinyard Software.

Miller, E. (2013, August 31). *Global terrorism database: Collection and coding* (Report to the Office of University Programs, Science and Technology Directorate). Washington, DC: US Department of Homeland Security.

O'Brien, R. (1985). *Crime and victimization*. Beverly Hills, CA: Sage.

Rosenfeld, R. (2004). Terrorism and criminology. In M. Deflem (Ed.), *Terrorism and counter-terrorism: Criminological perspectives* (pp. 19–32). New York, NY: Elsevier.

Schmid, A. P., & Jongman, A. J. (1988). *Political terrorism: A new guide to actors, authors, concepts, databases, theories and literature.* Amsterdam, The Netherlands: North-Holland.

Silke, A. (2003). Becoming a terrorist. In A. Silke (Ed.), *Terrorists, victims and society: Psychological perspectives on terrorism and its consequences* (pp. 29–54). West Sussex, England: Wiley.

Smith, B. L., Damphousse, K. R., Jackson, F., & Sellers, A. (2002). The prosecution and punishment of international terrorists in federal courts: 1980-1998. *Criminology & Public Policy, 1,* 311–338.

START Center. (2013). *Annex of statistical information: Country reports on terrorism 2012* (pp. 263–274). Washington, DC: US Department of State.

Sutherland, E. H., & Cressey, D. R. (1978). *Criminology* (10th ed.). Philadelphia, PA: Lippincott.

Wigle, J. (2010). Introducing the Worldwide Incidents Tracking System (WITS). *Perspectives on Terrorism, 4,* 3–23.

Playing in the Sandbox:
A Methodological Conversation

Nicole Rafter and Amy Farrell

When Michael Maltz invited me to contribute a methodological autobiography to this volume, I turned for help to Amy Farrell, whom I knew first as a graduate student (I chaired her dissertation committee) and now as a colleague (we teach in the same department). Amy is a topnotch methodologist, and I knew she would be able to help me figure out whether I did, indeed, have a methodological autobiography. We conducted four open-ended interviews structured around an academic life history. We transcribed the interviews and condensed those four interviews into this edited piece.—NR

* * * *

AF: It is probably best to do this as a life history piece—a methodological life history. Could you talk a little about your decision to go to graduate school and study criminal justice?

Background and Training

NR: I was living in the Berkshires with two little kids, teaching college English part-time, and I found myself teaching more and more courses with titles like "Crime and Punishment." One day at a faculty meeting the dean said, "Enrollments are down so

I will have to let go of all the part-timers; but they are all women and don't need to work anyway." I was angry but didn't yet have the language to explain why. This was the very early 1970s. But I thought "To hell with it, I'll go to graduate school in criminal justice." Sometimes people ask "Why did you go into that field?" and I say, "It must be genetic," but I was very attracted to the social class issues that even I, in my untutored way, could see in the field of criminology.

But I didn't know what to do next. I wrote to different schools for packets of information and got something from the University of Connecticut—where Albert Cohen used to teach. I saw his courses and his name. I had no idea who Albert Cohen was but liked the kinds of courses he was teaching. So I wrote to him, "Dear Albert Cohen, please give me advice about where I should go to graduate school"—something like that. He didn't answer for a long time. He had been on a sabbatical in Israel. Finally my letter made its way to him and he wrote back; I wish I had kept the letter—it was so sweet, giving me lots of advice. By then I had found out that one of the top schools in criminal justice—at SUNY Albany—was practically in my backyard, just an hour-and-a-half away.

I applied, got in, and got a research assistantship. I really loved it. It was a strange time for a woman to be in criminal justice because everything was highly gendered. People would sort of pat me on the head and say, "Isn't it nice that you

N. Rafter (✉) • A. Farrell
Northeastern University, Boston, MA, USA
e-mail: nicolerafter@yahoo.com

M.D. Maltz and S.K. Rice (eds.), *Envisioning Criminology: Researchers on Research as a Process of Discovery*, DOI 10.1007/978-3-319-15868-6_13, © Springer International Publishing Switzerland 2015

are going to work with juvenile delinquents, dear." As a result, I swore I would never take a course in juvenile delinquency, and I never did. And stupidly, in my annoyance, I swore I would specialize in men's maximum security prisons, which is what I did for a while. I took a lot of courses in prisons which were about men.

AF: So criminal justice wasn't seen as an area for women to specialize in? Again, a pat on the head, but we don't really expect you to be a scholar?

NR: Yes, but nobody used those words. I had one female teacher, Marguerite Warren. One day I went to the dean and said, "Would you please hire more women instructors?" and he replied, "What a strange question! When I went to Harvard Law School, I never asked myself whether the teachers were men or women."

AF: Privilege makes you not question things right? So you were interested in studying prisons because it was less feminine? A rejection of the notion of working with kids?

NR: That's right. I took a lot of courses with Don Newman, who chaired my dissertation committee. He was a delightful man but hard for me to relate to. When I was doing my dissertation research, I went to him and said, "In the annual reports of Sing Sing in the nineteenth century, there are Matron's Reports, and it is obvious that women were held there too. Can you explain this to me?" Don roared, "How the hell should I know?" I now understand that he had no reason to read these reports, but the roar took me aback.

My dissertation was on the history of the defective delinquency movement. I guess you want to know why I picked such an odd topic. I get interested in things for reasons I don't fully understand. The criminal justice school at SUNY Albany had a little library with several thousand books. One was the first history of eugenics, by Mark Haller. On one of its opening pages I saw the term "defective delinquents." I was amazed by the term and wondered how anybody could think that up. I knew there was a story there, and

that led me to eugenics. New York, as it turned out, had passed one of the first eugenic prison laws—to hold prisoners for life if they were found to be "feeble-minded"—and all the records were in the state archives.

I had a great time doing my dissertation, but I kept coming across those Matron's Reports. I told myself, "When I get out of here, I will try to find out something about early women prisoners."

AF: Were you interested in historical questions, the historical trajectory?

NR: Yes, Graeme Newman, who is still at SUNY-Albany, included historical materials in his courses. But even before that, I was interested in history. I can remember as a very little girl going to Westminster Abbey. My mother is English so we went to England after the Second World War. I loved to walk around the rooms—you could roam freely then—and try to imagine what had gone on in them. But I had never read history.

AF: Yet, people would say you are one of the top historical criminologists. So, you didn't have formal training in history but you always had an interest in history, maybe as a paradigm of thinking?

NR: Yes, but I don't think I realized that until now.

AF: When you were taking prison classes, what drove you to the archives, wanting to go back in history?

NR: Reading those words "defective delinquent" in Mark Haller's book; and then I started reading more about the eugenics movement. Once I got to the New York State Archives, I felt, This is where I belong for my whole life. Many years later, I got a fellowship to return to the New York State Archives to look at the records from the units that had held defective delinquents.

AF: Is it the hunt that is interesting? The peeling back the layers to see what you would find?

NR: Yes. Even when you don't know what you are looking for, something will be on the back of an envelope or playbill, and Damn! there it is!

AF: So you left graduate school having run into the Matron's Reports and hoping someday to do something with them? But you came to Northeastern first?

Partial Justice: Women in State Prisons, 1800–1935 (1985, 1990)

NR: When I came to Northeastern, in 1977, I had not finished my dissertation. I had two little kids and a husband back in the Berkshires trying to sell our rickety house. It was a really hard transition.

At the time, the National Institute of Justice had an "unsolicited" fellowship—money for projects that they had not designated themselves. This was a very good idea because it encouraged people who had offbeat ideas to apply. I wrote a proposal to study the history of women in prisons; this would be 1978. They gave me the grant, but about 10 days later, they took it away. I found out why: Senator [William] Proxmire, who used to give an annual Golden Fleece Award, had the year before almost given it to NIJ for supporting a historical study of Boston courts. Somehow NIJ held him off, but they swore they wouldn't fund another historical project.

NIJ gave me a chance to revise my proposal. Robert, my husband, who is such a mensch, and I were supposed to go to Provincetown—we'd gotten a sitter for the kids and were going to have a weekend to ourselves. I said, "I have to take along the typewriter and rewrite this proposal." Robert said, "Sure we can do that." I wrote a new proposal titled something like "Problems in the Women's Prison System: Origins and Development." I only had to rewrite the first 10 pages; the methodology was the same. NIJ gave me back the grant! I had an office downtown with two graduate students.

AF: Oh, you didn't have an office on campus?

NR: Northeastern didn't have room for me. I found a space in Copley Square—not the safest place at that time. I'd put a sign in the window that said something like Center for the Study of Women's Prisons, and ex-cons wandered in wanting to know more about that.

AF: So you had two graduate students

NR: Yes. They did the state-by-state research on the women's institutions, using runs of prison reports in the State House.

AF: And you did the archival prisoner research in your selected states?

NR: I did. At the time I was naïve about how I was going to go to (for example) Tennessee for 2 weeks when I had small children.

I had 10 days to work with the archival records of each prison. I had never seen the records I was going to use, so I began by trying to assess the raw number of cases I had to deal with and the length of time it would take me to record a single case on a form I had designed.

AF: Did they have a record for each inmate?

NR: For the early years, the women's names were just listed among the men's names in big prisoner registries; I had to pick them out. For later years, there was usually a separate record on each female inmate and these were collected in one spot. After I assessed the total number of female cases, I did a few practice cases, filling out my forms with information from the registry or case file. Let's say I could cover a single case in 20 minutes. I could then figure out how many records I could cover in 10 days.

AF: So that was your sample, how many you had and how many you could get done in the allotted time.

NR: Then I would randomly pick the first one, and if I had a skip interval of, say, 20, pick the 20th female case after the first one. But for the very early years, when the women's names were in the big ledgers, I covered every case. I was very interested in how those early state prisoners fared in men's institutions.

AF: What were you interested in knowing from the individual cases—their experience as female inmates?

NR: Yes, and I also wanted to understand racial and regional differences. I wanted to see if there were different models for how women were incarcerated. I also wanted to see if there were differences in conditions between men and women. Once or twice, I coded records in a room from which I could see where the women's unit had been. I could imagine what it would have been like to bring food in and out, for instance.

AF: Kind of like what you did in Westminster Abbey.

NR: Yes

AF: There was something about the physical space that was important and helped you recreate what it would have been like.

NR: Yes, and I loved that. I hadn't had any courses in methodology. After Stat I, I had managed to wiggle out of the requirements, or maybe there wasn't a requirement for Stat II. I am very good at wiggling out of requirements. As an undergraduate, the same thing. I now wish I could take your method courses. I was naïve and untutored back then.

The hardest part wasn't figuring out a methodology but doing field work in a strange city, on the cheap. In Nashville, I put myself up at a really horrible motel in the downtown, near the archives. I didn't want to be walking out in the empty streets at night to find food, so I lived off the motel's vending machines. Worrying about my kids. I probably put too much stress on myself.

AF: It is hard to do that type of field work.

NR: Yes, and lonely too. Thank god for archivists who took me under their wing, who asked me, "You want to come to dinner?" People were nice. Except for the archivist guy who just said, "You want to come home with me?"

AF: So you came back and wrote this up as *Partial Justice*.

NR: Yes. I can't believe how naïve I was. Originally I wrote 48 state narratives. Done! But then I thought, "That is very boring to read. I have to do this regionally." So I went back and kept reworking the material. My friend Nicolette Parisi took the data forms, coded them, and printed out the results—several hundred tables. I thought, "Oh, you just put the tables in the text." John Laub was here at Northeastern

by then, and he said, "I don't know if there is a rule, but you probably should not have more tables than pages of text." So I cut some tables.

AF: How did you know you wanted to make this into a book?

NR: I just took it for granted that that was what I was going to do.

AF: So how did you then decide about where to publish or who to publish with?

NR: Oh, what an awful problem that was! I went to a conference where the University of California Press was represented. There was a tall, elegant, UC editor; I told her about my book, and she said in the most condescending voice, "Oh, we wouldn't publish anything like *that*." I felt so bad that I couldn't approach anybody else. But Northeastern had a new press at that time, and I had been assigned as college liaison to it, so I submitted the manuscript to them. I did a couple of books with them.

AF: Did you have a sense of how groundbreaking or how important the historical work was?

NR: I didn't think it was groundbreaking or important.

AF: In retrospect do you see it?

NR: That question is hard for me. I thought I was doing something no one else did because it wasn't important. I was sort of off in the corner playing in the sandbox.

AF: I like your "off in the corner playing in the sandbox" idea.

NR: Maybe that is the title for this chapter.

You know who else was doing criminal justice history? Mary Gibson. I used to go to the Social Science History meetings, where there were good scholars doing qualitative and quantitative work within criminal justice. These meetings were always in November, so there was a clash with the ASC meetings and I didn't go often, but I did meet Mary. That was an important contact for me. Here was a woman, a feminist, who could sit down at the table with the big guys and talk about research in criminal justice.

AF: And she was a historian.

NR: Yes.

AF: So did she become a mentor or a colleague for you?

NR: A colleague. We did the Lombroso translations together.

Creating Born Criminals (1997)

AF: After *Partial Justice*, did you want to stay with work on women?

NR: I wanted to, very much, but I also wanted to turn my dissertation into a book. It was published as *Creating Born Criminals*, near the start of my other work on the history of biological theories of crime. I liked writing that book because I could set it up as a sort of narrative. It had a good guy and a bad guy, and I really fell in love with the good guy. Unfortunately, he died in the 1880s so we couldn't take it too far.

AF: What did you like about the good guy/bad guy?

NR: The good guy was a tragic figure. He was the first person who undertook to educate what he called idiots—people we would now say have mental disabilities. His name was Hervey Backus Wilbur. Dr. Wilbur was the first person to treat "idiots" with respect; he was sure he could cure them of their disabilities. At first he was successful: there was a kind of halo effect, the children lived in his home, and probably they were not severely disabled in the first place. They were kids who could be trained to exhibit normal behaviors.

But Dr. Wilbur, in the later part of his life, was forced to start a eugenics institution—the opposite of everything he ever wanted for people with disabilities. It was called the Newark Custodial Asylum for Feeble-Minded Women of a Child-bearing Age. He thought it was a terrible thing, to lock up "feeble-minded" women to prevent them from reproducing. But the State Board of Charities forced him to do it. The bad guy was Isaac Kerlin, who criminalized people with mental disabilities. So I paired them off. I had an introductory chapter; I think I must have rewritten it maybe 80 times, and then I threw it away. I've always wished I kept it.

AF: Was it a methods chapter?

NR: It was theoretical. But I felt it was boring and would keep readers from getting into the story. The first person to comment on the book was Neal Shover, and he said, "I read your new book but you don't have any theory in it." I had hoped that the theory would reveal itself slowly. I wish someone would ask me to do a second edition so I could add a few pages at the front. I would explain that *Creating Born Criminals* examines how, in the late nineteenth- and early twentieth-centuries, mentally disabled people were constructed as criminals and criminals were constructed as mentally disabled. For eugenicists, the equation went in both directions.

AF: For you, was the research question about that constructionist process?

NR: Yes, it was—about how the born criminals were created.

AF: This historical method—what made you choose it? That's what you've always done, but what do you think are the benefits of this particular type of inquiry?

NR: The value is twofold. First, at the time—the 1990s—a lot of people were doing institutional history, but no one was looking at institutions for people with intellectual disabilities; these people were really marginalized in all ways.[1] The second value lies in what we can learn about constructionist processes by studying the history of institutions for people with intellectual disabilities.

AF: You have many different areas of inquiry, but they all have used a very similar sort of methodology. You have this method down, of doing the historical work. You may have varied it a bit every time, but I'm wondering where the idea comes from. Do you see something in history that you want to understand, or do you see something in the

---

[1] James W. Trent later wrote a wonderful book on this: *Inventing the Feeble Mind: A History of Mental Retardation in the United States* (University of California Press, 1995).

modern context that you want to understand through its historical background? I'm wondering where the original question comes from? Not where finding the answer comes from, but where the original questions come from.

NR: I'm not sure, but I do see themes that persist in my work from the beginning. For example, take mental disabilities. I'm *still* working on that topic with my genocide book today. My sample includes people who were killed by Hitler because they were mentally disabled.

AF: You got sparked in your dissertation work on defective delinquents, and then you found key players along the way that made you want to peel back the layers further?

NR: I think a connective link is my interest in people who are neglected. You could read 50 books about the Holocaust, and you'd never find out there was this whole population that Hitler planned to kill the minute he started World War II.

AF: Then perhaps what draws the gender work and the work on the defective delinquents together is this interest in neglected populations.

NR: Overlooked populations. Ways in which social control systems react to marginalized populations.

AF: As a methodologist, I always think the questions drive the method. You apply the similar method to different questions. Those questions are framed in the same way because they require the same kind of method. So I'm interested in the parallels across the questions.

NR: I see the parallels in retrospect—you're drawing them out. I develop case studies and then compare them. But it seems to me that often I allow the questions to evolve from the research that engages me.

AF: What I know about you is that you get something that makes you passionate, and then you do more reading on that subject than anyone I have ever known. You're drawn by something that intrigues you,

then you want to know everything that there is to know about that. Where does that passion come from?

NR: Did I tell you about what the word "enthusiasm" means?

AF: No.

NR: It comes from Greek and means to be filled with god. Sometimes I do feel filled with a passionate spirit. Literally inspired.

Lombroso Translations (2004, 2006)

AF: Can you explain where Lombroso comes in and how your Lombroso translations relate to your earlier historical work on biological theories of crime?

NR: I told you about how I occasionally went to the SSHA meetings and met Mary Gibson. After that, she and I would sometimes—separately—write an article or book on the history of criminology, a topic that automatically leads to Lombroso. He wrote about biological theories of crime over a period of decades, and I became interested in how his ideas developed over time. Did this concept date from the end of his life or the beginning? One summer day, the thought struck me that we might be able to translate Lombroso. Mary knows Italian; as an Italian historian, she's fluent.

AF: And why did you want to translate Lombroso?

NR: To get at the chronology of his ideas. Did the born criminal concept come before or after his work on degeneration theory? So I called Mary up and said "Are you sitting down? I want to propose that we translate Lombroso together." She replied, "That's a very serious question. It will need a lot of reflection," and then, almost immediately, she said "Yes." So we both got very enthusiastic about it, and we went on to translate Cesare Lombroso's two main criminological books, *La donna delinquente* [*Criminal Woman*] and *L'uomo delinquente* [*Criminal Man*].

AF: This was a complete departure from your previous methods?

NR: Right—nobody had ever done anything like this. We had to decide first how to handle the many editions of *Criminal Man*. We knew of only one edition of *Criminal Women*, which had been partially translated into English as *The Female Offender*.

AF: And the earlier translations had covered only part of Lombroso's work, is that right?

NR: Yes, but even the parts of his work that *had* been translated were undatable. First we had to figure out how many editions *L'uomo delinquente* had gone through. Some consisted of a single volume, others of two or four volumes. So we were dealing with 11 Italian volumes covering 5 editions in all.

We decided to do *Criminal Woman* first because we thought it would be easiest. But there was no copy of the Italian version in this country, only a copy on microfilm in Yale; I had to get it printed. I began by translating, Italian dictionary in hand, part of the preface. But I didn't know then that this preface was extremely difficult to understand, even in Italian, or that Lombroso was often incoherent in his prefaces. After I had a draft—also incoherent—of this preface, I flew to New Jersey, where Mary lived, and we had a weekend to work together. I remember thinking "Oh Lord, what is she going to think of what I've got here?"

In the many years—11 in all—that we worked together on the Lombroso project, Mary never said one word that would make me feel like an idiot about not knowing Italian. She would say of a word or phrase, "I think it means this, but I'm not sure; yes, that might work." She was never condescending, always collaborative. Eventually we translated all of *Criminal Woman* and compared it to the 1893 English translation, finding a lot of telling differences between the two.

AF: And you used the microfilm copy from Yale to do all of it?

NR: We did for *La donna delinquente*; that was the only way we could get it. It was about 900 pages long. Mary skimmed it and picked out the passages to translate. We had to leave out a lot. We knew we would never get a contract for a 900-page translation; who would want to read it? Mary picked out the key passages in both books.

AF: Condensing them down?

NR: Yes. And then we developed a pattern. I would translate first, and then we'd get together and go over it. When I lived in Rome for a year, Mary happened to also be in Rome; she had a fellowship. So Mary would go and do her archival work on the other side of the Tiber in the morning; then she would walk across to our side for a late lunch with Robert and me. She and I would then work for the rest of the afternoon on the stuff I had translated that morning.

AF: Why did you go to Italy?

NR: When Robert retired, we decided that we were just going to go somewhere and have fun for a year. We picked Italy because we both wanted to learn Italian—he wanted to translate Italian poetry, and I had this Lombroso project. Mary and I did most of the work on *Criminal Man* back in the States. I didn't go to Italy because of Lombroso.

AF: And who published it?

NR: Duke University Press, which at that time had an editor who was very interested in race, and we had used the word "race" a couple of times in our proposal. Who would publish this? It was just sort of a cockamamie thing. We made a list of maybe 20 publishers we would try. Nothing worked out until this editor at Duke took an interest. And it has been good for Duke, too.

AF: They continue to sell the books?

NR: They sell the books. I was sure that if we could get a publisher, then sales would be steady, if small, because there is always going to be an interest in Lombroso. Although he too, like many of my subjects, is a sort of a marginal person, he's not marginal in criminology.

Shots in the Mirror: Crime Films and Society (2000, 2006)

AF: Where did you find yourself going after the Lombroso project? When did you start working on movies?

NR: My first movies book—*Shots in the Mirror*—began before the Lombroso translations, in a period of my life when I was pretty unhappy. Every night, going home from work, I would walk by a video store on Harvard Street and pick up a crime movie—I just needed to get away from my problems. Then one spring vacation, Robert and I went off on a holiday, and I took along a book along called *The Celluloid Closet*—a wonderful book about gays in the movies. It dawned on me that somebody could write a book about crime in the movies.[2]

AF: So *The Celluloid Closet* provided you with a sort of template? You could do that same kind of thing with crime films?

NR: It did. It made me realize you could look at movies from various points of view and use genres as case studies.

AF: And that set of work—in many ways, it's different, it's a departure from the methods that you used before. It involved less historical work?

NR: It was categorical: cop movies, court movies, prison movies, and so on. But I talked about their development.

AF: Every chapter had that trajectory to it, how that genre of film developed?

NR: That's right. So they were historical!

AF: But they didn't involve historical research in the same way.

NR: I did go back to the origins of each genre.

The Criminal Brain (2008; 2nd ed. forthcoming 2016)

AF: Were you also doing new research at this time on biological theories of crime? Were you asking new questions?

NR: I was asking new questions. When I decided to write the criminal brain book, I took on a big job because it was a history of biological theories of crime from the late

eighteenth-century onward. Fortunately I got fellowships from Oxford to work on it there. That was wonderful for my self-esteem, and it gave me access to documents like essays on phrenology from the early nineteenth-century. I wasn't using archival material there but I was using a whole lot of early published documents.

AF: What were the main questions you were trying to answer in *The Criminal Brain*, and what drove you to them?

NR: Several questions led me to the decision to write this book. First, I already knew a good deal about the history of biological theories of crime from working on *Creating Born Criminals* and the Lombroso translations. Second, I was fascinated by them. And third, I realized that biological theories were making a comeback in neuroscience and evolutionary psychology, and even on the fringes of criminology. These theories, which often imply that some people are biologically predisposed to commit crime, have tremendous potential for doing harm—for leading to bad public policy. I wanted to make their past comprehensible so readers could evaluate them properly—fairly, but with considerable caution based on the lessons of the past, such as those from the eugenics movement.

AF: Did your research on this book differ in important ways from your earlier research?

NR: In retrospect, I can see I was still categorizing types of knowledge, still treating groups of ideas—those of phrenology, for example—as a case. Subject matter aside, it wasn't too different from my first movies book. Methodologically, I was still looking for genres and then analyzing them historically.

The Crime of All Crimes (forthcoming 2016)

AF: What brought you to your current research on genocide?

NR: I got a Fulbright fellowship to teach in Linz, Austria. I was going to start on a history of

[2] Russo, V. (1987). *The celluloid closet*. Harper & Row (1st ed., 1981).

criminology, but I was so distracted by the fact that Linz had been Hitler's home town that I couldn't get started. His mother's house is still there; his school is there (grim thing that it is). He was everywhere, as were signs of the Old Fighters, the people who were National Socialists before Hitler came to power. Everywhere I turned, there were reminders of the Nazis.

Seven kilometers away was the Mauthausen concentration camp—one of the worst. It was not a death camp, but it was a camp for extermination by labor. I was transfixed by it. And then, with even more of a link to my earlier interests, down the road in the other direction, just 3 km away, was Hartheim Castle, which around 1900 had become an institution for mentally disabled people. When Hitler came to power, Hartheim became one of the six killing centers for the disabled. It had one of the first gas chambers—it's still there to see! And it became a training center for the SS and others who later went to Poland to design and run the gas chambers at Auschwitz and other death camps. So Hartheim was where they learned gassing—down the road from where I was living.

AF: All of this was sort of in your face, like was impossible to ignore?

NR: Literally in my face: Out of my apartment window I could see the balcony from which Hitler announced the Anschluss. The Nazis were inescapable, like the biggest magnet you ever saw; you couldn't help but be whammed into them. And so that's where the genocide book began.

AF: How did you get from the Nazis to your genocide book?

NR: I wanted to do something that would encourage criminologists to take genocide seriously. I thought it would do criminology a world of good if it had to look at something so big, so real, and also so diverse. I began by making a list of all the twentieth-century genocides—there were about 65 of them. Next I tried to figure out how many

genocides I could cover in a historical comparative criminological study and decided that eight was the magic number. I was quite ambitious. Comparative genocide at the time I started this book worked like this: three authors wrote about three genocides, A, B, and C, but seriatim, not all at once. One author wrote about the Nazis, another about the Cambodian genocide, and a third about a third genocide, and the editor wrote a general introduction. That's not comparative work really.

AF: Not even in the same category—it's just comparing across the divide but doing separate analyses. But why not just cover the Nazi genocide of the disabled—the genocide that drove your original interest? This need to compare across categories: where does it come from?

NR: Maybe it is a kind of psychiatric disorder—compulsive comparative criminology. I can tell you where it came from in this particular case. Several good books had already been written on the Nazi effort to exterminate the disabled, but that wasn't my primary interest in any case. I wanted to know what genocide in general looked like. I knew the Holocaust hadn't been typical, but I wondered if there was anything like a typical genocide. And I thought one way to find out would be through comparisons.

I also figured that a criminologist—me—might be prepared to do actual comparative work. But I wanted to capture the great diversity in these events. And so I took my 65 genocides and did frequencies by region over the twentieth-century. Africa had this many, South America had none, Central America had a few; you see what I mean? Using the frequencies, I selected a final sample that would be roughly representative of genocides throughout the world in the twentieth-century.

AF: And you're dealing with how many genocides in total?

NR: Eight, which I think is the biggest comparative study of genocides to date. It is a lot to handle. It's hard for me to think of eight things at once. Have you read the studies of probation and parole decision-making that find that at the most, people can only hold five or six variables in their mind at once? Eight genocides is almost too many.

AF: So you've been collecting archival records?

NR: No, I'm using only secondary sources.

AF: Things other people have written about these genocides?

NR: That's right.

AF: And then you're coding information out of that?

NR: For each genocide, I have a set of 36 questions to answer. What I had to do was to study each genocide in itself before I could begin to do the comparative work. Usually I read about 25 sources for each genocide.

AF: So you could ferret out what was the right information?

NR: I looked for various perspectives. It's very important to know the perspectives of the bad guys—the genocidists. That's one of my main conclusions. And once I felt that I could understand why they would do such a horrible thing, I felt that I was getting there with this particular genocide, getting to understand the dynamics.

Chicken or Egg?

AF: In a book on methods, one should (but often does not) learn that questions drive method. You obviously have similarities in your questions that drive you toward similar methods. Do you feel that's true?

NR: Yes.

AF: Do you feel that you begin with a method or with a question?

NR: I begin with questions because I'm usually working in the dark—I mean I've often done research on things that nobody asked about before, so I couldn't begin with methods. I had to begin with questions.

AF: How would you generally describe your methodological approach to the question that you asked?

NR: You tell me: what are my options?

AF: It seems that with many of your lines of inquiry, you begin with trying to answer the questions you've set by going back to the beginning. Like, what's the earliest thing you can find about this?—and then moving forward in a historical approach.

NR: That's true.

AF: You would try to delve as far back in the history as you can to peel that onion, and then move forward?

NR: Yes. Usually I have some idea how far back I need to go because I've been reading.

AF: Let's take the genocide project for example: Was there some period of time of reading and going back through historical work before you formulated your questions? Or did the questions come pretty quickly and then the historical reading?

NR: Living in Austria, I got to the big questions pretty quickly. Then I thought, why hasn't anybody looked at genocide from a criminological viewpoint? I began to think it would be good to encourage criminologists to look at genocide from a criminological point of view, although it took me a long time to figure out what I meant by that.

AF: And what do you mean by that?

NR: In criminology we aren't at all constrained by the legal definition of a crime but rather range all over the map with relevant questions: Who is most likely to commit this crime? To be victimized by it? Where does it occur most often? What proportion of offenders are caught? And so on. In dealing with genocide, one can look at these questions from an individual point of view— who, demographically, is most likely to engage in genocide? Some researchers are taking that tack, but I'm more interested in group-level questions, since by definition genocide is a crime of one group against people in another group. So I'm asking questions like, Which groups are most likely to commit this crime? Under what circumstances? Which groups are most likely to be victimized, and why? And so on.

AF: Is the genocide project like your research on the history of women's prisons in that both take a case-study approach?

NR: The latter used archival data, while in this case I have to use secondary data. However, in a sense I did develop my own data set because I had the 36 questions that I developed for each genocide, beginning with the antecedents of each and ending with the aftermaths. And then, say for the Armenian genocide, I read everything I could get my hands on and kept filling out the answers to my questions. I did it on the computer so some of my answers are very long. I did that for each of my genocides.

AF: So what makes it original is in a sense you've taken secondary sources and put them in a systematic format?

NR: That's right.

AF: And why did you make that decision?

NR: For one thing, I don't know the languages. I couldn't read Turkish sources for the Armenian genocide, or the Russian and Polish sources for the Katyn Forest Massacre, and so on. It was also necessary because I wanted to have a big sample and do genuinely comparative work, which I couldn't have done even if I could read Turkish sources on the Armenian genocide. I would have needed to read a minimum of 10–15 languages to do the research on these eight genocides from a variety of perspectives. And so I stuck to English.

AF: Did you use some kind of systematic process to develop the sources so that you looked at the same range of sources for each genocide?

NR: I tried to find out what the leading books were on each genocide, and the most recent books. I was very interested in feminist research. And I tried to find out if there were debates about some aspect of that particular genocide. If there were debates, I'd go for the books that raised the questions, where people argued with one another. And I tried to go back in time when it was possible or when it seemed relevant to read works from the time of the genocide. Thus I used different types of

sources for each genocide to some degree, but I always concentrated on answering my 36 questions.

AF: Did you cover government reports?

NR: Yes, when they were relevant. But I mainly used scholarly writing.

AF: For the genocide project, did you formulate the same sort of case-study method that you had used in previous projects, or did you do it in a different way?

NR: In a different way. For the women's prisons project, I was collecting data on *individuals* and then aggregating that in state-level case studies, from which I generalized to regions, using the various prisons' annual reports. But for the genocide book, I'm reading about events. When I started to read books that didn't cause me to fill out my questionnaire much anymore, I'd stop.

AF: So you reached saturation. I guess the book on films in many ways used a case-study approach as well?

NR: It did. I hadn't thought of that. I looked at police films, and courtroom films, and so on. I guess those were cases!

AF: Probably neither of the earlier works was as systematic as the case-study approach of your current work, where you have the same 36 questions that you're asking about every genocide; but you covered similar themes—every chapter has similar themes.

NR: Yes, I was systematic with the films book too. In that case—I think the introduction to the second edition talks about this—I watched all the police films, defined in a certain way, that had been released up to the time that I started to write.

AF: I'm also thinking about the structure of the chapters: although the chapters on police films, attorneys, and prisons weren't identical in format, they looked for the same sorts of data.

NR: Right. I was always looking at gender, social class, race.

AF: Did you consciously define those themes, or did they sort of just work out that way?

NR: For *Shots in the Mirror* I didn't have a form to fill out. It was inductive. I'd watch these movies and begin to see themes—or sometimes hidden themes; there a lot of homosexuality in some police films, for example.

AF: Whereas in the genocide work, you established these 36 questions through doing your first couple of genocides; right?

NR: And through reading.

AF: How did you learn to do this? Did this approach just come naturally? Where did you get your methods training along the way? You said earlier that you didn't feel like you got that methods training in graduate school, yet you developed a methodology and that's been pretty consistent across all your work.

NR: I didn't realize it was consistent until now. I always felt bad that I didn't have methodological sophistication. There is common sense to doing some research, so I just looked at the problem and figured out how I could answer it.

AF: But in addition to reading all the primary materials, do you find yourself also reading methodological works?

NR: Yes. And I try to learn from others' mistakes and omissions.

AF: Has there been a time that you took a deeper dive into a particular methodology or into methodological texts as opposed to studying examples?

NR: I did at the beginning of the genocide book. There are a number of books on comparative historical methods. Those were very helpful. They discuss what you can learn from doing comparative history and what you can't. Some people think you can use it to learn about causes. I didn't want to be merely descriptive in this book, but I also didn't want to talk about causes very much. I ended up talking about causes a lot more than I wanted to. It's pretty risky to talk about the causes of genocide because there are so many of them and because they are often surprising.

AF: So the causes are more complex than maybe can be rooted out?

NR: Yes. I also read a lot of the sociological and social psych literature on violence, and some of the biological literature too.

AF: Did you ever conceptualize the genocide book as something that would be integrated across themes or…?

NR: I hope it is! But I also have to tell the story of each of my eight cases. So I put them in different places in the book.

AF: Ah, to set the story up.

NR: I tell the story of one or two of my eight genocides in each chapter. Those stories could be the most interesting part of each chapter, or they may be something that people skip; I don't know. I mean, I like to tell stories; I like books that tell stories. Maybe it'll work and maybe it won't. But the reader has to know what the stories are.

AF: Exactly, and you can't include all eight in every chapter.

NR: No the reader wouldn't remember from chapter to chapter. So I give a very short summary of all eight genocides in Chap. 2; then in subsequent chapters I go back and expand. I locate the stories where they are most relevant thematically. So, for example, I tell the longer story of Rwanda in my gender chapter because gender played a big role in that genocide.

Conclusion

AF: Comparative work is a constant across your work, whether it is comparative in terms of different cases or across people. Does it seem natural for you to take a comparative approach?

NR: I guess so!

AF: Do you have an idea about why or what moves you in that direction?

NR: It seems commonsensical to me that if you want to find out what genocides are like, you'd compare some of them. But you know, Amy, it might be that there is not much in common in genocides after all. These phenomena are so very different.

AF: I guess maybe you did the same thing with the films project, approaching the topic from a criminological perspective.

NR: Right. To take a criminological approach comes naturally to me because I've been doing this kind of research and reading for a long time. By "criminological approach," I mean anything having to do with the study of crime—offender demographics, victim characteristics, place where the crime usually occurs, why the crime often goes undetected—all those sorts of things.

AF: Among the authors in this volume, some will have had significant formal methodological training and others would have come up with their own methodology along the way. I would argue very strongly that you would be someone whom others would identify as being groundbreaking methodologically—I mean among people who do historical criminology.

NR: There are only one or two of us!

AF: But there are very few that have done the work you've done, so you would be looked at as the model there. In the same way that someone else might be seen as the model of multilevel regression.

NR: I think it is important to consider the context in which someone works. As I was coming of age in criminology, issues began to emerge about gender, race, and other intersectionalities. So that's an agenda that has developed across people; it's been a mutual project for a lot of feminists and people who work on race. So I think that, too, makes a big difference in what people work on.

AF: But you take a very different approach than many people who have tried to address intersectionality issues. Not so many people have done that from a historical perspective.

NR: You asked before if I'm a question in search of a method. When I'm working, that's exactly what I am. . Until we started having these conversations, I didn't realize that I usually end up with the same method. Have you seen the movie *The Eternal*

Sunshine of the Spotless Mind? I keep reinventing the wheel because I forget that I invented it before.

AF: Do you naturally call upon comparative methods as you approach your questions?

NR: You've taught me that I do. You've revealed to me the eternal sunshine of my spotless mind.

AF: You seem to approach questions by saying, Let's tell the story up to now so we can understand how we got here. Do you think that that historical lens—actually a sociological and historical lens—leads you to certain kinds of questions?

NR: Since you've been asking that question so persistently, I think the answer must be yes.

AF: It doesn't have to be. Some would say that the questions that you ask are very different from each other because they deal with such different topics, from movies to prisons. But I'm wondering if there is a common thread that originates in a methodological perspective as well. Or do you really think you begin with a question and the method just comes naturally?

NR: The questions seem to descend on me, and then I spend a lot of time trying to figure out how to answer them. If I'd known I had a method all along—if you'd told me earlier—I would not have wasted so much time making mistakes.

AF: Are they really mistakes or do you learn from them?

NR: Yeah, I learn, but I also flounder about a lot.

AF: Along those same lines, would you say that your writing is your analysis, or do you find you have analytical periods and then writing periods?

NR: With the genocide book, I've certainly had an analytical period because it's taken so long to get the questionnaires filled out for all eight genocides, and then to analyze the cases using the computer analysis program NVivo.

AF: How did you find NVivo?

NR: Laura Siller, one of the graduate students I work with, and another student coded from my questionnaires. They took the answers to my eight questionnaires, some of which were 50–60 pages long, single-spaced. And the questions were of course numbered 1a, 1b, 2a, 2b, and so on. When they gave me data at the end, all the 1a answers were together for all eight genocides, so now I could look and compare across them instantly.

AF: That's an interesting way to use NVivo. You had already done all the data collection; they were helping you organize the data so you could find things.

What would be the best way to train people to do what you do? Or to answer questions in the way you answer them?

NR: As you've shown me, I use a case-study method. So I would get them to figure out what their cases were and to define them. And then I would get them to identify dimensions of their cases, and as they were collecting data I would have them focus on those dimensions in particular. A priority would be figuring out what they want to know.

I don't spend a lot of time with students training them in a specific way, but I do ask them to keep bringing me new iterations of their dissertation proposals. And I try to see where the proposal looks fuzzy or muddy.

AF: So does your contribution lie in helping people craft their question? Then you send them off on their own to learn how to answer it, and you guide them in that process?

NR: Yes, it is much like how I work with myself.

AF: So do you see your role as a senior faculty member, an educator, a mentor—all those things—as being to help students learn how to ask good questions?

NR: Yes, I do.

AF: Do you think if students learn how to ask good questions, they'll learn how to do the rest? Is asking good questions the hardest part?

NF: Yes, and I also encourage them to think outside the box. I have a student who said, "Finally I'm happy because I'm doing feminist research." When she first came here, all she wanted to do was to test theory X using Y data. I asked who her M.A. advisor had been, and she said_____.
I replied, He is a very good methodologist, but he's in the box, and she said, "Definitely." Natasha Frost[3] and I pushed her to do a feminist project. She is now having great fun. She told me it is always helpful to chat with me because I push her to think.

AF: How do you train students to ask the right questions? That is maybe one of the most important things that we do as social scientists.

NR: Having them write helps a lot. Tell them: Write it down, then put it aside for a couple of weeks and go back and look at it. Is this really what you want to do? How might you make this point differently? Help them critique their own work and their own thinking. That's what I do in the writing Practicum course. Students critique one another's work, but the goal is to get them to have editors in their own heads. I told them I want to turn them into an additional person: An editor who can look at their work and, if necessary, say, That's crap.

AF: How do you get people to ask good questions though—even creative questions?

NR: Some of them know already what they are passionate about, and others will never have any passion; but with most students, you find out through conversation.

AF: I like to have things come from students. That's better than just asking them to take off from something their advisor is doing.

NR: You do a wonderful job at that.

AF: You do, too. We're probably alike. It's not surprising, I learned it from you. I still like your notecard method. I tell students the trick that you taught me one time: write your hypothesis down on a notecard and tape it to your computer, and then write only what you need to answer that question. I still find myself doing that. I was doing it just today for something.

_____
[3] Another Northeastern colleague.

NR: Once I was advising some students to do that, and they said, Professor Farrell does that too!

This trick keeps me focused.

AF: So is there anything else...

NR: Yes. I have a question about a term I've been using in the genocide book to describe my approach. It is a cumbersome term, "historical criminological comparative research"; the "criminological" of course means "sociological" too and brings in a whole lot of other literatures as well. Do you think that historical comparative criminological research is what I've been doing all along?

NU: I would say so.

NR: That's good to know, now that I'm close to retiring!

AF: The notion of historical comparative criminological research describes almost all of the work you've done, although you may have employed other methodological tools as well. Your studies are similar to each other. When we started these interviews, you said you don't have a single method, but it seems like you absolutely do. You approach different questions in the same way.

NR: That's very encouraging; now I know what I do. And I will keep using the method but now more consciously because I have ideas for other projects down the line.

You've been very clever, Amy, in the way you invented a methodology that led me to understand my own methodology!

References

Lombroso, C. (2006). *Criminal man* (M. Gibson & N. H. Rafter, Trans.). Durham, NC: Duke University Press.

Lombroso, C., & Ferrero, G. (2004). *Criminal woman* (N. H. Rafter & M. Gibson, Trans.). Durham, NC: Duke University Press.

Rafter, N. H. (1985). *Partial justice: Women in state prisons, 1800–1935* (1st ed.). Boston: Northeastern University Press.

Rafter, N. H. (1990). *Partial justice: Women, prisons, and social control* (2nd rev. ed.). New Brunswick, NJ: Transaction.

Rafter, N. H. (1997). *Creating born criminals*. Champaign, IL: University of Illinois Press.

Rafter, N. H. (2000). *Shots in the mirror: Crime films and society*. New York: Oxford University Press.

Rafter, N. H. (2006). *Shots in the mirror: Crime films and society* (2nd rev. ed.). New York: Oxford University Press.

Rafter, N. (2008). *The criminal brain: Understanding biological theories of crime*. New York: New York University Press.

Rafter, N., Posick, C., & Rocque, M. (forthcoming, 2016). *The criminal brain: Understanding biological theories of crime* (2nd ed., rev.). New York: New York University Press.

Rafter, N. (forthcoming, 2016). *The crime of all crimes: Toward a criminology of genocide*. New York: New York University Press.

Getting Things Wrong Really Does Help, as Long as You Keep Trying to Get Things Right: Developing Theories About Why Homicide Rates Rise and Fall

Randolph Roth

How can we come up with new ideas in criminology that have a chance of being better than the ideas that have come before? That's a humbling question for scholars like me, whose insights have been born of failure. It's a daunting thing, even in a world of tenure, to work for a decade on a project, only to find that the data have made a hash of your hypotheses. As I put it to friends at the time, "my theories died a horrible death in the face of the evidence." It's tough to end up with a bigger puzzle than the one you started with and no responsible way to publish what you have found, because the data don't make sense in light of your initial theories or the theories of your colleagues. But that's the way many advances in knowledge come about, especially in criminology, where official data are of such poor quality and so limited across time and space that we have to gather our own data, project after project, without knowing what they will reveal. And the data, once gathered, almost always surprise us—indeed, I believe they will always surprise us if we are open to what they can tell us. But that's a wonderful thing, because it means, as I remind my students constantly, that we don't have to be geniuses to do original work in criminology. We just have to work long hours and trust that better hypotheses will emerge from the data.

Originality stems not only from failure, however, but from a willingness to persist despite failure. The costs of failure are considerable, in lost income, reputation, and opportunities; and success, if it comes with an original finding, also has its costs, in rejections and hostile reviews. Scholarship can get brutal, because the stakes are high: not only for ideologues who do not want to see their theories tested against evidence, but for scholars who are trying to get things right and have arrived at different conclusions. There are great satisfactions, however, in developing a novel theory, especially when we have an opportunity to work with colleagues at the cutting edge—colleagues who are open to new ideas and who know from experience that everyone's hypotheses, including their own, must be put to the test against fresh evidence and revised in light of new findings. That's the excitement of scholarship, as we work through trial and error toward getting things right.

I did not set out to write *American Homicide* (Roth, 2009) or develop a theory of why homicide rates have gone up and down in the modern and early modern era. I meant to write a very different book that focused on a very different set of theoretical questions. I began my career as a historian of northern New England, interested in why Vermont's revolution—the most radically egalitarian and democratic of any future state—had led by the 1830s and 1840s to levels of church membership and church attendance that were unsurpassed in the Protestant world

R. Roth (✉)
Ohio State University, Columbus, OH, USA
e-mail: roth.5@osu.edu

M.D. Maltz and S.K. Rice (eds.), *Envisioning Criminology: Researchers on Research as a Process of Discovery*, DOI 10.1007/978-3-319-15868-6_14, © Springer International Publishing Switzerland 2015

and to a flurry of religious revivals and reform movements that helped reshape society and politics in the antebellum North (Roth, 1987). I couldn't help but notice, as I completed my project, that my research in newspapers, court records, and other sources had uncovered evidence of remarkably few homicides or other violent crimes from the end of the Revolution into the 1840s. I noticed as well that northern New England's homicide rates were also extraordinarily low in the 1950s and 1960s, which led me to wonder "Why Northern New Englanders Seldom Commit Murder." That was to be the focus of my second book.

I decided to study New Hampshire and Vermont from colonial times to the present because I thought that they held the key to understanding how a democratic, pluralistic society like the United States could be nonviolent. Most scholars at the time focused on cultures of violence, almost to the exclusion of cultures of nonviolence. I already knew northern New England well enough to realize that the theories of "nonviolence" that could be extrapolated from the prevailing theories of violent cultures didn't apply to Vermont and New Hampshire. For instance, northern New Englanders were just as obsessed as antebellum white Southerners or twentieth-century urban African Americans with their personal honor, and they felt the sting of dishonor deeply, so much so that it could drive them to violence. They simply had better opportunities to develop the attributes that made a person "honorable" in society's eyes than antebellum Southerners or modern African Americans; and they had better means of defending their honor nonviolently, particularly through ironic or self-deprecating humor.

Consider the scorn heaped by the temperate majority in the early nineteenth century upon people who drank and their willingness to shame drinkers personally and publicly. When a church committee in South Newbury, Vermont, found that a habitual drunkard had backslid, it posted a notice at the post office announcing his excommunication. "Whereas Mr. Lyon has not kept his promise to reform, we the Church Committee return him to the outside world from whence he came.

By the church committee." The next day another notice appeared. "Whereas Mr. Lyon is so much worse than when he joined the church, we of the outside world refuse to accept him back. By the Outside Committee" (Roth, 2009: 192). The laughter that these responses provoked in church members and nonmembers alike, not to mention the place they received in community lore, affirmed the honor of the insulted members of the community and undermined the standing of those who had insulted them.

Spouse abusers also faced scorn and ridicule, but they too found ways to respond nonviolently to criticism from their neighbors. A volunteer at the New Hampshire State Library told me the story of a man named Perley who had abused his wife, Lucy, for years. When Lucy sued at last for divorce, a neighbor, Leonard Martin, was summoned to testify, because divorce was not a "no-fault" process in the final decades of the nineteenth century. Leonard told the truth as plainly as he could: Perley "was a drunk and was abusive to Lucy." From that moment, the men were sworn enemies. When they worked their fields on the opposite side of the road, they yelled at each other all day long, but Perley never threatened Leonard with violence. He trusted, in patient New England fashion, that God would punish Leonard for betraying his friendship. His closing line was always "Leonard, I'll see you in your grave," to which Leonard replied, just as patiently, "I'll bury you, Perley." God took his time: Perley lived to be 88. But Leonard, still vigorous, outlived him. After Perley's funeral, Leonard showed up to help the grave-diggers. They worked in silence until the last shovelful was tamped down. Then Leonard jumped on the grave, danced a jig, and yelled "There, I buried you, you son of a bitch!"

I'm still convinced that the peculiarities of northern New England's culture of honor and of its ways of coping with dishonor, where they have persisted, have deterred violence to this day. I believe faith and humor diminished violence, as did the egalitarianism of northern New England's postrevolutionary social order, which enabled the vast majority of women and men to achieve honor in their eyes and in society's. Self-employment and home ownership—the most important markers of status in New England society—were widespread, particularly in the early nineteenth century, as was participation in public life, thanks to churches, volunteer organizations, town meeting days, and the many offices and service obligations that were necessary to keep New England's townships running smoothly (Roth, 1987). I have since reframed the hypothesis in more general terms, because I concluded that the crucial factor in deterring or facilitating violence was not the particular attitude toward "honor" in a culture, but the legitimacy of the status hierarchy, which is premised on the selective distribution of honor and dishonor. Homicide rates are lower where people believe that the social hierarchy is legitimate, "that one's position in society is or can be satisfactory and that one can command the respect of others without resorting to violence" (Roth, 2009: 17–18, 23–26). But I discovered that the legitimacy of the social hierarchy is generally the "weak force" in driving homicide rates. Persistent social changes that make it harder for people to achieve honor within a society, such as the decline by a third of real wages for the working poor in Europe in the late sixteenth and early seventeenth centuries, the decline in self-employment in the northern United States in the nineteenth century, or the decline in high-paying factory jobs in affluent societies since 1960, led to slow, steady upward pressure on rates of violence for several decades, until people learned to cope with the new realities and find new ways to achieve honor. And nothing can generate violence more quickly than forcing a group of people suddenly to the bottom of the social hierarchy, as was the case with Africans forced into slavery or Europeans contracted into indentured servitude in the New World. On the whole, however, the influence of legitimizing or delegitimizing the social hierarchy is modest compared to the influence of other, more powerful forces.

What derailed my study was not my second thoughts about the role of honor and social hierarchies—those came later—but the data I amassed about violent crime and violent death in Vermont and New Hampshire. I gathered every scrap of data I could, from newspapers, diaries, inquests, case files, prison records, vital records, docket books, and local histories based on oral tradition or testimony. I used capture-recapture mathematics to account for unrecorded events and lost records, and I used a number of methods to estimate the populations at risk to be sure that the rates of violence I calculated represented real changes in violence, rather than artifacts of the demographic methods I used. And what I found came as a surprise. I discovered that the early nineteenth century—the period on which had I based my hypotheses—was the least violent in the area's history. By the late nineteenth century, the homicide rate in northern New England was as high as in London or Manchester, England. Child murders, spousal killings, and everyday murders among young men—they were all more common than they had been in the early nineteenth century. And I discovered, much to the dismay of someone with my democratic beliefs, that violence had been rare in northern New England in the mid-eighteenth century and that the Revolution had made things much worse for several decades. Something had gone terribly wrong.

I was also surprised to discover that the homicides that occurred in northern New England when the murder rate was higher had much in common with the homicides that occurred in more violent areas of the United States. Consider, for instance, an archetypally southern feud that ended in bloodshed in 1868 in Shrewsbury, Vermont. The Plumleys and the Balches had quarreled, sued, and fought for years over insults, boundary lines, and stray livestock. At their last meeting, arbitrators were assessing the damage done by Balch livestock to a Plumley cornfield. Ziba Plumley, the clan's aged patriarch, crippled in a fight with a Balch 3 years before, grew livid as it became clear that the arbitrators were going to find for the Balches. He ordered his son Horace to prod a Balch confederate, John Gilman, Jr., out of the cornfield at gunpoint. When the frightened Gilman begged Horace Plumley to turn the rifle aside, Ziba told Horace to shoot him, and Horace did. Ziba then pointed to the Balches present and told his sons to shoot them. A furious gun battle broke out at a distance of ten paces.

The Plumleys hit one Balch in the arm and another in the leg, but could not prevent the Balches from taking cover and returning fire. "God damn it," Ziba yelled at his sons, "Can't you shoot straight?" (*Rutland* [Vermont] *Daily Herald*, 3, 4, 5, 6, 12, 15, and 16 August 1868 and 8 April and 28 June 1869). For the sake of my premise, I wish these fellows had had their shootout somewhere in West Virginia.

The data from northern New England, however, held the key to developing macrohistorical theories of violence that are more robust and have fit the data from other places I have studied to date. When I separated by type the homicides I had found in New Hampshire and Vermont, I discovered that the patterns made sense in terms of New England's history. Murders of children by adult relatives or caregivers followed a long, smooth curve that was the inverse of the birthrate: high fertility meant a low child murder rate, and low fertility meant a high murder rate (Roth, 2001a, 2001b). Marital homicides and romance homicides jumped suddenly in the 1830s and 1840s: decades in which jobs opened up to women in education and industry, in which self-employment declined for men, and in which the ideal of companionate marriage took hold (Roth, 1999, 2009: 250–290). Homicides among unrelated adults peaked during periods of political turmoil: the Revolution, the Embargo crisis, and the sectional crisis.

It appeared, as I put it in the mid-1990s, that "state breakdowns and political crises of legitimacy produce surges in nondomestic homicides and that the restoration of order and legitimacy produces declines in such homicides" (Roth, 1997). The same pattern was evident on the national level in the twentieth century, for which comprehensive homicide statistics were available. "The theory can be extended to the twentieth century: the crisis of legitimacy in the 1960s and 1970s (especially in the eyes of African Americans) may have contributed to soaring homicide rates; and the establishment of state legitimacy through the New Deal, World War II, and the Cold War may have reduced homicide rates through the 1950s." The idea that there was a relationship between legitimacy and crime

dawned upon a number of scholars independently in these years, including psychologist Tyler (1990), criminologists LaFree (1998) and Eisner (2001), and sociologist Gould (2003).

I knew, however, that it would take more to confirm these hypotheses than evidence drawn from the history of Vermont and New Hampshire, my area of expertise. Who would believe a theory of interpersonal violence based on New Hampshire and Vermont? So I put these theories at risk against a wider range of evidence. I extended my research to the colonial period, to early modern Europe, and outward to the South, the Midwest, the West, and the urban East. Everywhere I looked, the domestic murder rate for children followed the inverse of the birthrate up to the end of the nineteenth century, when family planning became more effective and more widespread. Marital and romance homicides increased suddenly in the 1830s and 1840s across the northern United States and in England and northern France. Everywhere I looked, homicides among unrelated adults correlated with political events.

I conducted "natural experiments" to prove that correlation. I hypothesized, for instance, that the homicide rate would soar during the American Revolution and remain high for decades afterwards in the Georgia-South Carolina backcountry, where the Revolution was a genuine civil war. I also hypothesized that the homicide rate would hold steady or fall in the Shenandoah Valley of Virginia, which enjoyed political stability under patriot control throughout the Revolution, and where support for the war effort and the new federal government was stronger than anywhere else in the South. My research in local archives confirmed these hypotheses, which gave me greater confidence in my macrohistorical theories of violence (Roth, 2009). Still, research on these theories has truly just begun.

I have been gathering historical and contemporary data since 2009 on a wider range of places, with an emphasis on measuring feelings and beliefs that may deter or facilitate homicide. I have tried to find proxies for measuring political instability, legitimacy, and fellow feeling at the level of the community and the nation.

I discovered, for example, that for colonial and early national periods, the best correlate of the homicide rate among unrelated adults is the proportion of new counties in any decade that is named for national heroes—British heroes in the colonial period and American heroes in the early national period. When the proportion was high—an unconscious measure of the degree to which citizens felt a patriotic bond with each other and with the nation's leaders—deadly feuds, bar fights, robberies, and sexual assaults were uncommon. But when the proportion dropped, the murder rate rose.

The same was true for hate speech, a measure of fellow feeling at the community level. For example, consider the racially charged word "nigger," which in the nineteenth century represented contempt and hostility both for African Americans and for whites who opposed the extension of slavery to the territories or favored the abolition of slavery and racial equality. Or consider the politically charged phrase "slave power," which represented hostility toward slave owners and toward politicians and political organizations that sought to secure or strengthen the institution of slavery within the Union. The spike in the use of these terms occurred during the Mexican War, which is precisely the point at which the number of deadly riots and rebellions increased, the proportion of counties named after national heroes fell, and the homicide rate among unrelated adults jumped. I gathered these data to put my theories to the test, not knowing how things would turn out, but thus far my theories have held up well, even though many unanswered questions remain (Roth, 2012, 2014).

I hope more scholars will undertake long-term studies of crime and violence in particular places. Such studies are remarkably scarce. But they hold the key, I believe, to creating original theories. Novel theories jump out from the data, because nothing else fits. I know this may sound like mindless empiricism, but I prefer to think of it as mindful empiricism, as Francis Bacon envisioned. I have always likened social science history to Ohio State's run-first offense under football coach Woody Hayes, which was characterized by contemporaries as "three yards and a cloud of dust." To my mind, social science history is "three cubic yards of documents and a cloud of library dust." But as I tell my students, "if you want to be original, work!"

I believe, however, that there is another important quality besides industry that creative scholars in criminology share: persistence. As Mlodinow (2008) says in his wonderful history of statistical thought, what distinguishes successful people more than anything else, mathematically speaking, is that they don't give up in the face of adversity. They give themselves more chances to succeed, chances that improve their odds. They reflect, reconsider, and try again.

What helps scholars persist? First, I believe we must have the courage to see the world in our own way, even if few others share our way of seeing. As an undergraduate, I hoped I could someday make a contribution to understanding social problems by applying the skills I had learned as a young scientist and mathematician. By nature and nurture, I am most at home in math and science, temperamentally and intellectually. I was troubled by most social science I read at the time, because it struck me as too narrowly focused on the present to build strong theories about human behavior. But I believed that the fundamental causes of human behavior might be apparent if we were to study behavior across vast stretches of time and space, which would give us enough variation and enough "natural experiments" and comparisons to identify which historical circumstances were most likely to lead to certain outcomes.

I was impressed at the time by the histories I read and by the historians I studied with, because they were committed to looking at human behavior comparatively and contextually across time and space. That is why I became a social science historian—a field that was just coming into being when I embraced it in the early 1970s. The historical profession has since largely turned away from social science history because of an aversion to statistics, to the more quantitative forms of social science, and to midrange social theories (which strike many historians, I think wrongly, as decontextualized). The turn has been so pronounced that the profession has only a handful of scholars under the age of 50 who love math and use it regularly in their work, not enough to sustain social science history as my generation and the generation before envisioned it. And life hasn't been easy for those of us who remain in the profession. My colleagues and I have faced a steady stream of rejections from journals and publishers, who prefer cultural and narrative history; and we have faced innumerate attacks on our work, especially when we study controversial topics like the relationship between guns and violence or homicide rates in the Old West.

It has been heartening, however, to see the intellectual benefits of taking of an approach that is at once social scientific and historical, and it has been gratifying to see more and more social scientists take an interest in history and produce so many fine works in social science history. And most important in helping us persevere, we have a home in the Social Science History Association. The SSHA was a godsend for me, as it has been for many like-minded scholars who believe history offers the best hope of building stronger social scientific theories. It is a model support group for scholars who are willing to use whatever tools are at hand—mathematical, scientific, social scientific, and humanistic—to solve problems. And it is a good home for scholars whose projects take decades to complete, because that is closer to the norm among social science historians. It would have been much harder to tough out my project had my colleagues in the SSHA not taken an interest in my project's failures. They are used to being surprised by data and to discarding the theories they started with.

I should confess as well that I was able to persist for the 22 years it took to write *American Homicide* in large part because I am stubborn and because I never lost sight of why I became a scholar: to solve social problems. If it were easy to understand and remedy social problems, they would have been solved long ago, so I expected progress to be slow and hard won. And most important, I enjoy teaching, so much so that I have always seen myself as a teacher first and a scholar second. I have always worked hard on my scholarship, but its frustrations and disappointments have been easier to bear because I love my

"day" job, spending time with students and helping them as best I can master the skills of critical thinking, reading, writing, and quantifying, so they can do a better job of addressing the world's problems than my own generation has—hopefully in a less ideological, more scientific way.

There is a cost, of course, as every academic in a research university knows, to developing a reputation as a "teacher first." I learned through the grapevine that my chair attributed the failure of my initial project to my "overcommitment to teaching," and he would have sacked me if I didn't have tenure. But he got it backwards. Being a "teacher first" made it possible for me to complete a data project that no professionally ambitious scholar would have taken on. I cared only about the project and tried as best I could to ignore its effect on my career. And thank God for tenure. It's a wonderful privilege, hard earned by everyone who has it, and I was determined to use it as it was intended, to take risks and take the time to get things right.

Finally, I think it's easier to persist if we learn to view attacks we consider unwarranted or unfair as opportunities to improve and defend our work. I discovered, for instance, that some humanistic historians have a double standard when it comes to quantification. They feel justified—and rightly so, I should add—in writing with authority about the feelings and beliefs of people in the past, even though they offer no quantitative measures of the degree, for instance, to which people were more or less patriotic or more or less antagonistic toward people of different classes, races, or religions. Humanistic scholars who have immersed themselves deeply in the thought and culture of a particular time and place can, I believe, tell us more about people's feelings and beliefs than any opinion poll ever could. But when a social science historian like myself cites humanistic work to illustrate, say, the connection between a lack of fellow feeling and higher homicide rates, these same humanists dismiss the finding because the feeling hasn't been quantified to the nth degree, even though they have argued in their own nonquantitative work for the same changes in feeling that I describe. Their complaints were not made in bad faith, of course—I doubt they were conscious of what they had done—but their purpose was to belittle social science and the idea that something as remote as patriotic feeling could have an impact on the number of deadly bar fights. Their criticism was, I still feel, unfair, but it led me to redouble my efforts to find quantitative measures of the changes in feelings and beliefs on which my theories rest. I am relieved to report that to date, that search has supported most of the research of the humanistic historians I have relied upon, a finding that I hope will encourage more social scientists to look to humanistic historians when they study thoughts and emotions and their behavioral consequences.

Another criticism I have received from humanistic historians is the commonplace that correlation is not causation, so they insist that the correlations I have identified among feelings, beliefs, and behavior can't tell us anything about why people behave as they do and may in fact be spurious. It's a criticism based to a large extent on a misunderstanding of statistics and of science. Science often proceeds through the discovery of correlations that are so strong and so nonrandom that they cannot be based on chance: there has to be a causal connection between the two. I have taken the criticism to heart nonetheless, because it rests at its best on a demand that I identify more carefully the mechanisms by which abstract thoughts and feelings in the society at large affect day-to-day behavior. It's not a conscious process in the minds of potential murderers. They don't say to themselves, "I'm really disillusioned with my country and my fellow citizens, so I'm going to go out and kill someone in a bar fight so I can feel better." But there has to be a mechanism. I have been thinking about how endocrinology might help us understand how emotions, such as those triggered by movements up or down a social hierarchy, might change our hormone levels without us knowing it and increase the likelihood that we will be aggressive, either proactively or defensively (Roth, 2010).

But I have been heartened by the thoughtful challenges that my closest colleagues in social science history have posed for my theories. Why, as Richard McMahon has wondered, were Irish Catholics, like African Americans, able to maintain such low homicide rates over most of the nineteenth century, despite the hardships and oppression they suffered? How did they maintain a strong sense of solidarity or a culture that encouraged nonviolent (or at least less violent) means of resolving conflicts (McMahon, 2013)? Why, as Donald Fyson has wondered, were the French inhabitants of Quebec, like the Sinhalese in the interior of colonial Ceylon, able to maintain low homicide rates after they were conquered by Great Britain? Did the decision by the British to leave local institutions and leaders in place help preserve a sense that the government and social order were legitimate (Fyson, 2009; Rogers, 1987; Wood, 1961)? These are wonderful questions that will keep us busy for years to come—another good reason, in retrospect, to have stuck with my project long enough to develop a theory that could be worthy of testing by my colleagues.

References

Eisner, M. (2001). Modernization, self-control, and lethal violence: The long-term dynamics of European homicide rates in theoretical perspective. *British Journal of Criminology, 41*, 618–638.

Fyson, D. (2009, November 14). *Men killing men: Homicide in Quebec, 1760-1860*. Paper delivered before the Social Science History Association, Long Beach, CA.

Gould, R. V. (2003). *Collision of Wills: How ambiguity about social rank breeds conflict*. Chicago, IL: University of Chicago Press.

LaFree, G. (1998). *Losing legitimacy: Street crime and the decline of social institutions*. Boulder, CO: Westview.

McMahon, R. (2013). *Homicide in pre-famine and famine Ireland*. Liverpool, UK: Liverpool University Press.

Mlodinow, L. (2008). *The drunkard's walk: How randomness rules our lives*. New York, NY: Pantheon.

Rogers, J. D. (1987). *Crime, justice, and society in colonial Sri Lanka*. London Studies on South Asia, no. 5. London, UK: Curzon Press.

Roth, R. (1987). *The democratic dilemma: Religion, reform, and the social order in the Connecticut River Valley of Vermont, 1791-1850*. New York, NY: Cambridge University Press.

Roth, R. (1997). *National endowment for the humanities grant proposal and bibliography*. Retrieved from http://cjrc.osu.edu/sites/cjrc.osu.edu/files/grant-proposal-and-bibliography.pdf

Roth, R. (1999). Spousal murder in Northern New England, 1791-1865. In C. Daniels (Ed.), *Over the threshold: Intimate violence in early America, 1640-1865* (pp. 65–93). New York, NY: Routledge.

Roth, R. (2001a). Homicide and neonaticide in early modern Europe: A quantitative synthesis. *Crime, Histories, and Societies, 5*, 33–68.

Roth, R. (2001b). Child murder in New England. *Social Science History, 25*, 101–147.

Roth, R. (2009). *American homicide*. Cambridge, MA: The Belknap Press of Harvard University Press.

Roth, R. (2010). Biology and the deep history of homicide. *The British Journal of Criminology, 51*, 535–555.

Roth, R. (2012). Measuring feelings and beliefs that may facilitate (or deter) homicide. *Homicide Studies, 16*, 196–217.

Roth, R. (2014). *The importance of testing criminological theories in historical context: The civilization thesis versus the nation-building hypothesis. Criminology* online: Presidential session papers from the American Society of Criminology.

Tyler, T. R. (1990). *Why people obey the law*. New Haven, CT: Yale University Press.

Wood, A. L. (1961). Crime and aggression in changing Ceylon: A sociological analysis of homicide, suicide, and economic crime. *Philadelphia: Transactions of the American Philosophical Society, New Series, 51: Part 8.*

Twists, Turns, and Tears on the Path to the Cycle of Violence

Cathy Spatz Widom

When I was growing up, I thought I would become a lawyer, having been influenced by the Perry Mason television series that I watched as a child. However, I attended Cornell University on a full scholarship and found that majoring in pre-law did not seem an option. I majored in "Child Development and Family Relationships" and was exposed to Urie Bronfenbrenner's "ecological model" of development and to research. I was also taking courses in the School of Industrial and Labor Relations and designed a couple of studies as part of social psychology course requirements. I began to think about graduate school and decided to pursue social psychology.

After taking a year off working as an administrative assistant in Boston, I applied to Brandeis University to study social psychology and began my graduate work the following year. My career took a slight turn when I discovered the construct of psychopathy and became fascinated by these individuals. I was a teaching assistant in an abnormal psychology class and one of the students in the class was serving time in a Massachusetts correctional institution. At that time, Brandeis had a special program for inmates and this young man (Stanley Bond) was enrolled in the course and in my section that focused on murder, aggression,

C.S. Widom (✉)
John Jay College of Criminal Justice,
New York, NY, USA
e-mail: cwidom@jjay.cuny.edu

and violence. He disrupted the class, threw down a chair, and told the class that I didn't know anything about these topics. Fortunately for me, he did not come back to class. I learned that he went on to participate in the Brighton bank robbery where police officers were killed. Interestingly, two young Brandeis undergraduates (Kathy Power and Susan Saxe) took part in the robbery, but they went underground for several years and were among the first on the FBI most wanted list before being caught. The young man who had been in my class was caught almost immediately (like a true psychopath) and ended up serving time for the crime. Ultimately, he died in prison and I was told later that he had tried to escape but was caught between the bars of his cell and somehow did not survive. These experiences stimulated my interests in psychopaths and female offenders and sent me on a different direction in my work.

I conducted my dissertation research in England at Broadmoor Criminal Lunatic Asylum (a maximum security hospital) where the offenders had indeterminate sentences "at her Majesty's pleasure." It was a good place to study psychopaths because the British sent them all to this one facility. In the United States, I would have had to go to many facilities to get the number of psychopaths I needed for my dissertation research.

After finishing my dissertation, I was appointed an assistant professor at Harvard University in the Department of Psychology and Social Relations. I continued my research on

M.D. Maltz and S.K. Rice (eds.), *Envisioning Criminology: Researchers on Research as a Process of Discovery*, DOI 10.1007/978-3-319-15868-6_15, © Springer International Publishing Switzerland 2015

psychopaths and female offenders but was also beginning to realize that studying psychopaths in prison was a problem. We were letting the criminal justice and legal systems define what I believed was a valid psychological construct. Consequently, at that time, I began a study of what I called "non-institutionalized psychopaths" (Widom, 1977) and a separate series of studies of female offenders (Widom, 1978) at Massachusetts Correctional Institution at Framingham. However, as was fairly common at that time, my appointment as a junior faculty member was time limited and I needed to find another job.

I accepted a position at Indiana University in Bloomington and thought I would have a quiet life there, pursuing my research and teaching. After only a short time at Indiana, I was asked to become the chair of the department (now Criminal Justice) and could not refuse. So, for the next several years, my research was largely on the backburner and I was an administrator. When my chairmanship was almost up, I decided that it would be sensible to get a federal grant to restart my research career. Realizing that I had not written a large grant before, I turned to one of my more experienced friends (Wes Skogan at Northwestern) for advice and told him that I wanted to get a grant. I then proposed several ideas for topics and he politely made it quite clear that those ideas were not going to be successful. He sent me back to think about more and better ideas. I discovered that there was a strong belief that abused and neglected children became delinquents and violent offenders and I began to suspect that the evidence base was weak. I proposed that topic to Wes and he thought it might succeed. Although psychologists did not typically study "violence" at the time, I was clearly a hybrid—a psychologist and a criminologist. For a long time, my work has straddled both fields and, I believe, benefited from the cross-disciplinary work.

I took a sabbatical from Indiana University in 1987 and went back to Harvard. During that year, I spent considerable time reviewing the literature on the "violence-breeds-violence" hypothesis and ultimately concluded that our knowledge was extremely limited. I wrote and published this review paper in *Psychological Bulletin* (Widom, 1989c). At the time, I argued that the problems

with the existing literature and weak empirical research made it difficult to draw firm policy conclusions. Thus, I was clearly aware of the limitations of the earlier research, having scrutinized that literature. The challenge I set for myself was how to design a study that would answer what I thought was a straightforward question: Do abused and neglected children become delinquents, adult criminals, and violent offenders when they grow up?

Even though I recognized that a prospective longitudinal study would be the ideal design to provide answers to my question, I knew that this would not be possible for a number of reasons. First, we would have to wait 20 years if we began with a birth cohort of children. Second, despite its devastating impact, child abuse and neglect are relatively low base rate phenomena so that we would have to design a study with a huge sample of children at the beginning to be able to end up with a large enough sample of maltreated children. Searching methods books for possible designs, I discovered a standard research design referred to as "specialized cohorts" (Leventhal, 1982; Schulsinger, Mednick, & Knop, 1981). In this design, the matched cohorts who are free of the "disease" in question (in my study, violent or delinquent behavior) at the time of the study are assumed to differ only in the attribute that we were interested in (whether they had experienced child abuse or neglect).

There were also questions of how to define the sample of children and how to operationalize the construct. Should we use self-reports? But young children would not be able to tell us about their early experiences. Should we depend on parents to report? Parents might be unlikely to want to share information that they were abusing or neglecting their children. Should we use teachers or other professionals who come into contact with the children? Perhaps, but these individuals might not be privy to the abuse or neglect that occurred behind closed doors within the family environment. Ultimately, I decided that none of these options was acceptable and given the state of knowledge, it became clear that it would be safest and cleanest to use documented cases of abuse and neglect. The rationale for identifying the abused and neglected group was that their cases were serious enough to come to the attention of the authorities. Then, the question was where to obtain these cases. Juvenile court records are typically sealed, but this is where the information would be. So, I set out to convince a juvenile court judge to allow me access to the records. Eventually, I was able to convince a judge, although our agreement involved my signing a legal document that stipulated that if I violated the terms of the agreement and revealed any information about the individuals or cases, I would be immediately charged with a felony. Needless to say, after this, I was extremely careful about protecting the confidentiality of our data and made everyone who worked on the project sign a confidentiality agreement. The judge was exceptional and taking a chance on me, but I think he realized that the questions I was posing were important ones. When I went back several years later asking for more help from the same judge, I didn't have such a hard time convincing him of the value of the work.

The next challenge was to obtain a control group of children without such histories. I realized that the best "control" group would be children who grew up in the same neighborhoods and decided that by getting children in the same elementary schools, we could accomplish this goal. By this time, we had identified the sample of abused and neglected children. We applied to the school district superintendent to find out what schools our children went to (or whether they went to these schools) so that we could then find same sex, race, and age matches for these children in their schools and classes. However, according to the Family Educational Rights and Privacy Act, in order to obtain information about children in school, one needs to have their parents' permission. I explained to the school superintendent that I did not have any contact with these children and, thus, I could not ask their parents for permission. Similarly, in order to obtain children as matches, we could not ask their parents for permission, since we had no intention at the time of speaking to these children or interviewing them. After many months and the assistance of local officials, I was finally able to convince the school superintendent to provide us with the information we needed. We then paid school staff to search the records of the over 140 elementary schools that existed at the time and found that many of the schools had closed since these children were enrolled.

With these design characteristics worked out, I was able to convince the National Institute of Justice to fund the research. In this archival study, abused and neglected children were matched with a control group of children and both groups were followed up through an examination of official criminal records (Widom, 1989a, 1989b). Numerous papers were published describing the findings and the *Science* paper was awarded the American Association for the Advancement of Science Behavioral Science Prize in 1989.

Briefly, we found that abused and neglected children were at increased risk for delinquency, crime, and violence, compared to the controls, but the relationship was not deterministic and the majority of the maltreated children did not become delinquents or adult offenders. These findings were contrary to the prevailing belief at the time—that abused and neglected children became delinquents and adult offenders. Because of the strength of the design, however, I believe that people eventually came to accept the findings and eventually policies were implemented based on the findings and replications by others.

At the same time, the fact that not all of these maltreated children had become offenders led us to wonder whether there were other outcomes associated with early histories of child abuse and neglect and whether these children were drug addicts, alcoholics, in psychiatric hospitals, or even still alive. This was the late 1980s and there was very little serious research on the long-term consequences of child abuse and neglect.

At this point, what had been an archival study became a prospective longitudinal study and the next phase of this research involved tracing, locating, and interviewing these abused and neglected individuals and controls about 22 years after these childhood experiences. During the years 1989–1995, we located and conducted the first in-person interviews, collecting extensive information about psychiatric, cognitive, intellectual, social, and behavioral functioning.

When I had originally proposed a study to find and interview these people all these years after their early childhood experiences, program officers at NIMH were very skeptical. Indeed, they would not fund a study without pilot data showing that I could find these folks and interview them. However, I could not waste these precious individuals to get pilot data to prove to NIMH that it would be possible. Fortunately, NIJ staffers were willing to take a gamble on the project and funded us to conduct 700 interviews, and the assumption was that we would be lucky to get the 700. After completing interviews with 699, I decided that it was important to publish with the existing data to demonstrate to the funding agencies that other scholars involved in the peer review process had judged the work to be of high quality. I picked two topics about which I thought it would be safe to publish with only the 699 interviews completed, recognizing that I still wanted to interview as many of the original sample as possible. Both papers were published using the data from the 699 subjects. The academic performance paper (Perez & Widom, 1994) stands and the results did not change with the addition of the remaining interviews (total $N = 1,196$). However, the paper on antisocial personality disorder (Luntz & Widom, 1994) was published in the *American Journal of Psychiatry* using the 699 cases, and those results were not the same when we finished the final data collection. This was a painful and important lesson that I share with my graduate students. Other researchers and clinicians continue to cite the premature findings in the Luntz and Widom (1994) paper (based on the incomplete sample of 699) and do not cite the book chapter that describes the correct findings based on the full sample with 1,196 participants (Widom, 1998).

Since that time, the scope of the original study has been expanded to assess multiple domains of functioning potentially affected by childhood victimization, including mental health, alcohol and drug abuse, revictimization, and economic productivity, service utilization, and physical health outcomes. Published papers cover this range of topics and others. Throughout this process, I have collaborated with colleagues from many different disciplines (e.g., economics, genetics, anthropology, criminology, medicine, dentistry, pediatrics, psychology, psychiatry, public health, and statistics). We have now published over 130 papers or book chapters on the consequences of child abuse and neglect and have received numerous awards for this research. Despite the blood, sweat, and tears that I experienced during the various phases of this research, making the effort to design a methodologically strong study has turned out to be an extremely worthwhile and gratifying endeavor.

References

Leventhal, J. M. (1982). Research strategies and methodologic standards in studies of risk factors for child abuse. *Child Abuse and Neglect, 6*, 113–123.

Luntz, B. K., & Widom, C. S. (1994). Antisocial personality disorder in abused and neglected children grown up. *American Journal of Psychiatry, 151*(5), 670–674.

Perez, C., & Widom, C. S. (1994). Childhood victimization and long-term intellectual and academic outcomes. *Child Abuse and Neglect, 18*, 617–633.

Schulsinger, F., Mednick, S. A., & Knop, J. (1981). *Longitudinal research: Methods and uses in behavioral sciences*. Boston, MA: Martinus Nijhoff.

Widom, C. S. (1977). A methodology for studying noninstitutionalized psychopaths. *Journal of Consulting & Clinical Psychology, 45*(4), 674–683.

Widom, C. S. (1978). Toward an understanding of female criminality. In B. A. Maher (Ed.), *Progress in experimental personality research* (Vol. 8, pp. 245–308). New York, NY: Academic.

Widom, C. S. (1989a). Child abuse, neglect and adult behavior: Research design and findings on criminality, violence, and child abuse. *American Journal of Orthopsychiatry, 59*(3), 355–367.

Widom, C. S. (1989b). The cycle of violence. *Science, 244*, 160–166.

Widom, C. S. (1989c). Does violence beget violence? A critical examination of the literature. *Psychological Bulletin, 106*(1), 3–28.

Widom, C. S. (1998). Childhood victimization: Early adversity and subsequent psychopathology. In B. P. Dohrenwend (Ed.), *Adversity, stress, and psychopathology* (pp. 81–95). New York, NY: Oxford University Press.

The criminal justice system is rife with data, not quite as extensive as the "big data" found in genetics or social media analyses, but still somewhat formidable. Lynn Addington ("Research Adventures with 'Kinda Big' Data") describes her forays into studying one of the newer such data sets, the National Incident-Based Reporting System (NIBRS) collected by the FBI. Another substantial source of crime data, collected by the Bureau of Justice Statistics (BJS), has been studied extensively by Janet Lauritsen ("The Devil is in the Details") who explains her involvement in its study. Many of the newer analytic tools were developed by Kenneth Land ("Solving Criminological Puzzles") and his colleagues; he describes the questions that led to their development. These and other tools of the trade were used by Pamela Lattimore ("Upon Becoming a Criminologist") in major evaluations, by Philip Cook and Jens Ludwig ("Elusive Facts about Gun Violence") in their critique of studies of gun violence, and by Alex Piquero ("What's the Question?") in a number of studies, particularly in the areas of criminal careers and crime prevention. And Susan Turner ("Predicting Risk") also describes how seemingly straightforward analyses of data can be misinterpreted by governmental bodies.

Research Adventures with "Kinda Big" Data: Using NIBRS to Study Crime

Lynn A. Addington

My chapter is slightly different than the others in this volume. Rather than focusing on a particular topic to frame my discussion of developing research questions and addressing methodological challenges, I use a dataset as the basis for exploring these issues. Specifically, my focus is on the Uniform Crime Reporting (UCR) Program's National Incident-Based Reporting System (NIBRS). Mike and Steve asked the contributors to be informal and conversational in our entries, which proved to be much more challenging than it sounded. My conversations about NIBRS tend to be highly animated ones that quickly get into the weeds. One reason is that I am thrilled to meet anyone expressing even a passing interest in NIBRS as the NIBRS crowd tends to be rather limited (although our numbers are growing). Another is that I truly love my research (overall and with NIBRS in particular). It continues to amaze me that I am paid essentially to play with data, explore topics of my choosing, and derive the excitement of discovering something new and interesting. In an effort to bring some organization to the present conversation, I start with a brief description of NIBRS for the uninitiated before discussing my experiences using these data in my research.

Background

NIBRS in a Nutshell[1]

Since the 1930s, the Federal Bureau of Investigation (FBI) has collected crime data from law enforcement agencies as part of the UCR. Initially, the only feasible method for this data collection was aggregate counts from each jurisdiction. As technology evolved, the manner in which data could be compiled also changed. NIBRS is the new format used to collect crime data for the UCR. NIBRS gathers information at the incident level with greater detail (and associated research opportunities) than previously available with the UCR's traditional summary reporting system format.

NIBRS encompasses a number of substantial changes as compared to the summary reporting system. NIBRS covers a wider variety of offenses than the eight Part I (formerly known as Index) offenses captured by the summary

L.A. Addington (✉)
American University, Washington, DC, USA
e-mail: adding@american.edu

[1] Much of this section borrows from a previous discussion (Addington, 2010). Readers interested in more details about NIBRS and the UCR are directed to sources such as Addington (2009, 2014) and Barnett-Ryan (2007). Those interested in working with NIBRS data are strongly encouraged to refer to the National Archive of Criminal Justice Data's online NIBRS Data Resource Guide, the related NACJD-produced NIBRS codebooks, and the FBI's NIBRS website and online annual reports.

M.D. Maltz and S.K. Rice (eds.), *Envisioning Criminology: Researchers on Research as a Process of Discovery*, DOI 10.1007/978-3-319-15868-6_16, © Springer International Publishing Switzerland 2015

reporting system. These eight offenses include murder and nonnegligent manslaughter, forcible rape,[2] robbery, aggravated assault, burglary, larceny-theft, motor vehicle theft, and arson. NIBRS collects incident-level details for 46 Group A offenses, which include the original eight Part I offenses. Examples of these additional crimes range from kidnapping and sex offenses beyond rape (such as sodomy and sexual assault with an object) to vandalism, gambling, and fraud offenses.

The main difference between NIBRS and the summary reporting system is the collection of incident-level data.[3] For the Group A offenses, NIBRS collects detailed information within six segment levels: administrative, offense, property, victim, offender, and arrestee. Overall NIBRS can collect up to 53 distinct data elements to describe each criminal incident. Thirteen of these elements are required for all criminal incidents. Examples of these characteristics include incident date, location of the incident, and type of victim. Thirty-six of the other data elements are mandatory, but only if they are relevant to a particular crime. For example, a weapon must be reported for a personal crime like murder, but not for a property crime like theft. Up to 13 data elements can be used to describe individual victims. Depending upon the crime, these elements include victim demographics, injury, victim-offender relationship, and circumstance codes for aggravated assaults and homicides.

NIBRS is not without its drawbacks. One of the most significant limitations is its lack of national coverage and particularly the present exclusion of the largest police agencies. To participate, states must be certified to submit NIBRS data. This certification process is a lengthy one and not all states are certified. In addition, even in certified states, not all law enforcement agencies report their crime data in NIBRS format. As of 2012, 32 states were certified with 15 having 100% participation (JRSA, n.d.). Within these states, participating law enforcement agencies tend to be those covering smaller populations. Only one jurisdiction that serves a population over 1,000,000 (Fairfax County, VA) reports its data in NIBRS format.

My Dataset Is Bigger than Yours, But It's Still Not "Big Data"

Even though it lacks national coverage, NIBRS data files are huge as a result of the expansion of crimes and incident details. The most recently available public-use files are from 2011 and contain information for 5,020,847 incidents, 5,593,257 victims, and 5,753,416 offenders with 376 incident variables, 280 victim variables, and 368 offender variables. Although these files are big, they do not constitute "big data" as that concept is used in the data analytics field. Actual "big data" refers not to the size of the file but its features. These features typically are summarized as volume, velocity, and variety, which refer to the amount of information, the speed at which it is generated, and the range of sources from which it is derived (e.g., Franks, 2012; McAfee & Brynjolfsson, 2012). Unlike NIBRS or other secondary datasets with big data, "the data available are often unstructured—and not organized in a database—and unwieldy" (McAfee & Brynjolfsson, 2012). As such, I refer to NIBRS as "kinda" (or less colloquially "quasi") big data. This designation recognizes that the sheer size of the file creates its own set of challenges but these are different than the ones confronted by analysts working with big data. The discussion below provides illustrative examples of issues generated by the size of the NIBRS data files.

[2] In December 2011, the FBI announced changes in its definition of rape to remove the "force" requirement and to include victims of both genders and not just female victims. This new definition took effect in 2013.

[3] The summary reporting system does allow for incident-level details as part of its Supplementary Homicide Report (SHR), but the SHR is much more limited than NIBRS. The SHR only collects incident details for homicides. The SHR also collects fewer incident details than NIBRS. Finally the SHR, like the rest of the summary reporting system, does not provide any unique incident identifiers. This omission restricts the SHR's ability to update data to include, for example, subsequent clearance information.

Inspiration, Perspiration, and Luck: Using NIBRS for Research

In an often-cited quote, Edison described genius as 1% inspiration and 99% perspiration. While not "genius" by any stretch, my experience with research borrows from this framework as I have found it is a mix of inspiration (being "clever" and identifying areas and questions in need of exploration) and perspiration (investing a good amount of sweat equity in learning a topic or dataset) but adds the element of a healthy dose of luck (benefitting from good timing and opportunity). Inspiration and perspiration are necessary but not sufficient, as investing in a great idea does not always pan out. This takes a bit of luck.

My discussion below explores some examples of these elements—the ideas, the sweat, and the opportunities. This framework provides a handy means by which to organize my discussion, but the process is not so rigidly compartmentalized. The actual practice of research is much more fluid where one area interacts with another. Investing in learning a dataset, for example, can create opportunities or generate inspiration.

Getting Lucky

I view luck in a fairly broad way—it includes timing, happenstance, and opportunity. As this chapter overall illustrates, some of it is just kismet and some is creating your own opportunities through hard work and good ideas. I start with luck because one aspect concerns my initial introduction to NIBRS and its timing. This luck, though, also includes ideas that actually came to fruition and had some success in dissemination as a presentation or publication since so many ideas never see the light of day.

I would be willing to bet a good chunk of change that no one applies to a graduate criminology program (or any program for that matter) with the goal of analyzing NIBRS data. I certainly didn't.[4] Instead, I stumbled upon NIBRS

as the result of working on assignments for two graduate classes—one on measurement of crime and the other research design. At the time, NIBRS was barely getting off the ground. To help promote interest in both collecting NIBRS data among law enforcement agencies and using it among researchers, a series of government reports were published to showcase the utility of the data. From my coursework, I knew the research opportunities provided by the detailed homicide data from the SHR. The potential of incident-level police data for crimes beyond homicide intrigued me. Around the same time, the *Journal of Quantitative Criminology* published a special issue on NIBRS. This issue helped open the door for publishing NIBRS-based research in traditional academic outlets. I was fortunate not only to happen upon NIBRS but also to do so at a time when few researchers were using these data, but academic journals were willing to seriously consider articles relying on these data. This latter element is the "reality" of research and was necessary for me to take the calculated risk of continuing to work with these data.[5] In an ideal world, we all would conduct research for the pure joy of discovery and generating knowledge, but practical requirements of our profession dictate that some of this work sees the light of day and is disseminated in a tangible format.

Another aspect of luck is the next step of identifying a research project that actually pans out. Sometimes you have a great idea, and in theory it should work but in practice the data do not cooperate, the number of cases is too sparse, or the available measures lack the requisite precision. Luck also plays a role in dissemination. Other times, the great idea works in practice but others fail to see its brilliance and it just won't land in a journal. I will provide a few examples of both of these types of projects in my discussion about research ideas below.

---

[4] As a disgruntled attorney, I applied to graduate school with the goal of running from the law.

[5] Early on as I started to get interested in working with NIBRS, a few mentors and more established researchers cautioned me about the opportunity cost of working with these data given what they perceived as its limited utility and publication opportunities.

Sweating with the Data

The perspiration aspect of research is really sweat equity and that investment of time and effort to learn the intricacies of the data—the possibilities, limitations, and issues. For me, it required studying the codebook, documentation, and other data user resources, becoming familiar with the variables, and reviewing reports and articles using the data. This investment is not limited to NIBRS but rather cuts across datasets. It's just the nature of secondary data analysis. Doing it right—to analyze the data correctly, avoid glaring mistakes, and reap the greatest return—is a tedious and time-consuming exercise with few shortcuts. Initially, the investment seems enormous with limited returns. Ultimately (with a little luck as noted above), this work and understanding of the data pays off in dividends such as publications, presentations, and funded research.

I have worked with NIBRS data for about 15 years. When I first started, it was a nightmare. Any new dataset takes time to learn, but the size and nature of NIBRS files amplified the anguish. The data also were not terribly user-friendly. Running a fairly straightforward analysis required merging together several segments that contained millions of cases. For example, looking at arrests for intimate partner violence required merging three agency-level segments onto four crime-based segments that contained victim, offender, offense, and arrestee information. Adding to the challenge was the limited desktop computing capacity at the time. As a result, putting together the requisite file could take hours and seemed like an eternity. I tried to coordinate creating these files to start running before I left to teach a class or out to grab lunch. Not infrequently, though, I would return to find some glitch in the syntax or raw data resulted in a file with no cases or only one case. During this time, I learned (and liberally practiced) a whole slew of new curse words. Even when the files would merge, occasionally my research question would evolve and I would need a particular variable or segment that was omitted in the original file. This situation also prompted a string of choice expletives as I would have to go back and recreate the file. These failures made it that much more joyful when the files came together. So much so that I often broke out my "happy data dance" when things actually worked.[6]

While this introduction to NIBRS was painful and a significant investment of time, it gave me unique insights based on a comprehensive view of the data and variables as well as an appreciation of how the files fit together. It also forced me to become fluent in the intricacies of the data. To identify the files I needed to construct and try to minimize making mistakes and rerunning files, I worked to learn as much as I could by reading (and rereading) the codebooks and various reports. As I discuss below, this investment also proved to be beneficial over the years as it helped me generate research projects by knowing the available information in NIBRS as well as understanding its capabilities.

Over the years, the staff at the National Archive of Criminal Justice Data (NACJD) have made great advances in archiving NIBRS files in formats that are much more user-friendly.[7] The most current iteration of this evolution is the NIBRS Extract Files. These files come complete with all of the segment files already merged as well as providing helpful assistance in other ways such as converting the many string variables present in the original files into numeric values.

While the tedious file-building issues have been resolved, the underlying data files are still huge and continue to grow as additional agencies submit NIBRS data. As a result, the sweat equity requirement remains. Even with advances in computing speed, setting up the files and even obtaining a basic frequency take much longer than most researchers are accustomed. As such, it is important to identify the file needed at the onset in order to set up the correct one and to quickly cull the file into a manageable size by

---

[6] Despite Mike and Steve allowing the contributors an option to include video files with this book, I feel as though I have compromised my professional veneer enough by telling this story, let alone by showing my dance!

[7] The NACJD archives and disseminates NIBRS as well as other crime and criminal justice data.

only including the relevant cases. Once the requisite file is created, other issues arise with obtaining variables of interest. The benefit of NIBRS is that it contains a great deal of incident-level details including options for multiple responses for information such as weapons, injuries, and locations. These options, though, add to the complexity of the file and recoding the necessary variables. Finally working with NIBRS is like analyzing any other data. It requires checking and rechecking file recodes as well as confirming models and analyses.

Being Clever

Having inspired or clever research ideas might be a bit of an overstatement. While I have had some fleeting clever moments, much of my work with NIBRS is rooted in fairly basic, foundational work. For me, one motivating question is to test conventional wisdom, ask "is that really the case?" and see if the data support it. More often than not, I am surprised that no one has examined many of the basic assumptions we have about crime. With its incident-level details and large sample size, NIBRS is capable of exploring many of these open issues. In addition to starting with fairly simple research questions, my initial exploration and discussion of them tends to focus on basic, descriptive analyses. Many interesting patterns can be gleaned from frequencies and bivariate comparisons. I credit Mike for promoting this approach and emphasizing the need to visualize data before turning to more sophisticated multivariate modeling (e.g., Maltz, 2010). Overall this approach resulted in some "successes" but also some failures and some that succeed analytically but almost failed to see the light of day as a publication. I provide examples of all three below.

Two examples of successful projects arise from my analysis of NIBRS clearance data. One early project examined time to clearance and tested the assumption that murders clear quickly if they are going to clear at all. Plenty of anecdotal evidence supported this idea, but we lacked any national or multi-jurisdiction data to

formally test it. Since NIBRS identified the date of the incident and the date of any clearance, I was able to explore—and empirically confirm—this assumption as well as examine characteristics of cases that tended to clear quickly (Addington, 2007).

A second example illustrates a success but also an unintended research question since it started as a clearance research project but ended up as something quite different. A few years ago, I was asked to write a paper examining clearance patterns of homicides involving elderly victims. Given my work with NIBRS clearance data, I agreed since I thought it would be interesting—but also a fairly easy—project.[8] Almost immediately I ran into trouble when I could not identify a clear measure of who is elderly. I assumed that age 65 would be the go-to number. Instead I found no general consensus in the literature. While many researchers gravitated to age 65, not all did and no clear support existed for any particular demarcation. This revelation surprised—and frustrated—me. It also resulted in the paper I actually wrote on measuring elderly and the way in which different measures of elderly affect the findings obtained (Addington, 2013a).

These examples are two that worked. Often, though, what should work "in theory" and what happens "in practice" collide in an ugly way. I have a file drawer graveyard of these ideas. My favorite example is from several years ago after I had been working with NIBRS for a few years. My clever idea was to take the offender demographics of the cases known to police and see how closely these matched to the arrestee demographics. I thought it would be interesting to compare initial victim or witness descriptions of the offender with the person ultimately arrested. I spent hours putting together the requisite files, recoding the data, and running my analyses (see the sweat equity discussion above). I was floored by the findings—the offender and arrestee demographics matched almost perfectly.

---

[8] A lesson I continue to fail to learn is that something that sounds like it will be easy to do is a huge red flag that it will be anything but.

Some characteristics didn't surprise me too much. Matches on sex I expected but I thought some slippage would occur for race and even more for age given the literature on how poorly eyewitnesses estimate age. As I was beginning to write up these findings for publication, I spoke with a colleague at the FBI about my amazing discovery. At that moment, it became a lot less amazing. I realized my findings likely were the result of the FBI's early, informal practice of encouraging law enforcement agencies to overwrite and correct offender information using arrestee demographics. Although the practice was no longer encouraged for the years of data I was using, many agencies still continued it, and the changes were not flagged in the file in any identifiable way. So much for my remarkable findings and into the file drawer graveyard the project went.

Other ideas actually work analytically but become a challenge to "sell" to a journal because reviewers are critical of the idea. Confirming conventional wisdom often receives a "so what" review and little appreciation of empirically supporting a basic assumption that no previous work had tested. Challenging conventional wisdom can bring visceral reactions, especially from reviewers who built their research agenda on these assumptions. Trying something new and unconventional also can bring criticism even when it is characterized as a means of beginning a discussion of the issue. Recently a colleague and I confronted this latter challenge with regard to a methodological rather than a substantive issue (Addington & Perumean-Chaney, 2014). One challenge with NIBRS is its large sample size. As a result nearly everything analyzed is statistically significant. We wanted to begin to explore other ways of identifying "significance" and begin a larger conversation on how best to analyze NIBRS data as more researchers are using these data and no one is confronting this foundational issue. We used three different methods to illustrate ways to explore this idea. We received some negative reviewer feedback for trying to bring a bit of creativity to the problem, which surprised us. After two revise and resubmits, we were able to placate these concerns but also stay true to our original work.

Fluid Nature of the Research Process

As I mentioned above, my experience is that research is a dynamic practice where ideas, investment in the data, and luck all interact and build off one another. One example of this process is a recent project on cyberbullying using NIBRS data to examine the nature of these cases that come to the attention of police and how police handle them (Addington, 2013b). The idea arose in part out of my investment and work with the data. NIBRS does not collect data on cyberbullying per se, but it does collect information on whether a computer was used as part of the crime, the age of the victim, as well as the crime of intimidation. Based on my knowledge of the variables, I used these characteristics to generate a proxy measure of cyberbullying. Given these criteria, the number of cases dropped considerably, but I was lucky enough to wind up with enough cases to analyze. I also was lucky to find an editor willing to publish this work, especially in light of a reviewer who utterly hated my article, my idea, and my use of NIBRS data in this way. In contrast, I had presented this work to a group of state UCR analysts and they loved the idea, especially finding creative ways of using data elements collected by NIBRS.

Conclusion

This chapter provides some initial insights about my experiences conducting research with NIBRS. It is not designed to be an exhaustive guide for using NIBRS as many more issues exist when analyzing and working with these data. It also is just my own perspective about working with these data. Other NIBRS researchers would provide different accounts, especially those involved in current innovative uses of merging NIBRS with other datasets. Despite these caveats, a few themes likely are universal when conducting research relying on secondary datasets. One is that no substitute exists for investing in learning a dataset; confirming file builds, recodes, and analyses; and providing a documented record. This hard work is tedious, not particularly glamorous, and incredibly frustrating when the project fails. A second is being open to unexpected opportunities. The best-laid plans often do not work out, but in their place may be the chance to work on other projects and research questions that are just as interesting (and sometimes even more so because they are unintended). Finally is the need to pursue intrinsically interesting work. What is interesting varies from person to person, but intellectually stimulating projects make conducting tedious tasks easier, generating clever research simpler, confronting the inevitable failures more tolerable, and living the life of a researcher much more rewarding.

References

Addington, L. A. (2007). Hot vs. cold cases: Examining time to clearance for homicides using NIBRS data. *Justice Research and Policy, 9*, 87–112.

Addington, L. A. (2009). Studying the crime problem with NIBRS data: Current uses and future trends. In M. D. Krohn, A. J. Lizotte, & G. P. Hall (Eds.), *Handbook on crime and deviance*. New York, NY: Springer.

Addington, L. A. (2010). National Incident-Based Reporting System (NIBRS). In B. S. Fisher & S. P. Lab (Eds.), *Encyclopedia of victimization and crime prevention*. Thousand Oaks, CA: Sage.

Addington, L. A. (2013a). Who you calling old?: Measuring "elderly" and what it means for homicide research. *Homicide Studies, 17*, 134–153.

Addington, L. A. (2013b). Reporting and clearance of cyberbullying incidents: Applying "offline" theories to online victims. *Journal of Contemporary Criminal Justice, 29*, 454–474.

Addington, L. A. (2014). The development of the UCR and the NCVS and their contribution to criminology. In L. Dugan, D. Weisburd, & G. Bruinsma (Eds.), *Criminology and criminal justice—The history of methods and statistics*. New York, NY: Springer.

Addington, L. A., & Perumean-Chaney, S. (2014). Intimate partner violence: What separates the men from the women for victimizations reported to police. *Homicide Studies, 18*, 196–219.

Barnett-Ryan, C. (2007). Introduction to the Uniform Crime Reporting Program. In J. P. Lynch & L. A. Addington (Eds.), *Understanding crime statistics: Revisiting the divergence of the NCVS and the UCR* (pp. 55–89). Cambridge, England: Cambridge University Press.

Franks, B. (2012). *Taming the big data tidal wave: Finding opportunities in huge data streams with advanced analytics*. Hoboken, NJ: Wiley.

JRSA. (n.d.). *Status of NIBRS in the states*. Retrieved May 7, 2014, from http://www.jrsa.org/ibrrc/background-status/nibrs_states.shtml

Maltz, M. D. (2010). Look before you analyze: Visualizing data in criminal justice. In D. Weisburd & A. P. Piquero (Eds.), *Handbook of quantitative criminology*. New York, NY: Springer.

McAfee, A., & Brynjolfsson, E. (2012). Big data: The management revolution. *Harvard Business Review, 90*(10), 60–68. Retrieved from http://hbr.org/2012/10/big-data-the-management-revolution/ar

Elusive Facts About Gun Violence: Where Good Surveys Go Bad

Philip J. Cook and Jens Ludwig

The evidence base for the study of guns and violence begins with data on such fundamental issues as the number and distribution of guns, the number of people shot each year in criminal assaults, and the frequency of gun use in self-defense. It seems that these simple descriptive statistics should be readily available, and in fact the rhetoric of the Great American Gun War routinely includes reference to 300 million guns, or 100,000 people who are shot each year, or 2.5 million defensive gun uses (DGUs). But it turns out that such statistics should be viewed with considerable skepticism. Developing reliable estimates of basic facts in this arena is surprisingly difficult, even with the best of intentions.

There exist administrative data compiled by government agencies on each of these topics, but those data are incomplete, difficult to access, error-prone, or all of these. As a result, analysts have made extensive use of population surveys, which in principle can overcome the limitations of administrative data. For example, if you want to find out how many guns are in private hands, why not ask a representative sample of US households whether there is a gun on the premises, and if so,

how many? But it turns out even state-of-the-art survey methods can generate heavily biased estimates. The existence and nature of these biases has been a matter of heated debate in one of these areas, DGUs, because of its direct relevance to advocates' claims concerning the value of widespread gun ownership. But the word "bias" in this context does not refer to political bias, but rather a predictable error characteristic of a particular estimation method. The surprise is that the survey methods used to generate such error-prone estimates are not obviously deficient, but rather widely accepted in social science. Hence there are methodological lessons that go well beyond the arena of gun violence. Here we recount three examples in some detail. The point is not that surveys are useless, but rather that their accuracy should not be taken on faith.

Accepted practice for scholars who are assessing the accuracy of a survey-based estimate of some population statistic is to review the methods used to generate the data. Indications that the survey-based statistics may be off the mark include a sample frame that omits some of the population (e.g., those who lack a landline phone), a low response rate, poorly written questions or a response mode that is not reliable given the subject matter. If given the survey method it is reasonable to consider the respondents as representative of the relevant population (possibly after population weights are applied, and subject to normal sampling error), and their responses

P.J. Cook (✉)
Sanford School of Public Policy, Duke University,
PO Box 90245, Durham, NC 27708, USA
e-mail: pcook@duke.edu

J. Ludwig
University of Chicago, Chicago, IL, USA

M.D. Maltz and S.K. Rice (eds.), *Envisioning Criminology: Researchers on Research as a Process of Discovery*, DOI 10.1007/978-3-319-15868-6_17, © Springer International Publishing Switzerland 2015

to the survey items are in some sense credible, then the resulting estimate is to be taken seriously. (Of course it helps if the agency that conducted the survey has a good reputation.) Unfortunately it is less common to include in the assessment a comparison with other estimates of the same population statistic, or of related statistics. An assessment based solely on the survey procedures is akin to the approach of the appellate courts in reviewing a criminal case—the guilty finding is tested not by looking at new evidence in the case, but rather by assessing the process used to arrive at that verdict.

The problem is this: Sometimes a survey is well designed, but the resulting estimates are demonstrably wrong, and by a wide margin. For that reason, we believe that if getting a reasonably accurate estimate is important (and if it is not, why bother?), then the analyst should ask and attempt to answer the following prosaic question: "Given everything we know, both from the survey in question and other sources, is this particular estimate in the right ballpark?" We might call this a "plausibility test." It may seem like common sense, but a quick scan of reports of survey results will demonstrate that a discussion of procedure is far more common than a discussion of plausibility.

As an example, consider a survey-based estimate of the amount that Americans drink. High-quality surveys of the United States population that ask respondents whether they drink and if so, how much, can be used to generate estimates of the national average per capita consumption of alcohol. In that case there is an obvious check on the accuracy of the result—tax-paid sales of alcoholic beverages. (In recent year those sales have amounted to about 2.3 gal of ethanol per individual age 15 and over.) As it turns out, survey-based estimates are typically 40–60% of tax-paid sales, suggesting either that a great deal of beer and whiskey is poured down the sink every year, or that respondents underreport their true consumption. (Another possibility is that the heaviest drinkers tend to be nonrespondents or left out of the sample frame entirely.) In this case the availability of reasonably accurate administrative data (tax-paid sales) provides a valuable external standard by which to assess and correct survey-based estimates. That situation is more the exception than the rule, but in other cases there may be other approaches to "plausibility testing."

In what follows we consider three examples from the study of gun ownership and use (or misuse). The first example is gun ownership—the household prevalence of guns, and the number of guns in private hands. The second is the number of individuals who are shot and wounded in assault circumstances. And the third is the number of instances in which a private individual uses a gun to defend against crime. In each case the apparent bias in estimates based on population surveys is remarkably large.

How Many Guns in Private Hands?

Key statistics in the debate over the feasibility of gun control are the household prevalence of private gun ownership, and closely related, the number of guns in private hands. Administrative data on the prevalence of household gun ownership is almost entirely lacking. Data of that sort could in principle be generated through licensing or gun registration. At the federal level registration is only required for owners of machine guns and other weapons of mass destruction. A few states require licensing or registration, but compliance with those requirements is likely to be far less than 100%.

Sample surveys appear to offer a good alternative to administrative data. For example, the General Social Survey (GSS), conducted by the National Opinion Research Center, has long included questions on gun ownership. In 1999 it estimated that just 36% of American households owned at least one firearm, down from nearly 50% in 1980 (Smith, 2000, p. 55).[1] The most recent estimate (February 2014) from the reputable Pew Research Center survey finds that 37% of households had at least one firearm.

---

[1] The drop in household ownership may reflect the trend in household composition during this period; households are less likely to include a gun because they have become smaller and, in particular, less likely to include a man (Wright, Jasinski, & Lanier, 2012).

As it turns out, however, there appears to be systematic response error (bias) in "household prevalence" estimates of this sort. That bias was discovered by comparing the responses of husbands and wives to the same question (Cook & Ludwig, 1996). In the GSS sampling procedure, whether the husband or wife is selected as the respondent for a household that is headed by a married couple is determined randomly, so the same percentage should report a gun in the household. In fact husbands are consistently more likely than wives to report a gun, with the difference as high as 10 percentage points in some years (Ludwig, Cook, & Smith, 1998). And GSS is not the only survey with this problem. Using the National Survey of Private Ownership of Firearms (NSPOF) data, we found that if husbands' answers were to be believed, the estimated national stock of handguns would be twice as high as if we believed the wives' answers (Cook & Ludwig, 1996).

It is tempting to believe that the husbands are more accurate, since they are likely to be the primary owners and users of any guns, and may be better informed and less reluctant to admit to owning a gun in a survey. But it is not necessarily true that the gap is due to wives' underreporting—the husbands may be overreporting—since some respondents may want to overstate their gun collection to impress the interviewer. Still, at this point it is reasonable to suppose that responses to the question of individual gun ownership are more accurate than responses to a question about household gun ownership.[2] In the Pew survey cited above, 24% of adults indicated that they personally owned a gun, with men more likely to report ownership than women by a factor of 3 to 1.

Analysis of a two-generation survey in California found that the "household gun reporting gap" appeared when teenagers were asked about guns in the home—the boys were much more likely to say yes than the girls (Cook & Sorenson, 2006). In this survey there was enough information to determine that the difference in

response was accounted for by the difference in participation in gun sports, suggesting that the response is influenced by whether the respondent has first-hand knowledge of the existence of a household gun collection.

To determine the *number* of guns in private hands (as opposed to the prevalence of gun ownership) requires that a survey ask how many guns are in the household, and that question has been quite rare. We used the 1994 NSPOF to generate detailed estimates: we found that 25% of adults (most of them men) owned at least one gun, that the average gun-owning adult owned 4.4; multiplying up, we estimated the total number of guns in private hands as 192 million (one-third of which were handguns) (Cook & Ludwig, 1996).[3] Does that estimate meet the "plausibility" test? Perhaps. The federal government has kept track of the number of civilian guns manufactured, imported, and exported since 1899. By 1993 (when the NSPOF was fielded) the cumulative total of guns introduced into the US civilian market (manufactures plus imports minus exports) was 223 million. It makes sense that the cumulative total somewhat exceeds the stock in that year (223 vs. 192 million), since guns are durable but not immortal—over the decades, millions have been broken and discarded, or destroyed following confiscation by the police. So the survey-based estimate is not in obvious contradiction to the administrative record.

But before concluding that that estimate of 192 million guns was in the right ballpark for 1993, we should consider the quality of the administrative records used as a benchmark. They necessarily omit counts of off-the-books imports and exports. Most prominent in recent years has been the illegal (and unrecorded) exports to Mexican drug gangs, but there is nothing new about such exports—the United States has long been a source of guns smuggled to Canada, the Caribbean, and Central America. It is also true that there are unrecorded imports,

---

[2] NSPOF asks both about how many guns the respondent personally owned, and also how many guns were in the household. We considered the answers to the personal ownership question more reliable, and used them to generate the estimate of 192 million guns in private hands.

[3] The most detailed national survey on the subject since then (the National Firearms Survey) found that gun-owning households average 5.2 guns in 2004 (Hepburn, Miller, Azrael, & Hemenway, 2007). Note that the number of guns per gun-owning household differs from the number of guns per gun-owning individual.

such as military weapons brought back from war by American troops (Kleck, 1991, App. 1). If the illicit exports exceed the imports, then the result would be that the administrative data exaggerate the net flow of guns into the civilian market.

Thus we have no "bulletproof" way to estimate the number of guns in private hands. The best that can be hoped for is a ballpark estimate. If we accept the Pew estimate that one quarter of adults own at least one gun, that amounts to 60 million individual gun owners aged 18 and over. Some adolescents own guns as well, so perhaps the true number is 65 million. Estimating the number of guns per gun owner requires a replication of NSPOF-type questions, which has not been done. If the average number per gun owner is 4, then the total is 260 million; if 5, then we are up to 325 million (which is about equal to the cumulative total between 1899 and 2011). In any event, it should be understood that there is a wide range of plausible estimates.

How Many Gun Injuries from Assault?

The number of gunshot victims in assault cases includes those who die and are hence counted in the Vital Statistics program as gun homicides.[4] While not perfect, the Vital Statistics counts are generally presumed to be quite accurate. The challenge, then, is to estimate the number of assault cases where the victim is shot but does not die, since there is no national system for counting such cases.[5]

In principle, survey data of a nationally representative sample of households could provide a comprehensive estimate of nonfatal injuries. The National Crime Victimization Survey (conducted by the Census Bureau on behalf of the US Department of Justice) has asked the relevant questions of a nationally representative sample since 1973, and released annual estimates of the number of gunshot victims in assaults. These estimates turn out to be gross underestimates of the truth, despite the fact that the NCVS is an exceptionally well-crafted survey. One of us (Cook) first became aware that there might be a problem after comparing the estimated nonfatal injury rate with the known rate of fatal gunshot wounds in assault (homicides). The ratio of nonfatal (from NCVS) to fatal was 2:1, implying that fully one in three gunshot victims die. By considering a variety of sources of information on the case-fatality rate in assaults where the victim was shot, a consistent finding emerged— rather than a 1 in 3 death rate among victims of criminal shootings, the actual fatality rate is typically about 1 in 7 (Cook, 1985).[6]

Since that demonstration a new source of data has become available and helped confirm the magnitude of the true case-fatality rate. This source taps into the administrative data of a sample of emergency departments called NEISS, which provides (among other things) an estimate of the number of gunshot victims treated in emergency departments and the circumstances in which the injury occurred (assault, suicide, accident). If we divide the number of gun homicides by the total of gun homicides and nonfatal gun assaults treated in the emergency department (as estimated from NEISS data), the case-fatality rate in 2011 is 1 in 6 (11,101 homicides and 55,544 nonfatal injuries). That is in line with the 1 in 7 estimate, given the fact that some gunshot cases do not show up at an emergency room.

The bias in NCVS estimates has if anything become more pronounced in recent years. Here is a recent report from the Bureau of Justice

---

[4] The National Vital Statistics System is managed by the federal National Center for Health Statistics, which compiles reports from states.

[5] The police are likely to know about most of those cases (because medical staff are required to report in many states), and some of the cases that are not treated in emergency rooms will come to police attention as well (due to 911 calls). Unfortunately, police records on gunshot victims are not separately compiled as part of the FBI's Uniform Crime Reporting system, but rather are submerged in the much larger category of "aggravated assault with firearm" (which includes threats and attacks where no injury results).

[6] This estimate was subsequently confirmed and reported in a doctoral dissertation at the University of Maryland (Long-Onnen, 2000).

Statistics: "In the 5-year aggregate period from 2007 to 2011, a total of 46,000 nonfatal firearm victims were wounded with a firearm and another 58,483 were victims of a firearm homicide (Planty & Truman, 2014, p. 11)." The "46,000" is estimated from the NCVS, and implies that over half of all gunshot victims die. The report goes on to note that the estimate of nonfatal gunshot cases from the NEISS is far higher, over 250,000 during this period, and then observes "The differences noted between the NCVS and NEISS-AIP firearm injury estimates are due in part to a variety of technical issues…. Therefore, NCVS may miss injuries that involve persons who are homeless, victims who require lengthy stays in a hospital, and offenders who are incarcerated or placed in other institutional settings after the incident." While one might hope for a stronger statement—namely, something to the effect that "The NCVS estimate understates the true number by a factor of 5 or more"—the careful reader will still get the idea.

The likely reasons for the gross underestimate of nonfatal gunshot victims in NCVS is that they are underrepresented in the sample, and not just for the reasons noted in the quote above. A large percentage of assault victims are drawn from the ranks of youthful men who are difficult to contact because they have no regular address, and in any event may be reluctant to talk to an interviewer. (In these respects there is a good deal of overlap between the shooters and the victims.)

When it comes to estimating the number of nonfatal gunshot assaults, best practice may be to ignore the national survey estimates, and generate estimates instead by using an evidence-based multiplier of the official count of gun homicides. That work-around appears to provide fairly accurate estimates.

Note that the large bias in the NCVS estimates is with respect to a narrow category of victimization (shot during a criminal assault) that is concentrated among a group that may in practice be underrepresented in the survey sample. That would not be the case for estimating victimization rates for such crimes as burglary or auto theft.

How Many DGUs?

While guns do enormous damage in crime they also provide some crime victims with the means of escaping serious injury or property loss. The NCVS, despite its limitations (see above), is generally considered the most reliable source of information on predatory crime, since it has been in the field since 1973 and incorporates the best thinking of survey methodologists. From this source it would appear that use of guns in self-defense against criminal predation occurs on the order of 100,000 times per year (Cook, Ludwig, & Hemenway, 1997). Of particular interest is the likelihood that a gun will be used in self-defense against a residential intruder. Based on the NCVS data for the mid-1980s, only 3% of victims were able to deploy a gun against someone who broke in (or attempted to do so) while they were at home (Cook, 1991). Since about 45% of all households possessed a gun during that period, it appears that it was relatively unusual for victims to be able to deploy a gun against intruders even when they have one nearby.

In contrast are the results of several smaller one-time telephone surveys, which provide a basis for asserting that there are millions of DGUs per year (Cook & Ludwig, 1996; Kleck & Gertz, 1995). The best known estimate in this literature is 2.5 million (Kleck & Gertz, 1995). Why do these one-time surveys produce estimates that exceed the NCVS estimate by a factor of 25 or more? One explanation is that the NCVS only asks questions about defensive actions to those who report a victimization attempt, while the phone surveys ask such questions of every respondent. While as a logical matter it seems like it would make little difference, it is quite possible that some NCVS respondents fail to report a DGU because they did not think to report to the interviewer the criminal threat that initiated it. In that case the NCVS will include false negatives in its estimate of DGUs. On the other hand, survey questionnaires that ask an open-ended question about self-defense uses greatly expand the scope for false positives

(Cook et al., 1997; Hemenway, 1997a, 1997b).[7] Moreover, as the National Research Council's Committee to Improve Research Information and Data on Firearms notes, "fundamental problems in defining what is meant by DGU may be a primary impediment to accurate measurement" (Wellford, Pepper, & Petrie, 2005, p. 103; see also McDowall, Loftin, & Presser, 2000). When respondents who report a DGU are asked to describe the sequence of events, many of the cases turn out to have involved something other than an immediate threat, and in fact a majority of such self-reported cases were thought to be illegal by a panel of judges (Hemenway, Miller, & Azrael, 2000).

Perhaps the most compelling challenge to the survey-based claim that there are millions of DGUs per year derives from a comparison with what we know about crime rates. The 2.5 million DGU estimate is well over twice the total number of robberies and assaults committed with a gun, as estimated at that time in the NCVS, which in turn is far more than the number of gun crimes known to the police.[8] Likewise, the number of shootings reported by those who claimed to be defending themselves vastly exceeds any plausible estimate of the total number of gunshot cases in the United States. The Kleck–Gertz survey suggests that the number of DGU respondents who reported shooting their assailant was over 200,000, over twice the number of those killed or treated in emergency departments (Hemenway, 2004, p. 67).

This last point engendered a small skirmish in the "great American gun war" that dovetails nicely with our call for a plausibility test. Gary Kleck (1997) responded to his critics by asserting that the true number of gunshot cases greatly exceeds the number treated in emergency departments. He claims that many gunshot wounds are not life threatening, and professional treatment would be optional. He speculates that a high percentage of victims are implicated in criminal activity, and that they would hence want to avoid notice of the authorities by going to the hospital for treatment. His argument, then, is that the estimated number of self-defense cases in which the assailant is shot could plausibly exceed the number of *all* gunshot cases (assault, suicide, accident, self-defense) that resulted in death or treatment in an emergency department. This far-fetched claim was tested directly in a series of jail surveys by John May and David Hemenway (May, Hemenway, & Hall, 2002; May, Hemenway, Oen, & Pitts, 2000). These surveys found that a remarkably high percentage of them had been shot at some point in their lives and had the scars to prove it—but more than 90% of those who had been shot reported that they had indeed been treated in a hospital. Thus they would have been included in official statistics on the number of gunshot wounds, and Kleck's assertions are shown to be far off base. The estimate of 2.5 million DGUs, and its subsidiary estimates, do not pass the plausibility test.

The fact is that the estimated number of DGUs from surveys is highly sensitive to the sequence of questions, and in particular whether respondents are only asked about self-defense if they first report a victimization. It also matters that the respondent is given some help in placing events in time (so that when asked about the previous 12 months they do not bring in events that happened before that period). The latter problem, known as "telescoping," is also important in estimating victimization rates. One of the great strengths of the NCVS, as opposed to these one-time surveys, is that its sample retains a household

---

[7] The possibility of false negatives is also increased. But given the rarity of gun use in self-defense, the effect of the two types of error is not symmetric. Even a small false positive rate will have a large proportional effect on self-defense uses. That insight is due to David Hemenway (1997a, 1997b). For example, if 1% of respondents are false positives, that by itself would be nearly enough to produce the Kleck and Gertz estimate of 2.5 million. Given that a representative sample of the US public would include many who are demented, intoxicated, or have a political agenda around this issue, it would not be surprising to get that high of a false positive rate. It raises the larger question of when sample surveys *can* be trusted as the basis for estimating rare events.

[8] The National Crime Victimization Survey for 1994 estimated that 10.9% of the nearly 10 million personal crimes of violence involved guns, for a total of 1.07 million gun crimes (http://bjs.ojp.usdoj.gov/content/pub/pdf/Cvius945.pdf, Table 66). (In the vast majority of these cases the gun was not fired.)

for seven interviews, one every 6 months. The previous interview is used as a way of providing the respondent with a bracket in placing events in time in answering the question of whether he or she had been victimized in the previous 6 months. Without any framing to prevent tele-scoping, the number of gun victimizations bal-loons up. In fact, when the same respondents in the same sort of one-time survey are asked about both DGUs and about victimization by guns, they report many more victimizations than DGUs (Hemenway et al., 2000).

There are lessons here for survey methodology and for gun policy. The methodological lesson is that survey-based estimates of what appears to be a well-defined construct (use of a gun in self-defense during the last year or last 5 years) is hypersensitive to survey design, so much that estimates may differ by a factor of 25 or more. Another lesson for gun policy is that what some individuals consider to be a legitimate use of a gun in self-defense may be highly problematic in practice.

Unlike in the two previous examples, we do not have a good answer to the question of how many DGUs occur in a given year. Ultimately the ques-tion is not well defined—given the way these esti-mates are used in the gun debate, it appears that the goal is to ascertain the number of *legitimate* uses of guns, which is to say both legal and in some sense justified by the objective circum-stances. The survey respondents' memory and interpretation of what transpired are likely to be a shaky basis (at best) for deciding whether a survey-reported case should "count." That is all the more so given the prevalence of mental illness, sub-stance abuse, dementia—and pranksters—in any representative sample of the US population.

One might ask at this point whether any survey-based estimate of the incidence of a rare event is likely to be accurate, given the possibil-ity that even a small percentage of false positives can swamp the true events. The answer depends in part on the nature of the event (whether it is likely to engender false reports), and in part on survey design. The NCVS estimate of DGUs greatly reduces the scope for false positives by screening on whether the respondent reports being a victim of crime that included a personal confrontation (as well as bracketing the time period). Additionally, it may be useful to ask respondents who do report a DGU to give the details, which can then be assessed. This approach is analogous to medical screening for rare conditions, where if the initial test is posi-tive then more expensive tests are administered that have high specificity to the condition in question.

The bottom line is that the results from one-time open-ended surveys asking about DGUs tend to produce estimates that entirely implausi-ble. Scholars have documented this fact and pro-vided some explanation for where the surveys go wrong. Nonetheless, the notion that there are mil-lions of virtuous defensive uses of guns each year continues to be asserted by advocates for deregu-lating guns, including the National Rifle Association. To borrow from Al Gore, it is a con-venient "truth." The marketplace of ideas (and facts) in such a contentious area has the effect of elevating research results that suit predetermined purposes, rather than results based on the best science (Cook, 2013).

Thoughts on Methodology

Even surveys that meet the highest standards of current practice may produce heavily biased esti-mates. The results discussed here should encour-age skepticism and engender what might be called "plausibility tests"—common-sense com-parisons of the resulting estimates with other sources of information. Too often the review of scientific contributions is like appellate review of a criminal conviction—the court focuses on just the process rather than the outcome. For policy-relevant work it is important to test the conclu-sions against what else we know about the reality of the situation.

The problem is by no means limited to surveys used by criminologists. In his recent paper on reporting the uncertainty in economic statistics, Charles Manski (2014) notes that statistical agen-cies should (but do not in practice) report both sam-pling error and nonsampling error. In comparison

with reporting sampling errors, "It is more challenging for agencies to report nonsampling errors
for official statistics. There are many sources of
such errors and there has been no consensus about
how to measure them. Yet these facts do not justify
ignoring nonsampling error. Having agency analytical staffs make good-faith efforts to measure
nonsampling error would be more informative than
having agencies report official statistics as if they
are truths (p. 2)." The examples reported here may
provide some inspiration about just how to assess
nonsampling error.

The overarching theme highlighted by our
examples is the value for criminologists to take
the magnitude of social science estimates seriously. Taking them seriously means understanding the reliability of sources. As a leading pediatric
cardiologist told Jerome Groopman for his book
How Doctors Think, "you not only need to know
what people know, but how they know it"
(Groopman, 2007, p. 135). If what a criminologist
"knows" about a particular population parameter
is based on a survey, then it pays to check, not
only about the intrinsic quality of the survey, but
about the plausibility of the resulting estimate.

References

Cook, P. J. (1985). The case of the missing victims:
Gunshot woundings in the National Crime Survey.
Journal of Quantitative Criminology, 1, 91–102.

Cook, P. J. (1991). The technology of personal violence.
In M. Tonry (Ed.), *Crime and justice: An annual
review of research* (Vol. 14). Chicago, IL: University
of Chicago Press.

Cook, P. J. (2013). The great American gun war: Notes
from four decades in the trenches. In M. Tonry (Ed.),
Crime and justice in America, 1975–2025 (pp. 19–73).
Chicago, IL: University of Chicago Press.

Cook, P. J., & Ludwig, J. (1996). *Guns in America:
Results of a comprehensive national survey on
firearms ownership and use*. Washington, DC: The
Police Foundation.

Cook, P. J., Ludwig, J., & Hemenway, D. (1997). The gun
debate's new mythical number: How many defensive
uses per year. *Journal of Policy Analysis and
Management, 16*(3), 463–469.

Cook, P. J., & Sorenson, S. B. (2006). The gender gap
among teen survey respondents: Why are boys more
likely to report a gun in the home than girls? *Journal
of Quantitative Criminology, 22*(1), 61–76.

Groopman, J. (2007). *How doctors think*. Boston, MA:
Houghton Mifflin.

Hemenway, D. (1997a). The myth of millions of self-
defense gun uses: An explanation of extreme overesti-
mates. *Chance, 10*, 6–10.

Hemenway, D. (1997b). Survey research and self-
defense gun use: An explanation of extreme overesti-
mates. *Journal of Criminal Law & Criminology, 87*,
1430–1445.

Hemenway, D. (2004). *Private guns, public health*. Ann
Arbor, MI: University of Michigan Press.

Hemenway, D., Miller, M., & Azrael, D. (2000). Gun use
in the United States: Results from two national surveys. *Injury Prevention, 6*, 263–267.

Hepburn, L., Miller, M., Azrael, D., & Hemenway, D.
(2007). The U.S. gun stock: Results from the 2004
National Firearms Survey. *Injury Prevention, 13*,
15–19.

Kleck, G. (1991). *Point blank: Guns and violence in
America*. New York, NY: Aldine de Gruyter.

Kleck, G. (1997). *Targeting guns: Firearms and their control*. Hawthorne, NY: Aldine de Gruyter.

Kleck, G., & Gertz, M. (1995). Armed resistance to
crime: The prevalence and nature of self-defense
with a gun. *Journal of Criminal Law & Criminology,
86*, 150–187.

Long-Onnen, J. R. (2000). *Measures of lethality and
intent in the geographic concentration of gun homicides* (Dissertation). University of Maryland, College
Park, MD.

Ludwig, J., Cook, P. J., & Smith, T. (1998). The gender
gap in reporting household gun ownership. *American
Journal of Public Health, 88*(11), 1715–1718.

Manski, C. F. (2014). *Communicating uncertainty in official economic statistics*. Cambridge, MA: National
Bureau of Economic Research. Working Paper No.
20098.

May, J. P., Hemenway, D., & Hall, A. (2002). Do criminals
go to the hospital after being shot? *Injury Prevention,
8*, 236–238.

May, J. P., Hemenway, D., Oen, R., & Pitts, K. R. (2000).
Medical care solicitation by criminals with gunshot
wounds: A survey of Washington DC jail detainees.
Journal of Trauma, 48, 130–132.

McDowall, D., Loftin, C., & Presser, S. (2000). Measuring
civilian defensive firearm use: A methodological
experiment. *Journal of Quantitative Criminology,
16*(2), 1–19.

Planty, M., & Truman, J. L. (2014). *Firearm violence,
1993–2011* (Special Report NCJ 241730). Bureau of
Justice Statistics, US Department of Justice.

Smith, T. W. (2000). *1999 National gun policy survey of
the national opinion research center: Research
findings*. University of Chicago, NORC. Unpublished.

Wellford, C. F., Pepper, J. V., & Petrie, C. V. (Eds.).
(2005). *Firearms and violence: A critical review*.
Washington, DC: National Academies Press.

Wright, J. D., Jasinski, J. L., & Lanier, D. N. (2012).
Crime, punishment and social disorder: Crime rates
and trends in public opinion over more than three
decades. In P. V. Marsden (Ed.), *Social trends in
American life: Findings from the General Social
Survey since 1972* (pp. 146–173). Princeton, NJ:
Princeton University Press.

Solving Criminological Puzzles

Kenneth C. Land

The editors of this volume have identified their goal as describing "… how research is really done, not just focusing on the end result—new methods or data sets" that is, to provide "… case studies, not of the innovations themselves, but of the thought processes that led to these research ideas" (Maltz, 2013). The specific charge to me was "In particular, aside from producing a bumper crop of researchers, you've played with crime and related data in ways that broke new ground. Too many people have a tendency to grab some data sets, toss them into one of the [four standard general purpose statistical analysis software packages], look for a nice low p-value, and write a paper (and perhaps a career) using it—which is something not found in your work (and that of your former students). What we'd like you to do is explain how you approach problems, how you know whether your findings are significant, when you feel that a new statistical approach is needed" (Maltz, 2013).

This is a tall, but enticing order. My main contributions to criminological theory and research over the past four decades fall into five categories: (1) crime opportunity theory and research, (2) unemployment and crime rate fluctuations,

(3) structural covariates of crime rates, (4) finite mixture/latent trajectory models of delinquent/criminal careers, and (5) short-term effects of executions on homicides. In each case, I will attempt to address the objectives described by the editors, that is, to explain how the problem to be researched was articulated, how I approached each problem, and how innovations in theoretical concepts/propositions and statistical approaches are generated thereby. I then will identify some commonalities to my work on these five topics in the concluding comments section of the chapter.

Crime Opportunity Theory and Research

I joined the faculty of the University of Illinois at Urbana-Champaign in 1973 after serving as a staff member of the Russell Sage Foundation and as an Instructor in mathematical sociology at Columbia University in New York City. At the Russell Sage Foundation, I had worked with Dr. Eleanor Sheldon, one of the leaders of the "social indicators movement" of the 1960s, on the Indicators of Social Change research project at the Foundation. The first fruit of that work was an article in which I used my training as a mathematical/statistical modeler of social systems, to propose that

"… the term *social indicators* refer to social statistics that (1) are components in a social system model (including sociopsychological, economic,

Comments and suggestions for revision on an earlier version of this chapter by Pamela Wilcox and Michael Maltz are gratefully acknowledged.

K.C. Land (✉)
Duke University, Durham, NC, USA
e-mail: kland@soc.duke.edu

demographic, and ecological) or of some particular segment or process thereof, (2) can be collected and analyzed at various times and accumulated into a time-series, and (3) can be aggregated or disaggregated to levels appropriate to the specifications of the model. Social system model means conceptions of social processes, whether formulated verbally, logically, mathematically, or in computer simulation form. The important point is that the criterion for classifying a social statistic as a social indicator is its *informative value* which derives from its empirically verified nexus in a conceptualization of a social process" (Land, 1971, p. 323).

Pursuing this line of thought, I had coordinated (with Seymour Spilerman) a Conference on Social Indicator Models, that is, models that could be used to form indicators of the functioning of social systems and analyze their interconnections and changes over time. The conference papers subsequently were collected and published in a volume on this topic (Land & Spilerman, 1975) that includes a conceptual overview of social indicator models, seven chapters on Replication Models and six chapters on Longitudinal and Dynamic Models.

I then continued this work on social indicators and contemporary social change in American society at the University of Illinois. As part of this research project, I became interested in the very striking increases in crime rates in the United States in the 1960s and 1970s. The question of why these increases were occurring was a puzzle for which no criminological theories or research as of the mid-1970s could provide an explanation.

In thinking about how to explain these changes, I struck up a collaboration with Marcus Felson. The first fruit of this collaboration was a 1976 article (Land & Felson, 1976) that articulated a general framework for building models of social indicators, with a specific empirical application to post-World War II changes in crime rates and police expenditures in the United States. This article contained three conceptual-methodological tools for the development of dynamic macrosociological models: (1) how social changes are affected by opportunity structures, (2) how large-scale societal changes can be traced by demographic accounts of population flows into and out of social states, and (3) how

dynamic structural-equation models can be used to build models of social change. After publication of the 1976 article, I teamed up with Illinois colleagues Lawrence E. Cohen, Marcus Felson, and James Kluegel on a series of widely-cited articles that developed what came to be known as the **crime opportunity/routine activities theory of crime.**

A few years later, Duke University doctoral student Pamela Wilcox Rountree and I were interested in the question of how social contexts could modify and affect opportunity structures for crime, in particular, at the neighborhood level. We collaborated with Terance Miethe to study this problem for a sample of neighborhoods in Seattle, Washington. A key methodological innovation in our 1994 article (Rountree, Land, & Miethe, 1994) is that it was the historically first application in criminology of the statistical methodology of multilevel regression models that began to be developed in the late-1980s and early-1990s. These statistical models embed an individual-level or level-1 regression model with fixed effects for the explanatory variables/regressors within higher-level or level-2 contexts with the effects of measures of the contexts estimated as random effects. In turn, the contextual effects can affect the relationship of the level-1 regressors to the outcome measures at level-1 either through the intercept or constant terms of the level-1 regression models or by interactions of the contextual variables with the regression coefficients of the level-1 regressors. Statistically, the contribution of multilevel regression models is that they facilitate statistical modeling of clustered data, that is, observations within a larger sample that are likely to have correlated error terms or share variance due to unobserved variables, such as is the case for a sample of crime victimization data on individuals within neighborhoods of a city.

Suffice it to say that the insight into this use of multilevel regression models allowed Wilcox and Land to develop more subtle conceptualizations of how crime opportunities vary by social context and thus for understanding more fully the complexities of opportunity that were eventually synthesized and published in a book on **multi-contextual crime opportunity theory** (Wilcox,

Land, & Hunt, 2003). Specifically, with this methodological innovation, we were able to integrate the various single-level conceptualizations of routine activities theory had heretofore been studied in distinct domains—the macrolevel study of the relationship of changes in opportunity structures to changes in crime rates and the microlevel study of how opportunity affects individual odds of victimization. Wilcox and Land thus merged these two existing conceptualizations in which I had played a developmental role as described above and in the next section. Most recently, this line of theoretical and research contributions has been reviewed and updated in Wilcox, Gialopsos, and Land (2013).

Unemployment and Crime Rate Fluctuations

In the early-1980s, I worked with Illinois doctoral student David Cantor on puzzling findings regarding the relationship of unemployment and crime rates (the U–C relationship) in various studies that had been published up to that time. Most cross-sectional studies had found some evidence of a positive U–C relationship, which is consistent with strain theory predictions. But studies of the over-time relationship of unemployment and crime rates were inconsistent—often finding null relationships or a negative relationship, which contradicts theoretical expectations.

Building on my collaborations noted above with Cohen, Felson, and Kluegel on how opportunities for crimes affected their rates of occurrence, this collaboration led to the Cantor and Land (1985) article which developed what came to be known as the **Cantor–Land (C–L) model of the U–C relationship**. This model posited that an increase in the unemployment rate affects crime rates through two pathways—the most immediate (contemporaneous) effect being through reductions in crime opportunities as rates of circulation of people and goods slow with an increase in the unemployment rate (which is associated with an economic slowdown or recession) followed by delayed (lagged) increases in crime motivations

as individuals who became unemployed lose economic and social support and connection to mainstream social institutions. We used these two pathways and time-series models to explain the often weak or negative findings in prior studies.

The C–L model subsequently has stimulated a large number of subsequent research articles as well as methodological discussions—over 400 citations. On the whole, the Cantor–Land thesis has held up well over the years, with the Abstract of one of the most recent articles (Phillips & Land, 2012) stating:

> We present the most comprehensive analysis to date by empirically evaluating this [C–L] model with data on 400 of the largest US counties—and examine the effects of aggregation on results as these county data are combined to the state and national levels—for the years 1978–2005. For seven Index crimes at each of the three levels of analysis, and with or without controls for structural covariates at each level, the directional effects hypothesized by Cantor and Land are found for 78 out of 84 estimated relationships. Even after taking into account the lack of statistical independence of these estimates by drawing on recently developed statistical theory, this is a very unlikely outcome. In accordance with expectations based on theory and prior research, (a) some of these relationships are weak and not statistically significant, and (b) the strongest and most consistent patterns of relationships for both the crime opportunity and crime motivation effects are found for three property crimes: burglary, larceny, and motor vehicle theft.

Structural Covariates of Crime Rates

In the mid-1980s, as a member of the faculty of the University of Texas at Austin, I worked with doctoral student Patricia L. McCall on the puzzling lack of consistent findings of expected theoretical relationships between structural characteristics of areal units (such as states, metropolitan areas, cities, neighborhoods) to homicide and other crime rates. To develop some insight into this puzzle, I reached back to the partialling fallacy concept, which originally was identified in ecological studies of juvenile delinquency by Gordon (1968). The partialling fallacy in multiple regression analysis can be due to modest levels of collinearity, for instance when a regressor/covariate, denoted X_1, is more highly correlated (at, say, 0.6) with another regressor, X_2, than either is with the outcome variable (say, 0.45 and 0.5). In this case, regression estimation algorithms typically will assign all explained variance to the one of the two regressors that is (possibly very slightly) more highly correlated with the outcome variable, X_1, and no explained variance to the other regressor, X_2, even though both regressors are measuring attributes that share more variance than either has in common with the outcome variable of the regression. This may lead to the likely erroneous inference that one of the regressors is not contributing to the explained variance in homicide when in fact it is a substantively important covariate. Moreover, another study of the same outcome with a slightly different sample that reverses the degree of the correlations of the two regressors with the outcome variable, a reestimation of the regression may assign all explained variance to the other of the two regressors, X_2 in this case—leading to the apparent lack of consistency among studies.

To address the partialling fallacy problem in studies of structural features of ecological units, Land, McCall, and Cohen (1990) applied principal components analysis and index construction to simplify the regressor space. This produced consistent findings across three levels of areal units (cities, metropolitan areas, and states) and time periods (1960, 1970, and 1990) and unleashed an avalanche of subsequent studies over the next two decades—with over 800 citations of the 1990 article—that similarly found the concepts and methods of the article to be fruitful in empirical research.

McCall, Land, and Parker (2010) noted the impact of the Land et al., 1990 article on the macrolevel study of homicide rates, described the advances made by the article, and reviewed findings from studies published in the 20 years from 1990 to 2010 in order to determine which structural predictors identified in Land et al. continued to be prominent in the study of homicide and which structural predictors have surfaced in recent years as influential to crime rates. Using data on large samples of US cities for the years 1970, 1980, 1990, and 2000, McCall et al. (2010) then presented a systematic empirical assessment of the explanatory power of the covariates of homicide rates identified in the Land et al. study, finding support for the claims of invariance established in the 1990 article.

Subsequent research on homicide trends in US cities by McCall, Land, and Parker (2011) applied latent trajectory methods (more about this in the next section) to the analysis of changes in homicide rates among large US cities across recent decades. Specifically, annual homicide rates for 157 large US cities were analyzed for the 30 years from 1976 to 2005 to address the fundamental questions: Did all of the cities experience similar levels and patterns of rise and decline in homicide rates over these three decades? Or is there hidden or unobserved heterogeneity with respect to these temporal patterns, thus leading to the identification of more homogeneous groupings of the cities? And if latent homogeneous groupings surface, is membership due to specific structural characteristics found within those cities?

McCall et al. (2011) found evidence for the existence of four latent homicide rate trajectories. After identifying and classifying the cities into these four groups, multivariate statistical techniques were used to determine which social and economic characteristics are significant predictors of these distinct homicide trends. Criminal justice measures also were included as controls. Consistent with Land et al. (1990), this analysis found that larger cities located in the South with higher levels of resource deprivation/concentrated poverty, higher income inequality, higher percentages of the adult male population that are divorced, higher unemployment rates, higher percentages of youth, higher percentages of the population who are Hispanic and higher numbers of police per capita are more likely to be in a higher than a lower homicide rate trajectory group. Higher percentages of the population enrolled in colleges and universities and locations in states with higher incarceration rates also were found to be characteristics of cities associated with membership in a lower homicide trajectory group.

Reflecting on these latent trajectory research findings, it occurred to me that they could provide some insight into the long-standing puzzle in ecological studies of a lack of consistent findings regarding the relationship of measure of youth age structure to homicide and other crime rates. Briefly, the age–crime relationship has been the subject of extensive study in criminological research. At the individual level, most studies conclude that, relative to other age groups, young persons are more likely to be involved in crime as offenders and/or victims. However, findings at the macrolevel are inconsistent with regard to the nature of the age structure–crime rate relationship. These studies typically measure age effects via the size of the youth population (e.g., percent of a city or neighborhood population between ages 15 and 29) with the theoretical expectation, based on the individual-level age–crime relationship, that, net of other explanatory variables, the relative size of the youth population should be positively associated with crime rates. This expectation is not uniformly supported by empirical studies, which have found evidence of null, negative, and positive relationships (Land et al., 1990; McCall et al., 2010).

To address and solve this puzzling finding, McCall, Land, Dollar, and Parker (2013) developed the concept of differential institutional engagement and tested its ability to explain discrepant findings regarding the relationship between the age structure and homicide rates across ecological studies of crime. Specifically, McCall et al. (2013) hypothesized that differential degrees of institutional engagement—youths with ties to mainstream social institutions such as school, work, or the military on one end of the spectrum and youths without such bonds on the other end—account for the direction of the relationship between homicide rates and youth age structure. Using large samples of US cities characterized by varying degrees of youths' differential institutional engagement for the years 1980, 1990, and 2000, and operationalizing the differential institutional engagement concept as the percent of the population enrolled in college and the percent of 16–19-year-olds who are simultaneously not enrolled in school, not in the labor market (not in the labor force or unemployed), and not in the military, consistent and invariant results emerged. Positive effects of age structure

on homicide rates are found in cities that have high percentages of disengaged youth, and negative effects are found among cities characterized with high percentages of youth participating in mainstream social institutions. Recent research by Dollar, McCall, and Land (2013) has found that measures of differential institutional engagement function similarly to clarify the age structure–homicide rate relationship at the neighborhood level.

Finite Mixture/Latent Trajectory Models of Delinquent/Criminal Careers

In the 1990s, Daniel Nagin and I took on the ongoing debate in the 1980s and 1990s about the criminal career paradigm. In our first publication (Nagin & Land, 1993), two core questions in this debate were addressed: (1) At the level of the individual, does the age-crime curve follow a single-peaked function similar to that which characterizes average offending rates in the population or is it approximately constant with age? (2) Can the criminal career of an individual be adequately characterized by a model that does not include the structural elements of career onset and termination or, alternatively, intermittency (i.e., periods of activity interspersed with periods of inactivity)? The article also contributed a new perspective on an issue that is agreed upon by all parties in the criminal careers debate—the existence of pronounced and persistent individual differences in criminal involvement. A voluminous literature documents the association between such persistent differences in offending and time-stable individual differences, such as IQ, aggressiveness, impulsiveness, neurological deficits, and early socialization. The Nagin and Land article added to this literature by providing evidence that certain individual characteristics not only distinguish relative rates of offending at any given age, the primary focus of the extant literature, but also predict the trajectory of offending over age.

Nagin and Land (1993) addressed these questions about delinquent/criminal careers by introducing **finite mixtures of zero-inflated Poisson models** (more generally, finite mixtures of any family of frequency distributions) for longitudinal panel data—which became known as **latent trajectory models or group-based trajectory models**—to model the life-course development of delinquent/criminal careers. These models facilitated the study of "hidden heterogeneity" in longitudinal panel studies of offending from childhood to late adulthood in such a way as to permit the estimation of different underlying, relatively homogeneous groupings in the data and the characteristics of individuals and their contexts that predict membership in one trajectory or another.

The Nagin–Land 1993 article (with over 500 citations) and subsequent methodological articles and empirical applications stimulated many applications in criminology and, more generally, in many other areas of developmental/life-course research. For instance, Hamil-Luker, Land, and Blau (2004) assessed predictions of continuity and change in antisocial behavior over time as derived from population heterogeneity and life-course perspectives with respect to a rarely studied form of delinquent/criminal behavior, namely, cocaine use during the late-teenage and young adult years. They first examined the extent to which differential propensities toward antisocial behavior can be detected in a nationally representative sample of youth aged 14–16 in 1979. Based on self-reported delinquent and criminal activities in late adolescence, traditional cross-sectional latent-class analysis identified three groups of antisocial/rebellious respondents and a group of non-offenders. These groups then were followed into early adulthood by examining age trajectories of cocaine usage between 1984 and 1998. Latent-class trajectory models identified clusters of respondents who have similar age trajectories of cocaine use over time and provide parameter estimates that predict membership in those clusters. In support of the population heterogeneity perspective, Hamil-Luker et al. found that antisocial/rebellious youth have higher probabilities of cocaine use throughout early adulthood than non-offending youth. There is, however, much variation in drug use patterns

among the groups as they aged. In support of a life-course perspective, it was found that social ties to schools, families, religion, and the labor market help differentiate youth who refrain from, maintain, or desist from using cocaine through early adulthood.

Recent criminological applications also have applied to the study of the crime rate trajectories of areal units such as the McCall et al. (2011) article on the rise and fall of homicide rates in US cities described in the previous section. In brief, whenever there is reason to believe that observed longitudinal data contains hidden heterogeneity, the latent trajectory model may be quite applicable.

Short-Term Effects of Executions on Homicides

Does the death penalty save lives? More specifically, are homicides reduced when an offender who has received a capital punishment sentence is executed? I watched the research literature and debates of answers to these questions among criminologists from the 1970s to the 2000s. In the 1990s and early-2000s, a new round of research emerged using annual time-series panel data on the 50 US states for 25 or so years from the 1970s to the late-1990s that claims to find many lives saved through reductions in subsequent homicide rates after executions. This research, in turn, produced a round of critiques, which concludes that these findings are not robust enough to model even small changes in specifications that yield dramatically different results. A principal reason for this sensitivity of the findings is that few state-years exist (about 1% of all state-years) in which six or more executions have occurred. Another issue that emerged from this research and its critiques is that the annual time interval of these state-level panel studies might be too lengthy if, as Zimmerman (2004, pp. 187–188) hypothesized "… any deterrent effect of capital punishment, to the extent that it exists, is likely to affect the rate of murder initially (i.e., within the particular year a given execution takes place) but then tends to dampen quickly.

As such the deterrent effect of capital punishment appears to arise from the process of administering executions and not from the existence of a death penalty law."

To examine this short-term effects possibility, I worked with Raymond Teske of Sam Houston State University and Duke doctoral student Hui Zheng. We focused on Texas, a state that has used the death penalty with sufficient frequency to make possible relatively stable estimates of the homicide response to executions. In addition, we narrowed the observation intervals for recording executions and homicides from the annual calendar year to monthly intervals. We applied dynamic regression (DR)–linear transfer function (LTF) model building strategies with seasonal autoregressive integrated moving average (seasonal ARIMA) time-series models to these monthly data. Based on these time-series analyses and independent validation tests, the best-fitting model in Land, Teske, and Zheng (2009) implied that, from January 1994 through December 2005, evidence existed of modest, short-term reductions in homicides in Texas in the first and fourth months that follow an execution—about 2.5 fewer homicides in total. Another model suggested, however, that in addition to homicide reductions, some displacement of homicides may be possible from 1 month to another in the months after an execution, which reduces the total reduction in homicides after an execution to about .5 during a 12-month period. All in all, this study suggested that there is evidence of a small short-term deterrence effect of an execution, part of which may be displaced to a subsequent month.

Subsequent research by Land, Teske, and Zheng (2012) addressed the question: Do executions impact felony and non-felony homicides similarly? Again, this question was addressed by using monthly time-series data on executions and homicides in Texas for the years 1994–2007, with the homicide data disaggregated into felony murders (killings which occur in conjunction with the commission of another crime such as robbery, sex motive, and other felonious activities) and non-felony-type homicides (all other homicides). The results of the analyses of non-felony-type homicides produced two DR-LTF

seasonal ARIMA time-series models, one of which contains autoregressive terms that describe an exponentially declining quadratic decay across the months after an execution and the other of which contains only a lag–1-month term. Both models indicate a modest lag–1-month net reduction, a deterrence. The nonautoregressive model lag–1-month deterrent estimate is −1.4 and that of the autoregressive model is approximately −1.96 homicides in the month after an execution. Both of these estimates are larger than the corresponding nonautoregressive model lag–1-month estimate (−1.3) and the autoregressive model lag–1-month estimate (−1.6) for all homicides combined of Land et al. (2009). In addition, the cumulative deterrent effect of an execution on non-felony-level homicides estimated in the autoregressive model is 1.4 during a 12-month period.

By comparison, the Land et al. (2012) analyses of the felony-type homicide series produce a nonautoregressive time-series model estimated increase, a brutalization effect, in the month after an execution of approximately 0.5 homicides. Combining the two nonautoregressive models, estimated counterbalancing lag–1-month deterrent and brutalization effects produce a slight estimated net deterrent effect of 0.9 homicides in the model after an execution—which is not very different from the −0.5 net reduction estimated in the 2009 article. A key point is that these estimates indicate that the short-lived deterrence effect of executions is concentrated among non-felony-type homicides.

These findings of short-term effects of executions on homicides, modest though they are, go against the grain of the dominant contemporary view among criminologists that there is no deterrent effect of capital punishment. On the other hand, they have intuitive appeal. A couple of years ago, I was a participant in a conference that brought together a group of criminologists and other social scientists who study crime with the chiefs of police of major US and Canadian cities. In the process of having a conversation about this research with one of the chiefs of police, I drew the analogy of the short-term deterrence effects we found to the driving patterns on interstate highways of most of us, in which, while the posted speed limit is 65 miles per hour, many of us will be traveling at 70–72 miles per hour. When the flashing blue lights of a police car up ahead come into view, however, the universal reaction is to ease off the gas pedal and slow down. Some 3–5 min later, however, we are back to cruising at 70–72 miles per hour. The police chief responded, "Yes, that is universal. I do it as well, even though I know that guy works for me." The police chief said that the finding that the deterrent effect is concentrated among the non-felony-type homicides made sense as well, as, in his experience, many felony offenders are repeat offenders and can only be deterred by imprisonment. On the other hand, there can be a slight deterrent effect among ordinary citizens (those with no prior history of violent felony offense) from non-felony-type homicides because they are not fully cognizant of the limited applicability of the death penalty to felony-type homicides.

Commonalities

What are some common elements among the foregoing descriptions of five major topics in criminology that I have studied. As emphasized throughout the expositions, **the first common element is the occurrence of a puzzle within the body of existing and ongoing criminological research**. Puzzles often are created by a set of trends in the society for which existing theories and models of analysis do not yield an adequate explanation—for example, the very striking increases in crime rates in the United States in the 1960s and 1970s, a period of relative post-World War II economic prosperity, which led to the development of crime opportunity theory. Puzzles also can occur when empirical findings are contradictory or inconsistent—as in the case of the lack of consistency of findings on the over-time relationship of unemployment and crime rates with theoretical expectations and cross-sectional findings, which led to the conceptualization and empirical estimation of the Cantor–Land model, or the lack of consistent findings regarding structural covariates of homicide and other crime rates

in ecological studies, which stimulated the conceptualizations and statistical methodology for finding consistent structural relationships. Sometimes puzzles are created by analyses and arguments among criminologists themselves concerning certain aspects of crime phenomena—as in the case of the debates over the age-crime curve in the 1980s, which led to the development of latent trajectory model for going beneath the hidden heterogeneity of aggregate age-crime data, or in the case of the existence or nonexistence of deterrent effects of the death penalty, which stimulated our analyses of the short-term effects of executions.

The key point about puzzles is that they are not "normal science" in the sense of straightforward applications of conventional statistical models (e.g., regression models) to examine the applicability of one or another criminological theory to a new set of data, looking for statistically significant or insignificant effects. Rather, they often arise from the accumulation of inconsistent findings from such normal science analyses, or from the inability of conventional theoretical concepts and models to explain new patterns in data.

A second commonality is that progress towards solutions to such puzzles often requires conceptual and/or methodological innovations or innovative applications of existing statistical methodologies. Examples of conceptual innovations from the descriptions given above include the development of multilevel crime opportunity theory, the Cantor–Land model of how fluctuations in unemployment affect fluctuations in crime rates, and the development of the differential institutional engagement concept to explain how youth age structure affects homicide and other crime rates. Examples of methodological innovations and applications include the application of multilevel statistical analysis to represent multilevel crime opportunity mechanisms, applications of methods of time-series analysis to estimate and assess the Cantor–Land model, the application of partialling fallacy concepts to the puzzling lack of consistent findings regarding the relationship of structural covariates to homicide and other crime rates, the development of finite mixture models to shed light on the age-crime curve, and the application of sophisticated time-series analysis models to assess the existence and extent of short-term effect executions on homicides.

Such innovations require some level of creative ability both in the development of theoretical concepts and in the development or application of statistical models and methods. To address a question raised in the introduction to this chapter: How does one know when a new approach is needed? In my experience, the answer is when existing concepts and/or methods continue to produce inconsistent or puzzling findings. And the related question: How do you know whether your findings are significant? The answer is that this occurs when you reach that "Eureka" moment, when the work you and your collaborators have done on conceptual and methodological developments does, indeed, succeed in resolving the puzzles or inconsistencies that led to the research effort.

References

Cantor, D., & Land, K. C. (1985). Unemployment and crime rates in the post-World War II United States: A theoretical and empirical analysis. *American Sociological Review, 50*, 317–332.

Dollar, C. B., McCall, P. L., & Land, K. C. (2013, November). *Age structure and neighborhood homicide: A test of the differential engagement hypothesis.* Paper presented at the Annual Meeting of the American Society of Criminology, Atlanta, GA.

Gordon, R. A. (1968). Issues in multiple regression. *American Journal of Sociology, 73*, 592–616.

Hamil-Luker, J., Land, K. C., & Blau, J. (2004). Diverse trajectories of cocaine use through early adulthood among rebellious and socially conforming youth. *Social Science Research, 33*, 300–321.

Land, K. C. (1971). On the definition of social indicators. *The American Sociologist, 6*, 322–325.

Land, K. C., & Felson, M. (1976). A general framework for building dynamic macro social indicator models: Including an analysis of changes in crime rates and police expenditures. *American Journal of Sociology, 82*, 565–604.

Land, K. C., McCall, P. L., & Cohen, L. E. (1990). Structural covariates of homicide rates: are there any invariances across time and social space? *American Journal of Sociology, 95*, 922–963.

Land, K. C., & Spilerman, S. (Eds.). (1975). *Social indicator models*. New York, NY: Russell Sage.

Land, K. C., Teske, R. H. C., Jr., & Zheng, H. (2009). The short-term effects of executions on homicides: Deterrence, displacement, or both? *Criminology, 47*, 1009–1044.

Land, K. C., Teske, R. H. C., Jr., & Zheng, H. (2012). The differential short-term impacts of executions on felony and non-felony homicides. *Criminology & Public Policy, 11*, 541–563.

Maltz, M. D. (2013). *Invitation to contribute chapter.* Email correspondence, October 25, 2013.

McCall, P. L., Land, K. C., Dollar, C. B., & Parker, K. F. (2013). The age structure-crime rate relationship: Solving a long-standing puzzle. *Journal of Quantitative Criminology, 29*, 167–190.

McCall, P. L., Land, K. C., & Parker, K. F. (2010). An empirical assessment of what we know about structural covariates of homicide rates: A return to a classic 20 years later. *Homicide Studies, 14*, 219–243.

McCall, P. L., Land, K. C., & Parker, K. F. (2011). Heterogeneity in the rise and decline of city-level homicide rates, 1976–2005: A latent trajectory analysis. *Social Science Research, 40*, 363–378.

Nagin, D. S., & Land, K. C. (1993). Age, criminal careers, and population heterogeneity: Specification and estimation of a nonparametric, mixed Poisson model. *Criminology, 31*, 327–362.

Phillips, J., & Land, K. C. (2012). The link between unemployment and crime fluctuations: An analysis at the county, state, and national levels. *Social Science Research, 41*, 681–694.

Rountree, P. W., Land, K. C., & Miethe, T. D. (1994). Macro-micro integration in the study of victimization: A hierarchical logistic regression model analysis across Seattle neighborhoods. *Criminology, 32*, 387–414.

Wilcox, P., Gialopsos, B. M., & Land, K. C. (2013). Multilevel criminal opportunity. In F. T. Cullen & P. Wilcox (Eds.), *The Oxford handbook of criminological theory* (pp. 579–601). New York, NY: Oxford University Press.

Wilcox, P., Land, K. C., & Hunt, S. A. (2003). *Criminal circumstance: A dynamic multi-contextual criminal opportunity theory.* Chicago, IL: Aldine de Gruyter.

Zimmerman, P. R. (2004). State executions, deterrence, and the incidence of murder. *Journal of Applied Economics, 7*, 163–193.

Upon Becoming a Criminologist and Spending 30 Years Thinking About Interesting Things

Pamela K. Lattimore

My first step toward becoming a criminologist was to apply in the fall of 1981 to the economics PhD program at the University of North Carolina at Chapel Hill because I (1) really enjoyed macroeconomics as an undergraduate and (2) envisioned a career as an environmental economist. Two semesters of graduate-level macro quickly dissuaded me of the first notion ("Rational expectations, anyone?")—although, fortunately, I did find graduate-level microeconomics interesting. I was focused on environmental economics because prior to going to graduate school, I was a technical writer for the Environmental Protection Agency—so I was familiar with many of the issues ("flue gas desulfurization") and was convinced of the importance of environmental policy. Unfortunately, the world-class environmental economist at UNC left Chapel Hill the year I started grad school.

My second step toward becoming a criminologist was to start playing racquetball on a regular basis with Ann Witte (of Schmidt & Witte (1984, 1988)). (Daily racquetball is a requirement for surviving the pursuit of a PhD in economics.) In 1983, as the "Nothing Works[1]" refrain continued to gain steam, Ann was awarded a grant from the National Institute of Justice (NIJ) to conduct a randomized control trial evaluating the effectiveness of an interagency vocational training program for youthful property offenders (the Sandhills Vocational Delivery System). (Gary Gottfredson had a companion grant to help the two North Carolina prisons develop and implement the program in coordination with the North Carolina Department of Corrections and Employment Security Commission. Gary also designed and installed a PC-based management information system for the program and evaluation—cutting edge in the day!) She needed a project manager for this study. I needed employment—at least for the summer. So, with the following comment— "Sure, but I'm not at all interested in this area"— I was hired.

For the next 5 years, as I completed my graduate work, I became more and more involved in the complexities of correctional intervention— the problems faced by correctional populations (in this case, 18–22-year-old property offenders in the pre-crack era), the difficulties in designing and implementing programs in a prison environment, the challenges of identifying appropriate measures and finding data to approximate those measures, and the implications of statistical power on the efforts to find effective interventions when budgets and timelines are both short. I also had my first exposure to many good people, toiling in corrections and allied service agencies

---

[1] See Lipton, Martinson, & Wilks, 1975; Martinson, 1974; also Lattimore & Witte, 1985.

P.K. Lattimore, Ph.D. (✉)
RTI International, 3040 Cornwallis Road, Research Triangle Park, NC 27709, USA
e-mail: lattimore@rti.org

M.D. Maltz and S.K. Rice (eds.), *Envisioning Criminology: Researchers on Research as a Process of Discovery*, DOI 10.1007/978-3-319-15868-6_19, © Springer International Publishing Switzerland 2015

who were trying to effect change and make a difference. (I'll return to what we found shortly.)

Step three set the hook for the next decades. After finishing my coursework and passing my comprehensive exams, I needed a dissertation topic. Rational decision-making and decision-making under risk were emerging as a hot academic area. Following on the work by Gary Becker, Isaac Ehrlich, and others, Ann and colleagues had published a labor theoretic model of criminal choice. These models had their roots in the economic model of choice—expected utility theory. At the same time, psychologists Daniel Kahneman and Amos Tversky were beginning to publish results of experiments that showed that individual choices under uncertainty systematically violated the predictions of expected utility theory.[2] I spent the next 2 years comparing and testing expected utility and prospect theory models of criminal choice (Lattimore, Baker, & Witte, 1992).[3] With a dissertation that merged criminology, economics, and psychology, I didn't exactly fit the mold of the academic economist. Also, I had met Joanna Baker, a management scientist/operations researcher, who became a wonderful mentor and collaborator with whom I pursued other "non-economics" research, including, for example, applying acceptance sampling to optimizing drug testing regimens (e.g., Lattimore, Baker, & Matheson, 1996) and using survival models to predict "demand" for prison beds (Baker & Lattimore, 1994; Lattimore & Baker, 1992).

Step four was lucky timing on my part. In 1987, Richard Linster at NIJ began a visiting researcher program to bring researchers into the agency to conduct intramural research and to help guide extramural funding. Christy Visher was the first hire. I arrived 6 months later for what was sup-

posed to be a 2-year temporary appointment. Dick was a physicist and liked maximum likelihood equations. Dick, Christy, and I would spend the next few years working with data collected by the California Youth Authority (CYA) that provided extensive information on the characteristics of a randomly selected cohort of youth paroled between July 1, 1981, and June 30, 1982. Recidivism data were available through September 1985. Our models were hazard models using a special functional form Dick developed that would allow for changing influences of factors over time and could accommodate the fact that not all members of the cohort would eventually fail—although the latter was less of an issue since 88% of our sample "failed" (arrest or revocation) during our observation period. A number of papers concerning the recidivism characteristics of this cohort resulted from this data set over the following 20 years, attesting to the value of good data (e.g., Lattimore, Visher, and Linster (1995), presented the violent arrest findings from a competing hazards model (also see Visher, Lattimore, & Linster, 1991; Lattimore, Visher, & Linster, 1994; Lattimore, Linster, & MacDonald, 1997;[4] and Lattimore, MacDonald, Piquero, Linster, & Visher, 2004).

One year followed the next, and eventually I was hired as a full-time federal employee of NIJ, eventually ending up as a Division Director in NIJ's Office of Research and Evaluation (ORE), when Sally Hillsman was ORE Director. It was an exciting time during Jeremy Travis' tenure as NIJ Director. We conducted other intramural research, including an ambitious project with the Florida Department of Probation to use management information system data to generate risk scores for Florida's probation populations that updated "automatically." We also examined homicide trends, looking at panoply of factors associated with homicide in eight US cities as homicide rates reached their peak in the mid-1990s (Riley, Lattimore, Leiter, & Trudeau,

---

[2] Kahneman was awarded the Nobel Prize in economics 2002 for their work on decision-making, heuristics, and biases; Tversky died in 1996.

[3] I collected data at Sandhills Youth prison from volunteer inmates using a "luggable" Hewlett–Packard dual disk computer and a program in BASIC that I wrote to collect choices among certain and uncertain returns to "crime" and a certain sentence (plea bargain) versus an uncertain outcome at trial (Lattimore et al., 1992).

[4] In the mid-1990s, we had the good fortune at NIJ for graduate student John MacDonald to join us—first as a graduate intern and later as a full-time employee. John worked with us on many of our later studies of the CYA data. John is now the Chair of the Criminology Department at the University of Pennsylvania.

1997). It was at this time, too, that Jeremy began to shine the spotlight on prisoner reentry. Working at NIJ was exciting—in the midst of policymaking, an opportunity to meet the "best and brightest" in the field and an opportunity to support and see important work unfold. There was a lot of work, however, and a lot of meetings. In 1998, I realized that (a) I was never near my dry cleaners during the week when it was open (7 am–7 pm), and, more importantly, (b) regardless of my willingness to work long, long hours, I no longer had time to do my own research. So, pondering what to do next and remembering with fondness Chapel Hill and the Research Triangle area of North Carolina, I called Jim Collins (who was at RTI and had been an NIJ fellow) and asked if RTI had any openings.

Moving back to NC in the fall of 1998, I transitioned from working for an agency that gave out grant monies (and did a bit of intramural research) to a research organization wholly dependent on grants and contracts to pay the bills (importantly, our salaries). In 1998, RTI had a group of researchers working in the juvenile delinquency and criminal justice area. For example, RTI conducted the first randomized control trial of the Drug Abuse Resistance Education (DARE; e.g., Rosenbaum, Flewelling, Bailey, Ringwalt, & Wilkinson, 1994) and conducted early work on the relationship of drug use to crime, delinquency, and violence (e.g., Collins, 1990).

My first assignment at RTI was Project Director for a SAMHSA-funded multisite evaluation of jail diversion programs for individuals with co-occurring substance abuse and mental health problems, funded by the Substance Abuse and Mental Health Services Administration (SAMHSA) (Broner, Lattimore, Cowell, & Schlenger, 2004; Lattimore, Broner, Sherman, Frisman, & Shafer, 2003). This eight-site, quasi-experiment involved baseline, 3-month, and 12-month interviews with about 2,000 individuals identified at a police encounter. The programs were diverse, including diversion in lieu of arrest in some sites and diversion following adjudication in others. This study provided my first glimpse at the challenges of coordinating eight principal investigators in the development of an instrument, the difficulties in identifying and enrolling subjects ("Where did all the eligibles go?"), and (once again) the potential that differences in treatment between treated and comparisons would be much less than ideal.

RTI was where I began to write proposals and direct my own large projects. At NIJ, I reviewed (literally) hundreds of research proposals over the years—good preparation to some extent in beginning to develop your own proposals but hardly sufficient (as with books, you may be an excellent reviewer of others' work, but that doesn't mean you can write a book yourself). This stage in my career is where the "fun" began in earnest. Developing projects and laying them out in a proposal is (can be) a creative undertaking. (My colleague Jim Trudeau says writing the proposal is the best part—you don't have to worry, e.g., about where all the eligible participants are. And, as Mike Maltz reminded me, proposal writing often generates the dual fears of "(1) what if we don't get the project and (2) what if we DO.") At RTI, proposal writing is also a joint undertaking—we brainstorm ideas (approaches to evaluation design, recruiting, data collection methods, analytical methods), share writing, and engage in a vigorous pre-submission review process that inevitably leads to improved proposals. Grant proposals are different from contract proposals. When I was with the government, we used to describe contracts as for the government's benefit and grants as for the benefit of the grantee. Contract proposals respond to specific government-delineated scopes of work; grant proposals are (generally) investigator initiated (although NIJ, e.g., may sometimes specify what is to be evaluated). We also began to build the RTI criminal justice program—which was formally established as a program under my leadership in 2000.

I've had the good fortune to lead a number of important studies—beginning with the evaluation of the Safe Schools and Healthy Students Initiative for the Office of Juvenile Justice and Delinquency Prevention, a comparison of alternative treatments for drug-involved probationers for NIDA (e.g., Lattimore, Krebs, Koetse, Lindquist, & Cowell, 2005), the evaluation of the Juvenile Breaking the Cycle program for NIJ (e.g., Krebs, Lattimore, Cowell, & Graham, 2010), and the multisite evaluation of the Serious and Violent Offender Reentry Initiative for NIJ (SVORI; e.g., Lattimore & Visher, 2013). I also had the opportunity to participate in an important CDC-funded project identifying the prevalence and effects of traumatic brain injury among a prisoner release cohort (e.g., Shiroma et al., 2010). Currently, I'm leading the NIJ-funded HOPE Demonstration Field Experiment and the Evaluation of the FY 2011 Bureau of Justice Assistance Second Chance Act Adult Offender Reentry Demonstration Projects (SCA AORDP), as well as a DOD-funded project assessing the impact of deployment, traumatic brain injury, and PTSD on military workplace violence. The HOPE DFE is a randomized control trial assessing the impact of swift and certain sanctions on probationer outcomes and has provided me the excellent opportunity to work with Doris MacKenzie and Gary Zajac at Pennsylvania State University. Both the SVORI and the SCA AORDP evaluations have been or are being conducted in collaboration with colleagues at the Urban Institute.

All of these studies have required innovation and adaptability—nothing ever turns out exactly the way you plan. For example, for the HOPE evaluation, we expected that it would take 9 months to enroll and randomly assign 400 probationers in each of the four sites (sites to be determined when we wrote our proposal). In reality, enrollment began in August 2012 and concluded September 2014, and two of the four sites still fell short of the 400 target. The SCA AORDP involves a multisite evaluation of seven very different programs serving (somewhat) different populations—similar in some ways to what we encountered with the SVORI evaluation, but the programmatic and population differences are attenuated because the SCA AORDP evaluation involves three prison programs, three jail programs, and one police department program. The programs are similar because (1) they are focused on prisoner reentry and (2) they are funded by one Bureau of Justice Assistance funding stream.

The point about funding stream versus program evaluation has reinforced for me something that

I have thought a lot about since we began the SVORI evaluation in 2003—although we talk about conducting program evaluations, often what we are called upon by our sponsors to evaluate are initiatives.[5] The distinction in my mind is that initiatives are outcome focused—reduce recidivism, drug use, etc.—and the "how" and, to some extent, the "for whom" are left up to the individual program grantees. The distinction between program and initiative is crystallized by my simultaneously leading the SCA AORDP evaluation and the HOPE DFE evaluation. Whereas the SCA AORDP evaluation focuses on locally designed reentry programs (as with the SVORI evaluation), the HOPE DFE is a four-site replication of the Hawaii Opportunity Probation with Enforcement evaluation that tested a model predicated on drug testing and swift, certain, and modest sanctions for (any) violations of probation conditions (Hawken & Kleiman, 2009). The Hawaii HOPE evaluation suggested significant short-term effects. Angela Hawken and her colleagues at Pepperdine University are providing training and technical assistance to the four BJA-funded sites implementing HOPE to assist the sites in implementing HOPE with fidelity. As criminal justice interventions go, the HOPE (now the Honest Opportunity Probation with Enforcement) program is simple—judge gives a warning hearing, probation administers regular drug testing, probation officers report all probation violations to the judge, missed drug tests result in warrants and arrests, judge oversees violation hearings for all violations, all violations result in some consequences (e.g., short jail stays, community service) that escalate with repeated violations, and treatment resources are reserved for those who repeatedly fail random urine tests (i.e., those for whom the threat of sanctions is inadequate to lead to cessation of drug use). This "simple" intervention, however, requires substantial systems change. Results are not yet

---

[5] Note that the Safe Schools Healthy Students was also a federally funded initiative—school districts were given grant funds to implement programs to make schools "safer" and students "healthier." The choice of interventions was up to the district with the caveat that selected interventions be "evidence based."

available (we are awaiting arrest data for our outcome study), but the experience of the sites as they have struggled to implement HOPE underscores that even "simple" programs actually require considerable effort to change practice as usual.

In contrast to HOPE, the SCA AORDP and SVORI programs are/were locally designed to address the multitude of needs of prisoner populations. These needs include education and employment skills (almost always), as well as for many substance abuse treatment, mental health treatment, anger management, life skills, and often support for things like housing and transportation. The short-term findings from the SVORI evaluation document the challenges of implementing and finding positive results (Lattimore & Visher, 2013, p. 301):

> The results suggest that these SVORI programs were able to increase the number and types of services provided to male prisoners before release, but that overall level of service provision was well below 100%...

And the SVORI short-term findings (Lattimore & Visher, 2013, pp. 302–303)[6]:

> … we identified modest effects during the initial, some would call "critical," early period following release. For example, the SVORI program participants were more likely to report living independently and having a job with formal pay and benefits shortly after release. The SVORI program participants were also more likely to report that they had not used drugs and to test negative on the oral drug screen, although few of these differences were statistically significant…. SVORI program participants were less likely to report having committed crimes since release, driven primarily by a lower reporting of drug possession crimes. On the other hand, official measures of criminal behavior indicated little difference between SVORI and non-SVORI participants.

And, the findings from the Sandhills Vocational Delivery System randomized control trial (Lattimore, Witte, & Baker, 1990, p. 130):

---

[6] Note that a subsequent long-term follow-up of the SVORI evaluation participants showed longer times to arrest and fewer arrests after release for the evaluation participants when a follow-up period of up to 56 months was examined (Lattimore, Barrick, Cowell, Dawes, Steffey, Tueller, & Visher, 2012).

In this article, we provided evidence on the extent to which two North Carolina prisons (in concert with other state agencies) implemented a vocational rehabilitation program for young property offenders…. the VDS was less than fully implemented since only 16% of the Es began the four activities for which we had quantitative data …. Most Es, however, received some services… we found that although the VDS was not fully implemented, there is only about a 1 in 10 chance that the better postrelease arrest record of the experimental group is due to chance. There was a 10 percentage-point difference in the proportions of the experimental and control groups arrested following release from prison. Given the relatively weak implementation of the program, this difference that is significant at the 0.10 level is highly suggestive of the efficacy of the VDS program.

So, what have I learned over the past 30 years? One is that the findings from the most recent reentry study that I have completed (the SVORI evaluation) were quite similar to the findings from the first reentry study that I completed. I was actually quite surprised when I reread the 1990 *Evaluation Review* article (Lattimore et al., 1990) with the extent to which I am in some ways back where I started. I have recently been talking a lot with colleagues about what I now perceive as the unreasonable expectations we are placing on correctional systems to quickly implement complicated programs to address entrenched offender problems usually with modest funds and short time lines. SVORI grantees had about 3 years to implement and deliver their programs, which involved developing and implementing or arranging in-prison and post-release services to address multiple needs, and then the evaluation (and their grant funding) ended. The programs were supposed to achieve measureable, significant ("magic" $p < 0.05$) reductions in recidivism—even though in most cases, the interventions were directed not at criminal behavior per se but at potential mediators of criminal behavior (e.g., substance use or employment). This standard is higher than what the pharmaceutical industry faces with FDA—where new drugs only have to be *as effective* as current treatments. Our standards are higher than medical trials—where treatment goals may require extending survival a few weeks for a portion of the treatment population. Contrast this to the congressionally mandated requirement that Second Chance Act-funded programs reduce recidivism by 50% within 5 years.

And, from the conclusions from Lattimore, Baker, and Witte (1990, p. 117):

> Thus for inmate programs designed to affect recidivism, the degree to which the program deters postrelease criminal behavior (the program's effect size) is a critical factor in the ability of statistical tests to reveal significant differences in outcome when they exist. For a given sample size and significance level, the smaller the effect of the program, the lower the power of the statistical test. Given the apparent intractability of criminal behavior, it appears naive to assume that any program, even if fully delivered, will have a large effect on the behavior of a criminal population. Further, *few prison treatments are likely to be characterized by 100%* delivery and receptivity (response). Programs that are only partly implemented result in dilution of the treatment and, ceteris paribus, *reduce the power of any statistical test*. With an a priori assumption of "small effect," large samples and an acceptance of critical levels for significance tests other than 0.05 (e.g., 0.1 or even 0.2) may be appropriate.

References

Baker, J. R., & Lattimore, P. K. (1994). Forecasting demand using survival modeling: An application to U.S. prisons. *Australian Journal of Information Systems, 2*(1), 2–16.

Broner, N., Lattimore, P. K., Cowell, A. J., & Schlenger, W. (2004). Effects of diversion on adults with mental illness co-occurring with substance use: Outcomes from a national multi-site study. *Behavior Sciences and the Law, 22*, 519–541.

Collins, J. J. (1990). Summary thoughts about drugs and violence. In M. De La Rosa, E. Y. Lambert, B. Gropper, & NIDA Research Monograph (Eds.), *Drugs and violence: Causes, correlates, and consequences* (Vol. 103, pp. 256–275). Washington, DC: US Department of Health and Human Services.

Hawken, A., & Kleiman, M. (2009). *Managing drug involved probationers with swift and certain sanctions: Evaluating Hawaii's HOPE*. Washington, DC: U.S. Department of Justice, National Institute of Justice.

Krebs, C. P., Lattimore, P. K., Cowell, A. J., & Graham, P. W. (2010). Evaluation of the Juvenile breaking the cycle program's impact on recidivism. *Journal of Criminal Justice, 38*, 109–117.

Lattimore, P. K., & Baker, J. R. (1992). The impact of recidivism and capacity on prison populations. *Journal of Quantitative Criminology, 8*, 189–215.

Lattimore, P. K., Baker, J. R., & Matheson, L. A. (1996). Monitoring drug use using Bayesian acceptance sampling: The Illinois experiment. *Operations Research, 44*, 274–285.

Lattimore, P. K., Baker, J. R., & Witte, A. D. (1992). The influence of probability on risky choice: A parametric examination. *Journal of Economic Behavior and Organization, 17*, 377–400.

Lattimore, P. K., Barrick, K., Cowell, A. J., Dawes, D., Steffey, D. M., Tueller, S. J., & Visher, C. (2012, February). Prisoner reentry services: What worked for SVORI evaluation participants? Prepared for National Institute of Justice.

Lattimore, P. K., Broner, N., Sherman, R., Frisman, L., & Shafer, M. (2003). A comparison of pre-booking and post-booking diversion programs for mentally ill substance using individuals with justice involvement. *Journal of Contemporary Criminal Justice, 1*(19), 30–64.

Lattimore, P. K., Krebs, C. P., Koetse, W., Lindquist, C. H., & Cowell, A. J. (2005). Predicting the effect of substance abuse treatment on probationer recidivism. *Journal of Experimental Criminology, 1*, 159–189.

Lattimore, P. K., Linster, R. L., & MacDonald, J. M. (1997). Risk of death among serious young offenders. *Journal of Research in Crime and Delinquency, 34*, 187–209.

Lattimore, P. K., MacDonald, J. M., Piquero, A. R., Linster, R. L., & Visher, C. A. (2004). Studying the characteristics of arrest frequency among paroled youthful offenders. *Journal of Research in Crime and Delinquency, 41*, 37–57.

Lattimore, P. K., & Visher, C. (2013). The impact of prison reentry services on short-term outcomes: Evidence from a multi-site evaluation. *Evaluation Review, 37*(3–4), 274–313.

Lattimore, P. K., Visher, C. A., & Linster, R. L. (1994). Specialization in juvenile careers: Markov results for a California cohort. *Journal of Quantitative Criminology, 10*, 291–316.

Lattimore, P. K., Visher, C. A., & Linster, R. L. (1995). Predicting rearrest for violence among serious youthful offenders. *Journal of Research in Crime and Delinquency, 32*, 54–83.

Lattimore, P. K., & Witte, A. D. (1985). Programs to aid ex-offenders: We don't know "nothing works". *Monthly Labor Review, 108*(4), 46–48.

Lattimore, P. K., Witte, A. D., & Baker, J. R. (1990). Experimental assessment of the effect of vocational training on youthful property offenders. *Evaluation Review, 14*, 115–133.

Lipton, D., Martinson, R., & Wilks, J. (1975). *The effectiveness of correctional treatment: A survey of treatment evaluation studies*. New York, NY: Praeger.

Martinson, R. (1974). What works?—questions and answers about prison reform. *The Public Interest, 35,* 22–54.

Riley, K. J., Lattimore, P. K., Leiter, J., & Trudeau, J. (1997). Homicide trends in eight U.S. cities: Project overview and design. *Homicide Studies: An Interdisciplinary and International Journal, 1,* 84–100.

Rosenbaum, D. P., Flewelling, R. L., Bailey, S. L., Ringwalt, C. L., & Wilkinson, D. L. (1994). Cops in the classroom: A longitudinal evaluation of drug abuse resistance education (Dare). *Journal of Research in Crime and Delinquency, 31*(1), 3–31. doi:10.1177/0022427894031001001.

Schmidt, P., & Witte, A. D. (1984). *An economic analysis of crime and justice.* Orlando, FL: Academic.

Schmidt, P., & Witte, A. D. (1988). *Predicting recidivism using survival models.* New York, NY: Springer.

Shiroma, E. J., Pickelsimer, E. E., Ferguson, P. L., Gebregziabher, M., Lattimore, P. K., Nicholas, J. S., …, Hunt, K. J. (2010). Association of medically attended traumatic brain injury and in-prison behavioral infractions: A statewide longitudinal study. *Journal of Correctional Health Care, 16*(4), 273–286.

Visher, C. A., Lattimore, P. K., & Linster, R. L. (1991). Predicting the recidivism of serious youthful offenders using survival models. *Criminology, 29,* 329–366.

The Devil Is in the Details: Crime and Victimization Research with the National Crime Victimization Survey

Janet L. Lauritsen

In this essay I discuss some of my research experiences with the National Crime Victimization Survey (NCVS).[1] Having used the data for more than 15 years to conduct various types of analyses, I have learned that the more I use the data, the more questions I have, not just about the various methodological properties of the NCVS, but about other survey data sets that serve as the foundation for a good deal of criminological research. Much of what we currently know about the factors associated with crime and victimization is based on these types of social surveys, and the methodological features of any data set can have important effects on the substantive patterns uncovered in the data.

As most criminologists know, the NCVS has been used to gather self-report data about individual and household experiences with violence and property victimization continuously since 1973. Using a nationally representative sampling frame, interviews are conducted with all persons ages 12 and older in each sampled household. The sample size of the NCVS has varied over time, ranging from about 275,000 interviews per year in the 1970s to about 160,000 interviews in 2012. The sample size is much larger than is found in most surveys used in criminological research

because the key purpose of the data collection is to provide reliable and timely estimates of criminal victimization—a statistically rare event.[2]

Luck

I never planned to spend a large portion of my career assessing a variety of research questions with data from the NCVS. My first experience with the data began rather unexpectedly in 1997 when I was offered an opportunity to analyze internal NCVS files that included geographic information about survey respondents' place of residence.[3] Prior to that time, I had studied individuals' risks for victimization using data from the National Youth Surveys, the Monitoring the Future Surveys, and the British Crime Surveys. I had given relatively little thought

---

[1] I use the term NCVS here to refer to the NCVS and its predecessor, the National Crime Survey (NCS).

J.L. Lauritsen (✉)
University of Missouri, St. Louis, MO, USA
e-mail: Janet_Lauritsen@umsl.edu

[2] Further details about the methodology of the NCVS can be found in many places. For the most thorough report, see Groves and Cork (2008).

[3] This opportunity was made possible by an agreement brokered by Alfred Blumstein (then principal investigator and head of the National Consortium on Violence Research) and Jan Chaiken (then Director of the Bureau of Justice Statistics). This agreement allowed NCOVR-affiliated scholars to access internal NCVS files for Census-approved research projects through the secure Research Data Center at Carnegie Mellon University. Robert Sampson was a member of the NCOVR Advisory Board, and he and I had many discussions of how contextual analyses of these NCVS data might proceed. Without the NCOVR-BJS agreement or Sampson's support, these early NCVS analyses would not have been possible.

M.D. Maltz and S.K. Rice (eds.), *Envisioning Criminology: Researchers on Research as a Process of Discovery*, DOI 10.1007/978-3-319-15868-6_20, © Springer International Publishing Switzerland 2015

to working with NCVS data because, like many criminologists at that time, I thought that the data probably had already been fully exploited by researchers. If there were not enough "independent" variables in the data to address key theoretical hypotheses about victimization (such as lifestyle and opportunity indicators), conventional academic wisdom suggested that the work to understand and develop the data files for analysis might not be worth the effort. But because the internal (or "area-identified") NCVS files could be linked with Census data and therefore had the potential to assess compositional and contextual influences on crime across the United States, this was an opportunity that I could not turn down.

The timing of this research prospect was perfect because it came shortly after I received tenure. Most students are unaware of the nature of this rather grueling process, but simply put, new assistant professors must prove that they are excellent teachers, colleagues, and researchers in order to keep their jobs. To demonstrate excellence in research, the quality and quantity of published research articles (not ideas or plans) are closely assessed by the faculty at the assistant professor's university and elsewhere. I mention this issue because it soon became obvious that this project would require an extraordinary amount of data preparation work before analysis could begin.[4] Early in their careers, professors often are warned that they might not want to engage in original data *collection* because it is very time consuming and will lessen the amount of time for analysis and publication. But with secondary data analysis, this aspect of research is rarely discussed.

Over the years, I had learned enough about statistical methodology and data management to realize this new project would be unusually time consuming.[5] Very large and complex hierarchical

data files would need to be merged, and the limitations of the NCVS geographic codes were unknown because no one had done this before. Moreover, once the necessary files had been merged, the statistical capacity of the NCVS data to answer my research questions was unknown.

The challenge with creating and using the area-identified NCVS data was due, in part, to the fact that it was only possible to access the data, build the files, and conduct the analyses while at a secure Census Research Data Center (RDC) at another university approximately 600 miles away from home. Needless to say, this required a lot of travel and resulted in unusual work delays. Had I not recently been awarded tenure, I doubt I would have been able to undertake such a lengthy data development period for what, at the time, seemed to be an uncertain outcome. Almost 4 years passed between the time I began the approval process to access the area-identified data files until the appearance of a refereed journal article. Though I did not fully appreciate it at the time, the travel schedule necessary for accessing the data had the benefit of providing built-in time to think more carefully about my research questions and to read more deeply about what others already knew about the NCVS.[6]

Persistence

It is often said that hard work and persistence prepare one to take advantage of opportunities and this is certainly true when it comes to research. In quantitative research, students often believe that the hardest work lies in statistical modeling

---

[4] Brian Wiersema's NCVS expertise was critical to the development of the area-identified NCVS.

[5] As an undergraduate, I was a math and computer science major until the end of my junior year at which time I changed my major to sociology. During graduate school, I spent several years working as a consultant and data archivist in the Social Science Quantitative Lab at the University of Illinois where I helped students and faculty solve their data and statistical programming challenges.

[6] Researchers trained to use computers during the 1970s and early 1980s will recall keypunching computer code onto punch cards, submitting their batch jobs at the card reader, and returning the next day to pick up their output only to discover that they left off a period at the end of a line of code. Such frustrations can lead to greater attention to detail, and the waiting time between job submission and results provides time to think. Students today have no parallel experience with computers, but might imagine what this is like by thinking about having to wait 8 hours between the time they press the "enter" key at the end of a command and the time their results appear on the screen.

and not in data analysis per se. But data analysis should be thought of as a larger process that also involves understanding the full set of methodological decisions that were made prior to one's own efforts to model the data statistically. This includes understanding the intended purposes of the data collection, the properties of all of the variables under consideration, the sample design, the mode of data collection, and the strengths and weaknesses that inevitably characterize all data. This aspect of data analysis is often difficult to do because researchers often know relatively little about a particular data set beyond a few basic points such as the unit of analysis, sample size, levels of variable measurement, and perhaps survey participation rates and other issues typically found in a codebook or described in early publications resulting from the data collection.

But the NCVS is somewhat unusual in that it has been an ongoing survey since 1973 and there is a rich research literature evaluating the methodological features of the survey, including several reports by the National Academy of Sciences (NAS) (see, e.g., Penick and Owens (1976) and, more recently, Groves and Cork (2008)). Moreover, there are a series of publications sponsored by government agencies as well as studies conducted by researchers specializing in survey methodology, and these materials are highly important for understanding the history of methodological decision-making and how the NCVS data came to take their present form. The longer I worked with the data, the more I realized how naïve it is to begin to use the data without familiarizing oneself with this literature. But more importantly, these historical readings provide something rare in criminology—an accessible set of materials about the known strengths and limitations of a data source.

Like some but certainly not all researchers, I happen to find data limitations fascinating in and of themselves because they often reveal something interesting about the phenomenon under investigation. Reading through the NCVS methodological literature, for example, one learns how difficult it is to assess the reliability of victimization reports. It is not surprising, of course, that question wording can produce enormous differences in victimization rates. But we have also learned many other things about these respondents' reports, for example, that unbounded interviews produce more reports than bounded interviews, that reports of victimization tend to decline over time in longitudinal studies, and that some victims have a difficulty providing counts of the numbers of recent events they have experienced. But none of the existing research can tell us which estimates are more accurate, nor is this something that can be readily determined with any known methodology. "Reverse-record checks" are often thought of as a solution to this issue, but studies show that persons who reported victimizations to the police or to victim services agencies typically turn up large proportions (e.g., 30%) of "known" victims who deny having been victimized later when contacted by researchers (Biderman & Lynch, 1991; Kilpatrick, Beatty, & Howley, 1998). It seems unlikely that this denial is due to forgetfulness because this is the case even for serious crimes, but it is hard to believe this subsample of victims is a random draw from the population of victims. How these types of findings might affect our conclusions about important issues such as the risk for repeat victimization is largely unknown, but clearly such problems about the limitations of victimization data are worthy of further investigation.

I found that the more I read about the strengths and weaknesses of survey data, the more appreciation I had for what the NCVS could tell us about crime that was unique. At the same time, it was becoming increasingly clear that mastery of the data would require persistent attention to emerging findings about survey methodologies. Though courses in research methods often cover many of the critical issues involved in answering research questions, methods are not static and new information about data gathering techniques requires ongoing education.

On the Shoulders of Giants

In his head-spinning book on discoveries, Robert K. Merton (1965) discusses the origin of the phrase "on the shoulders of giants" and how it came to be attributed to Newton, even though many had used a variant of this phrase as early as

500 years before him. As a sociologist who also studied scientific practice, one of Merton's key arguments is not only that good research builds on the important work of others, but that so many [scientific] "discoveries" are not wholly new; they may have been "pre-discovered" by others whose work was hidden, ignored, or underappreciated for any variety of sociological reasons.[7] This latter insight became increasingly obvious to me as I moved into my next phase of research with the NCVS data.

After completing a series of analyses with the area-identified data, my access to those data ended.[8] But my questions about the NCVS only grew in number and scope. I became interested not only in the empirical evidence used in methodological decision-making but the social processes that affected how the data came to be structured as it is. Who made these decisions and why, and how did this process change over time? What factors, for example, led to the development of new rape and sexual assault, hate crime, and disability questions? Why were some questions, such as the lifestyle items, removed from the survey? Why are some measures, such as immigrant status, not available on the survey? Why did the sample size decline in some years? And so on. To begin to understand these larger processes, I applied for and received a Visiting Research Fellowship with the Bureau of Justice Statistics to investigate the methodological history of the NCVS.[9]

After arriving at BJS and talking with some of the statisticians there, I quickly realized how much more there was to learn about the NCVS and how little I knew about the logistics of an ongoing survey operation of this magnitude.[10] I was both overwhelmed at the sheer amount of research material buried in internal BJS and Census memos and excited to be granted the opportunity to learn about the data in ways that only a handful of other researchers outside of the agency seemed to know. It was during this project that I learned there were many hidden, ignored, and underappreciated researchers of the NCVS, and although there were certainly key figures in the development of the survey throughout its various phases (both within and outside the agency), it does not seem correct to refer to just one of them as the "giant" of the survey. Rather, unlike academic data collections that typically have one or more principal investigators who might be more readily identified as the "giants," the NCVS was a collective and institutionalized data enterprise that made it unlikely that many of the different types of researchers who contributed to the development of the data would receive personal credit for their scientific accomplishments.[11] I deeply respect commitments to this kind of collective scientific enterprise and to the principles and practices of a federal statistical agency (National Research Council, 2013).

The BJS and Census R&D memoranda as well as documents from outside researchers over the years were filled with interesting and important findings about the strengths and limitations of the data as well as discussions about potential changes to the survey, data user demands, answers

---

[7] As Michael Maltz informed me, "Stigler's law of eponymy" even more strongly states Merton's observations by claiming that "No scientific discovery is named after its original discoverer." For more fun, see http://en.wikipedia.org/wiki/Stigler's_law_of_eponymy where it is claimed that Stigler named "Merton as the discoverer of Stigler's law, consciously making Stigler's law exemplify itself."

[8] My access to the data ended when funding for access to the Census RDC ended. It would have been possible to submit another grant for Census approval and outside agency financial support necessary to access the data, but I decided to pursue other research issues that did not require area-identified information.

[9] For this opportunity, I am deeply grateful to Lawrence Greenfeld, then Director of BJS, and Michael Rand who so generously let me peruse the materials in his file cabinets.

[10] I am indebted to a great deal of people at BJS for their generosities during my first and subsequent fellowships.

[11] Sociologists might think of this process as similar to what Howard Becker's describes in his book *Art Worlds* (University of California Press, 1982)—the production of art as collective action rather than as an individual case study of the personality or life history of the artist or musician. For a less academic and more political example, see Elizabeth Warren's discussion of how some CEOs take too much credit for their contributions to the economy (http://articles.philly.com/2012-07-30/news/32924415_1_elizabeth-warren-american-crossroads-president-obama).

to questions from outsiders, etc. I was able to help bring some of this work to academic attention through a 2005 special issue of the Journal of Quantitative Criminology (Volume 21, Number 3), but a great deal more remained. Fortunately, much of the methodological history of the NCVS would come to be recorded in the summary report by the NAS Committee on National Statistics entitled "Surveying Victims: Options for Conducting the National Crime Victimization Survey" (Groves & Cork, 2008).[12] Indeed, it would be a great accomplishment if this level of methodological detail were known about all of the data sources that routinely appear in criminology journals because it would mean that the profession took seriously the limitations of its science.

With Countless Possibilities Come Many Challenges

My initial uses of the NCVS treated the data in ways that are similar to what is found in most survey data analysis—with the individual and his or her responses to the questions as the unit of analysis. This type of research question is most typical in victimization research: What factors are associated with an individual's risk for victimization? But the NCVS is also hierarchical in nature, and this provides the researcher with a wide range of research possibilities. Because the data collection is ongoing and the sample is designed to produce nationally representative rates of personal victimization (such as rape and sexual assault, robbery, and aggravated and simple assault) and household victimization (such as burglary, larceny, and motor vehicle theft), it is possible to configure the data to have multiple units of analysis, such as the

incident, the household, the person, or rates at either the national or selected subnational level (such as the metropolitan area or across urban, suburban, and rural areas).

The hierarchical nature of the data means that after downloading the public use file, one does not simply open up a data file and begin producing basic descriptive frequencies for a set of independent and dependent variables as might be done with other rectangular data sets. It is necessary for the researcher to think not just about a topic, but to formulate a specific research question because each question of interest may require a different data configuration, some of which will require much more time for data development. Take, for example, the topic of assault. One might be interested in learning whether certain demographic factors are correlated with an individual's risk for assault victimization or with certain types of assault (e.g., intimate partner, gun violence). One might be interested in whether these same factors are associated with the likelihood that an assault victim calls the police or whether the assault results in a serious injury. These types of issues can be answered by treating a year of data as cross-sectional and creating a person- or incident-level file.

But the NCVS has also been an ongoing data collection effort since 1973, and so important research questions about historical context also can be examined with these data: Have assault rates for different demographic subgroups changed over time in similar or different ways? Do different types of assault (such as intimate partner violence or stranger violence) have similar trends? How has the reporting of assault changed over time? etc. And because some temporal data also are available at the metropolitan area level, one can examine variations in such patterns over time and across places, thus expanding the range of contextual factors that can be considered as covariates of the various assault victimization rates. These types of questions (and more) can be studied with the NCVS data, but each question requires that the researcher set up the data appropriately before statistical analysis can begin.

---

[12] Toward the end of my research fellowship period, BJS was facing an enormous budget challenge in large part because the cost of the NCVS was increasing while agency funding was not. This challenge led BJS to commission the NAS Panel to study options for the NCVS as well as review all of the programs of the BJS. More than a year after my fellowship ended, I was asked by the NAS to serve as a member of that panel, during which time I refrained from contact with the agency.

In my experience, the key challenges that the NCVS researcher will face are that some of the necessary data configurations can be tedious to produce and the issues that need to be handled may vary by year of data collection due to changes in the files and data records. Moreover, these are issues that one can learn about only through trial and error as one works to set up the data for their own statistical modeling. Personally, I enjoy these aspects of data analysis, but I know that many do not. Nonetheless, I often remind students that if this kind of work was not viewed as drudgery by so many researchers, their research question was likely to already have been answered.

The Importance of Verification

One of the most valuable research practices that I was reminded of during my early fellowship at BJS is the importance of verification and replication. The tables and figures in each BJS publication must be verified by statisticians other than those who produced the analysis before the report can move to copy editing and publication. The obvious purpose of this is to eliminate mistakes in official statistical publications of the Department of Justice. Some mistakes might be small and of relatively little substantive import, but others may have large consequences if the erroneous information is used to justify changes in policy or practice. In either case, they are unacceptable. The institutionalized practices at the agency help ensure that neither type of mistake escapes notice.

Every researcher knows how easy it is to make a mistake, but the idea of having others external to the project reproduce and check our data and analyses is not often considered. The reasons for this may seem obvious; this type of work can be very time consuming for others to do, each of us has our own ways of doing work so that mistakes are detected and minimized, and these types of verifications (we hope) are unlikely to result in any changes to the results or substantive conclusions. In some research work, external verifications are not possible because the researcher is working with confidential data and the data

access agreements do not allow for data sharing. So if it is not practical or possible to have one's findings routinely verified by others, what else might researchers do to minimize error?

The most feasible option practiced by many researchers is to assume that someday, someone will want to replicate your published analysis in an effort to build on previously established findings. This is an especially useful assumption if one is using data that are publicly available or available to other researchers under special data access agreements. The practice of keeping good research records not only allows a researcher to more easily build on their own work at a later time, but it also has the benefit of allowing one to answer future questions from others about how they handled various data and analytic issues.

The idea that scientists should produce their research in ways that permit outside replication is not new. Writing about political science nearly 20 years ago, King (1995) argued that "the only way to understand and evaluate an empirical analysis fully is to know the exact process by which the data were generated and the analysis produced" (p. 444). However, his suggestions as to how this might be done resulted in a range of counterarguments about data and program sharing, and similar debates about these scholarly norms can be found in many other disciplines such as sociology (e.g., Freese, 2007), psychology (e.g., Open Science Foundation, 2014), and biology (e.g., Gelman, 2013).

Much of the debate centers on just how much of one's own intellectual work (particularly in the form of computer programs and data) one is expected to share with others, and scholarly norms about this appear to vary across disciplines and journals within disciplines. At one end of the spectrum are clearly stated expectations for the full sharing of materials, such as those required by the American Economic Association's journal *The American Economic Review*. Researchers who publish in this journal are required to submit their data, programs, and all instructions necessary for replication of the analysis at the time a paper is accepted for publication, and these materials are made available on the journal's website. At the other end of the spectrum are most journals in criminology and other social sciences where no clear policy is stated, and decisions about sharing this type of information with interested readers are ultimately left to the discretion of the individual researcher.

Regardless of a journal's specific policy about data or program sharing, published research is expected to contain all of the methodological details necessary for work to be replicated. I teach a graduate course in quantitative methods in which students are guided through the process of replicating a published article of their choosing. The research must have relied on publicly available data, and students are told to choose something they admire or would like to build on in their own future research. Inevitably of course, they quickly learn how many methodological decisions are made during data analysis, and oftentimes they find that the details necessary for replication are unclear or are not provided in the publication. After repeated unsuccessful attempts to uncover the original authors' decisions (with my guidance), they are then encouraged to contact the author(s) for further clarification. To date we have found every author to be responsive. However, in some instances, the author(s) was unable to recall, for example, how they made their case selections or handled missing data on some of their variables, and if this is the case, the students will then proceed based on their own decisions about how these issues should be handled. The student's final results may differ from the published findings, and the key issue here is whether the substantive meanings of the findings change. This practice of replicating another's research before building on it is critical to the scientific process and it should not be skipped. It is always informative in some way and can sometimes lead to the discoveries of important and consequential errors.[13]

---

[13]My favorite story about a classroom replication exercise involves Thomas Herndon, a graduate student in economics at the University of Massachusetts—Amherst. In 2013, he discovered a critical error in the work of Harvard economists Carmen Reinhart and Kenneth Rogoff in which they argued that high levels of government debt caused economic growth to slow considerably. See, for example, http://www.reuters.com/article/2013/04/18/us-global-economy-debt-herndon-idUSBRE93H0CV20130418.

Conclusion

As I thought about my experiences using the NCVS data over so many years, several themes became obvious to me. These included the good luck I had about the timing of my access to the area-identified data, the persistence that would be necessary to master many of the important aspects of the data, my growing appreciation for the collective efforts of those who developed the data, the seemingly endless analytic possibilities as well as challenges that users of the data face, and the importance of verification (especially with complex data) to ensure one's results are correct. These experiences are unlikely to be unique to NCVS data researchers, even though the data themselves are distinct in studies of crime and victimization and in the survey research world. And though it may sound cliché to say, none of these insights about data analysis would matter much if the research question under investigation is unimportant or misinformed.

References

Biderman, A., & Lynch, J. (1991). *Understanding crime incidence statistics: Why the UCR diverges from the NCVS*. New York, NY: Springer.

Freese, J. (2007). Replication standards for quantitative social science: Why not sociology? *Sociological Methods and Research, 36*, 153–172.

Gelman, A. (2013). *Replication backlash*, December 17th, Retrieved May 4, 2014, from http://andrewgelman.com/2013/12/17/replication-backlash/

Groves, R., & Cork, D. (Eds.). (2008). *Surveying victims: Options for conducting the national crime victimization survey*. Washington, DC: National Academy Press.

Kilpatrick, D., Beatty, D., & Howley, S. S. (1998). *The rights of crime victims—Does legal protection make a difference?* Washington, DC: National Institute of Justice.

King, G. (1995). Replication, replication. *Political Science and Politics, 28*, 443–499.

Merton, R. K. (1965). *On the shoulders of giants: A Shandean postscript*. New York, NY: The Free Press.

National Research Council. (2013). *Principles and practices for a Federal Statistical Agency* (5th ed.). Washington, DC: National Academy Press.

Open Science Foundation. (2014). *Reproducibility project: Psychology*. Retrieved May 4, 2014, from https://osf.io/ezcuj/wiki/home

Penick, B., & Owens, M. (Eds.). (1976). *Surveying crime*. Washington, DC: National Academy Press.

What's the Question?
Ask That and You Will Follow
the Path of Discovery

Alex R. Piquero

Introduction

My first week of graduate school in the Department of Criminology and Criminal Justice at the University of Maryland in September 1992 was quite memorable. In 1 week, Charles Wellford had us delve into the classic American Bar Foundation Survey on criminal justice as well as Packer's two models of the criminal process, Denise Gottfredson had us think about research design, and Doug Smith, well, he had us shaking in our pants as we started "introductory" to graduate statistics in criminology. But there was nothing "introductory" about that class. Why you may ask? Well, we didn't have the option of point and clicking anything. We used a statistical program called GAUSS, with its nonexistent help function and its user-driven code to make it do what you wanted it to do. It was in that first week of graduate school and the remaining 4 years of my graduate school career and the constant presence of Doug Smith that taught me the craft of research, one that was focused on (1) asking very specific and original research questions that could be answered (as best as possible) in a yes/no fashion and (2) whose findings were interesting regardless of how they came out.

That training and subsequent research experiences with faculty and colleagues alike are what taught me that research is not an outcome but a process, one that takes time, care, and attention. But to understand how I see research as a process of discovery, I need to take the reader through a brief, longitudinal journey about how I got to where I am, what I have learned in the process, and my hope for what my students will take away and improve upon in their own careers.

Graduate School

I was very fortunate to have a great set of faculty at Maryland, led by one of the world's most important criminologists, Charles Wellford, and which included Ray Paternoster, who would later become my mentor, colleague, and friend. Equally important I might add were a group of fellow graduate students who not only pushed me to be a better scholar but who have gone on to become both acclaimed researchers and dear friends. Three in particular stand out: Bobby Brame, Paul Mazerolle, and Steve Tibbetts—all of whom happened to be students of Ray's as well. Each of them was instrumental in helping me develop my craft in unique ways. First, however, some context.

I started graduate school at a time in criminology that I found to be very exciting. Gottfredson and Hirschi's *A General Theory of Crime* was

A.R. Piquero (✉)
University of Texas at Dallas, Richardson, TX, USA
e-mail: apiquero@utdallas.edu

M.D. Maltz and S.K. Rice (eds.), *Envisioning Criminology: Researchers on Research as a Process of Discovery*, DOI 10.1007/978-3-319-15868-6_21, © Springer International Publishing Switzerland 2015

out, stirring up the flames of debates regarding criminal careers and life-course research, and soon thereafter Moffitt's developmental taxonomy was published in 1993. My colleague and friend Paul Mazerolle, now a pro-vice-chancellor at Griffith University in Brisbane, Australia, located this article at McKeldin Library and circulated among all of us (I still have the one he gave me with his handwriting all over it!). Nagin and Land's 1993 article on the trajectory methodology ushered in a new way of describing offending patterns, and the four of us (Brame, Mazerolle, Piquero, and Tibbetts) took a class with Ray on testing criminological theory. From that course, several peer-reviewed articles were born, and countless idea for subsequent papers emerged—many of which have long since appeared in print. It was an exciting time, not only because issues surrounding developmental and life-course criminology were rampant with interesting empirical puzzles but because we all desired to use longitudinal data to assess life-course issues and we were learning methodological and statistical techniques from both Doug Smith and David McDowall, two of the best in their business.

I was also fortunate at that time to realize that studying developmental and life-course criminology questions was no easy task—but this made the discovery process more fun and more rewarding. What data challenges forced me to do was to ask very straightforward and specific research questions that, when coupled with dozens of other research questions and papers, would begin to form a coherent research base, akin to solving a crossword puzzle, one clue at a time.

My Academic Career

I started my academic career in 1996 as an assistant professor of criminal justice at Temple University in Philadelphia. I was surrounded by a stellar set of criminologists. Just to name a few, in my office to my left, John Goldkamp, leading criminal justice scholar on issues related to discretion in the criminal justice system and drug courts. Down the hallway to my right, Ralph Taylor, a leading figure in communities and

crime. On the other side of the hallway was Joan McCord, prominent theorist and life-course scholar, followed by Jim Fyfe, a great policing researcher, and, on the tenth floor, Jack Greene, an authority on police and public policy. And that was just in the criminal justice department!

But Philadelphia had much more to offer and two experiences stand out—both of which helped me in a pathway to furthering my road to discovery. In my first semester, I had the courage to cold-call Marvin Wolfgang, who was located in a townhome off the main campus of the University of Pennsylvania in west Philadelphia near Abner's Cheesesteaks. I spoke with his secretary, Esther, who scheduled a meeting with the two of us. Off I went to see the scholar who led two of the most famous and important criminal career studies in our field, the 1945 and 1958 Philadelphia birth cohort studies.

At our meeting, Professor Wolfgang grilled me big-time. He asked why I become interested in criminal career issues, what I had learned the most in graduate school, and what I wanted to learn in the future. I (think!) answered all of his questions well or at least well enough because he then allowed me to ask him questions regarding the birth cohort studies, criminal career analysis, and so forth. It was a very fortuitous meeting in several respects, and I am so glad I had the chance to meet him. What I learned from him about criminal careers was the power of arraying the data into transitions, what happens from one period to the next.

Soon thereafter, I had heard that a professor in the psychology department at Temple, Larry Steinberg, had just received a large grant from the MacArthur Foundation to launch a research network on adolescent development and juvenile justice. Having written a few articles on issues that I thought he would be interested in, I cold-called Professor Steinberg, told him who I was, and asked if he could spare a few minutes to meet with me. He agreed, and off I went to Weiss Hall where we met for a short bit of time. I must have passed that first test because he invited me to a Network meeting where he asked me to present some of my research to a group of academics and practitioners as well as some of the foundation staff. I did that and soon thereafter I became involved in the Network and right after that began involvement in a research project, Pathways to Desistance, that had become—and still remains—a prominent part of my research foci.

Before I discuss Pathways, it is important to also know that during my 4 years on the faculty at Temple, I was also fortunate to become integrated into an NSF-funded project, the National Consortium on Violence Research (NCOVR), chaired by Alfred Blumstein from Carnegie Mellon University, that brought together prominent violence and longitudinal research from around the world with the intention of sharing data, crafting research, and mentoring a cadre of pre- and post-doctoral students—many of whom would become academic leaders in their own right. NCOVR brought me into another set of research collaborations with leading criminologists in efforts to study criminal career issues, including Terrie Moffitt, David Farrington, and Daniel Nagin.

Pathways to Desistance

During the late 1990s, the Network decided to launch its own longitudinal study that sought to build upon some of the limitations of current studies. Namely, we were interested in understanding how serious youthful offenders transitioned from their offending pathways between adolescence and early adulthood. Although the details are more frightening than identifying the ingredients of a hot dog, suffice it to say, sitting around the room with a group of really smart social scientists and creating a research design, interview battery, and data collection mechanisms just pushed my thinking and skill set even higher. At the end of the day, we were able to follow over 1,300 serious youthful offenders in Philadelphia and Phoenix for a 7-year follow-up period. Numerous publications have come out of the Pathways project on a variety of topics, and many more are not only planned by various investigators, but a great many more will arise out of the fact that the original research team decided early on that much of the data would be archived for public use at ICPSR, where it has

been for a good while now. Pathways taught me not only how to work with an inter- and multidisciplinary team, but it also taught me how to be judicious and planful with respect to research questions, variable collection, and data quality.

The Cambridge Study in Delinquent Development

Earlier I noted that I was fortunate to become acquainted with David Farrington, a criminologist who needs no introduction. In the early 2000s, Farrington and I were discussing how much new criminal career information had emerged since the publication of the 1986 National Academy of Sciences report of the same. He suggested that we coauthor a review piece with Al Blumstein for Tonry's *Crime and Justice* series. Having never written one of these essays before—but certainly having read them all—I quickly agreed assuming it would be "a long review piece." That turned out to be a wild understatement on my part! I think we ended up with a draft of about 300 pages, to which David said "we should have written book!" which we ended up doing. But what I learned from working with Al and David was how they saw the field. Of course, it was much easier for them, as they had been contributing to that area of work for 30+ years. But what they were able to do, which I have slowly started to be able to do as well, is to see and interpret the overall contributions the studies have made to the criminal career area and criminology more generally. Contributions and knowledge allow one to see what has been done but more importantly where the holes are, and in the criminal career area, there were (and still are) a great many research projects and questions still to be studied. And that book David suggested, well, it has turned into not one but two books and dozens of articles thus far—all on various criminal career/life-course topics.

Still, I would be remiss if I do not share one of the most relevant insights that David taught me about the research discovery process. First and foremost, David is masterful in identifying "key aims and research questions." As one looks through his published work, it will be easy to see that what David does is he identifies a key, focused research question, one that can be answered yes or no and one that is interesting regardless of its outcome. Aha! Doug Smith and Ray Paternoster ring in my ear yet again.

Describe, Describe, Describe

It is not difficult to "see" research questions. They appear everywhere and at all times. But questions are more readily visible when one has a good description of the patterns that one is trying to explain. For me, I need to see the data or a visualization (in the Maltz sense) of what it is I am trying to understand, before I can go any further: plotting crime rates in a city over time will do the trick, as would plotting the number of offenses by age in a longitudinal study. As I tell my graduate students, I do not want to see any modeling whatsoever until I see the crosstabs, descriptives, and frequencies. I know this may come across as boring to some, but I firmly believe that a basic understanding of the data is a necessity when it comes to conducting research.

It is also the case that throughout my career, I have been mainly interested in asking and answering specific criminological theory and criminal justice research questions. Many of these questions either rely on or necessitate the use of longitudinal data, which offers its own set of promises and challenges. That said, I have tried to focus all of my efforts, regardless of the substantive topic that interests me at that time, on asking a very specific research question, one that can be answered yes or no and one that is interesting regardless of its outcome. This approach has helped me to be able to see the detailed colors of the Grand Canyon while still being able to describe the vastness of it all from 35,000 ft.

Research Discovery as a Process

I tell my students that science takes time and that science cannot be rushed. Fits and starts are all part of the knowledge discovery process.

In many ways, research is very much like a week's worth of New York Times crossword puzzles. On Mondays, it starts off easy—tempting you and creating a false sense of superiority. Tuesday, it's a tad bit harder, but still more than doable. Wednesday and Thursdays are a bit more challenging, Friday and Saturday, well everyone knows those—and Sunday, whoa! But the great thing about a crossword puzzle, just like in research, is that you can stop it for a bit, work on or do something else, and then come back to it and see things that you were not able to see before. Research then, like appreciating a crossword maker's clues and grid schema, is always filled with an "a-ha" moment, the kind when you finally solve a difficult clue or ask and answer a neat research question. Of course, the road to discovery in research does not end, as there is always a new set of questions, a new data source, or a new methodological technique that is in need of application and, as well, a new puzzle to solve.

So What Do I Do Before I Do Research?

I have been involved in a vast array of criminological and criminal justice topics, but much of my interest has centered on offender decision making and, in particular, how various risk and protective factors are implicated in longitudinal offending patterns. Before I set out to conduct a particular study, and assuming I have the data in hand, there are two things that I always do—neither of which are glamorous but both of which are, in my view, necessary. First and foremost, I read, read some more, and read as widely as I possibly can. This is a habit I picked up in graduate school, where weekly I would go to the library, sometimes by myself, other times with my colleagues, and I would go up and down the issues of the new journals—and not just in criminology/criminal justice. In fact, I learned a lot about the scientific process and craft of research by reading how researchers in other disciplines asked research questions and conducted their own studies—regardless of the topic. Journals in psychology, sociology, political science, public health, and even law are always filled with clever research studies, pitched in discipline-specific ways, with different methodological techniques and presentation styles. What I learned from that exercise—one that I do still to this day—is that science is a real craft, one that takes time, one that is focused on asking good questions, one that involves applying the most appropriate (and simplest) methods, and one that needs to speak to different audiences. I think one of the most a-ha moments was when I found a research article that dissected Bruce Springsteen lyrics. In short, reading both widely and frequently has helped me realize that oftentimes researchers in other disciplines are interested in similar substantive topics, asking similar questions, but doing it in a way that speaks to their audience.

Guided by my research questions, a second thing that I always do before I settle in to "do research" is I look at histograms, frequencies, descriptive, and crosstabs so I can understand and visualize the patterns in the data. Once I get a sense for the data, I return to my research questions, conduct the planned analyses, table them up, and then draft the results and conclusions. Importantly, I then put away the analysis for a few days. Subsequently, I reestimate the same models, without looking at the previous output, and then table them up and rewrite the results again. Why do I do this twice? I do so because it forces me to double-check my work and see how I have interpreted and written the same results, in order to ensure that I have estimated the analyses correctly and that I have interpreted the results in a similar manner.

Like I said, neither of these are very glamorous, but I find that reading widely and constantly checking one's own work are an effective way to producing the best possible science at that time. This read-run-write approach is also one that is repeated. That is, just because I have sat down and estimated models and written a paper does not mean that "it's done." It is only done for the time being, as I regularly share my finished research with several colleagues and graduate students for feedback. In this regard, I also purposely share my work with individuals at various stages of their careers and with a few who may

know little about the substantive topic or the methodological approach. Why? Because I hope that my research is read widely by different people in different disciplines and with different areas of interest. Quite often, I receive useful feedback regarding various aspects of my work that I had not thought about before. In the interests of producing the best science at the time, one's work is never really done.

So What Do I Do After I Do Research?

I have been fortunate to be asked to lecture to a wide variety of lay and academic audiences, testify before various public and government agencies, and give media interviews around various research studies that I have conducted. Each of these audiences represents a different constituency, each with different skills and interests. Early in my career, I was a bit hesitant to do this kind of post-research outreach; yet I have come to realize that this is simply another opportunity for getting research out of the standard academic circles and into the community. Whether people refer to it as public criminology or translational criminology, my goal has always been the same: to deliver the best possible science in ways that are useful and understandable to a varied set of audiences. I cannot say that it has always been successful, but the positives outweigh the negatives that come with preparing talks, meeting people, and sometimes disagreeing with persons who do not see or interpret the science in the same way that I do. Let me highlight two specific experiences where I was asked to translate research, research that took many hours and days of labor, into a few minutes.

In 2013, I was asked to give oral testimony to Attorney General Holder's Task Force on Children Exposed to Violence on the issue of early crime prevention. The Task Force was comprised of a variety of individuals from various walks of life. Off I went to Detroit, Michigan, and I had a set time to speak for a 3-min slot followed by 5 min of questions and answers from the Task Force. When I first received this invitation, I thought, as many academics do, "how am I going to communicate years and years of research from dozens of scholars across various disciplines, including my own research, in 180 seconds?!?" It came to me that the best way to do this, and I do not mean to dumb this down, was to think about how I would explain this area of research—namely, what the main findings were and what it means for public policy—to my parents at the dinner table. This forced me to get right to the point, in a way that persons who were not intimately familiar with the research would walk away understanding what the main issues were, what the main findings were, and what policy steps could be considered.

A second experience involved some research I have been involved in with Bianca Bersani and Tom Loughran regarding immigrant offending patterns. Our research was fortunate enough to be picked up by various media outlets, including Al Jazeera America for which I did a television interview for a segment they produced on the topic. The research we published used complicated methodological techniques, and the results clearly showed the lower offending rates of first-generation immigrants compared to their second-generation counterparts as well as native-born American youth. Again, I had to think carefully about how to relay those findings in a simple yet careful (because of the nature of the topic)

manner so that anyone tuning into the segment could understand what we did, what we found, and what it meant. Relatedly, my University's Development Office asked me to give a community lecture to several board members and their guests one evening in downtown Dallas on the topic of immigration. Talk about a varied audience. There were lawyers, doctors, CPAs, retirees, their children, and several other constituencies in the audience, and I was asked to lecture on my work on immigration and crime—without notes or a PowerPoint. So, once again, I had to think carefully about the audience and more importantly what I wanted to convey regarding this hot-button issue. My talk was aimed largely at talking about what people think the immigration/crime linkage to be, what our research has shown, and what we think some of the next steps are in this area of work. The talk was well received, so much so that I stayed for an hour longer talking to attendees who relayed my work to their own work (there were immigration lawyers in attendance) and draw several insights from it that they could use in their own careers. Experiences like that are, of course, delightful, but even more rewarding is seeing "a-ha" moments in the audience as you see persons think about research, its findings, and its application in ways that they had not done before.

Predicting Risk: Who Knew It Was Such a Risky Business?

Susan Turner

If one glanced at the working paper on the Center for Evidence-Based Corrections website entitled "Development of the California Static Risk Assessment, CSRA," the most likely reaction a reader might have is a yawn. He or she might think the project was pretty dry and uneventful. Not so. What began as a fast turnaround project, done in collaboration with our client, the California Department of Corrections and Rehabilitation, morphed into a saga that would try the patience of any researcher.

Setting the Stage

The state of California spends almost as much of the general fund on corrections as it does on higher education, despite a correctional population (prisoners and parolees) of about 190,000 compared to almost three million students in higher education institutions statewide. At the height of the prison population, more than 163,000 felons were incarcerated in 33 prisons throughout the state. The state prison system is responsible for the welfare, safety, and rehabilitation efforts of offenders while they are in their care and oversees large numbers of felons on parole supervision after their release from prison.

S. Turner (✉)
University of California, Irvine, CA, USA
e-mail: sfturner@uci.edu

Over the recent decades, California had fallen from a national leader in the supervision and treatment of offenders to one where inmates were dying unnecessarily from poor medical care, exacerbated by overcrowding. Recidivism rates were high—over two-thirds of offenders released from prison were reincarcerated within 3 years. The costs associated with the "churning" of offenders in and out of the prison system were high. Treatment and rehabilitation services were few and not well targeted to offenders who needed them.

California has enacted a large number of reforms to try and address the prison population and conditions over the past years. Most observers are aware of the recently passed Public Safety Realignment legislation, which has shifted responsibility for lower-level offenders from the state to the county level in 2011, reducing the prison population by tens of thousands. However, key to bringing the state and its treatment of offenders back to a level of professional leadership is their adoption of the "California Logic Model," in which assessing offenders' risk to the community (for public safety) and needs (for the delivery of treatment services) assumes a central role. The California Logic Model was developed by a special task force comprising national leaders drawn from the field and academia (CDCR, 2007). One of the first steps in the model is to reliably assess an offender's risk of recidivism. This "risk" then figures into supervision and

M.D. Maltz and S.K. Rice (eds.), *Envisioning Criminology: Researchers on Research as a Process of Discovery*, DOI 10.1007/978-3-319-15868-6_22, © Springer International Publishing Switzerland 2015

rehabilitation services for each offender. The concept of risk-based decision-making and delivery of services based on need is at the forefront of best practices in corrections and one, which until very recently, the California state prison system had not embraced.

The California Static Risk Assessment Instrument

Our project was to develop the risk assessment tool to be used by the state prison system, as recommended by the expert panel. Although the primary risk and need assessment system utilized by the state was and still is the Correctional Offender Management Profiling for Alternative Sanctions (COMPAS) system (Brennan et al., 2009), at the time validation studies were ongoing, and results would not be available in time to meet operational needs. COMPAS was also a tool that required administration by trained staff and can take anywhere from 10 min to an hour to administer (Northpoint, nd). The pressure was on to get a tool that could quickly produce risk scores for large numbers of inmates with a project deadline of about 4 months.

The state determined that the best option was to build a tool based on one that had been developed by the Washington State Institute for Public Policy. Washington State had created and validated a tool that used only 26 "static" measures (primarily prior criminal record) using automated criminal history files (Barnoski & Aos, 2003). The upside was that this tool was as predictive as a tool that combined both static and dynamic factors—buttressing California's interest in a static tool. The California instrument consists of 22 items, including two demographic items, one total felony conviction item, nine adult felony record items, nine adult misdemeanor record items, and one adult supervision violation item (Turner, Hess & Jannetta, 2009). Unlike the Washington version, the California version did not contain four items on juvenile prior record, because juvenile data appear rarely on automated criminal history data in the state.

Rapid Production

What set this project apart from many of the Center projects was the rapid turnaround required. Starting from scratch to a validated tool had to take place in 4 months—a drastically shorter time frame than many research projects normally operate. Our Center analyst dropped everything to become expert in processing California's automated criminal history records or "rap sheets." The Center had an "all hands on deck" approach, often feeling the "heat" of Sacramento on our figurative necks. What we didn't expect was the sheer amount of time it would take to "read" the rap sheets. Although the data were automated, vestiges of the old Common Business-Oriented Language (COBOL) system were apparent in the file structure and minimal documentation. (COBOL was developed in 1959 in an effort to establish a common business computer language.) Data were not entered into fields as expected; pointers would refer to a "comments" field, populated by whatever the data entry person felt was the best way to document an arrest outcome, sentence, etc. Countless hours were devoted to detecting "string patterns" in the comments field and translating them into acceptable offense codes and disposition information required by the tool. Nonetheless, following good practice, we were able to develop our models on half the data and validated the California tool on the second half. We met our targets and delivered our computer code to the state by the required deadline.

Skepticism in the Parole Ranks

As can often be the case, decisions made at the highest levels of an organization may not have an easy implementation when it comes to the staff who must put the changes into action. One policy change that incorporated the tool was the development of a parole violation decision-making tool that incorporated both the offender's risk level (from the tool) and the seriousness of the offense, in decisions about which sanction would be recommended for parole agent responses to parole violations. Only those violations that were the most serious, committed by high-risk parolees, would be recommended for a return to custody. This approach had proven successful in Ohio as a mechanism for reducing parole revocations (Martin & Van Dine, 2008; Martin, Van Dine & Fiakloff, 2009). A major impetus for this change in practice was the fact that California's prisons faced a large and rapid "churning" of parolees who were violated using a parole board process (as opposed to the courts) and spent an average of 4 months incarcerated before returning to the streets, driving up the prison population (Grattet, Petersilia & Lin, 2008). Our Center was involved in the training of parole agents for the parole matrix rollout, as well as conducting a process and outcome evaluation. In our training, it was quickly apparent that parole agents were not enamored of the tool—preferring to think that their experience and clinical judgment were more accurate and nuanced than any automated tool could ever be. As the tool was rolled out in a pilot program, in which the Center used a quasi-experimental evaluation design (we could not convince them to do a randomized trial), information on each agent's use of the tool was recorded by a database developed by the state to capture the tool's recommendations and actual parole agent decisions.

Of course, a major assumption of the pilot project was that agents would follow the tool's recommendation, except in the rare instances in which they could either "override" or "underride" the tool's recommendation, provided they gave reasons (such as treatment not being available). Did they? Once we received the data and began analyzing, we discovered that agents followed the parole matrix recommendations about two-thirds of the time—much less than expected and certainly not at a level at which one would expect the tool to make a big difference in revocations to prison. And in fact, we did not see any reductions in returns to prison or any changes in recidivism for those parolees participating in the "experimental" sites. We felt like air had been let out of our risk balloon (Turner et al., 2012).

Rolling Out Non-revocable Parole

The parole matrix was rolled out within the department without a great deal of public scrutiny or fanfare. Such was not the case in the rollout of Non-revocable Parole, another effort which utilized the risk tool. Non-revocable Parole, based on the risk-need and responsivity literature, was designed to "get smart" in the allocation of resources—to reduce resources devoted to "lower-level" parolees and use these resources to supervise and provide more services to higher-risk parolees. With Non-revocable Parole, lower-level parolees would be under no supervision by parole at all. They would, however, be subject to search-and-seizure conditions, in a compromise with law enforcement and prosecutors, who opposed the policy. Of course, if a parolee is not under supervision, he or she cannot be returned to prison for a parole revocation. Thus, one of the expected benefits would be reductions in the churning of parolees back into prison for parole violations, helping reduce the state prison population.

Eligibility criteria for the Non-revocable Parole program were quite restrictive. Only parolees who had no current or prior serious or violent offense (as defined by California statute), had no prior or current sex offense, were not validated prison gang members, had no conviction for a serious prison disciplinary incident, and had low or moderate risk to recidivate (as determined by the risk tool) were eligible. It was expected that perhaps 10% of the parole population would fit these criteria. The eligibility process required both an automated review of the parolee records and a manual screen to ensure accurate determination of prior record.

Shortly after the first parolees were placed on unsupervised parole, a firestorm erupted. In rolling out the program, several hundred high-risk parolees were erroneously released by our well-developed and validated risk tool. How could this possibly be? Apparently, some of the criminal history records used as input to the tool were incomplete due to some of old prior record history being stored in manual, as opposed to automated records.

State staff had not known this was the case. One can imagine an incomplete rap sheet would result in an incorrectly "low" predicted risk.

The state quickly gathered the information required to complete the rap sheets and rescore parolees. However, the damage had been done. The media saw this as an opportunity to criticize the entire effort. Headlines such as "California prisons: 'Non-revocable parole' is too dangerous" hammered the department and its theory-based program (Lieu, 2011). To add insult to injury, much of the news coverage was inaccurate. The public was led to believe that the tool was used to let offenders out of prison early, heightening concerns for public safety. The tool was never used to release inmates early, but the damage had been done.

Investigation by the California Inspector General

Spurred by concerns about the mishap with Non-revocable Parole, one of California's legislators called for an investigation by the California Inspector General, whose mission is oversight of the state's prisons and correctional programs. The Center found itself in the crosshairs of what seemed to be political sparring, designed to enhance a "tough on crime" narrative by facing off with the state. The Inspector General staff requested all forms of project materials, conducted phone interviews with Center staff, hired their own consultants to review our materials, and eventually met with our Center staff in a meeting that could only be described as inquisitorial and harassing, as if we were witnesses under cross-examination. However, the most distressing part of the process was the lack of expertise of the auditors assigned to the case. They were not trained researchers, did not understand what validation meant, and had an obvious agenda to discredit our work and the risk tool used as part of the Non-revocable Parole program. We felt immense pressure from them to disavow our own work. We would do no such thing.

It came as no surprise to us that the Inspector General report was extremely critical of the Non-revocable Parole program and the risk tool. However, we were faced with the question of how to respond to their flawed report. Should we ignore the report and hope that knowledgeable people would be able to see through the poor work on their part, or should we jump into what we knew was going to be a rough and tumble interchange? One of the good things about our relationship with the state is that we were able to consult and work with their staff to craft a response to the report. We did this by way of a letter to the Inspector General himself. The letter was short, addressing major flaws in their analysis, including their office creating their own manual risk coding scheme and proclaiming it was more accurate than the automated tool, when, in fact, they did not test their tool, as well as repeating incorrect assertions about the tool's use of juvenile records, which we had repeatedly corrected them on during their investigation. This was posted on the Center website (and remains there[1]). For example, the OIG insisted that their manual scoring system was better than our automated risk instrument because their method resulted in different risk levels from the automated scores. The problem with this was that they were comparing their tool to scores created by an out-of-date scoring algorithm. They also added additional items, not present in the automated tool. They claimed—without any validation with data—that their tool was more accurate.

One option we considered, but decided not to pursue, was bringing up the Inspector General staff on charges of harassment. That seemed like more than we could tackle at the time, so we did not go forward with this. However, we had a small sense of satisfaction when we found out later that the Inspector General staff member who had been one of the more problematic ones had been laid off in a subsequent reorganization at their office.

---

[1] http://sites.uci.edu/cebc/files/2013/06/Letter-to-OIG-5-25-11.pdf

Trying to Convince Critics on the Science

What was very apparent in our skirmishes with the risk tool was a misunderstanding on the part of practitioners, the public, and officials on the use of risk assessment in corrections. We felt it important to educate our audiences, as part of the research process. In our discussions about the tool, we would routinely place the tool in the context of risk assessments that happen in our lives. Car insurance policies are priced according to factors associated with risk (e.g., age, gender, zip code), as is health insurance (although less so now under the Affordable Care Act). It may be that some individuals classified as "low risk" exhibit risky behaviors (car accidents, illness, recidivism). Likewise, some individuals who are predicted to be high risk may never engage in high-risk behaviors. False positives may place someone under more supervision than is warranted. False negatives are more problematic for corrections—failure to identify someone as a high risk can result in a "Willie Horton" event,[2] which can destroy careers.

So off we went to try and explain how risk assessments work to the legislator who had called for the Inspector General investigation. Imagine bringing your dean, a University of California legislative liaison, and a campus communications director to a meeting with a legislator to discuss how our tool—and risk tools in general—works. It was both embarrassing and reassuring at the same time—embarrassing that we had to call on the "big guns" as part of our effort to educate the legislator but reassuring that our institution stood behind our research. The meeting with the legislator and staffers was very cordial. Our explanations were very well received. The most memorable moment came near the end of our meeting when the legislator commented that he was very supportive of risk assessment tools, as long as they were 100% accurate. Obviously, we had not been successful in our education attempt.

Sometimes You Just Don't Know What You Are Getting Into

As we reflect back on our work with the risk tool, we could never have imagined the challenges to the research process we would face. Some were in the actual conduct of the research, but many more were in the application of a research-based tool in a political environment in which being "tough on crime" still resonates with the public. Our work on the risk tool continues, however, despite the challenges we have faced. The tool serves a very valuable role in the tool kit of the state in their placement and supervision of offenders under their jurisdiction. Our Center is now involved with revalidation of the tool with the changing prison population resulting from California's recent Public Safety Realignment. Under realignment, lower-level offenders—those who are not serious, violent, or sex offenders—are now the responsibility of the counties and are not sent to prison from the courts nor supervised on state parole after release from prison. The state assumes the responsibility for the higher "stakes" individuals—those convicted of violent, serious, and sex offenses. From our perspective, one of the most ironic outcomes of our research is that counties are now interested in working with the state and the Center to use the risk tool computer code to predict the risk of recidivism for their county populations. One might say it's hard to keep good research down.

---

[2] Willie Horton, a felon serving a life sentence for murder, was released on a weekend furlough program from a Massachusetts prison in 1986. While on the furlough, he escaped and raped a woman. When Michael Dukakis, who was governor in 1986 and who supported the program, ran for president in 1988, his opponent used Willie Horton's picture in a negative campaign ad. Although the ad itself didn't cost the election, it damaged his run.

References

Barnoski, R., & Aos, S. (2003). *Washington's offender accountability act: An analysis of the Department of Corrections' risk assessment.* Washington, DC: Washington State Institute for Public Policy.

Brennan, T., Dietterich, W., & Ehret, B. (2009). Evaluating the predictive validity of the COMPAS risk and needs assessment system. *Criminal Justice and Behavior, 36*(1), 21–40.

California Department of Corrections and Rehabilitation (CDCR). (2007). *Expert panel on adult offender recidivism reduction programming: Report to the state legislature*. Sacramento, CA: California Department of Corrections and Rehabilitation.

Grattet, R., Petersilia, J., & Lin, J. (2008). *Parole violations and revocations in California*. Washington, DC: National Institute of Justice.

Lieu, T. (2011). Non-revocable parole is too dangerous. *Los Angeles Times*. Op-Ed.

Martin, B., & Van Dine, S. (2008). *Examining the impact of Ohio's progressive sanction grid, Final Report*. Washington, DC: National Institute of Justice.

Martin, B., Van Dine, S., & Fialkoff, D. (2009). Ohio's progressive sanctions grid: Promising findings on the benefits of structured responses. *Perspectives, 33*, 22–29.

Northpoint. (n.d.). *Select COMPAS questions asked by requesting agencies*. http://www.northpointeinc.com/files/downloads/FAQ_Document.pdf

Turner, S., Braithwaite, H., Kearney, L., & Hearle, D. (2012). Evaluation of the California parole violation decision-making instrument (PVDMI). *Journal of Crime and Justice, 35*(2), 269–295.

Turner, S., Hess, J., & Jannetta, J. (2009). *Development of the California static risk assessment instrument (CSRA)*. Working paper, Center for Evidence-Based Corrections, University of California, Irvine. http://ucicorrections.seweb.uci.edu/pubs#reports

Section 5

Visual and Geographical Tools

In recent years, there have been notable developments in using visual and geographical tools in studying crime and criminal justice. As computer-based crime mapping replaced the police standby of pin maps, researchers began to develop additional tools based on those maps. David Weisburd's use of hot spot analyses ("Small Worlds of Crime and Criminal Justice Interventions"), Elizabeth Groff's work with geographical information systems inside a police department ("Practitioner to Academic"), and Kim Rossmo's development of geographic profiling tools ("Rounding Up Twice the Usual Number of Suspects") are prime examples. Data itself can also be visualized. Some examples of its benefit are described by Jonathan Caulkins ("Systems Modeling to Inform Drug Policy") and Michael Maltz ("Sometimes Pictures Tell the Story"). And Matthew Hickman ("I Want You to Wear Something for Me") shows how officer stress can vary over time and space in response to calls for service, which can have a major effect on officer health and performance.

Systems Modeling to Inform Drug Policy: A Personal Odyssey

Jonathan P. Caulkins

Introduction

My primary goal is to discover, document, and disseminate previously unknown empirical regularities that are relevant to the amelioration of some societal problem. I trace that focus on relevance to my engineering-based, problem-solution mindset.

I grant that some subjects merit scientific investigation independent of practical purpose. Indeed, a portion of my research—which I will not discuss here—is devoted to a branch of applied mathematics called dynamical systems. Although we motivate those papers with prose that connect the models to some decision context, the papers are clearly written for academics; few actual policy makers consult them directly.

Yet I would limit basic research to eternal constants, such as mathematics or the nature of subatomic particles. Social phenomena, including crime and deviance, are heavily contextual; the few principles of social interaction that span all times and cultures tend to be banal. So in my

For *Envisioning Criminology: A Handbook of Emerging Research Strategies for Studying Crime and Justice*, Michael Maltz and Steve Rice (eds.)

J.P. Caulkins (✉)
Heinz College, Carnegie Mellon University,
5000 Forbes Avenue, Pittsburgh, PA 15213, USA
e-mail: caulkins@andrew.cmu.edu

opinion research in these domains should be grounded in a desire to be useful. That does not mean all research must be practical in an immediate sense. Academics should pursue phenomena that seem "curious" without understanding where that trail will lead. But having followed the trail, the acid test of whether those years of work were productive is whether the insights improve the understanding—directly or indirectly—of those who are working to ameliorate the problem that made the subject important in the first place.

With that preamble, I will sketch three particular discoveries, stressing the "history" of how they came about more than would be customary in a standard journal article. These are not my three most important findings. They are selected because they can be explained easily, are interesting in and of themselves, and illustrate principles I will state in the conclusion as my (perhaps biased) self-assessment of keys to success when conducting policy-relevant research.

To Begin at the Beginning, Study Initiation

The first vignette pertains to what drives trends in drug initiation. Figure 1 shows the number of Americans trying cocaine for the first time, by year, going back as far as the data will allow.

Technical aside: The trend is based on retrospective self-reports from 668,715 respondents to

Fig. 1 First-time initiation into cocaine use over time in the United States (millions)

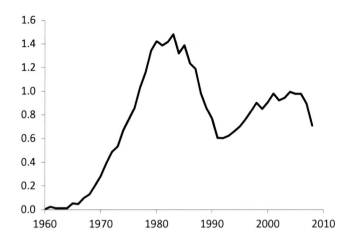

National Surveys on Drug Use and Health administered by SAMHSA from 1999 to 2010. There are obvious limitations to these data, notably that they rely on self-report. The data and their limitations are discussed in greater length in Caulkins (2008), but for present purposes, please accept the premise that the data are good enough to support the analysis which follows.

Figure 1 shows that trends in cocaine initiation have gone up and down very swiftly. This is completely inconsistent with what is perhaps the dominant—albeit implicit—view of drug-related phenomena in sociology and criminology. That view holds that drug use is best understood as a symptom of deeper underlying problems such as poverty, racism, homelessness, anomie, and the like. In effect, the mental model for many people is

$$\text{Drug Use at time } t = \beta_0 + \beta_1 * \text{poverty}_t + \beta_2 * \text{racism}_t + \beta_3 * \text{homelessness}_t + \ldots$$

One can see at a glance that this view is utterly inconsistent with the data, since those right-hand side variables do not soar and plummet nearly as quickly as do initiation rates. Since poverty, racism, homelessness, etc. do not change as rapidly as cocaine initiation, there must be other factors involved, and likely better ways of analyzing them than regression.

Engineers cut their teeth on differential equations, which sometimes come into play in the social sciences as well. I showed the cocaine

initiation graph to my colleagues with whom I work on those dynamical systems models mentioned above. They pointed me to the Bass model, and sure enough, it nails the question of what explains the patterns in drug-related initiation.

Frederick Bass (1969) invented his eponymous model to help manufacturers forecast demand for entirely new classes of consumer products. In the 1960s those would have been things like color televisions and microwave ovens. In later decades the model has been applied to pocket calculators, VCRs, and smart phones. Conventional time series or regression-based forecasting fails for a truly innovative product because there are no relevant historical data.

Instead, Bass suggested a simple differential equation model. The model embodies the following understanding of customers' new product adoption decisions. There are a few "innovators" who obtain a new product in response to general availability and marketing, but most are "imitators" who first acquire the product after hearing testimonials from friends who already use the product. The model has just two parameters, one related to the number of innovators and the other to the number of imitators.

It was easy to parameterize the model and observe that it fits the data on drug initiation remarkably well and it wasn't hard to understand why. While consumption of mind-altering substances by people who have become dependent may require modifications to conventional

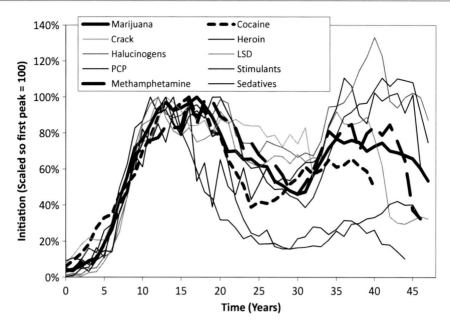

Fig. 2 Commonality across ten drugs in initiation trajectories. (Initiation counts scaled vertically so initial peak = 100 and shifted horizontally to adjust for differences across drugs in when they became widely available in the United States)

consumer theory,[1] no drug is "instantaneously addictive." So the behavior surrounding initiation and early use of cocaine is not appreciably different than the behavior surrounding initiation and early use of Twitter or Tumbler.

The bigger challenge was figuring out how to get anyone to believe this. The idea that differential equation models from marketing might help explain drug user behavior seemed natural to me, but most people to whom I broached the idea would dismiss it out of hand. So I developed a sequence of power point slides with which I have won converts to the core idea, even among those unfamiliar with differential equations.

The first slide shows the cocaine initiation data above. The next adds lines for the nine other substances for which suitable data exist. The advantage of looking at all substances is obvious. We want general principles, not explanations particular to one substance. Yet, when I announce

that I am going to examine together substances as diverse as methamphetamine and heroin or LSD and inhalants, people object. Medical audiences in particular say it doesn't make sense to lump together stimulants and depressants or substances that work through the dopamine system with those that work through the serotonin system. It's great fun to let audiences give voice to those concerns just before showing the graphs, because that hammers home the key conclusion.

The lines on the second chart are the raw data scaled vertically, so all hit an initial peak of 100. (Unscaled curves for drugs that are rarely used, like heroin, would be hard to see when plotted alongside drugs that are widely used, like marijuana.) The third slide just shifts the time axis. Rather than measuring time for every substance as years since Jesus' birth, I measure time relative to when that substance was first generally available in the USA. That's the 1960s for marijuana and heroin, 1970s for powder cocaine, 1980s for crack, 1990s for ecstasy, and so on.

The result (Fig. 2) shows a stunning overlap in the S-shaped growth curve for all ten

[1] Or not; those who subscribe to Rational Addiction Theory (RAT) contest this point.

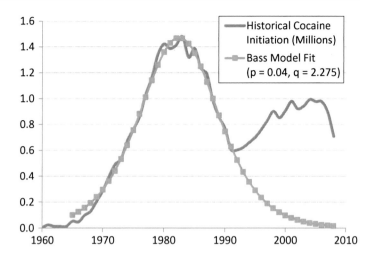

Fig. 3 Bass model fit to time series for cocaine initiation in the United States

substances. I have never bothered applying any formal statistical test to these curves; the eyeball test shows clearly that the initiation patterns are strikingly similar across substances. The final figure (Fig. 3) shows that tuning the two Bass model parameters (rates of imitation and adoption) to the cocaine data provides a remarkable fit to the rapid rise and subsequent trough in cocaine initiation. The Bass model is explicitly about *new product* adoption, so a different model is required to explain ongoing initiation for an established drug—e.g., cocaine after 1990, and that is a different story.

But the punch line is clear: initiation into the use of illegal drugs follows familiar models that apply to early adoption of any new product; we don't need a drug-specific let alone an illegal-drug-specific science. Indeed, similar models govern things like the diffusion of technology and rumors.

That drugs induce dependence, alter neural pathways, and are provided through black markets are all crucially important for understanding other aspects of drug policy, but not for explaining the rapid surge in use at the beginning of a drug "epidemic."

Drugs are Consumer Goods Provided Through Markets

I often coauthor with Peter Reuter, a great and deep thinker who co-founded RAND's Drug Policy Research Center. We use some stock phrases repeatedly because they pack a lot of meaning into a few words. One is, "Drugs are consumer goods that are produced, distributed, and sold through markets." Not everyone agrees with this viewpoint:

- Criminologists tend to see illegal drugs through a deviance lens, and by definition those who buy and sell illegal drugs are committing crimes.
- People in public health tend to view drugs through a medical lens, and ingesting neurotransmitters does have psychopharmacological and physiological effects.

But an equally valid lens is that drugs are consumer goods provided via markets. Some authors think deeply about why people use drugs, identifying many and diverse reasons. But if one wanted to get philosophical, one could develop comparably long lists of reasons why people "use" Cheerios or Cheez-its. Or one could just say it's because people like them.

Similarly one can work hard to understand why people become drug dealers (or fill other roles in the drug supply industry), just as one can think deeply about why people choose to be teachers or truck drivers, but at the end of the day, the main reason is money. There are people who supply drugs for ideological reasons, and much retail distribution occurs within social networks. But most drugs consumed in most countries are supplied through multilayered distribution chains that span international borders, and beyond friend-to-friend distribution at the very bottom of these supply chains, the primary motivation for participation is to make money.

That does not mean all drug market participants rationally maximize utility with perfect foresight, as envisioned by University of Chicago economists. The claim is only that participants are responding to monetary incentives, not that they are wise to do so. After all, even plants respond to the incentive of light—by growing towards it—and few think plants employ conscious utility maximization or higher order reasoning.

Prices are elemental to the study of markets, and price monitoring offers enormous advantages. Participants in illegal markets hide their activity, so the field is plagued by weak data. Enormous sums are spent counting users, but prevalence data are still limited in fundamental ways. Notably, a Pareto or 80/20 rule applies to drug consumption, as with consumption of most goods, meaning that a small minority of users account for the great bulk of consumption. For example, 20% of users account for 80% of consumption, and, thus, roughly 80% of consumption-related sequelae, including overdose and other health harms, crime committed for money to buy drugs, spending that becomes income for drug suppliers, etc. So counting users mostly means counting relatively infrequent users who do not drive the societal harms.

Also, when it costs $30 M to pin down the prevalence at one point in time, one tends not to have many data points. So traditional drug-data systems usually report only annually, or at best quarterly. This means that there are very few data points with which to analyze the drug market.

By contrast, prices, and the closely associated metric of purity, can be sampled at much higher frequency than can prevalence because the law of one price applies, meaning that there must be one consistent price throughout the market, as arbitrage eliminates large and persistent differences. So in principle there is no need to obtain price data from a large and representative sample of people. If everyone pays the same price, then one merely needs a large enough sample to overcome sampling variability, and it doesn't matter who the respondents are.

Of course the reality is more complicated, but the key insights remain: (1) Data series that can be sampled with high frequency are valuable and (2) Price and purity can be measured with much higher frequency than can traditional metrics, such as prevalence.

That was obvious to me from the outset, as an engineering student with a minor in economics. But the story of how that insight eventually bore fruit is interesting for purposes of this volume.

At first I naively assumed that others were already collecting, reporting, and analyzing price data. So I wangled an introduction to John Coleman, the Drug Enforcement Administration's special agent in charge of the Boston office (a wonderful man who offered wise and contrarian counsel at many points during my career). John arranged for me to get the security clearances necessary to visit the archives at the DEA's library in Washington, DC.

It immediately became clear that the DEA was not analyzing price data from a strategic perspective. DEA wanted to know prices well enough that its undercover agents could look like credible buyers, but it wasn't observing whether particular operations were disrupting markets sufficiently to create a spike in prices, which seemed to me to be a completely natural performance measure.

My first attempt to develop high-frequency time series failed utterly, but it laid the groundwork for later success. One of my advisors at MIT, Dick Larson, (rightly) insisted that I had to go see firsthand any system I wanted to analyze, so he arranged for me to spend a summer riding along with a narcotics squad going on raids, observing undercover purchases, listening to their stories, and on occasion taking drug dealers to dinner to pick their brains about their business practices. That summer the police were implementing a geographically focused crackdown on two select neighborhoods. I proposed using retail prices in those neighborhoods, relative to prices in similar neighborhoods as a barometer of the extent to which enforcement disrupted those two markets.

Within a day of getting out on the street, I realized the plan was hopelessly naïve because *almost every retail transaction was for $20.* That does not mean supply never varied or that customers never had to pay more per unit received. Rather, what changed was the amount in the bag, not the price of the bag. That is the opposite of gasoline. A gallon of gas is always essentially a gallon of gasoline, so the price at the pump is a good gauge of relative supply. Not so with drugs.

But I learned something valuable, and that is that *buyers have no precise knowledge of what is in the bag they are buying.* In particular, they had no idea as to the purity of the contents of the bag; purity could vary dramatically from purchase to purchase in ways not observable by the customer.[2]

A few years later, I was again working on the problem of creating price series, this time focusing on the DEA's System to Retrieve Information on Drug Evidence (STRIDE). STRIDE is an administrative system for keeping track of drug samples; informally, it ensures that the right bag of white powder gets associated with the right defendant in the right court room and that none of those bags of white powder go missing. But STRIDE's fields include a quantitative assay of purity and, if the sample came from an undercover buy, the amount the agent paid for that sample. That is, it offers transaction-level price data stamped with a specific date and location.

Others had produced price series with STRIDE, but their series were absurdly noisy unless averaged over large periods of time. When I reproduced their analyses, I immediately saw the problem. The standard approach took averages of the price paid per pure gram. That is, for each transaction, the number of dollars paid went in the numerator, and the product of the weight in the bag and purity of the drug went in the denominator: dollars divided by pure grams equals price per pure gram.

I wondered what happened to observations whose purity was zero, since dividing by zero is

undefined.[3] It turned out those observations were being discarded, yet observations with positive but exceedingly low purity were causing great mischief. Suppose purity is usually 20%, but 1 in 40 observations were 1% or 0.1% pure. If a given week or month happened to have none of the very low purity observations, the price appeared to be much lower than in a month in which there happened to be one or two such observations. So the existing STRIDE-based price series bounced around wildly.

This was silly.

I understood from having watched retail transactions that the users did not know what was in the bag. Sometimes, they got lucky and the drug was more potent than usual; sometimes they got ripped off and most or all of the white powder was mannitol or some other "cut." But to the extent that the seller and buyer had reached an agreement to transact at a particular price, it was not over the price per pure gram actually in the bag; the users never knowingly paid $20 for 0.5 g that was 0.1% pure. The agreed-upon price was the dollar amount (readily observed) divided by the weight in the bag (observed, albeit imperfectly given how small the bags are) times the purity the buyers *expected* the drugs to be, based on what they knew from other transactions in that area and time and of that size. So the smarter way to create a purity-adjusted price series was to first estimate the expected purity and then divide dollars paid by the expected pure quantity in the bag.[4]

---

[2] Indeed, as Peter Reuter and I elaborated later, often not even the seller knows what the purity is because a day or two earlier, the seller was in the role of ignorant buyer purchasing from a higher-level supplier. Thus, at the retail level, drugs are a "double-sided experience good" making the "lemons problem" of sustaining a market equilibrium particularly interesting. For more, see Reuter & Caulkins 2004).

[3] At that time we all understood zero purity observations to be "rip-offs." Later we learned that those 0's really meant the sample hadn't been assayed quantitatively; DEA used a 0 to mean "missing value." So ironically discarding the 0 observations is not crazy, but being suspicious about discarding data was a key step toward unraveling the mystery.

[4] I credit this insight to Al Drake's probability course at MIT, which taught me that when it comes to distributions, the expected value of a function is not the same as the function evaluated at the distribution's expected value. In this case, if X represents the distribution of transaction-level purity observations, $E[1/X]$ was not the same as $1/E[X]$. What matters to both user evaluation of efforts to disrupt markets is not the price of an individual transaction, but how much users spent per pure unit obtained over the 10–20 buys made over the course of a week.

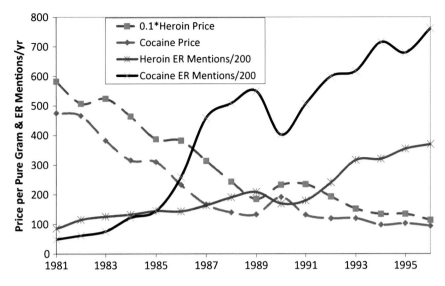

Fig. 4 Trends in purity-adjusted prices and emergency department mentions for cocaine and heroin in the United States

That simple insight led to several papers by me which paved the way for scores of papers by economists exploiting the now informative purity-adjusted price series (Caulkins & Reuter, 1998). Among the findings was that drug use is more responsive to changes in price than anyone had imagined (Gallet, 2014; Pacula, 2010). I had written a few papers along those lines, but the professional econometricians did a much better job of it.

The old view was that addicts had to get their fix and would do anything to get it. That mechanistic notion of human behavior is overly simplistic, as should have been obvious even then.[5] People tend to care about prices of things they spend a lot on. When rents go up, we live in smaller apartments; when the price of toothpaste goes up, we don't much alter our brushing habits. Expensive

illegal drugs (heroin, cocaine/crack, and meth) stand out in this respect. A small subset of very frequent users account for the bulk of consumption, and for most of them, drug purchasing dominates their "household" budget. Daily users of the expensive drugs often spend more than half of their disposable income on their drug of choice. No other product or commodity is like that.

Having passed the baton to economists to estimate the "elasticity of demand" for illegal drugs, there remained for me the challenge of convincing policy makers that prices mattered. I could point to mathematically dense papers in august journals that pronounced the elasticity to be such-and-so via this or that newfangled statistical technique, but that was rather useless. Esoteric econometrics might lead someone who already believed prices drove behavior to adjust their understanding of *how* responsive drug use was to prices, but the great bulk of people "knew" prices didn't matter, and no black box manipulation of Greek symbols was going to change their belief.

So I again developed simple graphs to communicate the key insight (Caulkins, 2001). First I display a graph like Fig. 4, showing how purity-adjusted prices for cocaine and heroin in the USA fell appreciably, particularly during the

---

[5] The idea that dependent users have no control over their consumption and so do not respond to incentives, such as price, is now clearly rebutted by how effective swift and certain schemes (such as HOPE, 24/7, and the Physicians' Health Programs) are at changing the behavior, but there were many years when the "brain disease" model of addiction led people to think that price and availability do not matter in the sense of shaping patterns of drug consumption.

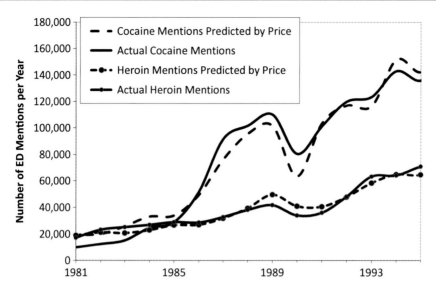

Fig. 5 Trends in emergency department mentions for cocaine and heroin juxtaposed with numbers that would be predicted by purity-adjusted prices alone

1980s, and emergency department (ED) mentions for those drugs were going up. But it is hard for the human eye to assess the strength of an inverse relationship. So I tell the audience that I will next apply an elementary constant elasticity demand model from Econ 101. That means nothing more than raising each price point in the time series to an exponent called the elasticity of demand and scaling the resulting graph vertically. To be clear, there are just two parameters: one exponent and one adjustment for scale.

I ask the audience how much of the jumps and wiggles in emergency department mentions they think can be explained by this terribly simple model, with just one independent variable (purity-adjusted price) and just one fitting parameter, besides the scaling constant. The most common reaction is, "Nothing. Price doesn't matter." Even those who concede that price might matter to some extent presume it has little explanatory power relative to variables they are accustomed to putting on the right-hand side of regressions, such as arrest rates, poverty, homelessness, anomie, strain, etc.

When I show the result (Fig. 5), almost every audience I've briefed has been stunned. It turns out that changes in (purity-adjusted) price alone can explain almost all of the considerable variation in health consequences over time for the two most important illegal drugs in the USA, meaning cocaine/crack and heroin.

I actually don't find Figs. 4 and 5 to be entirely persuasive. Over that extended time scale, omitted third variables could be driving changes in both price and ED mentions, but I have similar figures for the sharpest drop ever recorded in a major drug market, the so-called "heroin drought" in Australia (Degenhardt, Reuter, Collins, & Hall, 2005; Weatherburn, Jones, Freeman, & Makkai, 2002). I usually follow up Figs. 4 and 5 with a series of slides shown together in Fig. 6. The solid black line in the upper left panel shows the signature characteristic of the Australian heroin drought: a precipitous 80% decline in ambulance callouts for heroin overdose. (These data are specifically for the Australian state of Victoria.) It is clear that this decline must stem from a supply-side shock because heroin consumption is dominated by dependent users whose demand is extremely stable. So demand could not possibly have dropped 80% in a month. But there was a strong ideological bias against admitting that a supply-side event could have produced something as good as an 80% decline

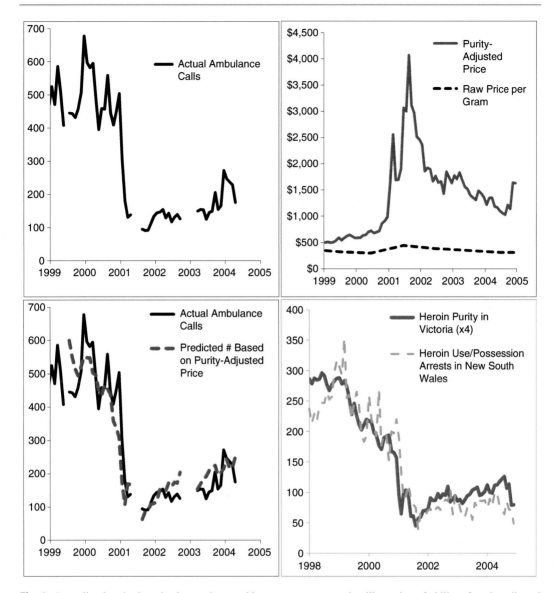

Fig. 6 Australian heroin drought time series provide even more persuasive illustration of ability of purity-adjusted prices to explain trends in adverse drug-related outcomes

in heroin-related harm.[6] Those who wanted to attribute the success to demand-side interventions pointed to a price series that purported to show little change in market conditions (dotted flat line upper right-hand panel). But that was a low-frequency (annual) series, and it did not adjust for purity.

When I spent a month visiting Australia's Drug Policy Modeling Program (DPMP), I discovered that the Victoria Police run what is perhaps the world's most thorough purity analysis system. Every single sample is quantitatively assayed. Those data had been used only tactically, e.g., to connect samples from different events and so build a cumulative case against defendants. They were rarely used for strategic market analysis. Yet the purity series (solid line, lower-right panel) revealed two important

---

[6] Cocaine was and still is secondary in Australia; heroin—and now to some extent meth—is the main problem.

features. First, purity had already been declining steadily for 2 years prior to the drought, indicating that the market was already under some stress. That was a surprise since the use had been rising, and people were writing articles about the "glut" in the market (e.g., Dietze & Fitzgerald, 2002). Second, purity dropped precipitously at the outset of the drought. So the purity-adjusted series (jagged solid line, upper-right panel) showed a sharp spike, even though the price series not adjusted for purity did not.[7]

Playing the same game of raising each purity-adjusted price point to a common exponent and scaling produces the dotted blue line in the lower left-hand panel of Fig. 6. It shows that purity-adjusted prices alone are sufficient to explain not only large but also very rapid changes in an important measure of drug-related morbidity.

The second act of the story was that some who grudgingly admitted the drought could be traced to a supply-side disruption clung to the idea that it must stem from local enforcement; the Australian Federal Police (AFP) and their interdiction efforts were "known" to be the height of drug war folly. But I collected high-frequency series from four different states and territories (Victoria, New South Wales, South Australia, and the Australian Capital Territory). All showed striking parallels in extent and timing of the decline, strongly suggesting that the origins of the drought were national, not due to local policing in one state. For example, trends in heroin purity in Victoria strongly parallel trends in low-level heroin arrests in New South Wales (lower right-hand panel of Fig. 6).

The easiest way to make sense of the drought is to note that before 2001, two very different types of operations delivered heroin to Australia: (1) "Mom and Pop" smugglers who would bring in 0.1–10 kg at a time, often on a commercial airline flight, and (2) large-scale operators based in Asia who secreted shipments of 100–250 kg at a time in commercial cargo, usually transshipped through third countries such as Fiji under the aegis of front companies set up for the purposes of camouflaging the heroin shipments. This bifurcated industry structure manifest in plots of the distribution of amounts seized by size of seizure: there were many seizures of less than 10 kg plus some of over 100 kg (which accounted for much of the weight seized even though they were not numerous). However, less heroin than one might have expected was being seized in lots of 10–100 kg. Large-scale operations were the low-cost way to smuggle heroin, but they require considerable operating scale–scale attained because the organizations were not Australia-specific or even Australia-based. Rather, they were based in Asia and shipped to other countries as well, including Canada.

A little arithmetic shows that the number of 100–250 kg shipments entering Australia each year couldn't be large, given Australia's population and user base, and, therefore, there weren't many of these large organizations. The AFP had been systematically dismantling their operations and achieved a notable success in Fall 2000 with its "Logrunner" operation (Hawley, 2002). Furthermore, AFP personnel had chatter suggesting that the few remaining organizations subsequently decided that the Australian market wasn't worth the bother, given the losses of their compatriots, so they shifted attention to exporting to other markets. That left the Australian heroin market served only by smaller, Mom and Pop operations, leading to a supply drought—and saving hundreds of lives.

The overall lesson, though, is that high-frequency data series can make sense of historical events in a way that traditional low-frequency time series cannot.

Cost Effectiveness of School-Based Prevention

My final example will be estimating the cost-effectiveness of model school-based drug prevention programs (Caulkins, Pacula, Paddock, &

---

[7] The beauty of the Victoria data was that there were so many purity observations that the purity series—and hence the purity-adjusted price series—could be plotted at extremely high frequency. We have proposed that this trick has general utility, particularly for jurisdictions that do not do many undercover purchases (see Caulkins, Rajderkar, & Vasudev, 2010).

Chiesa, 2002, Caulkins, Peter Rydell, Everingham, Chiesa, & Bushway, 1999, 2002). Early in my career, I played a supporting role in RAND's seminal *Controlling Cocaine* project (Everingham & Rydell, 1994; Rydell & Everingham, 1994). That project compared on common metrics the strategic performance in long-run market equilibrium of treatment and various supply-side programs (specifically, source country control, border zone interdiction, and domestic supply control interventions). A variety of metrics were employed, including the present value of kilograms of cocaine consumption averted per million taxpayer dollars spent.

The *Controlling Cocaine* project led to many insights, but the "horse-race results" captured the most attention (somewhat regrettably, since they were frequently misunderstood). The punch line repeated in media outlets was "treatment is seven times more cost-effective than enforcement" (even though that is not the right way to state the result).

One response to the work was "What about prevention?" Prevention was not included in the original work for lack of time and budget, so I wrote a proposal to the Robert Wood Johnson Foundation (RWJF) asking for funding to add school-based prevention to the set of strategies evaluated. The proposal said, more or less, "Everyone knows an ounce of prevention is worth a pound of cure," "Surely it makes economic sense to protect kids from starting drugs," and "That is confirmed by preliminary calculations based on effectiveness figures reported in peer-reviewed journals."

RWJF funded the project, which led to many wonderful insights but not, as expected, a slam dunk finding that school-based prevention was the most cost-effective drug control strategy.

Before telling the story, it is important to recognize that no empirical evaluation directly assesses reductions in kilograms of cocaine consumed over a lifetime. Rather, the empirical evidence concerning prevention pertains to relatively short-term effects (usually 18 months–5 years) on self-reported prevalence of the use of marijuana, alcohol, and tobacco by people in the program as delivered in the research evaluation.

What we wanted was actual (not self-reported) effects on quantity consumed (not prevalence) over the lifetime (not just 1.5–5 years) of cocaine (not marijuana, alcohol, or tobacco) by everyone affected directly or indirectly (not just on those in the program) for a program as implemented by a bureaucracy at scale (not just the investigator managed trial). So one has to build a modeling bridge between results as reported in the scientific literature and results that matter for policy.

After some work, we choose the outcome metric from the empirical evaluations that would make the best anchor for this bridge and reviewed the evaluation literature. There were literally thousands of published articles purporting to evaluate drug prevention interventions, but only a handful were based on rigorous randomized controlled trials (RCTs). So it was a simple matter to read all of those studies, extract their point estimates for the outcome of interest, plug them into our modeling bridge, and determine the resulting average and range of bottom-line cost-effectiveness results in terms of present value of kilograms of cocaine consumption averted per million dollars.

We were flabbergasted to find that (1) the average effect was more or less zero and (2) even the average among the most respected "model" programs was quite small. In particular, it was much smaller than in our preliminary calculations described in the proposal. Since the average effectiveness was essentially zero, we changed our goal from estimating the cost-effectiveness of school-based prevention as practiced in the USA to estimating the cost-effectiveness of *model* school-based programs.

There remained though a shocking gap between what we now concluded and what we projected in the proposal.

We did not intentionally deceive RWJF. Rather, the reason, in a nutshell, is a sort of publication bias that can arise when an evaluation reports only one or a few of very many measured outcomes. (Outcomes measured often include the effect on each individual drug at each of two or three follow-up times and evaluated in terms of past-month, past-year, and lifetime prevalence of use.) When preparing the proposal we took the average of the effects that the evaluations' authors

Table 1 Hypothetical data illustrating how prevention results reported in abstracts can exaggerate perceptions of effectiveness of an intervention

		Study #1 (%)	Study #2 (%)	Study #3 (%)	Study #4 (%)	Study #5 (%)	Average (%)
Marijuana	Past month	7.1	4.4	−8.1	18.6	19.7	8.3
	Past year	19.3	10.1	10.0	−7.5	6.1	7.6
	Lifetime	23.8	8.0	7.5	0.5	7.3	9.4
Alcohol	Past month	17.9	3.1	16.5	−2.6	10.0	9.0
	Past year	13.8	15.4	−2.5	7.3	15.1	9.8
	Lifetime	9.9	12.9	11.8	−0.5	−4.6	5.9
Cigarettes	Past month	12.4	4.1	12.4	11.5	8.8	9.8
	Past year	11.1	26.3	−2.4	4.4	7.4	9.4
	Lifetime	3.4	−4.7	21.2	5.5	18.3	8.8
Reported in abstract		23.8	26.3	21.2	18.6	19.7	

focused on—typically what they cited in the articles' abstracts. During the research project we had decided a priori which of the several dozen outcome measures we would use. It turns out—rather obviously in retrospect—that if you pick the measure ex ante and then average across articles, you get a much lower estimated effectiveness than if one averages the reductions in the measure which the authors highlighted.

Table 1 illustrates the point with hypothetical data. No matter which of the nine outcome measures (rows) one chooses, the average effect is less than 10%, even though all of the articles could (honestly) cite an effect of around 20%.

This bit of cold water did not endear me to funders or colleagues in the prevention world. I am fortunate that I discovered it while working at RAND, because RAND takes an almost perverse pride in its willingness to bite the hand that feeds it. Around this time, I'd watched RAND colleagues tell the Clinton Administration's Department of Defense that letting gays serve openly in the military would not jeopardize unit cohesion or readiness. That was not what the generals wanted to hear, and at the time the military provided more than half of RAND's revenues. Yet the RAND researchers didn't soften or spin the results to curry favor. In an era that places great pressure on academics to fundraise, it is good to spend time at an institution whose bedrock value is an unswerving devotion to objectivity.

In the end, we concluded that model school-based prevention programs are sound invest-

ments, mostly because of collateral reductions in the use of legal drugs and because the programs were cheap. I brief that point as, "prevention programs are cost-effective even though they are not very effective." It is an important distinction; e.g., notions that one could legalize drugs and prevent an increase in use by redirecting saved resources into school-based prevention are terribly naïve.

The oxymoronic character of the line "cost-effective despite not being very effective" worked so well that I coined four more and concluded my briefings with the following slide:

Insights Concerning School-Based Drug Prevention

- Prevention is cost-effective but not very effective.
- Drug prevention is not primarily about preventing drug use.
- You need to do prevention 15 years before you know you need to do it.
- Only one-quarter of program's impact on cocaine use comes from preventing participants from initiating cocaine use.
- Most uncertainty about cost-effectiveness is not due to uncertainty about cost or the evaluated effectiveness.

Each bullet point has the character of appearing to be nonsensical on its face and yet captures a deep insight once explained. For present purposes it is not necessary to resolve these conundrums; our two books (Caulkins et al., 1999, 2002) explain them fully, and Caulkins, Pacula, Paddock, and Chiesa (2004) provide the CliffsNotes versions. The key point is that I realized cleverness counts in communicating results, almost as much as it does in discovering them.

Concluding Recommendations

Reflecting on these three anecdotes and my career more generally, I could offer "tips" to an aspiring young scholar:[8]

- Develop expertise in a problem domain; institutional factors matter.
- Venture off campus and "get your hands dirty" observing the world.
- Be multidisciplinary, since the world is.
- The best ideas come from talking to people, not reading papers.
- Read broadly, not just deeply.
- Find good coauthors (especially when writing books).
- Explain results to decision makers in person; they won't read academic journals.
- Love teaching; there will be times when research is unfulfilling.
- Be the 1st not the 100th person looking at a problem from a particular perspective.
- Seek findings that were unknown a priori but are obvious ex post.
- Most important findings can be seen in simple graphs and descriptive statistics.

I'd also suggest organizing your finances so you can walk away from your job at any time. There is a lot of "game" in academe, and availability of funding often seems inversely related to the importance of the question asked. You'll be happier doing research you think is good and right, not just that which pays the mortgage.

Those tips mostly pertain to how, not why, and the why is important. I would discourage anyone from doing policy research because they want to change policy—a phrase which almost always implies "in a particular direction." Those who work to change policy in a particular direction are advocates, not scientists. A scientist can become an advocate, but once an advocate, never again a scientist. Those who try to do both diminish the credibility of the entire scientific enterprise, jeopardizing its place in society as an estate committed to objectivity and fact, not prejudice or partisan interest.

Rather, if you want to improve policy in some domain as a policy researcher, then

- Seek to inform, not sway policy makers.

Many academics seem to view policy makers as an enemy to be beaten into submission with overwhelming evidence. It is better to think of them as customers or as partners in a learning process just as students are.

Solving societal problems requires teamwork, and players on a team need to understand what their role is and what it isn't. As Laurie Anderson, NASA's first (and only) artist in residence noted, "My job is to make images and leave the decision-making and conclusion-drawing to other people."

My job is to create insights, and I am responsible for communicating them to decision makers. But I am not a decision maker. Nor am I an advocate. No one elected me, so my preferences for policy A over policy B should receive no more weight in the nation's decision making than the preferences of any other voter. If a duly elected representative fully understands the trade-offs and nonetheless supports policy B, that is her prerogative. It would be wrong for me to rework the analysis, or the presentation of that analysis, to bolster the case for policy A.

My friend and colleague Keith Humphreys likes to remind academics that we are a strange breed, far removed from the median voter. We are, obviously, more highly educated, but we also are more affluent, more liberal, more urban, and less religious. With those demographic eccentricities come values that shape policy preferences. So academics' policy preferences often depart from those of the electorate. Academics live in a

---

[8] Many of these tips parallel observations made concerning how operational analysis proved useful to policy makers during its genesis in World War II; see, e.g., Budiansky (2013), especially pages 146–147.

bubble, mostly interacting with others in the university world, so we can fall into the trap of thinking our values are universal. Nothing could be further from the truth.

Academics who analyze public policies should expect that now and again a democratic society will stably adhere to policies that are anathema to the analyst, despite mountains of evidence that amply demonstrate their folly—to the academic and to like-minded elites. At that point the academic has three choices: move to a technocracy, develop ulcers, or smile at how diverse society is. Many of my colleagues turn to Tums and Pepto-Bismol, but I prefer to remember that it takes all kinds to make a world and to have enough faith in the democratic process to believe that in the long run, better informed policy makers will, on average, produce better policy, even if the world does not turn on a dime the week after my latest paper gets published.

All scientific papers should conclude with limitations. Here the number one caveat is that I wouldn't recommend my path to all. It suited me but is somewhat high risk if the goal is to achieve stature in a conventional academic department and discipline. I was lucky, and taking career advice from people who have been successful is vulnerable to selection bias because it samples on the dependent variable.

References

Bass, F. M. (1969). A new product growth model for consumer durables. *Management Science, 15*, 215–227.

Budiansky, S. (2013). *Blackett's war: The men who defeated the Nazi U-boats and brought science to the art of warfare.* New York, NY: Alfred A. Knopf.

Caulkins, J. P. (2001). The relationship between prices and emergency department mentions for cocaine and heroin. *American Journal of Public Health, 91*(9), 1446–1448.

Caulkins, J. P. (2008). Implications of inertia for assessing drug control policy: Why upstream interventions may not receive due credit. *Contemporary Drug Problems, 35*(2–3), 347–369.

Caulkins, J. P., Pacula, R., Paddock, S., & Chiesa, J. (2002). *School-based drug prevention: What kind of drug use does it prevent?* Santa Monica, CA: RAND.

Caulkins, J. P., Pacula, R., Paddock, S., & Chiesa, J. (2004). What we can—And can't—Expect from school-based drug prevention. *Drug and Alcohol Review, 23*(1), 79–87.

Caulkins, J. P., Peter Rydell, C., Everingham, S. S., Chiesa, J., & Bushway, S. (1999). *An ounce of prevention, a pound of uncertainty: The cost-effectiveness of school-based drug prevention program.* Santa Monica, CA: RAND.

Caulkins, J. P., Rajderkar, S. S., & Vasudev, S. (2010). Creating price series without price data: Harnessing the power of forensic data. In B. Kilmer & S. Hoorens (Eds.), *RAND TR-755-EC Understanding illicit drug markets, supply reduction efforts, and drug-related crime in the European union* (pp. 165–196). Cambridge, England: RAND.

Caulkins, J. P., & Reuter, P. (1998). What price data tell us about drug markets. *Journal of Drug Issues, 28*, 593–612.

Degenhardt, L., Reuter, P., Collins, L., & Hall, W. (2005). Evaluating explanations of the Australian heroin drought. *Addiction, 100*, 459–469.

Dietze, P., & Fitzgerald, J. (2002). Interpreting changes in heroin supply in Melbourne: Droughts, gluts or cycles? *Drug and Alcohol Review, 21*, 295–303.

Everingham, S. S., & Rydell, C. P. (1994). *Modeling the demand for cocaine. MR-332-ONDCP/A/DPRC.* Santa Monica, CA: RAND.

Gallet, C. A. (2014). Can price get the monkey off our back? A meta-analysis of illicit drug demand. *Health Economics, 23*, 55–68. published online in 2013 at DOI:10.1002/hec.2902.

Hawley, M. (2002). Heroin shortage—the cause. *Platypus Magazine, 76*, 43–48.

Pacula, R. L. (2010). *Examining the impact of Marijuana legalization on Marijuana consumption: Insights from the economics literature.* Santa Monica, CA: RAND WR-770-RC.

Reuter, P., & Caulkins, J. P. (2004). Illegal lemons: Price dispersion in cocaine and heroin Markets. *Bulletin on Narcotics, LVI*(1–2), 141–165.

Rydell, C. P., & Everingham, S. S. (1994). *Controlling cocaine: supply versus demand programs.* Santa Monica, CA: RAND.

Weatherburn, D., Jones, C., Freeman, K., & Makkai, T. (2002). Supply control and harm reduction: Lessons from the Australian heroin 'drought'. *Addiction, 98*(1), 83–91.

Practitioner to Academic: An Interdisciplinary View from Both Sides of the Looking Glass

Elizabeth R. Groff

I can trace my interest in urban places back to childhood. As a child, I lived in a neighborhood near a small town. I walked or biked to school, the candy store, and a nearby park. Their proximity provided me with a large degree of independence at a young age. As an 11-year-old, my family moved to a larger home located in a suburban development that had been recently carved from farmland. The blocks there were three times as long as in my old neighborhood, and the houses sat much further from the street. The design of my new neighborhood emphasized privacy at the expense of shared community life. I rode a bus to my new school. No parks were within walking or biking range. My sense of isolation was overwhelming. Getting my driver's license at 16 meant I could access all these destinations via car but that experience shaped how I thought about human activity and urban form.

Twenty-odd years passed after high school graduation and I finally got around to finishing my bachelor's degree at the University of North Carolina at Charlotte. I entered college with the intention of studying organizational psychology, but a general education course in geography captured my interest. I was hooked by a subsequent course focusing on behavioral geography because it emphasized human behavior and urban form. My interest turned to the role of crime in urban

change during my last year as an undergraduate. I began by synthesizing the literature and creating a conceptual model of vulnerable environments that focused on what characteristics of places were associated with high crime rates. I was struck by the mismatch between the scale at which interactions played out (individual situations at addresses or at a location along a block or at an intersection) and the scale at which they were studied using quantitative data (census tracts as proxies for neighborhoods). I entered the master's program because there was just too much more to learn.

In graduate school, I immersed myself in three essential tools, methodology, statistics, and geographic information systems (GIS). For my master's thesis, I decided that I wanted to study the neighborhood characteristics associated with crime. This topic built on the foundation of that original literature review. My advisor, Dr. Owen Furuseth, negotiated funding for my study from the Charlotte-Mecklenburg Police Department (CMPD) and the Charlotte Housing Authority (CHA). The results of my research pointed to the salience of neighborhood characteristics for understanding crime rates. I was offered a position at CMPD and CHA after I graduated. My expertise in GIS increased my marketability. The utility of analytic mapping was just being recognized, and relatively few people were skilled in it. I took the position with the CMPD because I felt I could have a bigger impact on the quality of life in the city by working to prevent crime.

E.R. Groff (✉)
Temple University, Philadelphia, PA, USA
e-mail: groff@temple.edu

M.D. Maltz and S.K. Rice (eds.), *Envisioning Criminology: Researchers on Research as a Process of Discovery*, DOI 10.1007/978-3-319-15868-6_24, © Springer International Publishing Switzerland 2015

Gaining an Understanding of Operational Policing and Place

In 1995, I became the first GIS Coordinator at the CMPD. I owed my job to Dennis Nowicki (Chief) and Dr. Richard Lumb (an academic he had hired to direct his Research and Planning Bureau). Those two men were visionaries. They recognized the potential for analysis (and in particular analytic mapping) to aid law enforcement in preventing and responding to crime. Part of my job was to grow the technical skills of crime and research analysts at CMPD.

I had no formal training in criminological theory or policing so I spent a good deal of time talking with folks in different areas of the police department especially crime analysts and police officers. I quickly learned that police work focused on people and places. I gravitated toward the studying the role of places in encouraging or discouraging crime because of my geography background. I quickly began assembling a wide variety of data sets for use by crime and strategic planning analysts. A GIS is able to link databases describing places even if they lack a common identifier through the use of location. Although the city of Charlotte was a fairly early adopter of GIS and had a solid base map to build upon, many city departments were lagging behind in spatially enabling their data. I spent a good deal of time geocoding (i.e., converting addresses into X, Y coordinates which can be mapped) and even screen digitizing information. Screen digitizing is the process of data creation by using the mouse and cursor to draw features of the real world in GIS software.

There was a clear need for spatial analysis. Police and crime analysts realized that crime was concentrated in particular police beats but they lacked the tools to examine those concentrations without being tied to jurisdictional boundaries. GIS offered a way of identifying hot spots that crossed jurisdictional boundaries and that existed in only parts of beats. It also offered a way to communicate those hot spots to the community. It turned out that I had begun working with police at about the same time these benefits were being more widely recognized. The software Spatial and Temporal Analysis of Crime (STAC) had recently been developed by the Illinois Criminal Justice Information Authority. The term "hot spots" was part of the lingo I encountered in CMPD which made sense to me since geographers have long been interested in geographic concentrations. Chief Nowicki sent me to visit the Chicago Police Department (CPD). I spoke with several members of the CPD department and learned about their new computer mapping program (IRMA) that the officers were using. I also met with Michael Maltz, an academic collaborator of Chief Nowicki who had recently written a guidebook on crime mapping (Maltz, Gordon, & Friedman, 1990/2000). It was an illuminating visit.

One of my assignments was to support the team government initiative which focused on bringing all the resources of government to bear in a single neighborhood. With colleagues I conducted windshield surveys (i.e., collecting data by driving around neighborhood streets) of all characteristics suggested in the literature to be related to crime. I walked the streets of this single neighborhood and observed firsthand how the environment shifted from one block to the next. I created a database to hold those observations. The database described every address and every street in the neighborhood. Using GIS I was able to integrate that information with other data from other agencies and easily share it. The database allowed us to examine how those characteristics were related to the patterns of crime and calls for service at each address and across street blocks.

I attended meetings with the community and observed the important role of maps to communicate information but also to provide a common frame of reference. Again and again, team meetings began slowly because everyone had a different agenda. Putting a map up on the wall was a key to focusing the conversation. The map provided a common reference point for everyone. It was critical to getting citizen engagement and uniting the team behind a common goal.

We had a parade of researchers coming through the department because of Dennis Nowicki's commitment to being an active part of research. It was through those interactions that I learned to view research through the lens of the practitioners who were being asked to take on more work to support it. Successful researchers kept that in mind when asking for support from police staff. Chief Nowicki was committed to getting the word out about our successes in Charlotte. He funded my travel to present at conferences. These experiences highlighted the innovative nature of our activity at CMPD. I attended the very first crime mapping conference held by the National Institute of Justice's newly formed Crime Mapping Research Center (CMRC). The energy at the meeting was palpable and exposed me to innovative practices in other police departments around the world.

Building a Network and Growing My Research Portfolio

I wanted to be a part of those efforts, so I joined the National Institute of Justice's CMRC. While at the CMRC I was exposed to an even greater number of academics and practitioners. Most of the work involved "getting the word out" regarding the important contribution that GIS could make to criminal justice agencies. But I also contributed to the formulation of large-scale projects such as the US Department of Justice (DOJ) Strategic Approaches to Community Safety (SACSI) project. I immediately began drawing from my experience at CMPD to create a sample list of important place characteristics that sites should include to increase their analytic capacity. I interviewed representatives from each site to discover the types of information and analysis that would be useful to them. We also discussed potential links to data sets from other agencies that would help them better understand their crime problems. I wrote a paper describing that experience (Groff, 2000).

I collaborated with colleagues to conduct original research while at the CMRC. I used the Grier Heights data I had collected as part of the team government project in Charlotte-Mecklenburg to create a risk surface for residential burglary using address characteristic and raster GIS (i.e., a continuous surface of grid cells).

Nancy La Vigne and I discovered situational (e.g., proximity to a bus stop, street lighting, etc.) and house (e.g., renter-occupied, substandard, etc.) characteristics were associated with greater incidence of residential burglary. This finding demonstrated the potential for developing early warning systems dedicated to preventing crime rather than apprehending criminals. Additionally, we found there were clear hot spots and cold spots of residential burglary even within a high-crime neighborhood (Groff & LaVigne, 2001). My belief that the action at places was at the micro-level of addresses and street blocks was cemented by the combination of empirical evidence and my field experience as a practitioner.

During my time at NIJ, I had the opportunity to meet some of the smartest, most innovative scholars studying criminological issues. After 4 years at NIJ, I knew I wanted to continue my research on crime and place.

Developing My Knowledge, Skills, and Abilities

In 2002, I joined a nonprofit research firm called the Institute for Law and Justice (ILJ) and entered the Ph.D. program in geography at the University of Maryland. Along the way I also successfully pursued a master's in criminology. My experiences in those programs expanded my theoretical, methodological, and analytical knowledge. Specifically, I picked up more advanced statistical and computational techniques for examining crime and place in geography and a broader theoretical and methodological grounding in both disciplines.

By this time, the adoption of GIS by criminal justice agencies was in full swing. Although many more agencies had GIS and could make maps, the analytic capacity of those maps was often limited. My first project at ILJ was to assist with the development of their spatial analytic capacity at the Metropolitan Police Department (MPD). This involved identifying a list of place characteristics and their sources within the expansive Washington DC government. I interviewed command staff and police officers to ascertain the types of questions they would like the new computer system to answer. Along the way, I learned how another agency conducted the business of policing and what questions were as yet unanswered from a practical standpoint.

I discovered there were many benefits to having practical experience prior to returning to college for my Ph.D. I already had a framework of knowledge which I used to classify and process what I was learning in the classroom. Of course, this also meant that I was often skeptical of researcher's claims about practitioners. I could apply what I was learning immediately since most of it was immediately relevant to my job. In addition, I was encouraged to offer my practical experiences during class which may have enriched the educational value for other students.

As a student, I was building on my knowledge of geography and criminology and gaining structured exposure to the theoretical and empirical context for what I had been experiencing in practice. Along the way, I often encountered cases where the same phenomenon was viewed very differently by practitioners and researchers. One particularly jarring experience occurred in a policing class. The professor was presenting the phenomenon of crime concentration, commonly called "hot spots," as a discovery by academics when practitioners had recognized it for a long time. I recall a heated discussion ensued. As a student I was often confronted with examples of the gulf between research and practice. Researchers were unaware of interesting and relevant action research being conducted in agencies, and practitioners were unaware of important empirical findings that might make them more efficient or effective at their jobs. The good news is that the gulf was much wider then and has narrowed considerably in the last 10 years. A final advantage of my practitioner experience was that I could draw upon the diverse network of professionals I had assembled. This meant I had a wider variety of "sounding boards" for the new ideas I was exposed to during at the university. It also meant that I could obtain data more easily than my fellow students.

While I was a student at the University of Maryland, David Weisburd asked me to comment on a paper he had done examining longitudinal crime patterns on street 100 blocks (Weisburd, Bushway, & Lum, 2004). I commented that although the work was a tremendous contribution to our knowledge of temporal variation in crime concentrations, the geographical component was underexplored.

That discussion launched our ambitious research collaboration with the goal of retrospectively collecting data on the physical and social environment of street segments (both sides of a street between two intersections). David Weisburd, Sue-Ming Yang, and I wrote a grant proposal to the National Institute of Justice in 2005 which was subsequently funded. My research was once again focused on micro-level places.

Building on that initial study, we wanted to use a theoretically based unit of analysis and chose to draw from Ralph Taylor's work applying behavior settings theory to street segments. The initial work in Seattle had not used geography to define units of analysis but rather relied on the street address ranges to identify 100 blocks. But in the GIS many streets did not end at intersections but instead extended across them. This meant our GIS streets did not accurately reflect the theoretical framework we wanted to use. It required many hours editing the Seattle street centerline file so our street segment units of analysis matched our theoretical definition of street segments. We also had many long discussions about crime committed at intersections. These crimes were allocated to intersections rather than street segments, but certainly the crime at intersections affects the adjacent street segments. We decided to exclude all intersection crime because the type of incidents which happened at street corners was qualitatively different then on street segments.

We started with the place characteristics that I had identified over 10 years of practice and then conducted an exhaustive literature review to link them to an opportunity perspective or a social disorganization perspective. Via this exercise we identified additional data characteristics and set out to collect as much information as possible about each street in Seattle. Obtaining retrospective information about the physical and social environment of street segments was an arduous effort. Ironically, computerization was working against us. As computers replaced paper records, city departments began to incrementally update their files. Many did not save snapshots of their data at year end or note in each record the date of the update. For many data sets we wanted, the historical data simply did not exist. This is a wider issue in data archiving because local governments will be unable to produce historical records. Their history has been overwritten.

Our micro-level unit of analysis required we collect data at the address level. This was a challenge. We were fortunate that Seattle was an early adopter of GIS technology, but even with that advantage, going back further than the mid-1990s proved challenging for many characteristics. We also met some resistance from infrastructure departments due to terrorism concerns. However, our aggregated unit of analysis did prove advantageous when talking with departments who wanted to safeguard the identity of individuals but were still very interested in contributing their piece of the environmental pie. In the end, we obtained a wide variety of information about the characteristics of street segments over much of the time period.

When we analyzed the data, it turned out that the unit of analysis did not change the original finding; crime was concentrated across street segments over time just as it had been concentrated across street hundred blocks. Because our entire study was spatially enabled, we could conduct the first systematic examination of how place characteristics were distributed across space and how they were related to crime. Interestingly, each type of place characteristic (e.g., number of truant school kids, amount of housing assistance, and street lighting as examples) was concentrated at relatively few street segments across Seattle (Weisburd, Groff, & Yang, 2011). We also examined whether street blocks with similar crime changes over time concentrated in the same areas or spread throughout the city. We found the spatial distribution of temporal crime trajectories was most often heterogeneous. In other words, there was a tremendous amount of "block to block" variability.

Blocks with different crime trajectories were often near one another. High-crime street blocks were often adjacent to low-crime ones. This pattern would not have been revealed with data aggregated to larger spatial units and demonstrates the importance of examining trends at very local geographic levels. It also reinforces the importance of initiatives like "hot spots policing" which address specific streets within relatively small areas (Groff, Weisburd, & Yang, 2010).

We used multivariate statistics to answer the critical question of whether the street segments with high concentrations of risk factors were indeed the street segments with high crime levels. Some of the characteristics associated with significantly higher odds of being in the highest crime group of street segments were associated with opportunity theories of crime (employees, bus stops, public facilities, and status as an arterial road). Other characteristics were associated with social disorganization theories (lower housing values, housing assistance, physical disorder, and few active voters). Still others were associated with both theoretical frameworks (high-risk juveniles and truant juveniles) (Weisburd, Groff, & Yang, 2012).

Long-Standing Interests Coupled with New Methodology Produce a Dissertation Topic

While we were conducting the data collection for the Seattle study, I was searching for a dissertation topic. My experiences as a practitioner and researcher had cemented my interest in how context affects the nature and volume of criminal events as well as how the event-level processes produce the observed patterns of crime. These led me to try to test crime pattern theory and routine activity theory, but I had no data source for information describing human activity to model how offenders and targets come together in space and time. About that time I took one course in agent-based modeling and one in advanced model development. These two courses opened my eyes to computational methods and how they could be used to explore criminological theories in a virtual world. I learned that by using agent-based modeling software, I could set up a virtual society using a computer program and distribute characteristics of places and people (agents), so they were consistent with their distributions in a target city (in my case Seattle). Agents (people) in the model could make autonomous, goal-directed decisions based on the characteristics of their location and in a manner consistent with what theory would suggest. This allowed me to investigate the outcome patterns of virtual crime to find out if they had the same patterns as real crime.

I developed an offender decision-making model for street robbery (Groff, 2007a). Then I systematically manipulated the urban environment on which agents traveled and interacted. In one model the streets were a uniform grid. In all other models, agents traveled along the streets of Seattle (Groff, 2007b). In one model using a real street network, the agents traveled in a random fashion with no time schedule or specific destination. In another they had a time schedule which took them off the street and reduced their vulnerability to being a victim of street robbery. In the final model they had a time schedule and a set of locations describing the timing and locations at which they undertook their routine activities. These locations in the model were a reflection of the locations of housing, jobs, and recreation in Seattle. By comparing the crime patterns produced by these models, I could clearly demonstrate the importance of the street pattern and of routine activities to crime patterns. In my dissertation I was able to integrate my interest in places and urban form with findings from my empirical research on place characteristics to create a new and unique contribution to the literature on crime and place.

I have explored many topics over my career, but my fascination with crime and place, urban form, and human activity is still the core component of my research agenda and will continue to be in the future. I hope graduate students and other scholars take the following points away from my story:

- Careers like research projects often proceed in a nonlinear fashion. Flexibility and adaptation are critical attributes to develop.

- The inspiration for avenues of inquiry often comes from unexpected and even non-work-related arenas of life.
- An openness to experiencing life leads to new research paths.
- Fieldwork is invaluable for increasing understanding. The old truism "there is no substitute for experience" holds but with a twist. In research it should be there is no substitute for "experiencing."
- There is much to be learned from collaboration. Everyone looks at a situation from a different angle. The more angles we consider, the more potential we have for increasing our understanding via breakthroughs.

References

Groff, E. (2000). *Strategic approaches to community safety initiative (SACSI): Enhancing the analytic capacity of a local problem-solving effort.* Unpublished manuscript.

Groff, E. R. (2007a). Simulation for theory testing and experimentation: An example using routine activity theory and street robbery. *Journal of Quantitative Criminology, 23*(2), 75–103.

Groff, E. R. (2007b). 'Situating' simulation to model human spatio-temporal interactions: An example using crime events. *Transactions in GIS, 11*(4), 507–530.

Groff, E. R., & LaVigne, N. G. (2001). Mapping an opportunity surface of residential burglary. *Journal of Research in Crime and Delinquency, 38*(3), 257–278.

Groff, E. R., Weisburd, D., & Yang, S.-M. (2010). Is it important to examine crime trends at a local "micro" level? A longitudinal analysis of street to street variability in crime trajectories. *Journal of Quantitative Criminology, 26*, 7–32.

Maltz, M. D., Gordon, A. C., & Friedman, W. (1990/2000). *Mapping crime in its community setting: Event geography analysis.* New York, NY: Springer. Retrieved from https://www.academia.edu/589926/Mapping_Crime_in_Its_Community_Setting

Weisburd, D., Bushway, S., & Lum, C. (2004). Trajectories of crime at places: A longitudinal study of street segments in the city of Seattle. *Criminology, 42*(2), 283–321.

Weisburd, D., Groff, E., & Yang, S.-M. (2011). *Understanding developmental crime trajectories at places: Social disorganization and opportunity perspectives at micro units of geography.* Washington, DC: Office of Justice Programs, National Institute of Justice.

Weisburd, D., Groff, E., & Yang, S.-M. (2012). *The criminology of place: Street segments and our understanding of the crime problem.* Oxford, England: Oxford University Press.

"I Want You to Wear Something for Me": On the In Situ Measurement of Police Stress and the Potential Rewards of Channeling One's Inner Experimentalist

Matthew J. Hickman

It might be *cliché*, but I'm going to begin my essay with a popular quote: "The definition of insanity is doing something over and over again and expecting a different result." This quote is often attributed to Albert Einstein, but also to Benjamin Franklin, Mark Twain, and many other thinkers and innovators who were far more intelligent than I am and who knew a lot more than I ever will about making scientific progress. I think the quote is appropriate here because it very succinctly summarizes how I came to find myself riding in the front seat of a patrol car late at night, chasing intoxicated drivers through the streets of Seattle, with a rather remarkable police officer who agreed to be "wired up" with a GPS-enabled heart rate monitor, while I took copious notes (Hickman, Fricas, Strom, & Pope, 2011).

The Problem

During the winter of 2009, the Pacific Northwest experienced a horrible string of murders of law enforcement officers. It began with the killing of officer Timothy Brenton of the Seattle Police Department on October 31, followed a month later by the killing of officers Greg Richards, Mark Renninger, Tina Griswold, and Ronald

Owens of the Lakewood Police Department on November 29 and a month later by the killing of deputy Kent Mundell of the Pierce County Sheriff's Office on December 21. These shootings were not accidental nor were they the result of police-initiated contacts. They were not even the result of the mutual exchange of gunfire between police and suspects. In each of these incidents, the killers ambushed and shot officers as they sat in a patrol car, in a local coffee shop, or responded to a call for service.

For those outside of the region, these events may not have registered on personal radar screens. The connection between Maurice Clemmons, who killed the Lakewood officers, and the sentencing reductions that led to his parole under the administration of former Arkansas Governor Mike Huckabee was certainly a national politics news item (given that Huckabee was running for President at the time). Regardless, I can assure you that most people in Washington State were fully aware of what was going on. There were simply too many police funerals in a short period of time, complete with the symbolism of hundreds, if not thousands, of police vehicles, personnel, and bagpipers in procession and a degree of solemnity that is rarely matched by other memorial events.

In the wake of these killings, and amidst the very sliceable tension within the local law enforcement community, a police commander acquaintance of mine asked me what we "knew" about

M.J. Hickman, Ph.D. (✉)
Seattle University, Seattle, WA, USA
e-mail: hickmanm@seattleu.edu

police stress. In more elaborate terms, he wanted to know the current state of academic knowledge on the topic and whether there was anything I could point to that could help them to better understand and respond to what officers may be experiencing, particularly in the field. He wanted to know what could be done to improve our understanding of officer health and safety. He was clearly (and understandably) worried about his people.

So what did we "know" about police stress? Well, we know that police officers experience higher rates of disease than the general public, and this has been linked to specific job characteristics (such as shift work), as well as on a theoretical level to the repeated initiation of the fight-or-flight response (absent actual flight) and subsequent immunosuppression caused by accumulated chemical stress products. Other identified problems include post-traumatic stress disorder, suicide, domestic violence, substance abuse, as well as a broad range of negative performance indicators. Researchers have identified a variety of stressors both unique and not unique to the police occupation and generally distinguish organizational or administrative stressors from job- or task-related stressors. Some research shows that officers rank the types of stressors that citizens might expect to be stressful (such as killing someone or being physically attacked) as greater sources of stress relative to other stressors, while other research indicates that officers rank the administrative stressors imposed by their supervisors as a greater source of stress than the physical dangers of the job. There is variability in the officer-level correlates of stress, as well as the extent to which officer characteristics may mediate the effects of stressors on outcomes. However, differing definitions of stress (both chronic and acute), underdeveloped theory, and inconsistent measurement contribute to a situation where this evidence can be considered mixed at best. Finally, stress inoculation training is widely regarded as a positive means of countering police occupational stress.

Unfortunately, the expression on his face after I ran through my little on-the-spot summary spoke louder than words. He was clearly disappointed by the summary, but in a broader sense I think he was disappointed in the academy. He wanted to know when, where, and under what conditions officers were likely to experience actual, real-world, acute stress and what could be done about it on an operational level. He didn't want to hear about surveys or the (seemingly) vague connections between the job and a variety of long-term health consequences.

Instead of skulking back to my office and scanning the job market for positions outside academia (this happens more frequently than I'd like to admit), I seized the opportunity to think about what was "wrong" in this area of research and ways to try and make things better. We needed to know the *when* and *where* of stress, as well as the conditions surrounding stressful events. The problem, as I saw it, was that what we "knew" about police stress was structured almost exclusively by self-report survey methodology and, to a lesser extent, observational studies. The literature on police stress could thus be characterized more accurately as a literature on *perceptual* police stress, with some notable exceptions (such as the work on biomarkers for stress by Violanti et al. (2007) in Buffalo, NY, and other researchers engaged in the physiological measurement of stress). This same literature is naturally based on retrospective measurement and does not really try to directly assess (e.g., through physiological measurement) the stress that officers experience, as they experience it, during their routine work. A major problem with self-report methodologies is that police officers often don't realize that they are experiencing stress and therefore may not recall it accurately or meaningfully on self-report instruments. A recent meta-analysis of 103 studies of perceptual stress among police officers was unequivocal in its assessment: "The breadth and degree of missing data is staggering, the inconsistency of measurement substantial, and the shortage of methodologically rigorous studies disappointing" (Webster, 2013: 644).

To be sure, survey-based studies and observational research generate important and insightful information and should be part of a comprehensive approach to studying police stress, but their limitations can only be overcome by direct physiological measurement. Given the unique nature of police work, directly measuring the physiological responses of officers to various stimuli during their shifts would provide a more accurate assessment of the stress they actually encounter. This had been done at least once before in the context of establishing job requirements for police in Canada (Anderson, Litzenberger, & Plecas, 2002), but we also needed to do better at assessing stress within micro-contexts. We have ample evidence from the "hot spots" and place-based criminological literature that small proportions of a city space can generate large proportions of calls, incidents, arrests, and related police activity. To be fair, perceptual police stress research has examined variability across assignments and organizational units, but generally at levels of aggregation that mask the much more meaningful microlevel variation that my police commander acquaintance wanted to understand.

We needed to be able to "map" stress. If we could develop a literal stress map of a police service area, we could potentially inform deployment and dispatch strategies, as well as occupational health programs. Bottom line, what researchers and police executives really want to understand is the actual stress that police officers experience on a daily basis, in the course of their routine patrol activities.

Solution: Drink the "Juice"

For some reason, this saga got me thinking about sociologist Sudhir Venkatesh's recollections of being a young doctoral student, asking gangsters in Chicago public housing projects, "How does it feel to be black and poor?" and then providing them with the usual Likert-style response options (a story he humorously recounts in his popular book, *Gang Leader for a Day* (Venkatesh, 2008)). Venkatesh lived to see another day, but in all seriousness, he probably risked his life with that little methodological disaster. In *Gang Leader for a Day*, as well as his more recent book, *Floating City* (Venkatesh, 2013), the "rogue sociologist" wakes the reader up to the notion that many of the conventional methods of the social sciences come with serious limitations and are often misapplied, and we just don't pay enough attention to these

issues. While the ethnographic methods that Venkatesh favors also have limitations, we can probably all agree that measurement is the hardest part of what we do.

For some areas within criminology and criminal justice, I think we have to be willing to recognize that we may have learned all we can learn using particular research methodologies. In my opinion, the study of police stress via self-report survey methods falls into this category. I think we've pretty much learned all we can about police stress by having officers fill out surveys. *Yet we keep doing it!* As an aside, in the past couple of months leading up to writing this chapter, I have received three peer-review requests from journal editors for manuscripts reporting the results of survey-based studies of police stress. I agreed to perform these reviews (and I promise that I evaluated them fairly), but I couldn't help but think of that famous quote as I wrote up my reviews: "The definition of insanity is doing something over and over again and expecting a different result." Why, I wondered, are we still doing this?

At about the same time as I was experiencing the frustration of not being as helpful to my police acquaintance as I wanted to be, my wife, who will occasionally and very subtly suggest that I might try exercising more than I do, had just purchased what was (at the time) a rather sophisticated wristwatch-style product manufactured by Garmin. The watch continuously recorded an individual's heart rate via wireless communication with a chest-strap heart rate monitor. The idea was that athletes could use the device to record and analyze their performance and fine-tune their exercise routines. Because the device was manufactured by Garmin—one of the world's leading manufacturers of electronic products that exploit the Global Positioning System (GPS) for purposes of navigation on land, sea, and air—this clever little watch simultaneously recorded latitude and longitude. The GPS functionality was there not so much for recording and displaying where you had completed your exercise, as it was for calculating elevation change and factoring that into the analysis of your exercise. But it was there nonetheless: heart rate, latitude and longitude, date- and time-stamped, and recorded simultaneously and continuously. *Brilliant!*

My colleagues will attest to the fact that I am generally a "late adopter" of personal technology, but when it comes to research, I like to think that I'm actually pretty tech-savvy, and I am always on the lookout for new ways to collect data about social phenomena. I'll admit to being somewhat behind the curve on social media, but I'm getting there, and the research potential is seemingly limitless. At any rate, the potential utility of this Garmin heart-monitoring device for the problem that I was dealing with was quite obvious.

So I was starting to get excited about the possibilities; the "juice" was really flowing at this point. But I'm not the type to go too far into something without consulting other knowledgeable folks. This exercise turned out to be both disappointing and enlightening. I love it when someone says, "You can't do that," or "That won't work," or, more sarcastically and dismissively, "Good luck with that." It just makes me smile. Not only do such statements generally tell me all I need to know about that individual's personality, it also generally confirms that I'm on to *something*. And sometimes that *something* turns out to be something really worth pursuing. Maybe I expected these reactions to be a little more tempered, such as "*How* will you do that?" or "*How* will that work?" or, maybe even, "*How* can I help you with that?" But, to be fair, I think what was underlying some of these pessimistic attitudes was a fair question, and an important one at that: *Can it be done?* This is a natural and important question one asks as part of the research process. Speaking with the lead author of the one prior study that measured police stress in situ (Anderson et al., 2002) revealed some potential complications and pitfalls, but also some encouragement. This was essential juice.

You can design research studies on paper all day long. Beautiful studies! Research designs that will knock the socks off a grant review committee! We can tweak things for days, months, even years. We can go through lots of erasers (or wear out the backspace key on our computers). But eventually, it's all going to come down to just getting out there, getting your hands dirty, and giving it a try. Either someone's going to take a risk on you and fund this little endeavor or, more likely, you're just going to have to do it yourself on the cheap. And chances are it won't work the way you thought it would anyway. But that's part of the *joy* of science! Trial and error! Failure and success! Discovery! And, hopefully, a heck of a lot of *fun* along the way!

Could I even get someone to agree to do this? Well, the graduate program in criminal justice at my home institution, like many other similar programs, tends to attract a good mix of students: working professionals, traditional students, and others. I had an exceptional student who took several of my courses and who also happened to be a Seattle police officer, and he routinely offered to take me on ride-alongs while he was in the program. I had never taken him up on these offers, not because I wasn't appreciative of them but mainly due to lack of available time as well as conflicting schedules. But he had recently graduated from our master's program, so I felt that I might be able to approach him about piloting this study without any professor–student relationship concerns related to control over grades, and so forth. I asked him whether he was still willing to take me on a ride-along, and he enthusiastically replied that he would be happy to do so. I then ventured that, "I want you to wear something for me." In retrospect, maybe this wasn't the best choice of words. But I quickly followed up that I wanted to know if he would be willing to wear the heart rate monitor during the ride-along. He agreed (and I think he was actually quite a bit more curious than he let on, but perhaps we can chalk that up to the stoic persona of law enforcement), but he needed to get permission from his chain of command, which was complicated by the recent shootings as all civilian ride-alongs had been indefinitely canceled. After meeting with the higher-ups and explaining the purpose and goals of the research, an exception was made and we were good to go. The juice continued to flow.

I have my test subject, but am I getting in over my head on the subject matter? As it so happens, when I was hired at my home institution, all new faculty members were assigned to peer groups of four to five other new professors from across the university. My peer group included scholars in mathematics, philosophy, business, and nursing. While the primary role of these peer groups was to serve as a support network for new faculty navigating the politics and procedures of university life (many beers were thus consumed), the peer groups had the serendipitous benefit of leading to cross-disciplinary collaborations. In the present case, my collaboration on this police stress research with Jennifer Fricas, a professor in our College of Nursing. The idea was to use heart rate as a proxy for stress response, but what did I *really* know about stress physiology? I can read as well as anyone else, but I certainly didn't have the depth of knowledge that my colleague does in this area. Collaboration can lead to much more juice, and higher quality juice at that.

And so it was that in early 2010, on a third-watch weekend shift, I met my former student at his police precinct and gave him some instructions on how to rig himself up with the heart rate monitor in the locker room. Then, we headed out on his patrol shift to collect some data. Consistent with the aims and purpose of this book, I won't recount the details of the study here, but I will present one of the graphics that essentially tells the story and where I think this area of research should be headed.

Figure 1 depicts the point data that were collected during the pilot. The ellipse drawn within the map identifies a particularly stressful hit/run call that evolved into a DUI arrest at gunpoint. As the officer chased the vehicle through the city and began to realize that he was dealing with a noncompliant, potentially intoxicated, and dangerous subject, his heart rate steadily increases. After the vehicle was stopped and several opportunities for compliance were offered, the officer's heart rate maximized at the exact moment that he decided it was necessary to draw his sidearm and began advancing on the vehicle. This is depicted in the map by the largest graduated point marker to the right side of the ellipse. Other notable incidents from the officer's shift included a call to assist a repo-man confronted by an angry car owner wielding a base-

ball bat (due east of the DUI incident described above) and a call reporting screaming and a possible knife within a Seattle Housing Authority apartment building (northwest of the DUI incident). I believe that by collecting these data on a systematic basis from several officers within a study area, it would be possible to develop valid "stress maps" of a police precinct using common density estimation techniques. Taking things a step further, I believe that one day in the not too distant future, these types of bio-data will be collected and monitored continuously by sensors embedded in the body armor that officers wear. Such technology already exists and is in use by the military for the purpose of reporting information to field medical personnel. There is a long tradition of "trickle-down" in technology from military to civilian law enforcement markets, and it's just a matter of time. Many issues to be worked out, but the day will come.

The "Post-do"

Success! Now it was time to try and scale things up. I needed funding to do this on a larger scale, and that meant a grant proposal. I was convinced that the pilot would make for a substantially stronger proposal and that reviewers would bathe themselves in the juice. The test officer's commander turned out to be a very like-minded person, and when I met with him to give him my pitch about doing this research on a larger scale in his precinct, he immediately saw the potential benefits and enthusiastically supported me.

Next stop: the police guild. Welcome to the realities of conducting research on police officers. It's very unlikely that you will successfully conduct research on live officers without the blessing of the union. I'm being a little facetious here—in reality, the union was a very important stakeholder here because they have clear interests in officer health and safety generally, as well as the immediate well-being of specific officers who may participate in research studies. The union president was very interested in the research, saw the immediate benefit to the police, and was very encouraging. Most importantly, he pledged his

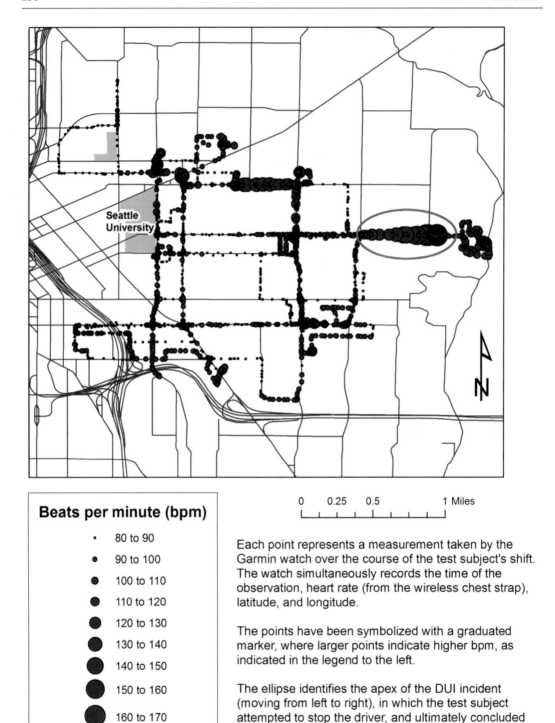

Beats per minute (bpm)

·	80 to 90
•	90 to 100
●	100 to 110
●	110 to 120
●	120 to 130
●	130 to 140
●	140 to 150
●	150 to 160
●	160 to 170

0   0.25   0.5   1 Miles

Each point represents a measurement taken by the Garmin watch over the course of the test subject's shift. The watch simultaneously records the time of the observation, heart rate (from the wireless chest strap), latitude, and longitude.

The points have been symbolized with a graduated marker, where larger points indicate higher bpm, as indicated in the legend to the left.

The ellipse identifies the apex of the DUI incident (moving from left to right), in which the test subject attempted to stop the driver, and ultimately concluded with a gunpoint arrest.

Fig. 1 Map of point data collected via GPS-enabled heart rate monitor

support as needed to help grease the wheels with officers and administrators.

A grant proposal was submitted under an appropriate solicitation, along with strong letters of support from the police department. The proposal was positively reviewed—no negative comments, anyway—but ultimately not selected for funding. This was obviously disappointing, but not really all that discouraging. The reality of grant work is that there are a lot of great ideas out there, but only a limited amount of funds available, and a set of funding priorities on the funder's side of the table. The floors of grant-making entities are covered in great grant proposals. It's just the nature of the beast. We tried again in a subsequent funding cycle, this time building the study into a multisite design and leveraging new and better technology available from colleagues at the Research Triangle Institute. Similar results, but we won't give up trying. Maybe someone else will get this going; for example, an interesting study monitoring the heart rates of a team of crime scene investigators was recently published (Adderley, Smith, Bond, & Smith, 2012). A little more of this type of work will help build the case for large-scale studies.

Where Is This Headed? Channel Your Inner Experimentalist!

I think our field would greatly benefit from more "experimentalists." I'm not referring to those who conduct their research by classical experimental design, although that is certainly something to which we might all aspire. As a starting point for discussion, and at the risk of drawing harsh criticism from fellow academics, I will rely upon the definition of "experimentalist" provided by *Wikipedia* (Experimentalist, n.d.):

> "Experimentalist" is a blanket term for all sorts of scientists engaged more in experimental activity than in the theoretical side of their sciences. The word "experimenter" emphasizes the person running an experiment, usually in a single instance; "experimentalist," by contrast, indicates a pattern in a person's approach to discovering knowledge. "Experimentalist" is also used in reference to a personality type that builds

up gradually to a work. Here the term is not limited to science, but is frequently used in relation to artists. Famous "experimentalists" could include Cézanne, Mark Twain or Robert Frost. The opposite of being an Experimentalist is to be a Conceptualist. Colloquially, an Experimentalist has been defined as "one who prefers to ascertain by finding out."

I think of Thor Heyerdahl's (1950) *Kon-Tiki* as a particularly inspirational work in this vein. Heyerdahl challenged the prevailing wisdom among anthropologists that Polynesia was settled by migration from the West; instead, Heyerdahl believed that, based upon similarities between the iconic statues of Easter Island and sculptures found in Peru from the pre-Columbian era, Easter Island was settled by migrants from Peru, to the East. To put it lightly, his theories were not well received by the academic establishment (and are still the matter of some debate). So what did he do? In 1947, he and his team of five men constructed a traditional raft out of balsa trees on the coast of Peru, erected a square-rigged mainsail, and sailed the damn thing on the prevailing winds and currents of the Pacific Ocean. They crossed nearly 3,800 nautical miles over 100 days, from Callao, Peru, to the Tuamotu islands of Polynesia. Sometimes, you just have to try it to find out.

When I say we need more experimentalists, I'm also thinking of the "tinkerer" personality—people who get enjoyment and reward out of fixing that which is broken, improving or modifying that which is not working well or not working as desired, and, when all else fails, creating from scratch a new means of accomplishing what needs to be accomplished through the tried-and-true process of trial and error. This more "tinkerer" conception of the experimentalist is a flavor of person one might have found working in Bell Laboratories (Gertner, 2012), or maybe the earlier years of the RAND Corporation (Abella, 2009). But this spirit of adventure and discovery is within us all. I recall when I was young, probably about 10 years old or so, I saw a small gas engine in our garage that had been removed from a lawn mower. I asked my father about it and told him I wanted to know how it worked. He gave me a toolbox full of wrenches and other tools and said, "Take it apart, and then put it back together. Then at dinnertime, *you* tell *me* how it works." Through that simple act, he led me down a lifelong path of tinkering with stuff: disassembling, fixing, modifying, and generally fiddling with all kinds of mechanical and electrical objects (often to my wife's chagrin). In a broader sense, he nudged me down the path of critical inquiry and a quenchless thirst for knowledge. We all have that, to some degree; we just need to channel it and carry that spirit into our professional work as well.

Unfortunately, the academy doesn't really have good support mechanisms for this essential form of applied research activity—the kind of stuff that is essential to ensuring that we are measuring what we intend to measure, and not slipping into the realm of what physicist Irving Langmuir (1953/1989) called "pathological science" (a situation where researchers—although well intentioned—fool themselves into studying that which isn't so, "… led astray by subjective effects, wishful thinking or threshold interactions" [1989: 43]). My home institution does not count experimentalist activity toward our annual performance reviews, unless it ultimately appears in a traditional peer-reviewed outlet. And the journal system, in its present form, does not really encourage or even allocate space for this type of work. Peer reviewers also tend not to appreciate this kind of work, seeing it as incomplete. An exception is the occasional "Research Note." (And just how does the Rank and Tenure Committee handle the "Research Note"?) In short, if my kind of "juice" speaks to you, you probably already know that there are very few *external* incentives for this type of work. But I'd really enjoy reading an electronic periodical that contains very brief summaries of things that people (experimentalists) are trying out, including pilot studies, early/preliminary findings, and general criminological tinkering—maybe *Criminology Letters* or something to that effect? Basically, I want a periodical version of the present book. Now that would be some serious juice!

The future of criminology and criminal justice will be in the real-time and place-specific measurement of what people are doing and what they are experiencing. Smartphones and other personal electronic devices will rapidly become a primary means of data collection for social scientists. These technologies have the potential to make data collection quite a bit more efficient, but it will also require the development of skills and techniques for handling and analyzing vast amounts of data and ensuring respect for privacy concerns. It's simply a matter of time, but we desperately need more researchers to get out there and get their hands dirty and try these things out. It's the only way to get the ball rolling, because if you wait for a funding agency to take a risk on a large-scale rollout of something like this, you may be waiting a while. We need more experimentalists. Just make it happen and have some fun because that's really what it's all about.

References

Abella, A. (2009). *Soldiers of reason: The RAND Corporation and the rise of the American Empire*. New York, NY: Harcourt.

Adderley, R., Smith, L., Bond, J., & Smith, M. (2012). Physiological measurement of crime scene investigator stress. *International Journal of Police Science & Management, 14*(2), 166–176.

Anderson, G., Litzenberger, R., & Plecas, D. (2002). Physical evidence of police officer stress. *Policing: An International Journal of Police Strategies & Management, 25*(2), 399–420.

Experimentalist. (n.d.). *Wikipedia: The free Encyclopedia*. Retrieved April 26, 2014, from http://en.wikipedia.org/wiki/Experimentalist

Gertner, J. (2012). *The Idea Factory: Bell Labs and the Great Age of American Innovation*. New York, NY: Penguin Press.

Heyerdahl, T. (1950). *Kon-Tiki*. New York, NY: Rand McNally.

Hickman, M., Fricas, J., Strom, K., & Pope, M. (2011). Mapping police stress. *Police Quarterly, 14*(3), 227–250.

Langmuir, I. (1953/1989). Pathological science (1953 speech transcribed by R. N. Hall). *Physics Today, 42*(10), 36–48.

Venkatesh, S. (2008). *Gang leader for a day: A Rogue sociologist takes to the streets*. New York, NY: Penguin Press.

Venkatesh, S. (2013). *Floating city: A Rogue sociologist lost and found in New York's underground economy*. New York, NY: Penguin Press.

Violanti, J., Andrew, M., Burchfiel, C., Hartley, T., Charles, L., & Miller, D. (2007). Post-traumatic stress symptoms and cortisol patterns among police officers. *Policing: An International Journal of Police Strategies & Management, 30*(2), 189–202.

Webster, J. (2013). Police officer perceptions of occupational stress: The state of the art. *Policing: An International Journal of Police Strategies & Management, 36*(3), 636–652.

Sometimes Pictures Tell the Story

Michael D. Maltz

Like so many others, I fell into a "life of crime" by accident. An electrical engineer by training, my first post-postdoc job was with an engineering consulting firm, where I was engaged in doing operations research, mostly for the US Navy. While I was there, in the late 1960s, the firm was commissioned to develop a new management information system for the Boston Police Department, and I was assigned to work on improving the BPD's communications system.

As the project wound down, I was approached by the federal agency sponsoring the work, the US Justice Department's Office of Law Enforcement Assistance (the predecessor twice removed from the Office of Justice Programs), to see if I would take a 2-year leave of absence and help put together the newly formed National Institute of Law Enforcement and Criminal Justice (now NIJ). When I broached the subject to my firm, they said that I could only take a 1-year leave, which I thought would be inadequate: from my experience in dealing with the Navy, I knew that it takes a year to learn your way around the bureaucracy and little time to make any progress.

So I quit and instead moved to Washington for what turned out to be a 3-year stint at NIJ.

But I had a bit of difficulty in dealing with the way research was done in the softer areas of criminal justice research. In fact, when I first became interested in studying crime and criminal justice, I was struck by the fact that most of the research in the field relied almost exclusively on numerical and statistical techniques to analyze data, with the holy "$p<0.05$" criterion being the sought-after standard of success; graphical analyses of data were few and far between (and its practice was dismissively called "data dredging"). You were supposed to propound a theory and test the data to see if it passed the ultimate test of "statistical significance": I had to learn just what it meant, since I had never taken *any* statistics course (just one on probability theory), let alone one that focused on social science.

As an undergraduate student in engineering, I was continually dealing with data that we had to present using graphs. We spent a great deal of time in the lab collecting data. Whether it was adding weight to a spring and measuring how much it stretched as a function of weight, or measuring the time it took for an object to fall different distances, or changing the voltage on the gate of a transistor and measuring how much the output voltage changed—all of these data collection exercises were followed by graphing the data. These as well as any of a hundred other examples imbued in me and my fellow students the value

M.D. Maltz (✉)
University of Illinois at Chicago, Chicago, IL, USA

Ohio State University, Columbus, OH, USA
e-mail: maltzmd@gmail.com

M.D. Maltz and S.K. Rice (eds.), *Envisioning Criminology: Researchers on Research as a Process of Discovery*, DOI 10.1007/978-3-319-15868-6_26, © Springer International Publishing Switzerland 2015

of visualization as a means of understanding data and the underlying theoretical concepts.[1]

After leaving NIJ, I began teaching research methods and statistics in a criminal justice curriculum, at the University of Illinois at Chicago, so I had to learn how social scientists use data. Untenured, I was not about to stick my neck out and bring engineering concepts into the classroom or in my research; instead, I buckled down and learned the "tried (tired?) and true" methods of social science. I used some good textbooks, but by and large there were no pictures—aside from figures showing how well data distributions fit the ubiquitous normal distribution curve.

Of course, I had to teach that kind of statistical analysis, since I had to prepare students for what they were likely to read in the criminology and criminal justice literature. Moreover, at that time, data collection (in the early 1970s) was a time-consuming and expensive effort, necessitating reading paper documents, coding them into (usually) numerical variables, and punching the coded data into computer cards. Therefore, data sets were usually random samples of a population, whether the population was of surveyed individuals or of records culled from a criminal justice agency. So it made sense to teach inferential statistics, i.e., how to infer characteristics of the whole population from a sample. But it still seemed to me that the statistical methods used at the time were pretty limited.

In my own research (especially after tenure!), I noticed that more and more agencies were generating computerized data sets, so obtaining large (or "biggish") data sets was not a problem. Granted, they are not as large as the "big data" sets, like the number of Twitter tweets or the characteristics of a genome, but they were large enough that most relationships were "statistically significant."[2]

I began by *looking* at the data, which I found to be, in a word, *fun*, like doing a jigsaw puzzle or finding "Where's Waldo" on a busy page. But there's a major difference between those activities and depicting data: you know beforehand that you have all the pieces of the puzzle and that Waldo is somewhere on the page, but you have no idea whether you will come up with a finding. When you do, of course, the enjoyment is that much sweeter. Described below (and in Maltz, 2009) are some data explorations that came out well (I've ignored the many that got me nowhere); to dig deeper into graphical methods for biggish data sets, see Unwin, Theus, and Hoffman (2006).

Recidivism. In 1976 Dick McCleary, currently on the faculty at the University of California, Irvine, joined me at the University of Illinois at Chicago. He was just finishing his Ph.D. in sociology at Northwestern University. His dissertation was on the parole process in Illinois, and he had some data that he and I decided to analyze. The data showed how many people in a particular cohort recidivated after release (Table 1).

At that time the standard measure of recidivism was the 1-year recidivism rate, the percent

Table 1 Monthly parole failures for 257 Illinois parolees

Exposure time (months)	Number failing during that month	Exposure time (months)	Number failing during that month
1	44[a]	12	3
2	9	13	0
3	8	14	0
4	9	15	2
5	6	16	2
6	5	17	2
7	5	18	0
8	3	19	0
9	2	20	0
10	2	21	0
11	3	22	3

[a]During the first 2 weeks, there were 29 failures

sample and were able to reduce the number of such findings to a more reasonable number. But in doing so they discarded 90% of the data, which to me, a data maven, is tantamount to committing a mortal sin.

---

[1] It also imbued in us what "linear" means, as used in linear regression, hierarchical linear modeling, and other techniques. And rare are the variables in social science that have a true linear relationship, so I also had a healthy skepticism of many findings based on linear analyses.

[2] Case in point: I once reviewed a report for a federal agency in which the data set was so large that every relationship was significant. So the researchers took a 10%

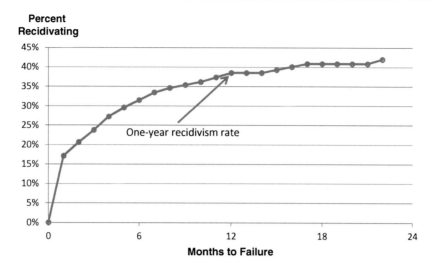

Fig. 1 Cumulative failures for 257 Illinois parolees

of releases who had been reconvicted[3] within 1 year. [In this case, the 1-year recidivism rate is 99/257, or 38.5%.] To us, however, this seemed to be an extremely limited measure. This became especially apparent after we plotted the cumulative distribution of his data, the total number of parolees in that cohort who recidivated over time (Fig. 1). That is, the 1-year recidivism rate was but a single point on the curve, and no use was made of how that point was arrived at—after all, it might have been arrived at because all 99 failed in the first 6 months, with none afterward, or because 8 or so failed every month, or in other ways of getting to 99 in 12 months. We felt that a better measure would be the percentage of parolees who *eventually* recidivated. As can be seen from the figure, it is logical to assume that relatively few, if any, of the parolees who hadn't (or hadn't yet) recidivated would do so in subsequent years.

Even better, it would be useful to portray the whole curve so that we would know how many would be expected to recidivate after any given number of years. In that way, we would be able to estimate how many parolees would be returned to prison in any given year and thus be useful in forecasting the prison population over time.

Since the figure resembles an exponential probability distribution, a distribution with which most people are familiar, it is logical to fit an exponential curve to the data. But this is not a standard exponential probability distribution: a standard probability distribution would approach 100% as time increases, while this 1 approaches a value closer to (and probably under) 120/257, or 46.7%. Such a distribution is called an incomplete distribution, since its final value is not 100%.[4]

Our question then became, is there a way to use the data to estimate the two parameters of interest for an incomplete exponential distribution, the maximum value (i.e., the percent of the group under study that is estimated to eventually fail) and how fast the maximum value is achieved? At that time neither of us was mathematically equipped to know how to do this.

A friend of mine, however, was. I posed the problem to Stephen Pollock, a faculty member in industrial and operations engineering at the University of Michigan, who directed us to a

---

[3]This is one definition of recidivism. Others include the percentage who were rearrested or indicted or who had violated parole; see Maltz (1984), Chap. 6.

[4]An earlier study did try to fit recidivism data to a *complete* exponential distribution, but it provided a less accurate fit.

method called maximum likelihood estimation (MLE). We learned how to implement it, then we looked at the way others had used MLE on similar problems, and we were able to develop techniques to analyze recidivism data to estimate those two parameters (Maltz & McCleary, 1977; Maltz, 1984).

We thought that we had developed a truly innovative method that could be widely applied and were quite proud of that fact. It wasn't until after we completed the article that we found out that we had reinvented the wheel. We soon discovered that someone had beat us to it by about 30 years: John Boag (1949) had used essentially the same method to estimate the proportion of patients cured of cancer (and how fast the uncured succumbed to cancer); and there had been a number of others in the interim who applied incomplete distributions in other biomedical applications. *Sic transit gloria mundi.*

Collusive Bidding. A few years later, Steve Pollock and I collaborated on another project, one that we hoped would result in some criminal or civil sanctions against the schemers but ultimately resulted only in an interesting exercise for us. It had to do with bidding collusion on road-building materials. The material in question is a prosaic product, the ribbed culvert pipe used under and alongside roads to keep water from washing out roads during rainstorms. It appeared that bidders would often submit the exact same (high) bids, except for one bidder, who submitted a lower bid that was accepted. Every county in the state had its own contracting department, and it appeared that the bidders were rotating as to which of them would submit the low bid for a given county. In addition, there were suspicions that they met together to decide who would win which bid, although the evidence was circumstantial.

We were approached by a district attorney in one of the counties to look at the evidence his investigator had collected. He had received funding from a grant from the Law Enforcement Assistance Administration (LEAA) to the National District Attorneys Association and used part of the money to explore this issue. [There is some irony in this fact, as will be noted below.]

The evidence we received from him consisted of a sheaf of handwritten pages that listed all of the bids submitted by every contractor over a number of years, for most of the counties in the state. During one of those years, the contractors apparently did not collude, and the winning bids were lower. During the next year, however, they again seemed to be colluding, according to the county purchasing agents. But the prosecutor was unclear as to how to analyze the bid data, so we were called in to help.

After entering the data into the University of Michigan mainframe computer,[5] we decided to graph the data. Since culvert pipe comes in different diameters and lengths, we converted each bid into a standard net unit price (in cents/ft) to include all pipe diameters. [Because of this, there are small differences in bids that are essentially equal; therefore, we treated bids within a few cents of each other to be essentially equivalent.] We still couldn't discern a pattern easily, because it's hard to find one by just looking at rows of numbers.

When you don't know what to do, it's not a bad first step to look at the data, which we did: we plotted the amount of each bid and the date (Fig. 2). I should note that the plotting hardware and software at that time were rather primitive, which is why we used numbers to denote number of bids, instead of markers or colors.

Since a number of counties had bids during the same week, we plotted the number of bids at a given price; thus, from Fig. 2, 31 bids at a net unit price of 285 cents/ft were made in the first week of January 1972, bids aggregated from a number of counties. Note also that only five bids were at lower prices during that week.

But it's not the specific numbers that are important here, but rather their pattern. Because the product is standard, what matters in these bids is the price and the price alone—the low bid *always* gets the contract. With that in mind, we then examined the visual patterns those numbers

---

[5] This was before there were PCs or Macs, let alone the easy-to-use versions of SPSS and SAS, and well before STATA and SYSTAT were created. The university had its own data-handling program, Osiris, into which the data were entered.

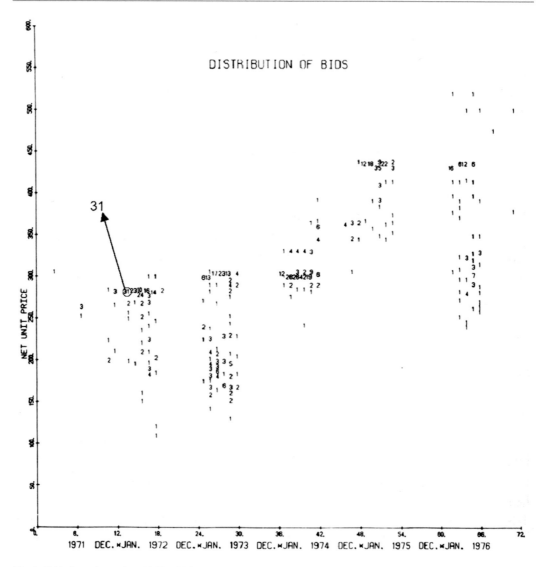

Fig. 2 Bids for culvert pipe, 1972–1976 bidding seasons

produce. A number of features of the bidding process are apparent from this plot:

- There is a bidding "season," from late fall to early spring, during which time different counties ask for bids.
- There appears to be a "standard" bid price for that season, which is used by most vendors; we called it the "list price."
- In 1972 a relative handful of bids were below the list price (45 of 174 bids, or 26%), while in 1973 this was true of over *twice* as many bids (103 of 182, or 57%).
- In 1974 almost all bids were at (or even above) the list price, with only a very few below it (12

of 152, or 8%)—and even those were not very far below list.
- In 1975 the list price went up considerably, and again relatively few of the bids were below it (31 of 133, or 23%).
- The bids in 1976 show even greater dispersion than in 1973, with a great many bids well below the list price (55 of 101, or 54%). Moreover, the median bid actually decreased between 1975 and 1976!

The bid data for each season is summarized in Fig. 3.

As can be seen, the percentage of bids below the list price was greatest in 1973 and 1976, in

Fig. 3 Number of bids, by bid year

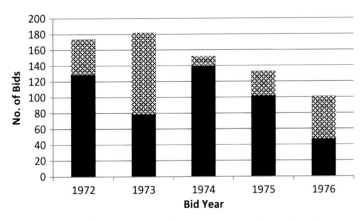

■ Number at or above list price   ⊠ Number below list price

both cases over half. These were our observations just by looking at the raw bid data. We then looked at the distribution of bids in each bidding season. That is, we plotted the fraction of bids that fell below a given price, as well as the fraction of *low* bids that fell below a given price. The distributions for the 1972–1976 bids (both all bids and low, or winning, bids) are shown below in Figs. 4, 5, 6, 7, and 8.

If all of the bids were the same, then the lines would be completely vertical; this would be the case if all bidders were to, literally, "fall into line." In 1972 about 80% of all bids were very close to the list price. And note that in the 1974 and 1975 bidding seasons, they were predominantly vertical as well, both all bids and low bids. So what happened during the 1973 and 1976 seasons? When we showed these figures to the prosecutorial staff, they had an answer; it confirmed what they knew about the bid situation:

- It turned out that the year 1973 was known as "the year of the price war" by them, when a number of vendors tried to collar more business by cutting their prices. This explains the increased number of bids below the list price.
- It appeared that the vendors decided against cutting prices (collusion?) during the 1974 and 1975 bidding seasons, as again most of the bids were at or near the list price.
- The apparent lack of competitive bidding in 1974 and 1975 prompted the beginning of the investigation and the issuance of subpoenas, which the officials felt was why the bidding was more competitive in 1976.

Additional graphical analyses (not shown here) showed how the bids seemed to rotate among vendors. That gave more support to the possibility that collusive bidding had reemerged after the price war.

Good news and bad news followed this graphical analysis. First the good news: all this was done using the actual data rather than inferential statistics. That is, we didn't have to assume anything about the data's normality, independence, heteroskedasticity, and the like. The prosecutor was pleased with this, because he felt that the figures could easily be understood by jurors. And we were pleased as well, because neither of us had ever testified in court and were looking forward to it and also because we were able to use our training to assist in a criminal case.

Now the bad news: it turned out that the prosecutor we had been working with came under indictment himself—for misusing federal funds (*not* those used to hire us)—so the case never went to trial, and as far as we know the (apparent) collusive behavior continued unabated.

And, of course, there was an additional benefit: Steve and I got a book chapter out of it (Maltz & Pollock, 1980).[6]

---

[6] A few years later, I was asked to perform the same kind of study by the World Bank, which had suspicions of collusion among contractors in bidding for medical-related contracts. I count this study as one of my failures, since they were all but certain that the bidders were colluding, but its traces were not apparent in the bid data that they provided me with. Sometimes data analyses aren't enough.

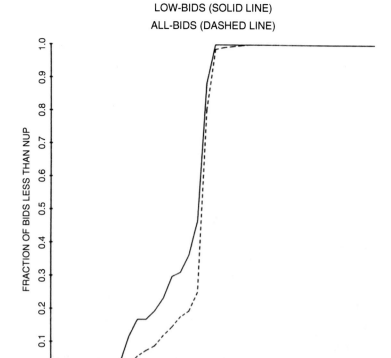

Fig. 4 Bid distribution, 1972 bidding season

WINTER 1972
LOW-BIDS (SOLID LINE)
ALL-BIDS (DASHED LINE)

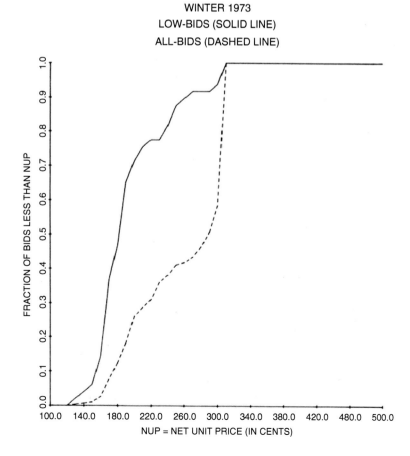

Fig. 5 Bid distribution, 1973 bidding season

WINTER 1973
LOW-BIDS (SOLID LINE)
ALL-BIDS (DASHED LINE)

Fig. 6 Bid distribution, 1974 bidding season

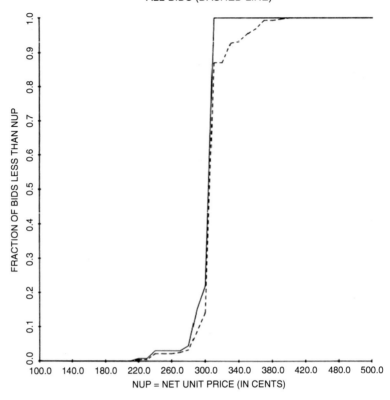

WINTER 1974
LOW-BIDS (SOLID LINE)
ALL-BIDS (DASHED LINE)

FRACTION OF BIDS LESS THAN NUP

NUP = NET UNIT PRICE (IN CENTS)

Fig. 7 Bid distribution, 1975 bidding season

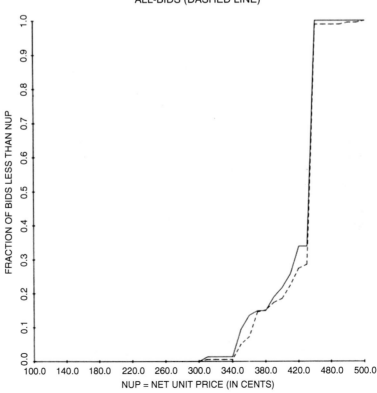

WINTER 1975
LOW-BIDS (SOLID LINE)
ALL-BIDS (DASHED LINE)

FRACTION OF BIDS LESS THAN NUP

NUP = NET UNIT PRICE (IN CENTS)

Fig. 8 Bid distribution,
1976 bidding season

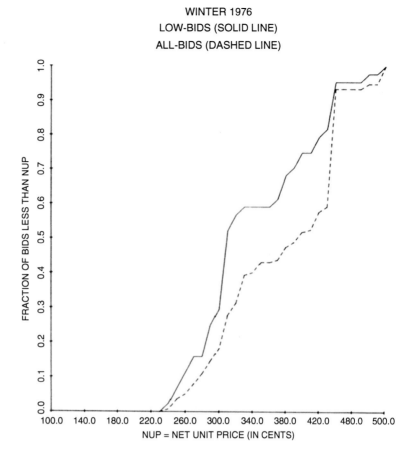

WINTER 1976
LOW-BIDS (SOLID LINE)
ALL-BIDS (DASHED LINE)

Homicide. This was pure serendipity. I was teaching a graduate course in statistical methods and was looking for a data set to use in class. To that end, I downloaded into SPSS a copy of the Supplementary Homicide Reports data set that Jamie Fox had made available on the National Archive of Criminal Justice Data website.[7] Since the victim-based data set has situations where there is more than one victim and more than one offender, as well as those where offenders are unknown, I decided to focus on one particular group of homicides: those in which one victim is killed by one known offender. In that way, we

would have ages of both the offender and victim.[8]

I had my teaching assistant run a crosstab of victim age vs. offender age for these cases and, to get an overview of the relationship, had her transfer the crosstab to a spreadsheet. We looked at the spreadsheet and were surprised by what we saw (Fig. 9). The maximum value, 1,213, was the number of 19-year-olds who killed 19-year-olds, but that was expected and not the main surprise: it was concentration of deaths above that point,

[7]A recent version is study ICPSR 24801, available at www.icpsr.umich.edu.

[8]Besides, cases with many victims and one or more offenders, and cases with many offenders and one or more victims, may be quite different than one-on-ones. Since we were just exploring, I decided that we should start at this point.

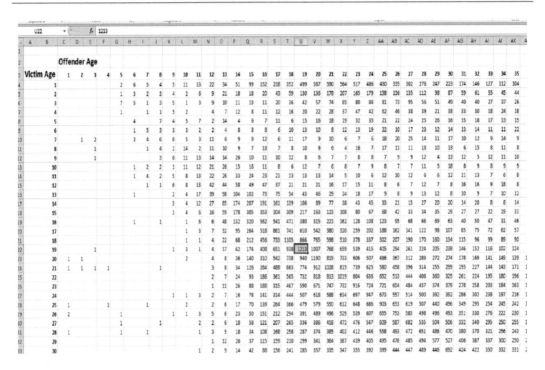

Fig. 9 Age of victim (↓) and offender (→) in one-on-one homicides

with victim ages 1–5, and the relative sparseness of deaths running diagonally to the southeast below those ages and above the peak.[9]

We then reduced the scale so the entire crosstab could be seen (Fig. 10).

The crosstab has an interesting shape, looking like a bird (of prey, of course) in flight, one with a visible tail stretching toward the lower right. The darker cells correspond to cells filled with more digits,[10] up to four in the upper left section of the main area. The dark area above that, in which victims' ages were between 0 and 6, was also interesting. This prompted me to plot the data as a 3D surface plot, which resulted in a very interesting picture (Fig. 11).

Note the secondary peak of homicides of young children, which is (literally) overshadowed by those committed by and against young adults. The diagonal tail in the lower right in Fig. 10 heads toward the lower right in Fig. 11, which is due to older offenders killing older victims, attributable to intimate partner homicide. It is much more pronounced in male-on-female and female-on-male homicides (Maltz, 1998).

Summary. As these examples show, depicting data can play an important part in understanding the processes generating the data. In the first case, it showed a pattern of recidivism obscured by using an inadequate measure of the phenomenon. In the second case, it showed some of the characteristics of collusive bidding that could be used both as evidence and as a means of detecting it. And in the third case, it showed some characteristics of one-on-one homicide that are usually not as salient as the more common 20-somethings killing each other.

---

[9] Note also the input errors in the far left columns. I doubt if there were any 2- or 3-year-old murderers.

[10] A 4-digit entry will have twice the ink of a 2-digit entry, so, for the mathematically inclined, the darkness of a cell corresponds to its logarithm to the base 10.

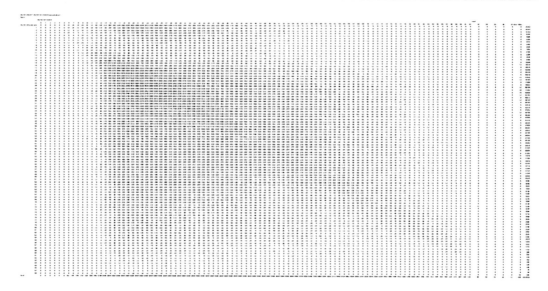

Fig. 10 Age of victim and offender: full spreadsheet

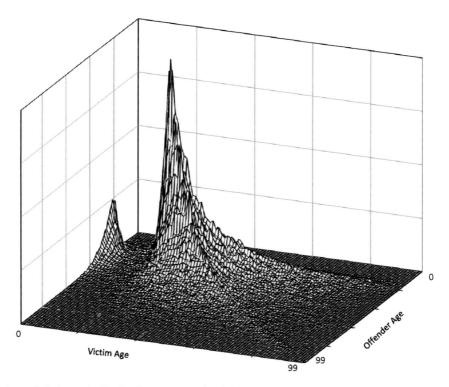

Fig. 11 Ages of victims and offenders in one-on-one homicides

Of course, not every data set will display its secrets as plainly as these ones have. It is, however, worth considering plotting a data set's variables as an initial step, if only to see if there are useful relationships that are not immediately apparent in the data set's variables. Another good reason for plotting them is to spot errors in the data, which happens more often than one might expect (Maltz, 2014).

A further concern is that, as Fagan (1993: 381) noted, "our methods grow more powerful and precise as we move ever further away from our data and the complex realities they represent." None of these pictures required the use of esoteric methods. What it did require is a desire to understand the data and an ability to deal with data graphically: not much else. It may be that too often graduate students are required to display their proficiency with new and complex statistical techniques, but spend too little time understanding the data that these techniques are designed to attack. And now that we're no longer dealing only with relatively small samples, but have fire hoses of data to deal with, a little more time devoted to playing with the data may pay off in greater insight.

References

Boag, J. W. (1949). Maximum likelihood estimates of the proportion of patients cured by cancer therapy. *Journal of the Royal Statistical Society, 11*, 15–53.

Fagan, J. A. (1993). Editor's introduction. *Journal of Research in Crime and Delinquency, 30*, 381–382.

Maltz, M.D. (1984). *Recidivism*. Orlando, FL: Academic Press. Internet version published in 2001. Retrieved from http://www.academia.edu/10061829/Recidivism.

Maltz, M. D. (1998). Visualizing homicide: A research note. *Journal of Quantitative Criminology, 14*(4), 397–410.

Maltz, M. D. (2009). Look before you analyze: Visualizing data in criminal justice. In A. R. Piquero & D. Weisburd (Eds.), *Handbook of quantitative criminology*. New York, NY: Springer.

Maltz, M. D. (2014). Visualizing data: A brief history. In G. Bruinsma & D. Weisburd (Eds.), *Encyclopedia of criminology and criminal justice*. New York, NY: Springer.

Maltz, M. D., & McCleary, R. (1977, August 3). The mathematics of behavioral change: Recidivism and construct validity. Evaluation Quarterly, 1, 421–438.

Maltz, M. D., & Pollock, S. M. (1980). Analyzing suspected collusion among bidders. In G. Geis & E. Stotland (Eds.), *White-collar crime: Theory and practice* (pp. 174–198). Beverly Hills, CA: Sage.

Unwin, A., Theus, M., & Hoffman, H. (2006). *Graphics of large datasets: Visualizing a million*. New York, NY: Springer.

"Rounding Up Twice the Usual Number of Suspects"

D. Kim Rossmo

Introduction

I was a police officer walking a beat in Vancouver's Skid Road when I began my graduate studies. While originally interested in mathematics I wanted something more exciting for a career, so after finishing my B.A. I joined the Vancouver Police Department. I planned to pursue a master's degree (and later a doctorate) in criminology; the idea was to use my police experience to inform my studies and for my graduate education to make me a better police officer. I believe I was successful on both counts.

I worked in busy areas to increase my opportunity to learn about crime and criminals. My police assignments included patrol, emergency response, Expo 86 (the 1986 world's fair), organized crime intelligence, and various task forces. I eventually became a detective inspector in charge of the Geographic Profiling Section, a specialized unit formed directly as a result of my Ph.D. research. Geographic profiling is a criminal investigative methodology for analyzing the locations of a connected series of crimes to determine the most probable area of offender residence (Rossmo, 2013). The technique is used to help detectives find the offender in "whodunit" investigations of

stranger serial crime through suspect prioritization.[1] As such cases can generate thousands of suspects and tips, police require methods for managing the challenges of information overload.

This chapter is about the origins, research, and development of geographic profiling. My doctoral research was based on the theories, concepts, and principles of environmental criminology. Crime pattern, routine activity, and rational choice theories provided the foundation for describing the mathematical relationship between offender movement and likelihood of offending. What follows is the story of this particular research effort, along with a discussion of some of its influences and challenges (interspersed with random musings). The pre-do/do/post-do structure was borrowed from this volume's editors, Mike Maltz and Steve Rice; before refers to the

D.K. Rossmo (✉)
School of Criminal Justice, Texas State University,
San Marcos, TX, USA
e-mail: krossmo@txstate.edu

[1] The title of this chapter comes from *Casablanca* (1942). Most people are familiar with the quote at the end of the movie when Vichy Police Prefect Captain Louis Renault commands a gendarme to "Round up the usual suspects" after Rick Blaine (Humphrey Bogart) shoots German Major Heinrich Strasser. Less well known is a similar statement by Captain Renault at the beginning of the film; when asked by Major Strasser what has been done regarding the investigation of two murdered German couriers, he replies, "Realizing the importance of the case, my men are rounding up twice the usual number of suspects." My point in using this quote for the chapter title is that geographic profiling provides a more effective and efficient method of prioritizing a criminal investigation than rounding up "twice the usual number of suspects."

M.D. Maltz and S.K. Rice (eds.), *Envisioning Criminology: Researchers on Research as a Process of Discovery*, DOI 10.1007/978-3-319-15868-6_27, © Springer International Publishing Switzerland 2015

selection of my dissertation topic, during refers to my doctoral research, and after refers to what followed my Ph.D. defense.

Pre-do

My first class as a new criminology graduate student at Simon Fraser University was on "The Ecology of Crime," taught by Professor Paul Brantingham. His course was an absorbing introduction to environmental criminology, a field previously unknown to me. As I had a background in mathematics, the subject was all the more fascinating with its focus on spatial and temporal crime patterns. Environmental criminology is the study of street networks, target backcloths, the ebb and flow of people, patterns, and the convergence of criminals and victims (Brantingham & Brantingham, 1984). I learned that crimes do not occur randomly in space; rather, their locations are the product of the built environment and the routine activities of offenders, victims, and guardians (Clarke & Felson, 1993). A new world of research possibilities opened up for me, and for my master's thesis I used geography of crime principles to analyze the interprovincial migration patterns of criminals wanted on outstanding warrants.

I later happened across a *Police Chief* article on the FBI's new Violent Criminal Apprehension Program (VICAP). On the cover was a map of the crime sites of a serial killer. The locations formed a geometric pattern that reminded me of some of the maps from our environmental criminology course readings. At the end of the class, Paul Brantingham had discussed crime pattern theory, a model of crime geometry that explained where criminals offended. I wondered if it would be possible to apply this theory and the principles of environmental criminology to mathematically analyze the patterns of serial murder locations. This eventually became the origin of the central question explored in my doctoral research (Rossmo, 1995).

I found only a few cases in which geography had been used in a police investigation during my initial background research. For example,

the Indian Police Service applied distance and time analyses for dacoities (rural banditry); during new moons, gangs of bandits would travel through the countryside under the cover of darkness to rob households in neighboring villages. Upon the report of a dacoity, the police would estimate where the offenders' home village was by using the time lag between the crime and sunrise and the average cross-country walking speed. In 1977, during the Hillside Stranglers investigation, the Los Angeles Police Department analyzed where murder victims were abducted, where their bodies were dumped, and distances between these locations (Gates & Shah, 1992). They viewed the problem in terms of Venn diagrams representing victim availability, offender capacity, and offender ability. In England, the Yorkshire Ripper inquiry accurately located the home city of the killer in 1980, using spatial mean and distance-time calculations (Kind, 1987).

My goal was to build on these efforts using environmental criminology theory and quantitative geographic methods. While serial murder is a fascinating subject, I originally chose it for simple data reasons as the crimes provided multiple locations for analysis; moreover, the media attention such cases generally receive made it possible to find detailed information on the crimes.

My research was done at an opportune time: the FBI's studies of serial murderers had led to the conception of behavioral profiling; it was now feasible to own a personal computer; and affordable geographic information systems (GIS) and desktop mapping systems were becoming available. These developments were important; scientific progress is more often the result of improved tools than advances in theory (Taleb, 2007). Finally, as I had a background in criminology, policing, and mathematics, the topic was a good fit for me personally.

Do

One of the most important principles I tried to follow during my dissertation research was to maintain a practical focus, which here meant viewing the problem from a police perspective. This approach influenced the initial definition of the research problem, the selection of the data, and the shape of the final analytic product. (The framework used in the research and development of geographic profiling is summarized in the Appendix.)

As one of the purposes of the research was the development of a tool useful for investigations of serial crime, my main analysis was limited to only information reliably known in a typical criminal case. In an unsolved murder or stranger rape, police usually know little or nothing about the offender. What they do generally know is where the crime occurred or the body was dumped. They can also often determine when the crime occurred (or at least the temporal order of the crimes in a series). Location and time therefore became my key variables.

While the FBI and a number of researchers had compiled lists of serial killers, a database of serial murder crime sites did not exist. This void meant I had to engage in long and extensive searches for crime addresses and location details, often needing to triangulate and integrate bits of information from a variety of different sources. In the end, this effort was well worth the time as it taught me much about the geography of criminals and the intimate details of crime locations.

One critical issue surrounded the exact definition of a crime site. It turns out that some offenses involve multiple locations, each with a different meaning in terms of offender decision-making, spatial independence, and profiling inference potential. For instance, a murder involves an encounter between offender and victim, an attack where threat or violence is first used, the murder itself, and then a body disposal (Rossmo, 2000). Consequently, depending upon how these cluster, a murder may include one, two, three, or four different locations. Unfortunately, some research in the area of crime mapping takes the expedient approach—a file of police reports is downloaded, crime addresses are geocoded, and the resulting data then analyzed. However, depending on definitions and report procedures, the

data may not be appropriate for the purposes of the research.[2]

This issue was underlined for me in a research project on stranger rape I was involved in some years later (Rossmo, Davies, & Patrick, 2004). In addition to the usual elements of location and date, the research data included a narrative summary of the crime. A stranger rape was defined as such if the victim and the offender did not know each other at the beginning of the day of the crime. However, we later noticed after reading the crime summaries that many of the incidents involved a scenario where the victim went to her local pub where she met the offender through friends or work colleagues. So while he was unknown to her at the start of the day, she, in fact, did know (at least) his first name, sometimes where he lived, and who his friends were. From an investigative perspective, the crime was not a "whodunit," and therefore not an incident we wanted to study for the purposes of this particular research project. The information in the crime narratives prevented us from analyzing a number of inappropriate cases and significantly biasing some of the spatial analyses.

Police investigations have to work from incomplete and sometimes erroneous information, so a robust methodology was essential for my dissertation research. A geographic profiling system is a model of real-world offender search behavior. Models require three qualities: (1) realism; (2) generality; and (3) precision (Levins, 1966). Tradeoffs are necessary in model building as an improvement in one quality usually weakens the other qualities, not unlike how higher power in a telescope reduces its field of view. In geographic profiling, realism translates into investigative utility, precision into analytic per-

---

[2] Criminological research often lacks an essential element in the scientific process. Science is based on observation and experimentation. Unfortunately, the tradition of observation so important in physics, chemistry, and biology is ignored in much modern criminology. Far too many researchers in our field analyze data with little appreciation for what it is, how it was generated, and what it really means, reducing crime to a few numbers, absent details and narrative. This is not a critique of quantitative analysis, only of sloppy quantitative analysis.

formance, and generality into police applicability (Rossmo, 2011). Model optimization requires finding the proper balance between these qualities. Crime occurs under a wide range of environmental and situational conditions. Importance was therefore given to developing a simple and generalizable model, and it was felt that minor improvements in precision should not come at the expense of robustness.

I received advice from a number of fellow investigators that informed and helped my research. For example, a subtle but important shift in the nature of the research problem followed suggestions from a senior police officer. Rather than trying to calculate an exact location for the offender's residence, the task was more realistically defined as the development of a method for suspect prioritization. This approach required me to create a mathematical algorithm for generating probability surfaces from crime site patterns. Detectives could then rank-order suspects by where their home address fell on the geoprofile; the higher the location was situated on the probability surface, the greater its geographic priority (see Figs. 1 and 2, below). For example, during Operation Lynx, a large-scale police inquiry of a rape series in England, detec-

tives used geographic profiling to prioritize the order in which they examined the fingerprints of over 12,000 suspects. This task had to be done by hand as police had only a partial latent print, insufficient for a computerized search. The offender's home was subsequently found in the top 3% of the geoprofile area. Information overload is a common problem in serial crime investigations and its management a necessary function.

Post-do

Completing and defending my dissertation was the end of the Ph.D. process. However, it was only the first step in terms of the development of geographic profiling as an operational police capability. It became evident that implementation required much more work: police agencies needed to become aware of the technique and how best to use it, a software system with functional investigative capabilities had to be built, and a training program had to be established.

Consequently, an operational geographic profiling software system named *Rigel* was developed to help meet the needs of police agencies

Fig. 1 Jeopardy surface of serial arsons

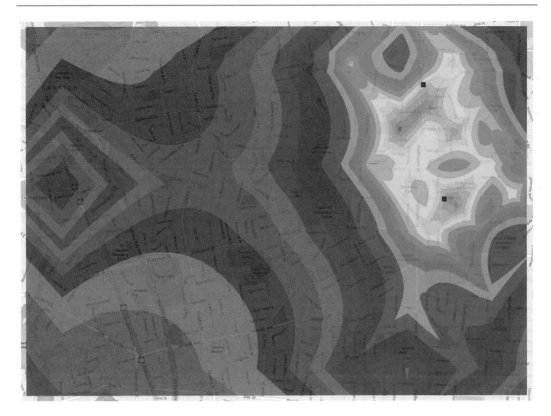

Fig. 2 GeoProfile of serial arsons with offender sites

for a suspect prioritization tool; the Royal Canadian Mounted Police (RCMP) was the first customer. An important element of geographic profiling is the visualization and manipulation of analytic results, which involve integrating the offender residence probability surface with a map of the area of the crime sites. Both three- and two-dimensional views are possible. The former, termed a jeopardy surface, shows the actual probability surface generated from the geographic profiling algorithm. The latter, termed a geoprofile, is more useful for police operational purposes as it allows specific streets, blocks, and areas to be ranked and prioritized. Figures 1 and 2 show a jeopardy surface and a geoprofile, respectively, based on the crimes of a serial arsonist in Saanich, British Columbia, Canada. This happened to be a solved case I was involved with so it became the first crime series the geoprofiling algorithm was tested on during my doctoral research. Dark red and orange designate the highest priority areas of the geoprofile, while gray

and purple indicate the lowest priority regions. The two blue squares are offender sites; the lower square marks the arsonist's home, the upper square his probation office (he was on probation for burglary during his arson series).

An essential aspect of this development was recognizing the limitations of any software system and determining those tasks better done by humans than by computers. It then followed that a proper training program had to be created. The Vancouver Police Department established a Geographic Profiling Section in 1995, and several other law enforcement agencies subsequently expressed interest in the technique. A formal training and certification program was developed, allowing the RCMP, Ontario Provincial Police, British National Crime Faculty, the Bureau of Alcohol, Tobacco, Firearms, and Explosives (ATF), and other organizations to implement their own capabilities.

Crime analysis techniques do not exist in isolation; there are always essential input and output stages. Before a geographic profile can be prepared, it is first necessary to determine which crimes were committed by the same serial offender. Subsequent efforts were therefore invested in the development of improved linkage analysis techniques. On the output side of the analytic continuum, a geographic profile is nothing more than a map; for it to have real-world impact, it must support investigative tactics useful to police detectives. Consequently, much thought was given to how a geoprofile could be applied for suspect prioritization, information management, spatial allocation of resources, and other investigative objectives. Any time a detective came up with a new investigative use for geographic profiling, the approach was documented and passed on in training courses and in future reports as appropriate.

It soon became clear that the real world was much more complex than the part I had bitten off for my research. As police investigators, literally from around the world, began to make more requests for geographic profiles in active investigations, greater case complexities were encountered in terms of crime location types, offender hunting behavior, and contextual environments. To respond to these real-world challenges, we resorted to theory, the power of which lies in its ability to answer unanticipated questions. Crime pattern theory and routine activity theory proved to be very useful in providing a roadmap for geographic profiling. This iterative process of operational problem, theory application, and real-world feedback was also invaluable for furthering our understanding of offender spatial behavior and in suggesting ideas for new research explorations.

The early decision to develop a robust and versatile methodology paid off. While the original research was on serial murder, geographic profiling has now been applied in cases of rape, robbery, arson, bombing, kidnapping, burglary, auto theft, credit card fraud, and graffiti. It turns out that other sciences are similarly interested in methods for finding things. Consequently, a number of collaborative research studies on the applications of geographic profiling in biology, zoology, and epidemiology have now been completed. The technique has been used to analyze

great white shark predation, variations in bat foraging in Scotland, bumble-bee search patterns, and the origins of invasive algae in the Mediterranean Sea. Epidemiological researchers have applied the model to locate mosquitogenic water sources from malaria cases in Cairo and contaminated drinking wells from cholera deaths. Intelligence applications in counterterrorism and counterinsurgency have also been advanced. With the emergence of asymmetric warfare, military analysts, now interested in crime analysis tools, have used geographic profiling to trace IED (improvised explosive device) bomb makers and rocket storage sites.[3] Criminology has traditionally borrowed from the natural sciences, so it was most rewarding to now see these fields adopting methods from criminology.

Conclusion

The realization of geographic profiling by law enforcement confirmed the real-world impact of my doctoral research on criminal investigations. This was greatly satisfying, not only in terms of recognition for my dissertation, but more generally in validating my research approach. It also highlighted the importance of operationalization, including the development and implementation of software systems, training courses, awareness programs, and organizational procedures and policies. Substantial follow-up efforts to translate the academic into the operational were required to make the most of the opportunities opened up by the research.

Interest in geographic profiling by police detectives was not completely unexpected. What was surprising, however, was the attention from scientists in other fields—biology, epidemiology, zoology, botany, veterinary medicine, intelligence, military defense—and the variety of novel

---

[3] See Martin, Rossmo, and Hammerschlag (2009), Le Comber, Nicholls, Rossmo, and Racey (2006), Raine, Rossmo, and Le Comber (2009), Stevenson, Rossmo, Knell, and Le Comber (2012), Le Comber, Rossmo, Hassan, Fuller, and Beier (2011), Rossmo and Harries (2011), Rossmo, Lutermann, Stevenson, and Le Comber (2014).

research applications they found for the technique. It was very exciting to have geographic profiling travel across disciplines, a rather rare event in criminology. This outside interest also provided strong evidence of the utility of environmental criminology generally, and the theoretical works of Paul and Patricia Brantingham, Marcus Felson, and Ron Clarke, specifically.

I am going to conclude by taking the opportunity provided by the purpose of this book to offer a few suggestions on research to graduate students and new scholars (and whoever else might wish to listen).

First, try to do research of significance and value. Know the "why" as well as the "what" and the "how" of your research. The purpose of publishing our work is to share it, not to merely add another check mark for some artificial performance metric. It says something (negative) about our profession when we measure "success" by how often our publications are cited by other academics, rather than by how our ideas and writing impact the real world of prevention, practice, policy, and justice.

Second, understand the problem. If you want to improve practice, make the effort and take the time to appreciate the practitioner's function, including the resource limitations and legal restrictions within which he or she must operate.

Finally, know your data. It is the primary connection between your research and the real world.

Researchers can only make a difference if their research matters. While that sounds trite, it is also an oft-ignored truism. A senior professor once told me that one of the Ivy League universities used to require only a single publication from new professors for tenure; however, the article had to be one of "significance." Even if you are not an Ivy League scholar, this challenge is still worth remembering.

Appendix

The approach followed in the research and development of geographic profiling is outlined in the following framework:

- Data
  - Algorithmic input limited to only data reliably known in a police investigation.
  - Development of improved techniques for crime linkage.
  - Use of a robust methodology to minimize information sensitivity.
- Analysis
  - Analytic labor divided between computers and humans.
  - Theory-based processes, adaptable to new and different circumstances.
  - Assumptions clearly articulated to avoid misapplications.
  - Ongoing refinement of training program.
- Utility
  - Use of addresses, a common database element, as a prioritization metric.
  - Algorithm generalizability.
  - Users able to visualize and manipulate analytic results.

References

Brantingham, P. J., & Brantingham, P. L. (1984). *Patterns in crime*. New York, NY: Macmillan.

Clarke, R. V., & Felson, M. (Eds.). (1993). *Routine activity and rational choice*. New Brunswick, NJ: Transaction.

Gates, D. F., & Shah, D. K. (1992). *Chief*. New York, NY: Bantam Books.

Kind, S. S. (1987). Navigational ideas and the Yorkshire Ripper investigation. *Journal of Navigation, 40*, 385–393.

Le Comber, S. C., Nicholls, B., Rossmo, D. K., & Racey, P. A. (2006). Geographic profiling and animal foraging. *Journal of Theoretical Biology, 240*, 233–240.

Le Comber, S. C., Rossmo, D. K., Hassan, A. N., Fuller, D. O., & Beier, J. C. (2011). Geographic profiling as a novel spatial tool for targeting infectious disease control. *International Journal of Health Geographics, 10*, 35–42.

Levins, R. (1966). The strategy of model-building in population biology. *American Scientist, 54*, 421–431.

Martin, R. A., Rossmo, D. K., & Hammerschlag, N. (2009). Hunting patterns and geographic profiling of white shark predation. *Journal of Zoology, 279*, 111–118.

Raine, N. E., Rossmo, D. K., & Le Comber, S. C. (2009). Geographic profiling applied to testing models of bumble-bee foraging. *Journal of the Royal Society Interface, 6*, 307–319.

Rossmo, D. K. (1995). *Geographic profiling: Target patterns of serial murderers* (Unpublished doctoral dissertation). Simon Fraser University, Burnaby, BC.

Rossmo, D. K. (2000). *Geographic profiling*. Boca Raton, FL: CRC Press.

Rossmo, D. K. (2011). Evaluating geographic profiling. *Crime Mapping: A Journal of Research and Practice, 3*, 42–65.

Rossmo, D. K. (2013). Geographic profiling. In G. Bruinsma & D. L. Weisburd (Eds.), *Encyclopedia of criminology and criminal Justice* (pp. 1934–1942). New York, NY: Springer.

Rossmo, D. K., Davies, A., & Patrick, M. (2004). *Exploring the geo-demographic and distance relationships between stranger rapists and their offences* [Special interest series: Paper 16]. London, UK: Research, Development and Statistics Directorate, Home Office.

Rossmo, D. K., & Harries, K. D. (2011). The geospatial structure of terrorist cells. *Justice Quarterly, 28*, 221–248.

Rossmo, D. K., Lutermann, H., Stevenson, M. D., & Le Comber, S. C. (2014). Geographic profiling in Nazi Berlin: Fact and fiction. *Geospatial Intelligence Review, 12*(2), 44–57.

Stevenson, M. D., Rossmo, D. K., Knell, R. J., & Le Comber, S. C. (2012). Geographic profiling as a novel spatial tool for targeting the control of invasive species. *Ecography, 35*, 704–715.

Taleb, N. N. (2007). *The black swan: The impact of the highly improbable*. New York, NY: Random House.

Small Worlds of Crime and Criminal Justice Interventions: Discovering Crime Hot Spots

David Weisburd

My interest in hot spots of crime goes back to qualitative work that I conducted before finishing my dissertation at Yale. Indeed, one might say that my pursuit of what was later to be termed crime and place (Eck & Weisburd, 1996) or the criminology of place (Sherman, Gartin, & Buerger, 1989; Weisburd, Groff, & Yang, 2012) came as an accident. In my acceptance speech for the Stockholm Prize in 2010 I noted paraphrasing a well-known book at the time (which was titled, *All I Really Need to Know I learned in Kindergarten*; Fulghum, 2004) that everything I needed to know about hot spots of crime I learned in the 72nd precinct in New York City (1984–1985).

Stanton Wheeler, one of my mentors at Yale, and one of the founders of the Law and Society movement, had put me in contact with Jerry McElroy (then Research Director) at the Vera Institute of Justice in New York City. They were looking for a young researcher to lead an evaluation of one of the first Community Policing programs (this was 1984). I was unemployed and needed to work to support my family. At Vera, where Sally Hillsman was the co-leader of their research group (and later Research Director for the National Institute of Justice under Jeremy

Travis), they were not only a good research group but also a friendly and supportive one. I had a great interview and they offered me a Research Associate position, and a high salary (as compared with academic venues).

In retrospect this was a defining moment in my career not only for its impact on how I came to think about hot spots of crime, but also for the degree of knowledge it gave me about policing. But as an aside, some academics I knew at the time thought I was making a big mistake and this would have a negative impact on my career. Vera was not an elite academic institution, but rather a policy-oriented research organization. Such policy interest was assumed to be a bit too close to the real world. Indeed, one Israeli mentor of mine told me that this could hurt my chances of getting an academic position in Israel—where my wife's family lived and where we intended to live after I received my PhD. Fortunately for me, I followed my gut both in terms of what seemed like a really interesting job and also in terms of having some money to live on.

This work at Vera was to have a dramatic impact on the direction of my career. Before this work, I had never really seen crime and justice in action. I was primarily a quantitative criminologist, and here I was running a project that was primarily a qualitative one. But visualization often starts with the look and feel of places, and that is what happened here. My job was to walk the streets 4 days a week with patrol officers that had

D. Weisburd (✉)
The Hebrew University, Jerusalem, Israel

George Mason University, Fairfax, VA, USA
e-mail: dweisbur@gmu.edu

M.D. Maltz and S.K. Rice (eds.), *Envisioning Criminology: Researchers on Research as a Process of Discovery*, DOI 10.1007/978-3-319-15868-6_28, © Springer International Publishing Switzerland 2015

been assigned to nine beats that were considered "bad areas" (see Weisburd & McElroy, 1988). The important point here is that the image of Vera and indeed criminology at the time was that crime was spread across "bad parts of town." Indeed, we were going to evaluate the program by examining crime changes in each of the beats patrolled which varied in size between 12 and 30 square blocks.

But after a few weeks in the field, it became apparent to me that the idea that there were bad neighborhoods belied the realities of crime in communities and the realities of how the police worked. We didn't spend our time walking around the whole beat that was assigned (these were foot patrols). In fact, what happened was that we spent most of our time at a few "bad places" often a street segment between two intersections with a good deal of street activity or a few problematic facilities. This led me to the concept of "small worlds" of crime that was to inform the way I have thought about crime, or visualized it since. There were not bad neighborhoods in the visual sense I had of that earlier. There were bad places in such neighborhoods. The overall area might be poor or disadvantaged, but most of the streets seemed to have little crime.

Moreover, police work was focused on those places. And this was to have a very strong impact on the way I thought evaluation work in policing should proceed. The Vera study was going to use the beats to evaluate community policing interventions. My argument was that it was unfair to evaluate the program in the large areas of beats as defined by Vera, and indeed the larger geographic areas that were the focus of most policing evaluations at that time. We should be evaluating such interventions in the small worlds where the police actually worked. My concern from a statistical perspective was that the impacts of policing would be watered down in the "larger worlds" of evaluation research. This became a central issue in my later work. One of the impetuses for the work on hot spots policing was my observation here that we would miss the impacts of police programs unless we carried out the evaluation at the same geographic level as the main part of the intervention. That didn't happen at Vera in part because we did not have the data to carry out such an evaluation.

My experience in the 72nd Precinct led me to respect the importance of practitioner knowledge about crime and justice. But it also pointed to the disjuncture between policing and the science of policing. Peter Neyroud and I were to come back to this issue in a paper we wrote for the Harvard Executive Session in Policing in 2011. We argued that police needed to take "ownership" and responsibility for police science, and recognize its value for advancing police practices (Weisburd & Peter, 2011). Simply stated, the police would have to integrate scientific knowledge into their work. But we also argued that academics would have to make the scene of policing, recognizing the value of practitioner experience and knowledge. My experience in New York suggests that we have much to learn from practitioners. But systematic development of knowledge will demand a restructuring of the relationship between policing and science that also requires the police to value and have knowledge about science.

I only worked at Vera for about a year, as I moved to the Rutgers School of Criminal Justice the next Fall to take on a faculty position. Rutgers, unlike many traditional criminology or sociology programs at the time, saw my field experience as an important positive part of my application package. Importantly at Rutgers I had an opportunity to extend my thinking on "small worlds" of crime. Again, it was somewhat serendipitous. We were looking for a visiting distinguished professor for that year and the Dean of the School, Ronald Clarke, asked me to serve on the committee. The other senior professors on the committee were quite busy, and it ended up that I did the phone interviews and made the recommendation. One of the candidates was Lawrence Sherman. We had the same mentor at Yale, Albert J. Reiss Jr., and Reiss told me that Larry would be a fantastic person to bring to Rutgers. Eventually others agreed, and Larry was brought on board. Ron was very interested in seeing me advance my work and accordingly he suggested that a key part of Larry's obligation should be to work with me. When Larry and I started speaking about our interests it became quickly apparent that we had much in common.

Larry was working at the time on completing a study in Minneapolis in which he randomly allocated police to carry out problem-oriented policing at specific addresses in Minneapolis. What he learned in identifying the addresses was that a very large proportion of crime was found at just a relatively small number of these places. This led to his important 1989 article on the Criminology of Place (Sherman et al., 1989) which was written while we were working on our own study of hot spots of crime. Larry and I quickly had a common language. His hot spots of crime, and my "small worlds" of crime and police activity, identified the same opportunities for advancing policing. We began to talk a good deal about its implications at our weekly meetings at Rutgers. We quickly focused our discussions on an idea that would radically alter the conventional assumptions about what the police could do to prevent crime. The key was our shared belief that if crime was clustered, police activities should be clustered—just as occurred naturally in New York. But this time we expected to use that idea in the context of a large study to challenge traditional skepticism regarding police effectiveness.

Studies of policing in the previous decade provided a very strong narrative regarding the inability of the police to prevent crime. David Bayley summarized this well when he wrote on the first page of his influential book *Police for the Future* (1996:3):

> The police do not prevent crime. This is one of the best-kept secrets of modern life. Experts know it, the police know it, but the public does not know it. Yet the police pretend that they are society's best defense against crime. This is a myth.

Though Larry and I were to begin our hot spots policing study a few years before this work was published, David summarized what was the prevailing wisdom about police effectiveness at the time. And he was not antipolice, but rather simply summarizing what was known and being said by others (see Weisburd & Eck, 2004). A few years later our Minneapolis Hot Spots experiment (Sherman & Weisburd, 1995) was to be the first in a series of studies that showed the police could prevent crime, but they had to focus their efforts on those small worlds where the action of crime was found.

Larry and I set out to design a study that would be able to overcome the dominant beliefs about police effectiveness at the time. For that reason we set out to conduct one of the largest experimental field trials in crime and justice, and certainly in policing. We felt that only a randomized experiment would provide the type of persuasive evidence that would challenge prevailing assumptions. The innovation in our study was that the police focus on hot spots of crime. But identifying the hot spots turned out to be much harder than we had expected. In Larry's original study of problem-oriented policing in Minneapolis, he ended up assigning the same buildings to treatment and control conditions because there were often hot spot addresses that were in the same building or building complex. We needed to find a way to place our data geographically. Neither of us had any idea how to do this, but we had heard about this new software, MapInfo, that allowed you to place street addresses on a map. We set out to work with the software and my assistants (including Lisa Mayer and Antony Petrosino) and I worked night and day for months on simply trying to geocode crime calls to the 3,000 top addresses in the city (with three or more crimes). Today most police data has an initial geocoding rate much beyond 90%. I think we had to hand geocode more than half the data at the time.

But when we were done we had the first detailed map of hot spots of crime that any of us had seen. We did not have a printer that would allow us to produce a single map with all of the points, so we divided the city into a large number of areas (something like 50 I seem to remember) and printed each area on regular-letter size paper. We then scotch-taped the pieces together and put them on the wall of the Center for Crime Prevention Studies (which I directed). We were all amazed. It was simply an epiphany. I remember staring at this picture with others, and realizing that it had changed our understanding of crime. There were other groups that were working on environmental criminology at the time (e.g. see Brantingham & Brantingham, 1991), but I suspect that we were one of the first to look at such a visualization of the crime problem. And it reinforced not only the situational perspective of crime which was a strong idea at Rutgers at the time because of Ron Clarke, but also the visualizations I had developed in my head from the Vera study.

It is really too bad that we didn't save this scotch-taped map. It showed how crime moved down arterial roads and how it stopped at physical barriers such as rivers or bridges. It showed that the high-crime addresses clustered on specific street segments, much as the crime in New York. This finding was to inform the design of the Minneapolis study as well as my more general thinking about the importance of street segments in understanding crime. Importantly, this visual exercise (supported by field observations of the places) led to the definition of hot spots in the Minneapolis Hot Spots Experiment and in Larry's paper published in *Criminology* (Sherman et al., 1989).

At Rutgers I already began to consider new theoretical perspectives that had received little attention in my formal academic training. Ron Clarke was one of the pioneers of opportunity theories in criminology through his work on situational prevention. He and I also had a weekly tea during which we spent a good deal of time talking about criminology. Looking at the map of the distribution of crime reinforced those discussions. Ron stressed the mundane everyday impacts of small changes in opportunities on crime (see Clarke, 1980, 1983). I remember seeing on the map how physical barriers "stopped" crime and wondering how criminologists had ignored such perspectives. The predominant criminological focus at the time, and perhaps still today, is concerned with criminal motivation. The map I viewed suggested that a concern with opportunities for crime at places was critical to our understanding of the crime problem.

My later thinking about social disorganization and crime places, and the importance of street segments as "activity spaces" or small micro-communities was also apparent in this visual portrait of crime in the city (Weisburd et al., 2012). And in this, the crime maps brought me closer to earlier theoretical perspectives in criminology. Social disorganization theory focuses on structural factors in communities that affect the ability of citizens to exercise informal social controls. It

has been primarily applied at macrogeographic levels (e.g., see Sampson & Groves, 1989; Shaw & McKay, 1942). Visualizing crime in communities pointed to the variability of crime within larger areas, and raised the question of whether social disorganization theory had relevance for understanding crime at place. My point is that looking at the data is key to advancing theory. In my case it both moved my interests to opportunities for crime, and led me to consider later on traditional theory in a different way.

This finding of variability of crime within communities was reinforced in two later studies. The scotch-taped map showed clearly that most of the streets in the so-called bad areas were relatively free of crime, and that there were crime hot spots even in the "better" parts of town. In the Jersey City Drug Hot Spots Experiment (see Weisburd & Green, 1995; Weisburd, Green, & Ross, 1994) Lorraine Green (now Lorraine Mazerolle) and I developed a visualization of this (see Fig. 1). The drug hot spots we identified (through a narcotics tip line, emergency calls to the police, and arrest information) were found throughout the city. Indeed, a senior commander in Jersey City was surprised to see one pop up right around his house in a middle class area. But even in the southern part of the city which was seen as overrun by drugs, most of the streets (even those right off the main boulevard where the drug markets were located) had little drug crime.

The best visualizations of this idea and the hot spots idea that came from my walks with cops on the beat 30 years ago were developed in a longitudinal research program in the criminology of place in Seattle Washington. In 2004 Shawn Bushway, Cynthia Lum, Sue-Ming Yang, and I published a paper that used group-based trajectory models to classify the streets in Seattle (about 25,000) by crime patterns over a 14-year period (Weisburd, Bushway, Lum, & Yang, 2004). The visualization of this analysis (see Fig. 2) clearly shows the chronic hot spots of crime that the community policing officers in New York patrolled. In this figure the top line representing just 1% of the streets in Seattle produced almost 25% of crime over the entire period examined.

Fig. 1 Drug hot spots in Jersey City (*Source*: Weisburd, David, Lorraine Green, and Debra Ross. (1994). Crime in Street Level Drug Markets: A Spatial Analysis. *Criminologie*, 27(1): 49–67)

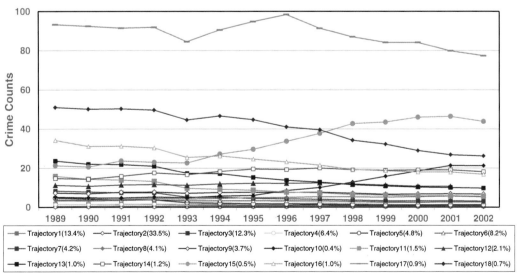

Fig. 2 Trajectories of crime at street segments in Seattle Washington (*Source*: Weisburd, David, Shawn Bushway, Cynthia Lum, and Sue-Ming Yang. (2004). Trajectories of Crime at Places: A Longitudinal Study of Street Segments in the City of Seattle. *Criminology*, 42(2), 283–322)

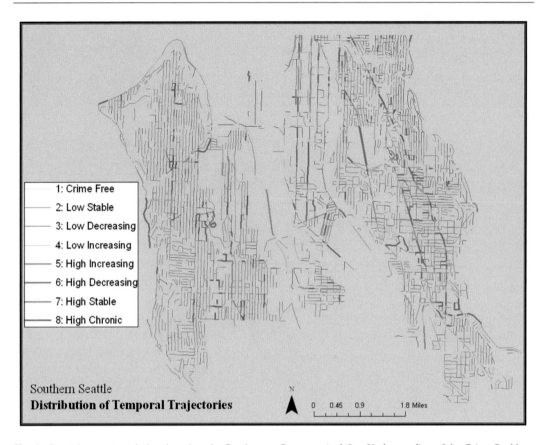

Southern Seattle
Distribution of Temporal Trajectories

Legend:
1: Crime Free
2: Low Stable
3: Low Decreasing
4: Low Increasing
5: High Increasing
6: High Decreasing
7: High Stable
8: High Chronic

N

0   0.45   0.9   1.8 Miles

Fig. 3 Street-by-street variation in crime in Southern Seattle (*Source*: Weisburd, David, Elizabeth Groff and Sue-Ming Yang. (2012), *The Criminology of Place*: *Street* *Segments And Our Understanding of the Crime Problem.* Oxford: Oxford University Press)

I think the best visualization we have produced of the variability of crime within neighborhoods was developed by Liz Groff, Sue-Ming Yang and me for our book, *The Criminology of Place* (2012). Figure 3 is a map of the Southern areas of Seattle which are generally defined as the bad parts of town. The darker red colors are the hot spot streets. As can be seen there are a number of them in this part of Seattle. But what is most striking is the predominance of the green and yellow streets, which are streets with little crime. This visualization shows that we have to pay attention to the "small worlds" of crime. Summarizing up to communities or neighborhoods will simply miss a great deal of the variability of the crime problem in cities. This was an observation developed while I walked the streets

of New York, and it revised my own image of crime in the city. It was one we were able to show visually to others some 30 years later.

References

Bayley, D. (1996). *Police for the future*. New York, NY: Oxford University Press.

Brantingham, P. J., & Brantingham, P. L. (1991). *Environmental criminology*. Prospect Heights, IL: Waveland Press.

Clarke, R. V. (1980). Situational crime prevention: Theory and practice. *British Journal of Criminology, 20*, 136.

Clarke, R. V. (1983). Situational crime prevention: Its theoretical basis and practical scope. In M. Tonry & N. Morris (Eds.), *Crime and justice: An annual review of research* (pp. 225–256). Chicago, IL: University of Chicago Press.

Eck, J., & Weisburd, D. (Eds.). (1996). *Crime and place.* Monsey, NY: Willow Tree Press.

Fulghum, R. (2004). *All I really needed to know I learned in kindergarten.* New York, NY: Ballantine Books.

Sampson, R. J., & Groves, W. B. (1989). Community structure and crime: Testing social-disorganization theory. *The American Journal of Sociology, 94,* 774–802.

Shaw, C. R., & McKay, H. D. (1942). *Juvenile delinquency and urban areas. A study of rates of delinquency in relation to differential characteristics of local communities in American cities.* Chicago, IL: University of Chicago Press.

Sherman, L. W., Gartin, P., & Buerger, M. E. (1989). Hot spots of predatory crime: Routine activities and the criminology of place. *Criminology, 27,* 27–55.

Sherman, L., & Weisburd, D. (1995). General deterrent effects of police patrol in crime 'Hot Spots': A randomized study. *Justice Quarterly, 12*(4), 625–648.

Weisburd, D., Bushway, S., Lum, C., & Yang, S.-M. (2004). Crime trajectories at places: A longitudinal study of street segments in the City of Seattle. *Criminology, 42*(2), 283–322.

Weisburd, D., & Eck, J. (2004). What can police do to reduce crime, disorder and fear? *The Annals of the American Academy of Political and Social Science, 593*(May), 42–65.

Weisburd, D., & Green, L. (1995). Policing drug hot spots: The Jersey City drug market analysis experiment. *Justice Quarterly, 12,* 711–735.

Weisburd, D., Green, L., & Ross, D. (1994). Crime in street level drug markets: A spatial analysis. *Criminologie, 27*(1), 49–67 (In French).

Weisburd, D., Groff, E. R., & Yang, S.-M. (2012). *The criminology of place: Street segments and our understanding of the crime problem.* New York, NY: Oxford University Press.

Weisburd, D., & McElroy, J. (1988). Enacting the CPO role: Findings from the New York City pilot program in community policing. In J. Greene & S. Mastrofski (Eds.), *Community based policing: Rhetoric or reality.* New York, NY: Praeger.

Weisburd, D., & Peter, N. (2011). Police science: Towards a new paradigm. *New perspectives in policing.* Cambridge, MA: Harvard Executive Session in Policing.

Index

Made in the USA
Coppell, TX
14 November 2020

41299755R00181